For Zion's Sake

Christian Zionism and the Role of John Nelson Darby

'Few dedicated Christian scholars with an evangelistic ministry have been attacked more unfairly than John Nelson Darby, who did more to promote the doctrine of the pre-tribulation Rapture of the Church than any other person. Darby did not invent it, of course, for it is both Biblical and ancient, but he popularised it during the nineteenth century. This well researched and readable book carefully sets the record straight and makes a valuable contribution to prophetic studies.'

Dr Tim LaHaye

Minister, Educator, Author, and Co-Founder of The Pre-Trib Research Center, Liberty University, Lynchburg, Virginia, USA

'Wilkinson's impeccable documentation and reasoning from Scripture thoroughly refute the myth that Darby got his doctrine of the pre-tribulation Rapture from a Scottish girl and two Jesuit priests. Primary historical sources cited herein clearly demonstrate the contrary. I highly recommend this excellent treatment of a controversial subject that has confused many.'

Dave Hunt

Author, International Conference Speaker, and Co-Founder of The Berean Call, Bend, Oregon, USA

'In our day when there is such confusion as to the different streams of Christian Zionism (some of which I can endorse but some I cannot), and due to the personal attacks on John Nelson Darby, many believers are confused about whether they should support Israel, and others who do support Israel often do not fully understand why. This work is greatly needed to clarify these issues, and should be read by all who wish to understand Darby, Zionism, and Israel.'

Dr Arnold G. Fruchtenbaum

Author, and Director of Ariel Ministries, San Antonio, Texas, USA

'This book represents a major step forward in the study of the origins and impact of Christian Zionism. *For Zion's Sake* balances scholarly rigour with personal commitment in a fine work of historical and theological reflection.'

Dr Crawford Gribben

Author, and Senior Lecturer in Early Modern Print Culture, Long Room Hub, Trinity College, Dublin, Ireland

'Dr Paul Wilkinson has provided a vital service in affirming Darby's legacy and pivotal role in modern Evangelicalism's renewed understanding of the central place of Israel in Biblical eschatology and its support of the cause of Zionism. In the process he offers a much-needed clarification of Christian Zionism, distinguishing its many current forms from the classical dispensational Restorationism of Darby's theological system. In addition he has given the recent opposing movement springing from replacement theology and political revisionism a proper name – Christian Palestinianism – identifying its tenets with a precision it has rarely done for itself. In the final analysis, Dr Wilkinson has restored Darby's reputation as having been a pious visionary used by God at a crucial time in history to formulate for His Church a comprehensive and coherent theological system that provided the Biblical foundation for Christian Zionism. For any student of ecclesiastical and political history, as well as systematic and historical theology, this book is essential reading.'

Dr Randall Price
Author, President of World of the Bible Ministries, and Distinguished Professor of Jewish Studies, Liberty University, Lynchburg, Virginia, USA

'With so much confusion and misinformation today concerning dispensationalism, Christian Zionism, and the role of J.N. Darby, Wilkinson's work is a breath of theological and historical fresh air. I am deeply grateful for his fine scholarship and the balanced way in which he makes his case. This work should quickly become a standard on Christian Zionism and Darby's influence on this important movement.'

Dr Mark Hitchcock
Author, Adjunct Professor at Dallas Theological Seminary, and Pastor of Faith Bible Church, Edmond, Oklahoma, USA

STUDIES IN EVANGELICAL HISTORY AND THOUGHT

A full listing of all titles in this series
appears at the close of this book

For Zion's Sake

Christian Zionism and the Role of John Nelson Darby

Paul Richard Wilkinson

Foreword by Thomas Ice

MILTON KEYNES · COLORADO SPRINGS · HYDERABAD

First published 2007 by Paternoster

Paternoster is an imprint of Authentic Media
9 Holdom Avenue, Bletchley, Milton Keynes, MK1 1QR, UK
1820 Jet Stream Drive, Colorado Springs, CO 80921, USA
OM Authentic Media, Medchal Road, Jeedimetla Village,
Secunderabad 500 055, A.P., India
www.authenticmedia.co.uk
Authentic Media is a division of IBS-STL UK, a company limited by guarantee
(registered charity no. 270162)

13 12 11 10 09 08 07   7 6 5 4 3 2 1

British Library Cataloguing in Publication Data
A catalogue record for this book is available from the British Library

ISBN 978-1-84227-569-6

Typeset by Paul Richard Wilkinson
Printed and bound in Great Britain
for Paternoster
by Nottingham Alpha Graphics

Series Preface

The Evangelical movement has been marked by its union of four emphases: on the Bible, on the cross of Christ, on conversion as the entry to the Christian life and on the responsibility of the believer to be active. The present series is designed to publish scholarly studies of any aspect of this movement in Britain or overseas. Its volumes include social analysis as well as exploration of Evangelical ideas. The books in the series consider aspects of the movement shaped by the Evangelical Revival of the eighteenth century, when the impetus to mission began to turn the popular Protestantism of the British Isles and North America into a global phenomenon. The series aims to reap some of the rich harvest of academic research about those who, over the centuries, have believed that they had a gospel to tell to the nations.

Series Editors

This book is dedicated to my Lord and Saviour Jesus Christ, who was, and is, and is to come. To God be the glory!

Contents

Foreword

John Nelson Darby is the most influential Evangelical that most Evangelicals have never heard about. Not only was Darby influential in formulating modern dispensationalism and pretribulationism, but he was also a pioneer in the development of a consistent Israelology, which today provides the theological basis for the majority of Christian Zionists. Dr Paul Wilkinson has done a thorough and masterful job of mining the depths of Darby's extensive theology and bringing it out into the light so that friend and foe alike can better understand exactly where so many current Evangelical beliefs originate.

Even though primitive forms of Restorationism began to appear in England by the late sixteenth century, it was not until Darby's formulation of a clear Christian Zionist theology in the mid-nineteenth century that it began to reach maturity. Dr Wilkinson puts on display the key elements that Darby moulded into a consistent Christian Zionist theology which has exerted great influence within contemporary Evangelicalism throughout the world.

The key starting point for Darby's Christian Zionism is his high view of Scripture and his consistent application of a literal hermeneutic often known as the historical, grammatical, contextual method. Coupled with a desire to glorify Jesus Christ in all that he did, Darby's Christian Zionism is built upon the New Testament doctrine that the Church was a mystery not revealed in the Old Testament, and therefore a distinct phase in God's single plan for history. Just such a view of the Church allowed Darby to take all of the promises to Israel literally without the need to resort to replacement theology, which has, since post-Apostolic times, plagued the Church and encouraged anti-Semitism. Darby's understanding of the Israel/Church distinction enabled him to develop a consistent Christian Zionist theology.

For Zion's Sake makes another important contribution with its honest presentation of Darby the man. This is important for anyone seeking to understand and evaluate the development of his theological system. Critics have accused Darby of being self-serving and deceptive, especially in the development of his pretribulational doctrine. Dr Wilkinson clearly demonstrates, however, that there is no historical basis to link Darby's development of the pre-trib Rapture with spurious influences like the Scottish lassie, Margaret MacDonald, or Edward Irving and the Irvingites. Instead, he demonstrates that the best explanation of the historical evidence is that Darby was an extremely capable and well-trained student of Scripture, and derived his doctrine of the Rapture from his own personal study of the Bible. Dr Wilkinson argues that to scurrilously suggest otherwise is to defame Darby's character and misrepresent one who showed throughout his life that he was a man of integrity to whom the Word of God, and not human influence, was paramount. Darby clearly exhibited all through his life the skills necessary to exegete Scripture, and the where-with-all to produce original thought. Confirmation that much of his thinking was the product of Evangelical biblical exegesis is seen in the way that his teachings have resonated throughout the world, even in our own day.

Aided by his analysis of Darby's contribution to the development of a clear Christian Zionist theology, Dr Wilkinson intelligently interacts with the many critics who oppose the biblical case for the restoration and future destiny of the nation of Israel. Whether exposing older forms of Replacement Theology, or more recent movements such as 'Christian Palestinianism', he exposes the sub-biblical nature of the various attacks upon Christian Zionist theology. Darby has been castigated for his biblical teaching on the restoration of Israel and the return of Christ, but as Dr Wilkinson demonstrates, his teachings present the 'blessed hope' of the Church, and not the fuse to Armageddon. After all, Darby believed that events leading up to Armageddon and the return of Christ were of a supernatural nature, and that it would be impossible for any group of people to set off a chain of human events which would result in the fulfilment of prophecy. He believed that if God did not bring these events to pass, they would not happen. As we have seen, the hand of the Lord has already been at work in the restoration of the modern state of Israel.

Dr Paul Wilkinson has done everyone a favour by so copiously outlining Darby's beliefs, and putting into perspective his contribution to Evangelical theology in general, and Christian Zionism in particular. *For Zion's Sake* demonstrates that Darby has produced one of the most comprehensive and coherent theological systems in the recent history of the Church. His importance and impact has remained hidden for too long. This book deserves a wide reading by anyone, scholar or interested layman, who desires to gain a clearer understanding of the history and significance of many of the issues that are at the forefront of Evangelicalism, especially in relation to the important topic of Christian Zionism.

Dr Thomas Ice
Executive Director
The Pre-Trib Research Center
Liberty University
Lynchburg
Virginia, USA

Acknowledgements

I would like to thank Professor Philip Alexander at Manchester University for supervising the thesis which forms the basis of this book, and Jeremy Mudditt and Dr Anthony R. Cross at Paternoster for assisting me with its publication.

I would like to thank Dr Thomas Ice at the Pre-Trib Research Center for kindly agreeing to write the Foreword. Dr Ice has greatly encouraged all of us at Hazel Grove Full Gospel Church with his enthusiasm for this work. I am also grateful to my brothers in Christ who have generously endorsed it. May all be encouraged in their service to the Lord and His people.

I would like to thank my parents, Anne and Geoff, for supporting me as only parents can. I love them dearly. May they, and the rest of my family, soon come to know the One who called me to this work, that we may walk together in His grace and truth. I would also like to thank my grandfather, Harry Wilkinson, for loving me with the love of Christ as he eagerly awaits His upward call.

I would like to pay tribute to my dear friends, Andrew and Pat Robinson. Andrew is the pastor of Hazel Grove Full Gospel Church in Stockport, Cheshire. He and his wife Pat have discipled me in the Christian faith for many years. Their devotion to the Lord Jesus Christ, and the sacrifices they have made in faithfully serving God's people, have made all this possible. I thank the Lord for the love, perseverance, and godly wisdom He has given them as a couple. Andrew is a true shepherd of God's flock, and it is an honour to serve alongside him and Pat in the work of the Lord. I thank them both for the sacrifices they made during the preparation of this book, and thank Andrew for the invaluable assistance he gave me throughout. I could not have done it without him, and I could not wish for a truer and more faithful friend.

I would like to thank all my brothers and sisters at Hazel Grove Full Gospel Church, and those connected with the fellowship, who have committed themselves to this work and supported me in so many ways. May we remain faithful to the Lord, to one another, and to the work He has called us to for His Name's sake, ever rejoicing that our names are written in heaven.

Finally, I would like to acknowledge the eternal debt I owe my Lord and Saviour Jesus Christ, who gave His life that I might live. I have known the Lord Jesus since the day He saved me at York University, in February 1990. Without the steadfast love, mercy, and grace I have received from Him each day, this book would not have been possible. *For Zion's Sake* serves no purpose unless it serves His.

Paul Richard Wilkinson
Hazel Grove Full Gospel Church, Stockport, Cheshire, UK
September 2007

Abbreviations

CBA	Christian Brethren Archive, John Rylands University Library, Manchester, UK.
CW1-34	The Collected Writings of J.N. Darby, 34 Volumes.
L1-3	Letters of J.N.D., 3 Volumes.
M4-5	Miscellaneous Writings of J.N.D., Volumes 4 and 5.
N&C1-7	Notes and Comments on Scripture, 7 Volumes.
N&J	Notes and Jottings from Various Meetings with J.N. Darby.
S1-5	Synopsis of the Books of the Bible, 5 Volumes.

With the exception of book, pamphlet, and sermon titles, the spelling of the Puritan era has been brought into the conventions of the twenty-first century.

Unless otherwise stated, Scripture quotations are taken from the Holy Bible, New International Version, Copyright © 1973, 1978, 1984 by the International Bible Society.

Chapter 1

Defining Christian Zionism

*'For Zion's sake I will not keep silent, for Jerusalem's sake I will not remain
quiet, till her righteousness shines out like the dawn, her salvation like a
blazing torch' (Isa. 62:1).*

Introduction

The world is waking up to the realisation that the establishment of the modern
State of Israel in 1948 cannot be explained simply in terms of political Zionism,
but must take account of a powerful, groundswell movement among Christians
which has been running alongside. Based on a literal interpretation of the Bible,
this movement influenced British foreign policy in the Middle East in the
nineteenth and early twentieth centuries, culminating in the Balfour Declaration
of 1917, and is having a major impact on current American foreign policy in
the region. This movement is known as Christian Zionism.

In an interview published on 18 August 2005 in the Arabic newspaper, *Al-
Sharq Al-Awsat*, Mahmoud al-Zahar, a senior Hamas leader, declared: 'We do
not consider the West as an enemy but we believe Christian Zionism is
criminal.'[1] More recently, Ahmed al-Tamimi, a Hamas cleric, cited Christian
Zionists as the enemy of Hamas and 'the greatest danger to world truth, justice,
and peace.'[2] In a 2003 article for the Internet magazine, *theGlobalist*, Michael
Lind introduced readers to John Nelson Darby, claiming that 'Mr Darby's
peculiar version of Christianity has shaped the American South for generations.
And now, through conservative Southern Republicans like George W. Bush, it
is shaping the Middle East and the world.'[3] Darby has been described by one

---

[1] Jerusalem Newswire Editorial Staff, 'Hamas: Christian Zionism is our Enemy',
Jerusalem Newswire, 22 August (2005), <http://www.jnewswire.com/article/527, 5 June
2006>.

[2] Stan Goodenough, 'Christian Zionists are our Enemy: Hamas Authority has pro-Israel
Christians in its Sights', *Jerusalem Newswire*, 9 May (2006), <http://www.jnewswire.
com/article/896, 5 June 2006>.

[3] Michael Lind, 'George W. Bush's Holy War', *theGlobalist*, 23 March (2003), <http://
www.theglobalist.com/DBWeb/StoryId.aspx?StoryId=3025, 27 July 2006>.

critic as 'the most influential figure in the development of Christian Zionism', and 'its greatest apostle and missionary'.[4]

John Nelson Darby, the founder of Plymouth Brethrenism, did indeed make a pivotal contribution to the development of Christian Zionism, but I will demonstrate how his doctrines have been misrepresented and misused by Brethren and non-Brethren scholars alike. The lack of critical research into the origins of Christian Zionism, and the 'somewhat blinkered' attitude of academics who have viewed the predominantly dispensationalist theology of Christian Zionism as having 'little intrinsic religious or theological value',[5] will be addressed and challenged.

At a time when conflict in the Middle East shows little sign of abating, and with much of the blame being laid squarely at the feet of Christian Zionists, the need to define this movement, trace its origins, chart its historical development, and evaluate its impact has never been more necessary. I will compare and contrast Christian Zionism with Jewish Zionism, and set it against an emerging movement which will be defined as Christian Palestinianism. Darby's life and ministry will be evaluated, and certain biographical works corrected, before an outline of his eschatology is given. After exploring the history of British Evangelical belief in the restoration of the Jews, the myth that Darby stole the doctrine of the pretribulation Rapture from his contemporaries will be exploded. The phenomenal impact of Darby's doctrines on the American Church will then be charted and compelling reasons given as to why America has superseded Britain as the patron of Israel and bastion of Christian Zionism. This book reveals the truth behind Darby and his message, and spotlights the imminent return of the Lord Jesus Christ as the centrepiece of his theology.

Jewish Zionism

According to Max Dimont, Zionism simply means 'a return to Zion', an ideology which has 'permeated Jewish thinking ever since the earliest days of the Diaspora'.[6] Rufus Learsi maintains that faith, land, and people 'are the strands that enter into the fabric of Jewish history', and that 'the resumption of national life in the ancient land is a basic credo of the Orthodox faith.'[7] Similarly, David Aune describes the Land of Israel as 'the indispensable setting

---

[4] Donald E. Wagner, *Anxious for Armageddon* (Scottdale, PA: Herald Press, 1995), pp. 88-89.

[5] Philip S. Alexander, 'Dispensationalism, Christian Zionism and the State of Israel', *Presidential Lecture for the Manson Society* (Manchester: Faculty of Humanities, University of Manchester, 2001), p. 1.

[6] Max I. Dimont, *Jews, God and History* (New York: The New American Library, Inc., 1962), p. 393.

[7] Rufus Learsi, *Fulfilment: The Epic Story of Zionism* (New York: The World Publishing Company, 1951), p. 122.

for the playing out of the eschatological drama.'[8] As we shall see, this interrelationship between faith, land, and people, which provides the basis for our understanding of Zionism, is firmly rooted in the Hebrew Scriptures, which are replete with references to 'Zion'. Zion is synonymous with the city of Jerusalem (Ps. 48:1-2), the Land of Israel (Isa. 51:3), and the Jewish people themselves (Isa. 51:15-16). So central is Zion to Jewish identity that the psalmist wrote from exile, 'If I forget you, O Jerusalem, may my right hand forget its skill' (Ps. 137:5). Its centrality is also enshrined in later Jewish writings such as the *Midrash Tanchuma (Kedoshim 10)*, which reads:

> As the navel is set in the centre of the human body, so is the land of Israel the navel of the world...situated in the centre of the world, and Jerusalem in the centre of the land of Israel, and the sanctuary in the centre of Jerusalem, and the holy place in the centre of the sanctuary, and the ark in the centre of the holy place, and the foundation stone before the holy place, because from it the world was founded.

Chaim Weizmann, 'the one man who embodied Zionism for the world outside Palestine',[9] described the Jews of the Diaspora as 'a sort of disembodied ghost'. Addressing the Palestine Royal Commission on 25 November 1936, he made the following statement:

> I believe the main cause which has produced the particular state of Jewry in the world is its attachment to Palestine. We are a stiff-necked people and a people of long memory...Whether it is our misfortune or whether it is our good fortune, we have never forgotten Palestine, and this steadfastness, which has preserved the Jew throughout the ages and throughout a career that is almost one long chain of inhuman suffering, is primarily due to some physiological or psychological attachment to Palestine. We have never forgotten it nor given it up.[10]

Nahum Sokolow, Weizmann's successor as president of the World Zionist Organisation (WZO), spoke in a similar vein of the 'everlasting, all-absorbing and unconquerable idea of a national future' for the Jewish people, which had accompanied them 'from the cradle to the grave' and was 'the secret of their long existence'. Sokolow claimed that there was 'no parallel in history.'[11]

---

[8] David E. Aune and Eric Stewart, 'From the Idealised Past to the Imaginary Future: Eschatological Restoration in Jewish Apocalyptic Literature', in *Restoration: Old Testament, Jewish, and Christian Perspectives*, ed. by James M. Scott (Leiden: Brill, 2001), p. 153.

[9] Golda Meir, *My Life* (London: Futura Publications Limited, 1978), p. 160.

[10] Quoted in Wilbur Smith, *Israeli-Arab Conflict and the Bible* (Glendale, CA: Regal Books, 1967), p. 62.

[11] Nahum Sokolow, *History of Zionism 1600-1918: Vol. I* (London: Longmans, Green and Co., 1919), p. xv.

Religion, Art, and Folklore

The *Amidah*, or *Shmoneh Esreh* ('Eighteen Benedictions'), is 'the most ancient, central and characteristic'[12] prayer of Talmudic Judaism. The tenth benediction, known as the *Kibbutz Galuyot*, calls upon the Lord to regather the exiles, while the fourteenth, fifteenth, and seventeenth benedictions call for the restoration of David's kingdom, the hastening of the Messiah, and the restoration of Temple service. This restorationist theme is found in every aspect of Jewish life, from the grace after meals to Jewish rites of circumcision, marriage, and death. It is also apparent in the three major festivals of Passover, Pentecost, and Tabernacles, the observance of which 'brought the fragrance of the orchards and vineyards of Palestine' into the slums and ghettos of Europe, and 'fed the nostalgia for the ancient homeland'.[13] Their commemoration also brought that same fragrance into the Nazi death camps.[14]

The Centrality of Eretz Yisrael

The destruction of the Second Temple and the rise of Christianity, which was messianic and Jewish by definition, had a marked effect on the eschatology of rabbinic Judaism. In addition, the failed revolt under Bar Kokhba in AD135 effectively ended belief that military action, in the Maccabean spirit, could usher in the messianic age and restore Israel's nationhood. Even so, pseudo-messiahs like Sabbatai Zevi (1626-1676) periodically 'flashed across the skies of Jewish history',[15] rekindling ancient hopes of a national, messianic revival. Two of the most eminent Jewish sages who upheld the belief in Israel's restoration were Maimonides and Nachmanides. Maimonides (1135-1204) taught that the Messiah would arise to restore David's kingdom and 'gather the dispersed of Israel',[16] while Nachmanides (1194-1270) called for the immediate resettlement of the Land by the Jews to fulfil the *mitvoth*, or 'commandments', associated with it. Thus Jewish messianism remained 'a broad constellation of ideas'[17] throughout the Middle Ages.

At the beginning of the nineteenth century, Claudius Buchanan, an Anglican

---

[12] Stefan C. Reif, 'Some Notions of Restoration in Early Rabbinic Prayer', in Scott, *Restoration*, p. 281.

[13] Learsi, *Fulfilment*, p. 21.

[14] *Shema Yisrael: Testimonies of Devotion, Courage, and Self-Sacrifice 1939-1945*, trans. from *The Shema Encyclopedia* by Yaakov Lavon (Southfield, MI: Targum Press, Inc., 2002).

[15] Joseph Adler, *Restoring the Jews to their Homeland: Nineteen Centuries in the Quest for Zion* (Northvale, NJ: Jason Aronson Inc., 1997), p. 27.

[16] Gershom Scholem, *The Messianic Idea in Judaism* (New York: Schocken Books, 1974), p. 29.

[17] Moshe Idel, *Messianic Mystics* (New Haven, CT: Yale University Press, 1998), p. 265.

missionary to India, was surprised to discover Hebrew literature relating to the restoration of Israel in the homes of the Malabari Jews he visited. He recorded his observations in *Christian Researches in Asia*:

> Ever since I came among these people, and heard their sentiments on the prophecies, and their confident hopes of returning to *Jerusalem*, I have thought much on the means of obtaining a version of the NEW TESTAMENT in the Hebrew language, and circulating it among them and their brethren in the East...I have had many interesting conferences with the Jews, on the subject of their present state; and have been much struck with two circumstances; their constant reference to the DESOLATION of Jerusalem, and their confident hope that it will be one day REBUILT.[18]

Buchanan's research, which has been overlooked by Zionist historians, provides an important first hand account of the restorationist hope that was still alive in the Jewish Diaspora. W.D. Davies believes that this attachment to *Eretz Yisrael* ('the Land of Israel') has 'remained tenaciously present in the depth of the consciousness of many Jews',[19] an attachment he describes as 'a kind of umbilical cord' and 'the essence of Judaism.'[20] However, despite the migration of individuals to the Land, the nineteenth century was well advanced before anything was collectively done by the Jewish people to facilitate their return. Until then their hope was largely expressed through prayerful longing.[21]

The Jewish Question

In 1842, German philosopher and theologian, Bruno Bauer, published *Die Judenfrage* ('The Jewish Question'), a hostile appraisal of Jewish life in Europe which called upon the Jews to renounce their attachment to Zion. This call was already echoing through the synagogues of Reform Judaism. Founded by Israel Jacobson in Seesen, Westphalia, the Reform movement sought to harmonise modernity with tradition, radically pruning liturgy and ritual in what has been described as 'a demythologising trend within Judaism'.[22] In November 1890, at a Chicago conference of Christians and Jews organised by the Christian Zionist, William E. Blackstone, the Reform Rabbi, Emil G. Hirsch, declared:

---

[18] Claudius Buchanan, *Christian Researches in Asia*, 3rd edn (Edinburgh: 1812), pp. 216-218.

[19] W.D. Davies, *The Gospel and the Land: Early Christianity and Jewish Territorial Doctrine* (London: University of California Press, 1974), p. 158.

[20] W.D. Davies, *The Territorial Dimension of Judaism* (London: University of California Press, 1982), pp. 36, 53.

[21] Margaret Brearley, 'Jerusalem in Judaism and for Christian Zionists', in *Jerusalem Past and Present in the Purposes of God*, ed. by Peter W.L. Walker (Carlisle: The Paternoster Press, 1994), p. 106.

[22] Walter Riggans, *Israel and Zionism* (Edinburgh: The Handsel Press, 1988), p. 14.

> We modern Jews do not wish to be restored to Palestine. We have given up hope
> in the coming of a political personal Messiah. We say, 'the country wherein we
> live is our Palestine, and the city wherein we dwell is our Jerusalem.' We will not
> go back…to form again a nationality of our own.[23]

The Jewish Enlightenment movement known as the *Haskalah* also emerged at
this time, and can be traced back to the philosophical writings of the 'German
Socrates',[24] Moses Mendelssohn. The *Haskalah* sought to foster a local
patriotism among the Jewish people through a process of cultural assimilation.
Notable assimilationists, such as Claude Montefiore, maintained that Jews
could become citizens and patriots wherever they lived. Religious concepts
were spiritualised and Jewish nationalistic themes transcended, exile no longer
being viewed as Divine retribution but as a Divine commission to the Gentile
world 'to act as its teachers and its guides'.[25] Known as *Maskilim*, its most
prominent disciples were Yehuda Leib Gordon, Lev Levanda, Moshe Leib
Lilienblum, and Eliezer Ben Yehuda, the man who was to become 'the pre-
eminent creator of the modern Hebrew language'.[26] These men had 'drunk deep
at the fount of enlightenment'.[27] However, following the Russian pogroms,
which broke out on the final day of Passover, 1881, a despondent Levanda,
'filled with corroding despair', realised that there could never be a Jewish home
in a Gentile land. He urged his fellow Jews:

> go now to the only land in which we will find relief for our souls that have been
> harassed by murderers for these thousands of years. Our beginnings will be small,
> but in the end we will flourish.[28]

Although the Russian pogroms helped shift Jewish opinion, the call to return
had already been voiced in the writings of a number of key Jewish intellectuals.

In his book, *Sh'ma Yisrael* ('Hear O Israel', 1834), Serbian Rabbi Yehudah
Alkalai appealed to his fellow Jews to return to their ancient homeland and so
hasten their redemption. Described as 'the earliest proto-Zionist',[29] Alkalai was

---

[23] Quoted in Yaakov Ariel, *On Behalf of Israel: American Fundamentalist Attitudes
toward Jews, Judaism, and Zionism, 1865-1945* (Brooklyn, NY: Carlson Publishing
Inc., 1991), p. 70.

[24] Martin Gilbert, *Letters to Auntie Fori: The 5,000-Year History of the Jewish People
and their Faith* (London: Weidenfeld & Nicolson, 2002), p. 161.

[25] *The Zionist Idea*, ed. by Arthur Hertzberg (Westport, CT: Greenwood, 1959), p. 23.

[26] Howard M. Sachar, *A History of Israel from the Rise of Zionism to our Time,* 2nd edn
(New York: Alfred A. Knopf, 1996), p. 62.

[27] Learsi, *Fulfilment*, p. 44.

[28] Sachar, *A History of Israel*, p. 13.

[29] David J. Goldberg, *To the Promised Land: A History of Zionist Thought from its
Origins to the Modern State of Israel* (London: Penguin Books, 1996), p. 6.

profoundly affected by the Damascus 'blood libel'[30] of 1840, which inspired him to write *The Third Redemption* (1843) and *The Offering of Judah* (1843). Polish Rabbi Zvi Hirsch Kalischer drew *his* inspiration from an Italian nationalist movement known as the *Risorgimento*, and wrote *Emunah Yesharah* ('The Right of Faith', 1843) and *Drishat Zion* ('The Quest for Zion', 1862). Moses Hess was profoundly influenced by Kalischer's work. Described as 'the first true Zionist visionary',[31] Hess realised that the only solution to the Jewish Question was a Jewish homeland. He too was captivated by the *Risorgimento*, which inspired him to write *Rome and Jerusalem* (1862). The Odessan physician, Leo Pinsker, added to the impetus with his highly influential *Auto-Emancipation* (1882), which has been described as 'the first fully-formed articulation of a Zionist doctrine directly stated as a solution for the Jewish problem'.[32] In the minds of these proto-Zionists, assimilation could not guarantee a Jewish future in Europe.[33] With the rise of political anti-Semitism in Germany towards the close of the nineteenth century, many Jews became convinced that a new solution to the Jewish Question was urgently needed.

In 1883, a young Jewish patriot by the name of Nathan Birnbaum helped found *Kadimah*, the first nationalist fraternity of Jewish students in Western Europe. Two years later he launched the first Jewish journal, in German, to promote resettlement in *Eretz Yisrael*; it was in the 1 April 1890 edition of *Selbstemanzipation* ('Self-Emancipation') that the term 'Zionism' was coined. In 1893, he published *The National Rebirth of the Jewish People in its Own Country as a Means to Resolve the Jewish Question. An Appeal to all Noble-Minded Men of Good Will*, calling for an international congress to be convened to consider his proposals. Birnbaum's solution to the Jewish Question effectively prepared the way for a movement which finally 'put feet to ancient hopes and dreams for a Jewish homeland.'[34] Before we examine this movement and the influence of its 'central and seminal figure',[35] Theodor Herzl, attention must be given to a cultural ideology which had developed during the nineteenth century and which saw the colonisation of 'Palestine' as the means of regenerating Jewish culture and countering the influence of *Haskalah*.

---

[30] Jews were falsely accused of murdering a Capuchin monk and his Arab servant in order to extract their blood for use in the preparation of Passover *matzah*.

[31] Geoffrey Wheatcroft, *The Controversy of Zion* (London: Sinclair-Stevenson, 1996), p. 47.

[32] Ben Halpern, *The Idea of the Jewish State*, 2nd edn (Cambridge, MA: Harvard University Press, 1969), p. 15.

[33] Eliezer Schweid, 'The Rejection of the Diaspora in Zionist Thought: Two Approaches', in *Essential Papers on Zionism*, ed. by Jehuda Reinharz and Anita Shapira (London: Cassell, 1996), p. 149.

[34] Stanley A. Ellisen, *The Arab-Israeli Conflict: Who Owns the Land?* (Portland, OR: Multnomah Press, 1991), p. 59.

[35] Hertzberg, *The Zionist Idea*, p. 45.

Cultural Zionism

Sir Moses Montefiore (1784-1885), the undisputed leader of Anglo-Jewry for much of the nineteenth century, was one of the pioneers of cultural Zionism, first visiting the Land in 1827 and later establishing the Fund for the Cultivation of the Land in Palestine by the Jews. The main driving force in Eastern Europe was Rabbi Samuel Mohilever, who helped to establish the *Chibbath Zion* ('Love of Zion') movement which, in the wake of the Russian pogroms, blazed a trail to the Holy Land under the banner, 'On to Palestine'.[36]

The name most synonymous with cultural Zionism is Asher Ginsberg, who wrote under the pseudonym, Ahad Ha'am ('one of the people'). Described as 'the undisputed moral philosopher'[37] of the Zionist movement, he was critical of the settlement activities of *Chibbath Zion*, believing that the answer to the Jewish Question was to make *Eretz Yisrael* a 'national spiritual centre of Judaism'[38] free of European values. Ginsberg was one of the most outspoken critics of Theodor Herzl, the man who effectively transformed Zionism from 'closet philosophy' into 'a mass movement and a maker of history'.[39] Despite Ginsberg's criticisms, 'the vast majority'[40] of those involved in the *Chibbath Zion* movement joined Herzl and the political movement he established.

Political Zionism

The trial and public demotion in Paris of Captain Alfred Dreyfus in 1894 was the spark which ignited 'the zionist fire'[41] in Theodor Herzl, Dreyfus having been wrongly convicted of treason and sentenced to life imprisonment on Devil's Island. At his demotion, the Parisian crowd shouted, *'A mort les juifs!'* ('Death to the Jews!')[42] Although he was 'embarrassingly ignorant of Judaism and Jewish history',[43] this episode convinced Herzl, an assimilated Jew, that anti-Semitism had arisen as a result of the emancipation of his people.[44] If France, which was the first nation to grant full rights to its Jewish citizens in 1791, could treat a man of Dreyfus' stature so disgracefully, what hope was there for European Jewry as a whole? Within eighteen months Herzl had

---

[36] Dimont, *Jews*, p. 397.

[37] Goldberg, *To the Promised Land*, p. 111.

[38] Leonard Stein, *Zionism* (London: Ernest Benn Ltd., 1925), p. 92.

[39] Hertzberg, *The Zionist Idea*, p. 40.

[40] *Encyclopaedia Judaica: Vol. XVI* (Jerusalem: Keter Publishing House Ltd., c.1971), p. 1041.

[41] Claude Duvernoy, *The Prince and the Prophet* (Christian Action for Israel, 1979), p. 71.

[42] In 1906, he was exonerated, reinstated, and awarded the Legion of Honour Medal.

[43] Goldberg, *To the Promised Land*, p. 30.

[44] *The Complete Diaries of Theodor Herzl: Vol. I*, ed. by Raphael Patai (London: Herzl Press & Thomas Yoseloff, 1960), p. 9.

published *Der Judenstaat* ('The Jewish State'), in which he resurrected the 'very old'[45] idea of restoring the Jewish homeland. This Zionist manifesto was conceived 'in a burst of obsessive energy'[46] during his time as correspondent for the *Neue Freie Presse*, and in February 1896 it 'broke upon the world like a bolt of thunder',[47] rekindling 'with prophetic vision'[48] the restorationist dream which, for centuries, had been 'politically inarticulate and therefore practically ineffective'.[49] This 'prophet in a hurry'[50] was in no doubt: 'The Maccabeans will rise again.'[51]

Despite opposition from the Executive Committee of the Association of German Rabbis, which denounced Zionism for undermining the Jewish obligation 'to serve with all devotion the Fatherland'[52] to which the Jews belonged, the modern Zionist movement was officially launched by Herzl on 29 August 1897 at the First Zionist Congress in Basle, Switzerland. In his opening address at the Stadt Casino Concert Hall, Herzl described Zionism as 'a home-coming to the Jewish fold even before it becomes a home-coming to the Jewish land',[53] stating as one of its objectives 'the transformation of the Jewish question into a question of Zion'.[54]

In order to secure 'a publicly recognised, legally secured home in Palestine', Herzl believed that Jewish 'self-awareness and national consciousness'[55] needed to be strengthened and international support solicited. Politically rather than theologically motivated, Theodor Herzl alienated the Orthodox Jewish communities by centring responsibility for Israel's restoration on the Jewish people rather than on the Jewish Messiah. As he wrote in *Der Judenstaat*, 'Shall we end by having a theocracy? No, indeed…Every man will be as free and undisturbed in his faith or his disbelief as he is in his nationality.'[56]

Between Herzl and the Orthodox community lay the middle way of the 'religious' Zionists. Rooted in *Hasidism*, they believed that working towards the restoration of the Jewish State was not incompatible with the belief that

---

[45] Theodor Herzl, *The Jewish State*, 6th edn (London: H. Pordes, 1972), p. 7.

[46] Virginia H. Hein, *The British Followers of Theodor Herzl: English Zionist Leaders, 1896-1904* (New York: Garland Publishing Inc., 1987), p. 1.

[47] Abba Eban, *My People: The Story of the Jews* (New York: Behrman House, Inc., 1968), p. 330.

[48] Walter Clay Lowdermilk, *Palestine: Land of Promise* (London: Victor Gollancz Ltd., 1944), p. 15.

[49] Joseph Heller, *The Zionist Idea* (New York: Schocken Books, 1949), p. 215.

[50] Walter Laqueur, *A History of Zionism* (New York: Schocken Books, 2003), p. 135.

[51] Herzl, *The Jewish State*, p. 79.

[52] Sachar, *A History of Israel*, p. 44.

[53] WZO, 'Theodor Herzl's Opening Address to the First Zionist Congress', <http://www.wzo.org.il/en/resources/view.asp?id=1367&subject=28, 1 May 2006>.

[54] Herzl, *The Jewish State*, p. 14.

[55] Laqueur, *A History of Zionism*, p. 106.

[56] Herzl, *The Jewish State*, p. 71.

only the Messiah could facilitate Israel's redemption. In 1902, Rav Yitzchak Yaacov Reines, a man of 'original and intrepid mind',[57] established the *Mizrachi* organisation in Vilna, Lithuania, with its slogan, '*Am Yisrael B'Eretz Israel al pi Torat Israel* – the Jewish people in the Land of Israel living according to the Torah of Israel'.[58] However, the 'leading prophet of religious Zionism'[59] was Abraham Isaac Kook, a Talmudic scholar from Latvia and the first Ashkenazic Chief Rabbi of the new *yishuv*.[60] In his book, *The Jewish Destiny and Nationhood* (1901), Kook emphasised the unique interrelationship between the people and the Land, arguing that neither could be redeemed in isolation. One of Kook's contemporaries, the Orthodox Hungarian Rabbi Yissakhar Shlomo Teichthal, also emphasised the uniqueness of this relationship after being 'converted' from his anti-Zionist position during the Holocaust. Teichthal laid much of the blame for Jewish suffering at the feet of the *Haredi* sect of Orthodox Judaism, which opposed the Zionist movement. He also believed that assimilated Jews had sold Israel's birthright 'for a portion of lentil stew of the nations', and called upon his people to return to the Land with this impassioned appeal: 'After all the suffering which has befallen us, and all the pain caused us by our own stepmother, the lands of exile, only Eretz Yisrael, our genuine mother, can comfort us.'[61]

Although Herzl had signalled his intent to secure a home in 'Palestine', he was willing to consider other territorial options, including Argentina, Cyprus, the Sinai Peninsula, and Uganda. In the wake of the Kishinev pogroms of 1903, Herzl believed that the British 'Uganda Proposal'[62] offered the Jews a *nachtasyl* ('night shelter'), or place of temporary refuge, until a permanent home in 'Palestine' could be secured. However, after concerted opposition from its 'most implacable opponent',[63] Menahem Mendel Ussishkin, Herzl was given an ultimatum to reject Uganda or leave the Zionist movement. It was at this point that Herzl became convinced of the unbreakable bond between the Jewish

---

[57] Learsi, *Fulfilment*, p. 123.

[58] *Encyclopaedia of Zionism and Israel: Vol. II*, ed. by Raphael Patai (New York: Herzl Press, 1971), p. 791.

[59] Jacob Agus, 'Preface 1', in *Abraham Isaac Kook: The Lights of Penitence, The Moral Principles, Lights of Holiness, Essays, Letters, and Poems*, ed. and trans. by Ben Zion Bokser (New York: Paulist Press, 1978), p. xi.

[60] The name given to post-1881 Jewish settlers in the Land who had fled the pogroms.

[61] Yissakhar Shlomo Teichthal, *Em HaBanim Semeha: Restoration of Zion as a Response during the Holocaust*, ed. and trans. by Pesach Schindler (Hoboken, NJ: KTAV Publishing House, Inc., 1999), pp. ix, 68, 195.

[62] Nathan Ausubel, *The Book of Jewish Knowledge: An Encyclopedia of Judaism and the Jewish People, Covering all Elements of Jewish Life from Biblical Times to the Present* (New York: Crown Publishers, Inc., 1964), p. 532.

[63] Sachar, *A History of Israel*, p. 62; cf. Joseph Klausner, *Menahem Ussishkin: His Life and Work* (London: The Joint Zionist Publication Committee, 1944), pp. 40, 61-62.

people and their 'ever-memorable historic home'.[64] The Uganda proposal was finally rejected at the Seventh Zionist Congress in 1905, a year after Herzl's death.[65] In a meeting in Manchester the following year, a perplexed Arthur Balfour, then leader of the Conservative Party, asked Chaim Weizmann to explain this decision. Weizmann later recalled the conversation which ensued:

> 'Mr Balfour, supposing I were to offer you Paris instead of London, would you take it?' He sat up, looked at me, and answered: 'But Mr Weizmann, we have London.' 'That is true,' I said. 'But we had Jerusalem when London was a marsh.'[66]

After Herzl's death, Weizmann sought to reconcile the practical and political factions which had arisen within the Zionist movement by developing a 'synthetic' form of Zionism. At the Eighth Zionist Congress in 1907, he laid considerable stress on the need to generate support for the Zionist cause among Diaspora Jews. Without undermining the importance of political diplomacy,[67] Weizmann advocated practical initiatives which would promote *aliyah*, raise awareness of Jewish settlements in the Land, and encourage support for the Jewish National Fund (JNF). The JNF was established at the Fifth Zionist Congress in 1901 with the express purpose of purchasing land for Jewish settlers, much of which was acquired from absentee landlords at exorbitant cost. As Weizmann ruefully observed, 'We found we had to cover the soil of Palestine with Jewish gold.'[68] In a report printed in *The Geographical Magazine* in 1936, Michael Langley described how land was being acquired 'by right of purchase' from Arab landowners 'who have grown rich on the sale of acres, hitherto fallow'.[69] In 1934 alone, £7 million had been spent on just 28,000 acres. Former Palestinian terrorist, Walid Shoebat, corroborates the report with a first-hand account of how many of his fellow Arabs, including his grandfather, sold land to the Jews 'because they got good prices for it and it had little other value to them.'[70]

---

[64] Herzl, *The Jewish State*, p. 30.

[65] Dismayed by the decision, a number of delegates withdrew from the WZO to form the Jewish Territorial Organisation. Under Israel Zangwill's leadership, the goal of these 'territorial' Zionists was to secure political sovereignty in *any* viable territory.

[66] Chaim Weizmann, *Trial and Error: The Autobiography of Chaim Weizmann* (London: Hamish Hamilton, 1949), p. 144.

[67] Unhappy with Weizmann's approach, Vladimir (Ze'ev) Jabotinsky quit the WZO and in 1925 established the Revisionist Zionist Alliance. Its objective was to put pressure on the British government to secure a Jewish state on both sides of the Jordan River.

[68] Weizmann, *Trial and Error*, p. 316.

[69] Michael Langley, '"Back to the Land" in Palestine', *The Geographical Magazine*, July (1936), 187-198.

[70] Walid Shoebat, *Why I Left Jihad: The Root of Terrorism and the Return of Radical Islam* (USA: Top Executive Media, 2005), p. 162.

In his diary entry for 3 September 1897, Herzl declared: 'At Basel I founded the Jewish State,' and then, as if gifted with prophetic insight, continued: 'If I said this out loud today, I would be answered by universal laughter. Perhaps in five years, and certainly in fifty, everyone will know it. The foundation of a State lies in the will of the people for a State, yes, even in the will of one sufficiently powerful individual'.[71] Remarkably, fifty years later, on 29 November 1947, the United Nations General Assembly voted in favour of Resolution 181, which called for the partition of Western 'Palestine' and paved the way for the establishment of the modern State of Israel. Moshe Dayan described the vote as 'the victory of Judaism' in fulfilling the 'age-old yearning – the return to a free and independent Zion.'[72] Like Moses, however, Herzl was destined to see the Promised Land 'only from afar'.[73]

Rebirth of a Nation

Partisanship proved to be the strength of the Zionist movement, drawing into the fold Jews from every position along the ideological spectrum.[74] However, with the exception of religious Zionists, most of its leaders were not theologically driven when speaking 'for Zion's sake' (Isa. 62:1). Despite attempts made by the Reform movement to sever the connection between the Jewish people and the Land, the evidence is clear: Zionism *is* integral to Judaism. In portraying the Jewish religion as 'a triangle the corners of which are faith, people and land', Marmur rightly argues that the absence of any one corner 'constitutes a distortion of Judaism'.[75] All three were brought into sharp focus at 4 p.m. on Friday, 14 May 1948, as David Ben Gurion, 'the messenger of pioneering socialism',[76] proclaimed to the listening world the Declaration of Independence of the modern State of Israel. Drawing upon Biblical history and the age-old attachment of the Jews to the Land,[77] he declared that the Zionist

---

[71] *The Complete Diaries: Vol. II*, ed. by Patai, p. 581.

[72] Moshe Dayan, *Story of My Life* (London: Sphere Books Limited, 1978), p. 83.

[73] Lance Lambert, *The Uniqueness of Israel* (Eastbourne: Kingsway, 2002), p. 145.

[74] Learsi, *Fulfilment*, p. 122.

[75] Dow Marmur, 'The Future of the Jews', in *Renewing the Vision: Rabbis Speak Out on Modern Jewish Issues*, ed. by Jonathan Romain (London: SCM Press Ltd., 1996), p. 178.

[76] Abba Eban, 'Introduction', in *Israel: The First Forty Years*, ed. by William Frankel (London: Thames and Hudson Ltd., 1987), p. 10.

[77] Israel's national anthem, *HaTikvah* ('The Hope'), reads: 'As long as the Jewish spirit is yearning deep in the heart, With eyes turned toward the East, looking toward Zion, Then our hope - the two-thousand-year-old hope - will not be lost: To be a free people in our land, The land of Zion and Jerusalem.'

dream had been fulfilled.[78] After a period of 'quaking instability', the 'centre of gravity of the Jewish people'[79] had finally come to rest. No longer would the Jews be 'driftwood on the current of history',[80] for Israel now had 'a Place on the Map' and the wandering Jew 'a home to return to.'[81] Golda Meir, one of the signatories to the Scroll of Independence, described her reaction: 'The State of Israel! My eyes filled with tears and my hands shook. We had done it. We had brought the Jewish State into existence – and I, Golda Mabovitch Meyerson, had lived to see the day...The long exile was over.' With Herzl's prophetic words fifty years earlier in mind, she declared: 'And so it had come to pass.'[82]

The re-establishment of the Jewish State has been described as 'the most spectacular event in nearly two millennia of Jewish history'.[83] As far as Christian Zionists are concerned, Israel's rebirth was indeed a miracle, but one they believe foreshadows a far greater event - the return of the Jewish Messiah.

Christian Zionism

Christian Zionism is an umbrella term under which many Christians who support Israel have congregated. However, although there is broad agreement among those who acknowledge God's prophetic purposes for Israel, and who point to 1948 as the fulfilment of prophecy, there is considerable disagreement relating to the interpretation of those scriptures which speak of the Rapture of the Church, the identity and role of the Antichrist, the Great Tribulation, and the Second Coming. I believe that Christian Zionism, properly defined, incorporates the following key elements:

1. A clear, Biblical distinction between Israel and the Church.
2. The any moment, *pre*-tribulation Rapture of the Church.
3. The return of the Jews to the Land.
4. The rebuilding of the Temple.
5. The rise of the Antichrist.
6. A seven-year period known as the Great Tribulation.
7. The national salvation of the Jews.
8. The return of Christ to Jerusalem.

---

[78] Quoted in William L. Hull, *The Fall and Rise of Israel: The Story of the Jewish People during the time of their Dispersal and Regathering* (Grand Rapids, MI: Zondervan Publishing Company, 1954), pp. 321-323.

[79] Herman Wouk, *This is My God: The Jewish Way of Life*, Revised edn (London: Collins, 1979), p. 259.

[80] Learsi, *Fulfilment*, p. 408.

[81] Jill Hamilton, *God, Guns and Israel: Britain, the First World War and the Jews in the Holy Land* (Stroud: Sutton Publishing Limited, 2004), pp. 251-253.

[82] Meir, *My Life*, p. 185.

[83] Rufus Learsi, *The Jews in America: A History* (New York: The World Publishing Company, 1954), p. 230.

9.   The thousand-year reign of Christ on earth.

In presenting this working definition, I have no wish to alienate any Christian friend of Israel. However, such a definition is necessary in order to dispel confusion, correct misunderstanding, and provide a sound, *Biblical* foundation on which to base that 'friendship' and support. Consequently, I will, on occasion, quote from those who would not subscribe to my definition, but whose contributions I consider to be of value.

The Zionist Badge

According to Edward Flannery, without Christian Zionism 'it is highly unlikely that the present State of Israel would have come into being so rapidly as it did'.[84] The *Encyclopaedia of Zionism and Israel* also credits Christian Zionism with having had 'a direct bearing'[85] on the Zionist movement, while Lawrence Epstein suggests that too few people realise 'how much Christians have contributed to the Zionist movement and to the nation of Israel'.[86]

Described as 'an American premillennialist Christian with a pro-Zionist orientation',[87] G. Douglas Young, founder of the Israel-American Institute of Biblical Studies in Jerusalem, wrote the following letter to the *Jerusalem Post* dated 26 October 1975:

> Sir, – I have been accused of being a Zionist – a Christian Zionist – by some of my co-religionists in Israel and in the administered areas. I would like to take this means of thanking them for this compliment. In spite of being a Christian, my Jewish friends in Israel and elsewhere have labelled me a Christian Zionist and for this I want to thank them too and to let them know what a warm feeling this gives me. I feel sorry for my Christian friends, and apologise for some of them, who are silent and have not yet identified publicly with Zionism, perhaps because they do not understand it or because they fear other consequences. I have always thought that it was a grand thing when the King of Denmark and his subjects wore the

---

[84] Edward H. Flannery, 'Christian Zionist Ethos should be Revived', *Providence Journal-Bulletin*, 26 April (1997), <http://pqasb.pqarchiver.com/projo/results.html?Qry Txt=christian+zionist+ethos&submit=Go, 6 June 2006>.
[85] *Encyclopaedia of Zionism and Israel: Vol. II*, ed. by Patai, p. 948.
[86] Lawrence J. Epstein, *Zion's Call: Christian Contributions to the Origins and Development of Israel* (London: University Press of America, 1984), p. ix.
[87] Yaakov Ariel, 'How are Jews and Israel Portrayed in the Left Behind Series? A Historical Discussion of Jewish-Christian Relations', in *Rapture, Revelation, and the End Times: Exploring the Left Behind Series*, ed. by Bruce David Forbes and Jeanne Halgren Kilde (New York: Palgrave Macmillan, 2004), p. 145.

yellow patch when the Nazis tried by this means to single out the Jews in that country. Now I am glad to be able to wear a similar identifying pin.[88]

Young's letter is helpful. Many Christians have chosen to wear the Zionist badge as a mark of solidarity with the Jewish people and the Jewish State, and as a way of distancing themselves from those within the Church who have replaced Israel theologically and opposed her politically. In his book, *Standing with Israel: Why Christians Support the Jewish State* (2006), Jewish writer David Brog describes Christian Zionists as 'the ideological heirs of the righteous Gentiles who saved Jews during the Holocaust', and those who today are 'putting on the yellow star'.[89]

The term favoured by historians when surveying Christian interest in the return of the Jews to the Land has been 'Restorationism', but this label is too broad and all encompassing and fails to account for theological intricacies. Since Christian Zionism is fundamentally eschatological, any survey which fails to get to grips with this theological vocabulary will be flawed. Although it is not easy to distinguish between the eschatological constellations which at first glance appear identical, care must be taken so that a correct identification of 'Christian Zionism' can be made.

The Fundamentals of Christian Zionism

The Christian Zionist badge has been indiscriminately pinned on members of the professing Church. This is particularly evident among liberal Protestants who have expressed solidarity with the Jewish State, either on humanitarian grounds, or to atone for crimes committed against the Jewish people in the name of Christianity, or simply as a means of upholding Biblical concepts of liberation and social justice. However, the history of this liberal movement is relatively recent compared to its fundamentally Biblical, Evangelical, and eschatologically-driven counterpart, and its impact marginal by comparison. One only has to consider the success of Hal Lindsey's *The Late Great Planet Earth*, which sold 28 million copies during the 1970s, and the remarkable phenomenon of the *Left Behind* series of Rapture novels, which have frequently topped best-seller lists and 'blown the lid off previous publishing records',[90] to appreciate the scale of a Christian Zionist tradition concerned, first and foremost, with pursuing a *Biblical* 'Road-map' to peace. Liberal Protestant theologians and sympathisers of Zionism, such as Paul Tillich and Reinhold

---

[88] Quoted in Calvin B. Hanson, *A Gentile, With the Heart of a Jew* (Nyack, NY: Parson Publishing, 1979), pp. 294-295.

[89] David Brog, *Standing with Israel: Why Christians Support the Jewish State* (Lake Mary, FL: FrontLine, 2006), pp. 229, 9.

[90] Mark Hitchcock and Thomas Ice, *The Truth behind Left Behind: A Biblical View of the End Times* (Sisters, OR: Multnomah Publishers, Inc., 2004), p. 13.

Niebuhr, may have hung their solidarity on scriptures concerned with social justice and liberation, but Christian Zionism as outlined in this book begins and ends with the Bible, and, more specifically, with a consistently literal interpretation of Biblical prophecy. As Elishua Davidson summarises, 'the whole prophetic biblical word is a blueprint for the future of Israel, the nations, and the world.'[91] Members of the Church of Jesus Christ of Latter Day Saints ('Mormons'), the Jehovah's Witnesses, and particularly the Christadelphians have often been included in historical surveys of Restorationism and Christian Zionism, but this simply muddies the waters. Owing to their heterodoxy, these movements must be treated separately and their theology distinguished from that which is fundamentally Protestant and Evangelical.

Classifying Christian Zionists

It is difficult to pinpoint precisely when the 'Christian Zionist' label was first used. In his diary entry for 5 September 1896, Theodor Herzl mentions 'the Christian Zionist Baron Manteuffel', whom he later describes as 'a Christian Zion enthusiast'. Two English clergymen, 'Mr. Biddulph' and 'Mr. Bramley Moore', are mentioned by Herzl in his diary as 'a Zionist'[92] and 'an ardent Zionist'[93] respectively. Also, during his closing speech at the First Zionist Congress in 1897, Herzl singled out one of the Christian observers at the Congress, Jean Henri Dunant, as a 'Christian Zionist'.[94]

Historians have frequently juggled with labels in attempting to classify Gentile interest in the restoration of the Jews. These have included 'Judeophile', 'philo-Semite', 'proto-Zionist', 'Gentile Zionist', 'Millenarian Zionist', 'Humanitarian Zionist', 'Protestant Zionist', 'British Zionist', and 'Restorationist'. They have invariably listed in the same category names such as Brightman, Cromwell, Simeon, Shaftesbury, Disraeli, Eliot, and Balfour, creating artificial and misleading genealogies in the process. As the *Encyclopaedia of Zionism and Israel* has rightly stated, Christian Zionism is 'a purely Christian affair' whose goals have 'remained theological'.[95] Far from being a contradiction in terms,[96] it is the most appropriate label for distinguishing a fundamentally Biblical, Evangelical, and eschatological interest in Israel's restoration from other expressions of pro-Israel sentiment.

---

[91] Elishua Davidson, *Islam, Israel, and the Last Days* (Eugene, OR: Harvest House Publishers, 1991), p. 120.

[92] *The Complete Diaries: Vol. II*, ed. by Patai, pp. 461, 535, 711.

[93] *The Complete Diaries: Vol. III*, ed. by Patai, p. 1159.

[94] *Encyclopaedia Judaica: Vol. VI*, p. 270. Dunant founded the International Committee of the Red Cross, inspired the Geneva Conventions, and received the first Nobel Peace Prize.

[95] *Encyclopaedia of Zionism and Israel: Vol. II*, ed. by Patai, p. 948.

[96] N.T. Wright, 'Jerusalem in the New Testament', in Walker, *Jerusalem*, p. 74.

The Church and Israel

Christian Zionists make a clear distinction between Israel and the Church, insisting that the Church is neither the 'new', 'true', nor 'spiritual Israel'. According to Lewis Sperry Chafer, founder of Dallas Theological Seminary, 'Israel has never been the Church, is not the Church now, nor will she ever be the Church.'[97] According to Ramon Bennett, 'When we speak of Israel's God or, the God of Israel, we speak of the God of the physical nation of Israel – the Jewish people, not the Church. Israel is not a synonym for the Church.'[98] Rob Richards, former UK director of the Church's Ministry among Jewish People (CMJ), is even more succinct: 'Israel is Israel is Israel'.[99]

Christian Zionists believe that God is working out uniquely separate, albeit interrelated, purposes with Israel and the Church. This distinction is rooted in the Abrahamic Covenant, which has been described as 'the basis of the entire covenant program',[100] 'the fountainhead of Bible prophecy',[101] and 'absolutely pivotal in the entire structure of prophetic truth'.[102] Thus although the Church is comprised of 'Abraham's seed' (Gal. 3:29), it does not fulfil 'the yet unfulfilled provisions of that covenant'[103] which pertain to the nation of Israel, and which the prophets spoke so much about. Consequently, Paul's statement that 'all Israel will be saved' (Rom. 11:26), described by Skevington Wood as 'a *crux exegetica* in prophetic interpretation',[104] speaks not only of the salvation of *individual* Jews prior to Christ's Second Coming, but of the future, *national* salvation of Israel when He returns to reign in Jerusalem. Israel thus exists as a nation *outside* the Church, 'with all of God's promises and plans for her

---

[97] Lewis Sperry Chafer, *Systematic Theology, Volume IV: Ecclesiology – Eschatology* (Dallas, TX: Dallas Seminary Press, 1948), p. 311.

[98] Ramon Bennett, *Saga: Israel and the Demise of Nations* (Jerusalem: Arm of Salvation, 1993), p. 23. According to Peter Richardson, the transfer of the name 'Israel' to the Church finds its 'fixed point' in the *Dialogue with Trypho, a Jew*, a second-century work by Justin Martyr. Nowhere 'from the close of the NT canon to Justin' is the Church said to be Israel. (Peter Richardson, *Israel in the Apostolic Church* [Cambridge: Cambridge University Press, 1969], pp. ix, 16.)

[99] Rob Richards, *Has God finished with Israel?* (St Albans: Olive Press, 1994), p. 21.

[100] J. Dwight Pentecost, *Things to Come: A Study in Biblical Eschatology* (Findlay, OH: Dunham Publishing Company, 1958), p. 70.

[101] Thomas Ice, 'Why Futurism?', in *The End Times Controversy: The Second Coming Under Attack*, ed. by Tim LaHaye and Thomas Ice (Eugene, OR: Harvest House Publishers, 2003), p. 401.

[102] Arthur Skevington Wood, *Prophecy in the Space Age: Studies in Prophetic Themes* (London: Marshall, Morgan & Scott, 1964), p. 38.

[103] Charles Caldwell Ryrie, *The Basis of the Premillennial Faith* (Neptune, NJ: Loizeaux Brothers, 1966), p. 156.

[104] Skevington Wood, *Prophecy in the Space Age*, p. 51.

remaining in full force'.[105] Christian Zionists make a further important distinction by insisting that the salvation of both the nation and the individual is mediated through the New Covenant in Christ. As Steve Maltz writes, 'There's no fast track to paradise for the chosen people,' since 'Jews are not saved through Judaism, but through Jesus, like everyone else.'[106]

A notable opponent of Christian Zionism is Charles Provan, who argues that 'the Israel of the Old Testament' has been 'deposed' by the Church, to which all privileges and promises have been 'transferred'.[107] He strings together numerous proof-texts in an attempt to prove that Israel's promised blessings have been 'applied en masse' to the Church, and that Jewish and Gentile believers 'are now members of the true nation of Israel'. Zion is now said to be 'devoid of all geographical connotations, and refers to the Church'.[108] W.J. Grier finds support for this replacementist view in the inserted headings of the King James Bible when he writes: 'Israel and Judah are evidently the Israel of God, the New Testament Church. So the Authorised Version headings, which refer Old Testament prophecies to the New Testament Church, evidently have the support of the New Testament itself.'[109] This defiling[110] of God's word through '*man*-made headings',[111] and the supersessionist doctrine underpinning them, have been denounced as 'a theological trap door'[112] through which many, like Provan, have fallen. Theologically this delegitimises the Jewish people and the Jewish State, and helps to foster anti-Semitism in the Church.[113]

The Church has consistently spiritualised Israel's blessings while interpreting her judgments literally. Basilea Schlink considers the transfer of

---

[105] Dave Hunt, *Global Peace and the Rise of Antichrist* (Eugene, OR: Harvest House Publishers, 1990), p. 28.

[106] Steve Maltz, *The People of Many Names: Towards a Clearer Understanding of the Miracle of the Jewish People* (Milton Keynes: Authentic Media, 2005), pp. 50, 168.

[107] Charles D. Provan, *The Church is Israel Now* (Vallecito, CA: Ross House Books, 1987), preface; *cf.* Gary North, *Rapture Fever: Why Dispensationalism is Paralyzed* (Tyler, TX: Institute for Christian Economics, 1993), pp. xii-xv; Greg L. Bahnsen and Kenneth L. Gentry, Jr, *House Divided: The Break-Up of Dispensational Theology* (Tyler, TX: Institute for Christian Economics, 1989), pp. 164-174.

[108] Provan, *The Church is Israel Now*, pp. 1, 39, 56.

[109] W.J. Grier, *The Momentous Event: A Discussion of Scripture Teaching on the Second Advent* (London: Banner of Truth, 1970), p. 47. These headings include those inserted above Isaiah 30, 34, 43-45, 50, 54, and 64.

[110] John R. Rice, *The Coming Kingdom of Christ* (Murfreesboro, TN: Sword of the Lord Publishers, 1979), p. 95.

[111] Sydney Watson, *The New Europe: A Story of Today and Tomorrow* (London: William Nicholson & Sons Limited, 1915), p. 190.

[112] Tom Doyle, *Two Nations Under God: Why Should America Care About Israel and the Middle East* (Nashville, TN: Broadman & Holman Publishers, 2004), p. 52.

[113] Marvin R. Wilson, *Our Father Abraham: Jewish Roots of the Christian Faith* (Grand Rapids, MI: Centre for Judaic-Christian Studies, 1989), p. 264.

one without the other to be 'untruthful and impossible'.[114] To paraphrase Michael Brown, one could no more convince the Jews in exile that God's promise of restoration was figurative than one could convince them that their captivity was to be understood figuratively also. Consistency in interpretation demands that the 'literality of the promised restoration would have to be just as real as the literality of the threatened judgment.'[115] As the Lord Himself declared, 'As I have brought all this great calamity on this people, so I will give them all the prosperity I have promised them' (Jer. 32:42).

The Land of Israel

Despite centuries of Diaspora wandering, the Jewish people have maintained a 'Holy Land-centred faith',[116] their hearts longing for the promised return to Zion. Christian Zionists insist that the Land of Israel, the Jewish people, and the city of Jerusalem are 'inextricably bonded together in a covenant relationship'.[117] As Moishe Rosen points out, 'God promised Abraham more than a nation of descendants. He promised a land.'[118] This interrelationship between the people and the Land is said to be 'the key which unlocks many prophetic secrets.'[119] Johann Kurtz, in his *History of the Old Covenant* (1859), expressed it this way: 'As the body is adapted and destined for the soul, and the soul for the body; so is Israel for that country and that country for Israel.'[120]

Although many Jews have now returned to the Land, and the State of Israel has been re-established, Christian Zionists insist that Israel's present territory is only a fraction of what was promised to Abraham (Gen. 15:18) and confirmed to Moses and Joshua (Num. 34:3-12; Josh. 1:4). As Carment Urquhart wrote in 1945, 'Palestine will never belong, by any real right of possession, to any people but the Jews…When the Jews repent and accept the Lord Jesus they will be given not only Palestine but also all the rest of the great Land of Promise, and will be a blessing in the midst of the whole earth.'[121] So central is the Land to their theology that Christian Zionists have described it as 'the most important

---

[114] M. Basilea Schlink, *Israel My Chosen People: A German Confession before God and the Jews* (London: The Faith Press, 1963), pp. 66-67.

[115] Michael L. Brown, *Israel's Divine Healer* (Carlisle: Paternoster Press, 1995), p. 184.

[116] David Dolan, *Israel in Crisis: What Lies Ahead?* (Grand Rapids, MI: Fleming H. Revell, 2002), p. 16.

[117] Hugh Kitson, *Jerusalem, the Covenant City* (Steyning: Hatikvah Ltd., 2000), p. 27.

[118] Moishe Rosen, *Overture to Armageddon? Beyond the Gulf War* (San Bernardino, CA: Here's Life Publishers, Inc., 1991), p. 106.

[119] C.I. Scofield, *Prophecy made Plain: Addresses on Prophecy* (London: Pickering & Inglis, n.d.), p. 69.

[120] Quoted in Smith, *Israeli-Arab Conflict*, p. 54.

[121] Carment Urquhart, 'The World-wide Jewish Problem', in John Urquhart, *Wonders of Prophecy: The Testimony of Fulfilled Prediction to the Inspiration of the Bible* (London: Pickering & Inglis Ltd., 1945), p. 195.

piece of real estate on earth',[122] 'God's geographical centre',[123] 'the geographical platform on which the story of the Bible is staged', 'the focal point of the universe – for the outworking of the purposes of God',[124] 'the centre of Divine dealings with nations',[125] 'the spiritual navel of the world',[126] 'the epicenter of human history',[127] and 'ground zero for the end times'.[128] In a similar vein, Jerusalem has been depicted as 'a miraculous entity',[129] the only city on earth 'not up for negotiation with anyone at any time for any reason',[130] and 'ground zero for the future activities of the Antichrist' and for 'God's gracious redemption.'[131] In his address to the Israeli Knesset on 5 December 1949, Prime Minister David Ben Gurion declared that 'Jewish Jerusalem is an organic and inseparable part of the State of Israel, as it is an inseparable part of the history and religion of Israel and of the soul of our people.'[132] Christian Zionists agree, although they assert that Jerusalem's importance rests ultimately in the fact that it is 'the city where God's Son died for the sins of the world.'[133] It therefore follows eschatologically that the Second Coming of Christ cannot be divorced from the place to which He will return, nor from the people to whom He will return. As Sydney Watson writes, 'the Jewish question is infinitely more closely enwrapped with the fact of our Lord's near return, than many speakers and writers give prominence to.'[134]

---

[122] Mark Hitchcock, *Is the Antichrist Alive Today?* (Sisters, OR: Multnomah Publishers, Inc., 2002), p. 46.

[123] John Wilkinson, *God's Plan for the Jew* (London: The Messianic Testimony, 1978), p. 89.

[124] Ronald B. Allen, 'The Land of Israel', in *Israel, the Land and the People: An Evangelical Affirmation of God's Promises*, ed. by H. Wayne House (Grand Rapids, MI: Kregel Publications, 1998), pp. 18, 28.

[125] C.F. Hogg and W.E. Vine, *Touching the Coming of the Lord* (London: Oliphants Ltd., 1919), p. 111.

[126] Ramon Bennett, *The Wall: Prophecy, Politics and Middle East 'Peace'* (Citrus Heights, CA: Shekinha Books, Ltd., 2000), p. 268.

[127] Joel C. Rosenberg, *Epicenter: Why the Current Rumblings in the Middle East will Change Your Future* (Carol Stream, IL: Tyndale House Publishers, Inc., 2006), p. 265.

[128] Hitchcock and Ice, *The Truth behind Left Behind*, p. 155.

[129] Randall Price, *Unholy War: America, Israel and Radical Islam* (Eugene, OR: Harvest House Publishers, 2001), p. 83.

[130] John Hagee, *Jerusalem Countdown: A Warning to the World* (Lake Mary, FL: FrontLine, 2006), p. 48.

[131] Charles H. Dyer, 'Jerusalem: The Eye of the Storm', in *Storm Clouds on the Horizon*, ed. by Charles H. Dyer (Chicago, IL: Moody Press, 2001), pp. 77-78.

[132] Jerusalem Post, *Front Page Israel: Major Events 1932-1979 as Reflected in the Front Pages of The Jerusalem Post* (Jerusalem: The Palestine Post Ltd., 1978), p. 132.

[133] Charles H. Dyer, *The Rise of Babylon: Sign of the End Times* (Wheaton, IL: Tyndale House Publishers, Inc., 1991), p. 58.

[134] Sydney Watson, *In the Twinkling of an Eye* (London: W. Nicholson and Sons, n.d.), p. vii.

Christian Zionists cite the Abrahamic Covenant as the basis of Israel's right to possess the Land, claiming that God's promises to Abraham were 'quite specific and unambiguous',[135] having been sealed by an unconditional and everlasting covenant (Gen. 12:1-7; 15:18-21; 17:6-8; 26:3; 28:13-15; Heb. 6:13-17).[136] Murray Dixon notes that 'God was the sole signatory'[137] to this covenant, since only He passed through the animal pieces (Gen. 15:12-21). The inference drawn from Ancient Near Eastern custom is that in so doing, God invoked a curse upon Himself, should He ever break His promise. Tatford adds that 'No provision was made for its revocation, and it was not subject to amendment or annulment.'[138] Christian Zionists insist that this unconditional covenant, unlike the 'conditional contract'[139] of Sinai, has not been abrogated or superseded by the New Covenant. Whereas *occupation* of the Land was conditional upon obedience to the law of Moses, *ownership* was eternally guaranteed on the basis of God's unilateral oath. Therefore despite periods of protracted exile, the relationship between the Jewish people and the Land was only '*interrupted*' and not '*severed*',[140] the return from exile being dependent entirely on God's faithfulness to His covenant with Abraham. As the psalmist declared, God 'remembers His covenant for ever, the word He commanded, for a thousand generations, the covenant He made with Abraham, the oath He swore to Isaac' (Ps. 105:8-9; *cf.* Luke 1:54-55, 68-73). Paul confirms this in his letter to the Galatians when he writes:

> The law, introduced 430 years later, does not set aside the covenant previously established by God and thus do away with the promise. For if the inheritance depends on the law, then it no longer depends on a promise; but God in His grace gave it to Abraham through a promise (Gal. 3:17).

Although Christian Zionists cast those who deny Israel's future restoration in the role of the 'stay-at-home son' (Luke 15:11-32),[141] they insist that it is not on the basis of merit that God is restoring Israel, 'but because He is a covenant-

---

[135] Frederick A. Tatford, *Five Minutes to Midnight* (London: Victory Press, 1970), p. 76.
[136] John F. Walvoord, *The Millennial Kingdom* (Grand Rapids, MI: Zondervan Publishing House, 1969), pp. 149-152.
[137] Murray Dixon, *The Rebirth and Restoration of Israel* (Chichester: Sovereign World, 1988), p. 39.
[138] Frederick A. Tatford, *The Middle East Problem: Israel in History and Prophecy* (Scarborough, ON: Everyday Publications Inc., 1983), p. 9.
[139] Charles Lee Feinberg, 'The Rebuilding of the Temple', in *Prophecy in the Making: Messages Prepared for Jerusalem Conference on Biblical Prophecy*, ed. by Carl F.H. Henry (Carol Stream, IL: Creation House, 1971), p. 103.
[140] Wilkinson, *God's Plan for the Jew*, p. 19.
[141] Steve Maltz, *The Land of Many Names: Towards a Christian Understanding of the Middle East Conflict* (Milton Keynes: Authentic Lifestyle, 2003), p. 23.

keeping Sovereign who has regard for His own reputation'.[142] In the words of Dave Hunt, 'God's integrity is tied to Israel'.[143] This inextricable link between the honour of God's Name and the restoration of the Jews to the Land is highlighted in the following Biblical prophecy:

> Therefore say to the house of Israel, 'This is what the Sovereign Lord says: It is not for your sake, O house of Israel, that I am going to do these things, but for the sake of my holy name, which you have profaned among the nations where you have gone. I will show the holiness of my great name...Then the nations will know that I am the Lord, declares the Sovereign Lord, when I show myself holy through you before their eyes' (Ezek. 36:22-23).

If, as supersessionists believe, the Abrahamic Covenant was conditional, then, according to George Peters, 'everything else is conditional; *then* the foundations of Christian hope crumble away beneath us, and *nothing stable remains.*'[144] In other words, if Israel has been rejected by God and replaced by the Church because of her failures, 'can it not be equally argued that the Church has miserably failed God also?'[145]

Can These Bones Live?

In his series of addresses on prophecy, Cyrus Scofield dismissed claims that the promised restoration of Israel was fulfilled when 42,360 Jewish exiles returned from Babylon (Ezra 2:64). According to the prophet Jeremiah, the Israelites had been promised an exodus 'out of the land of the north and out of all the countries where [God] had banished them' (Jer. 16:14-15; 23:7-8), an exodus that would eclipse their flight from Egypt. Scofield questioned how the return of so few from Babylon could 'efface by its greater splendour the amazing events of the exodus'.[146] Since the re-establishment of the State of Israel in 1948, there has been a dramatic increase in Jewish immigration from around the world.[147] Christian Zionists generally believe that the collapse of the former

---

[142] Dolan, *Israel in Crisis*, p. 19.

[143] Dave Hunt, *Judgment Day! Islam, Israel and the Nations*, 2nd edn (Bend, OR: The Berean Call, 2006), p. 261.

[144] George N.H. Peters, *The Theocratic Kingdom of our Lord Jesus, the Christ, as Covenanted in the Old Testament and Presented in the New Testament: Vol. II* (Grand Rapids, MI: Kregel Publications, 1978), p. 48.

[145] Charles L. Feinberg, *Israel at the Centre of History and Revelation*, 3rd edn (Portland, OR: Multnomah Press, 1980), p. 105.

[146] Scofield, *Prophecy made Plain*, p. 82.

[147] The airlift of Jews from Yemen ('Operation Magic Carpet', 1949), Iraq and Iran ('Operation Babylon', 1950-1952), and Ethiopia ('Operation Moses' and 'Operation Queen of Sheba', 1984-1985; 'Operation Solomon', 1991) have been described as 'remarkable examples of immigration'. (Lilli Myss, *A Call to the Nations: Warning Signals for the Coming Russian Exodus* [Chichester: New Wine Press, 1999], p. 178.)

Soviet Union in 1991 was a judgment from God upon a communist regime which had refused to allow Jews to leave the country. In the years immediately following the collapse, 750,000 Russian Jews emigrated to Israel in line with Jeremiah's 'second exodus' prophecy.[148] Russia is typically identified by Christian Zionists as 'the land of the north' (Jer. 16:15; 23:8; *cf.* Isa. 43:6), and as a major player in the end-time prophecies of Ezekiel 38-39.[149]

Described as 'the Magna Carta of Zionism and of Jewish history',[150] Ezekiel's vision of the dry bones (Ezekiel 37) has been interpreted by Christian Zionists as prefiguring the literal re-establishment of the 'seemingly dead nation'[151] of Israel, which occurs in two distinct stages. First, the Jews are restored to the Land in unbelief (representing the joining together of the dry bones), and are then spiritually restored by the breath, or Spirit, of God, signifying their acceptance of the Messiah. As Charles Spurgeon declared in a sermon at the Metropolitan Tabernacle in 1864,

> The meaning of our text, as opened up by the context, is most evidently, if words mean anything, first, *that there shall be a political restoration of the Jews to their own land and to their own nationality*; and then, secondly, there is in the text, and in the context, a most plain declaration, *that there shall be a spiritual restoration, a conversion in fact, of the tribes of Israel*...There will be a native government again; there will again be the form of a body politic; a state shall be incorporated, and a king shall reign...I wish never to learn the art of tearing God's meaning out of His own words...Let this be settled...that if there be meaning in words, Israel is yet to be restored.[152]

Christian Zionists point to the following statistics as evidence that the first stage of Ezekiel's vision has been progressively fulfilled. In May 1839, William Tanner Young, the first British consul in Jerusalem, reported to Foreign Secretary Palmerston that there were approximately '9690 [Jewish]

---

[148] Myss, *A Call to the Nations*, p. 19.

[149] See John F. Walvoord and Mark Hitchcock, *Armageddon, Oil, and Terror: What the Bible says about the Future* (Carol Stream, IL: Tyndale House Publishers, Inc., 2007), pp. 87-114; Rosenberg, *Epicenter*, pp. 81-157.

[150] Claude Duvernoy, *Controversy of Zion: A Biblical View of the History and Meaning of Zion* (Green Forest, AR: New Leaf Press, 1987), p. 61.

[151] Tim LaHaye, 'Twelve Reasons why this could be the Terminal Generation', in *The Return: Understanding Christ's Second Coming and the End Times*, ed. by Thomas Ice and Timothy J. Demy (Grand Rapids, MI: Kregel Publications, 1999), p. 188.

[152] Charles Haddon Spurgeon, *The Restoration and Conversion of the Jews: A Sermon Preached on Thursday Evening, June 16th, 1864...at the Metropolitan Tabernacle, Newington, in Aid of the Funds of the British Society for the Propagation of the Gospel amongst the Jews* (Pasadena, TX: Pilgrim Publications, n.d.), pp. 428-429; *cf.* Charles Haddon Spurgeon, *12 Sermons on the Second Coming of Christ* (Grand Rapids, MI: Baker Books, 1993), pp. 137-138.

Souls'[153] in the Land. This figure had risen to 66,000 by the end of the First World War,[154] and according to *The Jewish Year Book 2006*, there are now 5.24 million Jews living in Israel.[155] Christian Zionists also draw attention to the way the Land itself has revived since the Jews began returning, proving that there is 'a special connection between the fruitfulness of the Land of Israel and the Jewish people'.[156] For example, in 1936, *The Geographical Magazine* reported that over 5 million cases of Jaffa oranges were being exported annually from Israel, a figure which, it was predicted, would rise significantly over the next few years.[157] Such reports have been hailed as evidence of an 'ecological miracle, unrivalled in the twentieth century', which occurred as the returning exiles 'transformed the land that had lain desolate'[158] for nearly two millennia 'into a smiling countryside'.[159] The mountains have again produced 'branches and fruit for [God's] people Israel' (Ezek. 36:8), the desert has yielded 'the cedar and the acacia, the myrtle and the olive' (Isa. 41:19), and Israel has quite literally filled 'all the world with fruit' (Isa. 27:6). American soil conservationist Walter Clay Lowdermilk described the 'herculean task' of those who were restoring 'the ancient fertility of the long-neglected soil' as 'the most remarkable' he had seen 'while studying land use in twenty-four countries'.[160]

Reviving the Hebrew Language

Inspired in his youth by a Hebrew translation of *Robinson Crusoe*, Eliezer Perlman believed that the Zionist dream could only succeed if the Jews had 'a Hebrew language' with which to 'conduct the business of life.'[161] Described by Sachar as a 'sparrow-chested little Russian Jewish philologist',[162] Perlman

---

[153] 'WM.T. Young to Viscount Palmerston, F.O.78/368 (No.13), 25 May 1839', in *The British Consulate in Jerusalem in Relation to the Jews of Palestine 1838-1914, Part I: 1838-1861*, ed. by Albert M. Hyamson (London: Edward Goldston Ltd., 1939), p. 5.

[154] Doreen Ingrams, *Palestine Papers 1917-1922: Seeds of Conflict* (London: John Murray, 1972), p. 44.

[155] *The Jewish Year Book 2006*, ed. by Stephen W. Massil (London: Vallentine Mitchell, 2006), p. 149.

[156] Rebecca J. Brimmer, 'Israel-Miracle Nation', in Rebecca J. Brimmer and Bridges for Peace Leaders, *Israel and the Church: God's Road Map* (Jerusalem: Bridges for Peace International, 2006), p. 134.

[157] Langley, '"Back to the Land" in Palestine', 202.

[158] Kitson, *Jerusalem*, p. 99; *cf.* Noah W. Hutchings, *25 Messianic Signs in Israel Today* (Oklahoma City, OK: Hearthstone Publishing, 1999), pp. 71-107.

[159] Maurice Edelman, *Ben Gurion: A Political Biography* (London: Hodder and Stoughton, 1964), p. 83.

[160] Lowdermilk, *Palestine*, pp. 14-19.

[161] Robert St. John, *Tongue of the Prophets: The Life Story of Eliezer Ben Yehuda* (Gordon City, NY: Dolphin Books, 1952), pp. 23-26, 38.

[162] Sachar, *A History of Israel*, p. 82.

became enamoured with the Hebrew language, the revival of which he believed was integral to Israel's restoration. Later adopting the surname Ben Yehuda, he wrote an article in 1879 for the Viennese newspaper, *HaShahar* ('The Dawn'), in which he argued the case for Jewish nationalism:

> If, in truth, each and every nation is entitled to defend its nationality and protect itself from extinction, then logically we, the Hebrews, also must have the same right...If we care at all that the name of Israel should not disappear from this earth, we must create a centre for the whole of our people, like a heart from which the blood would run into the arteries of the whole, and animate the whole. Only the settlement of *Eretz Israel* can serve this purpose.[163]

After making *aliyah* with his wife in 1881, Ben Yehuda set about establishing Hebrew as the common tongue of the Jewish settlers, compiling one of the most comprehensive dictionaries ever produced. Unprecedented in the history of the nations, a language long forgotten had been revived, and by 1916 forty percent of the Jewish population in *Eretz Yisrael* spoke Hebrew as their first language. So 'formidable'[164] was Ben Yehuda's achievement that three days of official mourning were observed when he died. Christian Zionists consider the revival of the Hebrew tongue to be part of the process of Israel's restoration, and 'arguably'[165] the fulfilment of Zephaniah's prophecy: 'For then will I turn to the people a pure language, that they may all call upon the name of the Lord, to serve Him with one consent' (Zeph. 3:9; KJV).

The Magna Carta of Christian Zionism

Immediately prior to His Ascension, Jesus spent forty days teaching His disciples about the kingdom of God (Acts 1:3). At the end of that period they asked Him, 'Lord, are you at this time going to restore the kingdom to Israel?', to which He replied, 'It is not for you to know the times or dates the Father has set by his own authority.' Christian Zionists believe that Christ's answer 'ratified to the apostles the promise that was given of old',[166] namely that Messiah would one day 'reign on David's throne and over his kingdom' (Isa. 9:7; *cf.* Luke 1: 31-33). As God had emphatically declared,

> I will not violate my covenant or alter what my lips have uttered. Once for all, I have sworn by my holiness – and I will not lie to David – that his line will continue for ever and his throne endure before me like the sun (Ps. 89:34-36).

---

[163] Quoted in St. John, *Tongue of the Prophets*, pp. 42-43.

[164] Sachar, *A History of Israel*, p. 84.

[165] Kitson, *Jerusalem*, p. 89.

[166] Adolph Saphir, *Christ and Israel: Lectures and Addresses on the Jews* (London: Morgan and Scott Ltd., 1911), p. 67.

The *immediate* priority for the disciples, however, was to proclaim the Gospel to the ends of the earth. So central is Acts 1:6-8 to Christian Zionism that it has been described as 'the "Magna Carta" of Zionism in the New Testament'.[167]

Christian Zionists also draw attention to the declaration Peter made in Solomon's colonnade that Jesus could not return 'until the period of restoration of all things about which God spoke by the mouth of His holy prophets from ancient time' (Acts 3:21; NASB). The Greek word translated 'restoration' is *apokatastasis*, which occurs only once in the New Testament. Meaning to set back in order again or to restore to its former state, it was used in Peter's day of the transfer of estates back to their rightful owners. Since the prophets had spoken at length about Israel's restoration, Christian Zionists believe that Peter must have had this in mind. George Peters asks whether God could have trifled with 'the dearest, most heart-felt hopes of a nation' by using 'language *pre-eminently calculated* to excite the same', answering his own question with an emphatic, 'No! God's Word is *the truth*, and the grammatical sense – the sense which all men agree is the most legitimate in language – contains *the plain truth, which God will fulfil* at the appointed time.'[168]

The Prophetic Clock of World History

In one of his *Addresses on Prophecy*, Cyrus Scofield claimed that the fig tree spoken of by Jesus in His parable (Matt. 24:32-33) is 'everywhere, and always, a symbol of Israel'. He believed that Jesus was telling the Church 'to watch the fig tree, not for the fullness of leaves, but for the first starting buds, the first indications of renewed life in Israel, religiously and nationally.'[169] With the re-establishment of the State of Israel on 14 May 1948, the nation began to bud again. This momentous event has been described as the 'paramount prophetic sign'[170] of Christ's return, the 'infallible sign of the approach of the end times',[171] the 'greatest miracle of our time',[172] a 'wrench in amillennial thinking',[173] and 'an earthquake shock to traditional Christian theology'.[174] Israel had been 'born in a day' (Isa. 66:7-8), a day, according to John Walvoord, when 'expositors of Biblical prophecy no longer need to depend entirely on the prophetic Word for their hope of Israel's restoration. Before the

---

[167] Duvernoy, *The Prince and the Prophet*, p. 7.
[168] Peters, *The Theocratic Kingdom: Vol. II*, pp. 73, 461-472.
[169] Scofield, *Prophecy made Plain*, p. 126.
[170] Hal Lindsey, *The Late Great Planet Earth* (Basingstoke: Marshall Pickering, 1988), p. 43.
[171] Tim LaHaye and Jerry B. Jenkins, *Are We Living in the End Times?* (Wheaton, IL: Tyndale House Publishers, Inc., 1999), p. 47.
[172] Joseph H. Hunting, *The Set Time is Come* (Carnegie: The David Press, 1980), p. 17.
[173] Arnold G. Fruchtenbaum, *The Footsteps of the Messiah: A Study of the Sequence of Prophetic Events* (Tustin, CA: Ariel Press, 1984), p. 65.
[174] H.L. Ellison, *The Mystery of Israel* (Exeter: The Paternoster Press, 1966), p. 11.

eyes of the entire world the seemingly impossible has occurred.'[175] The re-establishment of the Jewish State proved that the Abrahamic Covenant had not been abrogated. When asked by Frederick the Great for a proof of the existence of God, his physician replied, 'Your majesty, the Jews.' As Gordon Wenham observes, 'Two hundred years later, after the holocaust and the establishment of the state of Israel, readers of Gen 17 even more skeptical than Frederick might be forced to agree.'[176]

Israel has been described as 'God's time clock',[177] 'God's barometer',[178] 'God's prophetic clock',[179] 'the powder keg fuse for the final world conflict',[180] 'the divine touchstone of world politics', and 'the evidence that God is the God of history'.[181] In the words of Leonard Sale-Harrison, 'Watch the Jew, consider his movements in the light of the Word of God, and you have your finger on the time of the great world-movements which are still to take place.'[182]

Christian Zionists pay close attention to the seventy 'sevens', or 'weeks', of Daniel's prophecy (Dan. 9:20-27), which are said to represent seventy seven-year periods. According to Mark Bailey, 'Daniel sits at a fulcrum between Israel's past and Israel's future.'[183] Richard W. De Haan describes the interval between the sixty-ninth and seventieth week as a break in God's dealings with Israel, arguing that 'God's timeclock that had been ticking off the 69 weeks of Daniel's prophecy stopped, and will not commence again until the Lord takes out the Church.'[184] Christian Zionists maintain that the sixty-ninth week of Daniel's prophecy closed with the crucifixion of Jesus and the destruction of the Temple, and that the seventieth week relates to 'God's unfinished business'[185] with Israel. The present, intervening period has been described as a

---

[175] John F. Walvoord, *Israel in Prophecy* (Grand Rapids, MI: Zondervan Publishing House, 1962), preface.

[176] Gordon J. Wenham, *Word Biblical Commentary, Genesis 16-50* (Dallas, TX: Word Books, 1994), p. 32.

[177] LaHaye and Jenkins, *Are We Living in the End Times?*, p. 62.

[178] Leonard Sale-Harrison, *The Remarkable Jew*, 11th edn (London: Pickering & Inglis Ltd., 1939), p. 219.

[179] Derek Prince, *Promised Land: The Future of Israel Revealed in Prophecy* (Grand Rapids, MI: Chosen Books, 2005), p. 20.

[180] Hitchcock and Ice, *The Truth behind Left Behind*, p. 73.

[181] Lance Lambert, *Till the Day Dawns* (Eastbourne: Kingsway, 1982), p. 97.

[182] Sale-Harrison, *The Remarkable Jew*, p. 119.

[183] Mark Bailey, 'The Tribulation', in Charles R. Swindoll, et al., *The Road to Armageddon* (Nashville, TN: Word Publishing, 1999), p. 51.

[184] Richard W. De Haan, *Israel and the Nations in Prophecy* (Grand Rapids, MI: Zondervan Publishing House, 1968), p. 87.

[185] Hal Lindsey, *The Rapture: Truth or Consequences* (London: Bantam Books, 1985), p. 5.

'gap',[186] 'intermission',[187] or 'parenthesis'[188] in God's plan for the Jewish nation. As Clarence Larkin explains, prophecies relating to Israel's restoration were postponed at the end of the sixty-ninth week because of their connection to events immediately preceding Christ's *Second* Coming. He illustrates his point by suggesting that the prophets 'saw the future as separate peaks of one mountain',[189] unaware that a valley lay in between. In other words, prophecies relating to the coming of the Messiah and Israel's restoration refer to two separate advents separated by the 'hidden' valley of the Church (cf. Eph. 3:9). Mark Hitchcock suggests that, when understood correctly, this parenthetical period 'drops in like a puzzle piece that allows many of the end-time events...to fit together'.[190]

The Midnight Cry

Christian Zionism, as defined in this book, teaches that the next event on God's prophetic calendar is the 'imminent', 'impending', or 'any moment' Rapture of the Church (cf. Matt. 24:39-41; Luke 17:30-37; 1 Cor. 15:51-54; 1 Thess. 4:15-17; 2 Thess. 2:1). According to Michael Rydelnik, 'Messiah Jesus can return for the church at any time – even as you read this paragraph.'[191] Hitchcock describes the Rapture as 'a sign-less event',[192] meaning that no prophecy *needs* to be fulfilled before the Rapture takes place. Although the consistent appeal of the Lord Jesus and His Apostles was for the Church to be watching, waiting, preparing, and longing for His return, the Apostle Peter warned that scoffers would arise 'in the last days' and mockingly ask, 'Where is this "coming" He promised?' (2 Pet. 3:4). Sadly, many Church leaders today are scoffing at the

---

[186] W. Graham Scroggie, *The Unfolding Drama of Redemption: An Inductive Study of Salvation in the Old and New Testaments: Vol. I* (Grand Rapids, MI: Kregel Publications, 1994), p. 426.

[187] Arno Froese, *The Great Mystery of the Rapture* (West Columbia, SC: The Olive Press, 1999), p. 295.

[188] C.I. Scofield, *The Scofield Bible Correspondence School Course of Study, Vol. I: The Old Testament*, 7th edn (London: Morgan and Scott, n.d.), p. 160.

[189] Clarence Larkin, *The Greatest Book on 'Dispensational Truth' in the World: Dispensational Truth or God's Plan and Purpose in the Ages*, Revised edn (Glenside, PA: Rev. Clarence Larkin Est., 1920), p. 7.

[190] Mark Hitchcock, *Could the Rapture Happen Today?* (Sisters, OR: Multnomah Publishers, 2005), p. 107.

[191] Michael Rydelnik, 'Israel: The Linchpin in God's Program for the Future', in Dyer, *Storm Clouds*, p. 26.

[192] Mark Hitchcock, *Iran: The Coming Crisis* (Sisters, OR: Multnomah Publishers, 2006), p. 11; cf. Louis A. Barbieri, 'The Church: Watching for our Blessed Hope', in Dyer, *Storm Clouds*, p. 45.

midnight cry[193] being sounded by Christian Zionists, without realising that 'we are well past the eleventh hour' and that 'time is fast running out.'[194]

Refuting the post-tribulationist position, which unwittingly advocates a form of replacement theology by applying scriptures relating to the Great Tribulation to the Church, Reuben Torrey writes: 'It is an absolute impossibility for an intelligent man to be watching for an event that he knows cannot occur for some years.'[195] According to a correct Christian Zionist reading of 1 Thess. 4:17, 'true Christians'[196] will be 'caught up' (Gk. *harpazo*) by the Lord Jesus from the earth *prior* to the commencement of the seventieth week of Daniel's prophecy. The Greek word, *harpazo*, has a number of meanings, each one representing a different aspect of the Rapture. As Kenneth Wuest notes, it means 'to carry off by force', 'to rescue from the danger of destruction', to transfer by divine power 'a person marvellously and swiftly from one place to another', 'to claim for one's self eagerly', and 'to snatch out and away'.[197] Christian Zionists believe that this event is foreshadowed in both Testaments by the 'catching away' of Enoch (Gen. 5:24; Heb. 11:5), Elijah (2 Kgs. 2:1, 11), Philip (Acts 8:39), and Paul (2 Cor. 12:2-4),[198] indicating that the Rapture will take place 'unexpectedly and unannounced'.[199] When speaking of the Rapture, Christian Zionists distinguish between true and false believers in the Church, insisting that 'Christendom is not Christianity'.[200] As Wuest explains,

> The nominal Christian, that person merely identified with the visible church by membership, and not possessing a living faith in the Lord Jesus as Saviour, will be left on earth to go through the terrible times of the Great Tribulation.[201]

Many Christian Zionists believe that once the Rapture has occurred, 'all professing Christendom will unite under the authority of Rome'[202] and 'accept

---

[193] Joseph A. Seiss, *The Last Times and the Great Consummation: An Earnest Discussion of Momentous Themes*, Revised edn (Philadelphia, PA: Smith, English & Co., 1863), pp. 33, 135, 265.

[194] Sam Gordon, *Hope and Glory: Jesus is Coming Again, The Timeless Message of 1 & 2 Thessalonians* (Greenville, SC: Ambassador International, 2005), p. 165.

[195] R.A. Torrey, *The Lord's Return* (Belfast: Ambassador, 1997), p. 111.

[196] Sir Robert Anderson, *Unfulfilled Prophecy; and The Hope of the Church*, 2nd edn (London: James Nisbet & Co. Ltd., 1918), p. 89.

[197] Kenneth S. Wuest, 'Great Truths to Live By', in *Wuest's Word Studies from the Greek New Testament, Volume III* (Grand Rapids, MI: Wm. B. Eerdmans Publishing Company, 1973), pp. 138-142.

[198] Hitchcock, *Could the Rapture Happen Today?*, pp. 52-61.

[199] Tony Pearce, *The House Built on the Sand* (Chichester: New Wine Press, 2006), p. 90.

[200] T.W. Carron, *The Christian Testimony through the Ages* (London: G. Morrish, 1956), p. 6.

[201] Wuest, 'Great Truths to Live By', p. 139.

[202] Chafer, *Systematic Theology*, p. 354.

the Antichrist',[203] having been deceived by his counterfeit signs and wonders (1 Thess. 2:9).

A further distinction is made between the Rapture and the Second Coming, the Church being caught away *before* the final seventieth 'week' begins and *before* Jesus returns to Jerusalem to establish His millennial reign on earth. Torrey refers to this as 'two stages in the one coming.'[204] According to Tim LaHaye and Thomas Ice, 'Christians have long debated whether or not there is a single passage in the Bible that reveals the two phases of Christ's coming separated by the Tribulation period.' LaHaye and Ice believe that, 'when properly understood, 2 Thessalonians 2:1-12 is such a passage.' They maintain that the subject of these verses is 'the whole second coming of Jesus Christ', the Rapture being found in the words 'our being gathered to Him' in verse 1, and the subsequent glorious appearing being found in the words 'the lawless one will be revealed, whom the Lord Jesus will overthrow with the breath of His mouth and destroy by *the splendour of His coming*' in verse 8. As they note,

> What's important to observe is that Antichrist's coming is clearly located between the two phases of Christ's coming...This alone makes a clear case for the pretribulational Rapture sequence of events: first we have the Rapture, then the man of sin is revealed, and finally he is destroyed by the brightness of the glorious appearing of Jesus.[205]

Detractors of this position interpret 'the day of the Lord' in verse 2 as synonymous with the Rapture, rather than with the glorious appearing of Christ at the end of the Great Tribulation period. Consequently, they argue that the Church cannot be raptured 'except there come a falling away first, and that man of sin be revealed' (verse 3). The Greek word *apostasia* has traditionally been interpreted *metaphorically* to denote 'a falling away' of the believer from the faith. However, LaHaye and Ice note that the earliest translations of the English Bible, including the Wyclif Bible, Tyndale's New Testament, the Coverdale Bible, the Cranmer Bible, and the Geneva, or 'Breeches', Bible, rendered it 'departure', but can find no reason why the King James version translates it as 'a falling away'.[206] Wuest points out that 'falling away' is an *interpretation*, and not a translation.[207] He sheds further light on this discrepancy by observing that the root verb of *apostasia* is *aphistemi*, which occurs fifteen times in the New Testament and is translated 'depart' eleven times in the King James version. As

---

[203] Anderson, *Unfulfilled Prophecy*, p. 60.

[204] Torrey, *The Lord's Return*, pp. 42-43.

[205] Tim LaHaye and Thomas Ice, *Charting the End Times: A Visual Guide to Understanding Bible Prophecy* (Eugene, OR: Harvest House Publishers, 2001), p. 38.

[206] LaHaye and Ice, *Charting the End Times*, p. 38; *cf.* H. Wayne House, 'Apostasia in 2 Thessalonians 2:3: Apostasy or Rapture?', in Ice and Demy, *The Return*, pp. 147-182.

[207] Wuest, 'Great Truths to Live By', p. 141.

he explains,

> It is used once in connection with departure from the faith (1 Timothy 4:1). The very fact that the qualifying words 'from the faith' are added, shows that in itself the word does not have the idea of a defection from the truth...The predominant meaning of this verb in the New Testament, therefore, is that of the act of a person departing from another person or from a place.[208]

Thus, for example, Satan 'departed' from Jesus (Luke 4:13), the angel 'departed' from Peter (Acts 12:10), and Anna 'departed not' from the Temple (Luke 2:37). As E. Schuyler English asks, '*Why do we assume that this departure must be from the faith?*...And since the definite article suggests strongly that the departure was something with which the Thessalonians were familiar, why do we think of the departure as apostasy?'[209]

Christian Zionists maintain that the true believer should expect Christ 'at any moment', and 'not look for Him in connection with some predicted event for which signs have been given to Israel and not to the Church.'[210] Froese draws the following logical conclusion:

> If you are waiting for the Great Tribulation, then you cannot be waiting for Jesus. If you are waiting for the appearing of the Antichrist, then you cannot be waiting for Jesus.[211]

True believers are never told to 'fear Antichrist'[212] because they will not be here; the comfort Paul spoke about in 1 Thess. 4:18 is in knowing that 'Jesus could come today.'[213]

Antichrist and the Great Tribulation

Christian Zionists believe that at the beginning of Daniel's seventieth week a charismatic world leader known as the Antichrist will 'burst upon the scene with great power and authority',[214] and be 'readily hailed as a saviour.'[215]

---

[208] Quoted in LaHaye and Ice, *Charting the End Times*, pp. 39-40.

[209] E. Schuyler English, *Re-Thinking the Rapture* (Neptune, NJ: Loizeaux Brothers, 1954), p. 69.

[210] Wuest, 'Great Truths to Live By', p. 140.

[211] Froese, *The Great Mystery of the Rapture*, p. 351.

[212] Todd Strandberg and Terry James, *Are You Rapture Ready? Signs, Prophecies, Warnings, Threats, and Suspicions that the Endtime is Now* (New York: Dutton, 2003), p. 71.

[213] Froese, *The Great Mystery of the Rapture*, p. 18.

[214] David Brickner, *Future Hope: A Jewish Christian Look at the End of the World*, 2nd edn (San Francisco, CA: Purple Pomegranate Productions, 1999), p. 41.

[215] James Montgomery Boice, *The Last and Future World* (Grand Rapids, MI: Zondervan, 1974), p. 72.

Contrary to the Protestant Reformed tradition, they emphasise the *political* rather than religious nature of Antichrist, describing him as 'the world's final false Messiah',[216] 'a master diplomat',[217] 'a supreme Dictator',[218] the 'Roman Dictator',[219] 'the New World president',[220] 'a mighty Kaiser...endowed with the superhuman powers of Satan'[221] who will 'assume the prerogatives of deity',[222] 'the most brilliant and benevolent leader in history',[223] 'a great humanitarian',[224] 'the ultimate humanist',[225] a 'man of war',[226] a 'master of deceit',[227] a 'man of unique intelligence and personal charisma'[228] who will 'mesmerize most of the world's population'[229] with his 'demonically produced miracles',[230] 'the great persecutor of Israel',[231] 'the incarnation of evil on earth',[232] 'an idolatrous human abomination',[233] 'a kind of inverse messiah',[234] 'a counterfeit god-man',[235] 'the devil's henchman',[236] 'Satan's masterpiece',[237] 'the culminating manifestation of Satan',[238] Satan's 'front man in the final climax of satanic rebellion against God',[239] 'a superman who will serve as Satan's counterfeit of

---

[216] Hitchcock and Ice, *The Truth behind Left Behind*, p. 134.

[217] LaHaye and Jenkins, *Are We Living in the End Times?*, p. 279.

[218] Watson, *The New Europe*, p. 66.

[219] Lindsey, *The Rapture*, p. 4.

[220] Froese, *The Great Mystery of the Rapture*, p. 226.

[221] Anderson, *Unfulfilled Prophecy*, pp. 72-73.

[222] Walvoord and Hitchcock, *Armageddon, Oil, and Terror*, p. 67.

[223] Hunt, *Global Peace*, p. 7.

[224] Larkin, *The Greatest Book on 'Dispensational Truth' in the World*, p. 122.

[225] Hal Lindsey, *The Final Battle* (Palos Verdes, CA: Western Front, Ltd., 1995), p. 165.

[226] Hitchcock, *Is the Antichrist Alive Today?*, p. 27.

[227] Lindsey, *The Rapture*, p. 150.

[228] Derek Prince, 'Epilogue: Drama in Three Acts', in Lydia Prince, *Appointment in Jerusalem* (Eastbourne: Kingsway Publications, 1984), p. 182.

[229] Strandberg and James, *Are You Rapture Ready?*, p. 96.

[230] Lindsey, *The Final Battle*, p. 163.

[231] Paul N. Benware, *Understanding End Times Prophecy* (Chicago, IL: Moody Press, 1995), p. 149.

[232] Brickner, *Future Hope*, p. 43.

[233] Erich Sauer, *The Triumph of the Crucified: A Survey of the History of Salvation in the New Testament* (Carlisle: The Paternoster Press, 1994), p. 120.

[234] Thomas S. McCall and Zola Levitt, *Satan in the Sanctuary* (Chicago, IL: Moody Press, 1974), p. 89.

[235] Fruchtenbaum, *The Footsteps of the Messiah*, p. 144.

[236] Gordon, *Hope and Glory*, p. 261.

[237] Arno C. Gaebelein, *The Conflict of the Ages*, Revised edn (Neptune, NJ: Loizeaux Brothers, 1983), p. 150.

[238] William E. Blackstone, *Jesus is Coming* (Chicago, IL: Fleming H. Revell Company, 1932), p. 107.

[239] Brickner, *Future Hope*, p. 44.

the King of kings and Lord of lords',[240] and 'the closest counterfeit of Christ that Satan can produce'.[241] Christian Zionists generally believe that the Antichrist will be hailed as the Messiah by 'Mystery Babylon' (Rev. 17:5), which they have described as a 'Harlot Church',[242] a 'false religious system',[243] a 'one world faith',[244] and a 'one-world super-church'. The head of this 'counterfeit bride of Christ'[245] is believed to be the Roman Catholic Church, which Dave Hunt describes as 'the largest and most dangerous religious cult that ever existed', and 'the most powerful and effective enemy of Christianity in history'.[246]

Antichrist has also been identified by many Christian Zionists as the future 'head of the European Union',[247] which is regarded as a prototype of the ten-kingdom alliance referred to in Rev. 17:12-18. This alliance is said to depict the 'Revived Roman Empire', which will 'rule the entire planet' and establish a 'New World Order' (*cf.* Dan. 2:33). In his book, *Rome, Babylon the Great and Europe* (2003), Bob Mitchell draws attention to the woman riding the beast in Revelation 17. He believes that this image is represented in the bronze statue outside the Council of Europe building in Strasbourg, and on European Union postage stamps where a woman (Europa) is depicted riding a bull (Zeus).[248]

Masquerading as a man of peace, Christian Zionists maintain that the Antichrist will convince the world that he has 'the ability to solve the Middle East problem'.[249] According to Dan. 9:27, he will do so by initiating a seven-year peace treaty with Israel, before breaking it halfway through, at which point he will seek to enforce 'a "final solution" of the Middle East conflict'.[250] The ensuing three-and-a-half-year period is generally equated with the 'day of the Lord' (*cf.* Isa. 13:6; Ezek. 7:19; Joel 3:14; Zeph. 1:7), the 'time of trouble for Jacob' (Jer. 30:7), and the time of 'great distress, unequalled from the beginning of the world until now – and never to be equalled again' (Matt. 24:21). As Stephen Boreland notes, the 'geographical locations', 'cultural

---

[240] Chafer, *Systematic Theology*, p. 346.

[241] Hunt, *Global Peace*, p. 8.

[242] Keith A. Macnaughtan, *Israel and the Coming King* (Murrumbeena: The David Press, 1974), p. 15.

[243] Hunt, *Global Peace*, p. 128.

[244] Davidson, *Islam, Israel*, p. 124.

[245] Fruchtenbaum, *The Footsteps of the Messiah*, p. 161.

[246] Hunt, *Global Peace*, p. 136.

[247] Hagee, *Jerusalem Countdown*, p. 101.

[248] Bob Mitchell, *Rome, Babylon the Great and Europe* (Cambridge: St. Matthew Publishing Ltd., 2003), pp. xi, 133, 142-150.

[249] Tatford, *Five Minutes to Midnight*, p. 72.

[250] David Dolan, *Israel at the Crossroads: Fifty Years and Counting* (Grand Rapids, MI: Fleming H. Revell, 1998), p. 280. Joel Richardson identifies parallels between the Antichrist and the Islamic 'Mahdi'. (Joel Richardson, *Antichrist: Islam's Awaited Messiah* [Enumclaw, WA: Pleasant Word, 2006], pp. 65-67, 187-191.)

inferences', and 'religious implications'[251] of the Olivet Discourse all relate to the Land of Israel and the Jewish people, not the Church. In other words, it has 'a Jewish cast'[252] from beginning to end. Referred to as the Great Tribulation (Rev. 7:14), this period will be marked by 'an incremental intensifying of God's judgment',[253] or 'divine wrath',[254] upon the earth (Rev. 6:16-17). As Wuest points out, 'the promise to the Church is that it has been delivered from the wrath to come (1 Thess. 1:9-10, 5:8; Rom. 5:9)', adding that the Bible 'expressly states who will be the objects of the divine wrath during the tribulation period, namely, Israel and the ungodly of the Gentile nations.' If the Church was destined to suffer, then surely 'the Bible would make note of that fact along with the mention of the above two companies of individuals.'[255]

Christian Zionists believe that as the Great Tribulation 'reaches its intensest horror',[256] the Antichrist will cause those left behind to take the 'mark of the beast' (666) as a sign of allegiance to him, without which they will be unable to trade (Rev. 13:16-18; 14:9-11; 20:4).[257] This will mark 'the point of no return'[258] when, for the first time in history, people will be given 'a deadline for declaring their allegiance to Christ and the gospel'.[259] According to LaHaye, 'Mark of the beast technology is already here!'[260]

The Third Temple

Most Christian Zionists foresee the day when Antichrist will set himself up as God in a rebuilt Jerusalem Temple,[261] in spite of the fact that 'two Arab shrines now stand on the only site on earth where this Temple may stand.'[262] They

---

[251] Stephen Boreland, *Some Golden Daybreak: A Defence of the Pretribulation Rapture* (Pearl Publishing Press, 2001), p. 49.

[252] English, *Re-Thinking the Rapture*, p. 44.

[253] Strandberg and James, *Are You Rapture Ready?*, p. xiv.

[254] Paul D. Feinberg, 'The Case for the Pretribulation Rapture Position', in *The Rapture: Pre-, Mid-, or Post-Tribulational?*, ed. by Gleason L. Archer et al. (Grand Rapids, MI: Academie Books, 1984), p. 58.

[255] Wuest, 'Great Truths to Live By', p. 140; cf. Thomas Ice, 'The 70 Weeks of Daniel', in LaHaye and Ice, *The End Times Controversy*, pp. 310-311.

[256] C.I. Scofield, *The Scofield Bible Correspondence School Course of Study, Vol. III: Synthesis of Bible Truth*, 14th edn (Chicago, IL: Moody Bible Institute, n.d.), p. 614.

[257] Thomas Ice and Timothy Demy, *The Coming Cashless Society* (Eugene, OR: Harvest House Publishers, 1996), pp. 121-132.

[258] Fruchtenbaum, *The Footsteps of the Messiah*, p. 176.

[259] Hitchcock and Ice, *The Truth behind Left Behind*, p. 143.

[260] Tim LaHaye, 'The Signs of the Times Imply His Coming', in *10 Reasons why Jesus is Coming Soon*, ed. by John Van Diest (Sisters, OR: Multnomah Books, 1998), p. 204.

[261] Thomas Ice and Randall Price, *Ready to Rebuild: The Imminent Plans to Rebuild the Last Days Temple* (Eugene, OR: Harvest House Publishers, 1992), pp. 197-207.

[262] Rosen, *Overture to Armageddon?*, p. 114.

generally follow John Nelson Darby in asserting that the 'temple' (Gk. *naos*; 2 Thess. 2:4) spoken of by the Apostle Paul is the future, *literal* Temple in Jerusalem, and not 'the Christian Church.'[263] They also recognise the significance of groups such as the Temple Mount Faithful who, in 1990, attempted to lay the cornerstone for a third Temple, and the Temple Institute, which has all but completed preparations for reinstating the sacrificial system.[264] Its founder, Rabbi Yisrael Ariel, explains that the Temple Institute is

> dedicated to every aspect of the concept of the Holy Temple of Jerusalem, and the central role it fulfilled, and will once again fulfil, in the spiritual wellbeing of both Israel and all the nations of the world. The Institute's work touches upon the history of the Holy Temple's past, an understanding of the present day, and the Divine promise of Israel's future...The Temple Institute's ultimate goal is to see Israel rebuild the Holy Temple on Mount Moriah in Jerusalem, in accord with the Biblical commandments.[265]

Christian Zionists believe that there is a prophetic link between the Third Temple and the Jewish festival of Hanukkah, which commemorates the rededication of Zerubbabel's Temple in 164BC following its desecration by Antiochus Epiphanes IV in 167BC. They maintain that this desecration foreshadows the 'abomination of desolation' referred to in Matt. 24:15 and Dan. 9:27,[266] and regard the Islamic Dome of the Rock as a precursor to it.

Based on a literal reading of Ezekiel 40-46, many also believe that the sacrificial system will be reinstated in the *millennial* Temple, but only in a memorial capacity akin to the Lord's Supper. As Darby explains, 'If Israel will have sacrifices, as well as an earthly temple and priesthood, they will be only commemorative signs of the one great offering of Christ.'[267] Controversy rages over preparations to rebuild the Temple, which Lindsey predicts will be 'the fuse that will ignite the final battle – Armageddon.'[268] As Joel Rosenberg points out, the Temple Mount is 'the most dangerous square mile on the planet.'[269]

The Second Holocaust

Christian Zionists generally agree that the Great Tribulation will climax with

---

[263] Scroggie, *The Unfolding Drama of Redemption: Vol. III*, p. 55.

[264] Ice and Price, *Ready to Rebuild*, pp. 105-114, 120-130.

[265] The Temple Institute, <http://www.templeinstitute.org/main.htm, 1 August 2006>.

[266] Erich Sauer, *The Dawn of World Redemption: A Survey of the History of Salvation in the Old Testament* (Carlisle: The Paternoster Press, 1994), pp. 170-171. Some have distinguished between a 'tribulation Temple' and a 'millennial Temple'. (*cf.* Ice and Price, *Ready to Rebuild*, p. 197; Hutchings, *25 Messianic Signs*, pp. 136-139.)

[267] J.N. Darby, *Letter* [1860], L3:325.

[268] Lindsey, *The Final Battle*, p. 93.

[269] Rosenberg, *Epicenter*, p. 191.

the besieging of Jerusalem (Zech. 12:2-3; 14:2), when Israel will be placed by God 'in a vice grip'[270] until she is 'completely surrounded, cut off, and alone.'[271] With prophetic insight the psalmist wrote: 'With cunning they conspire against your people; they plot against those you cherish. "Come," they say, "let us destroy them as a nation, that the name of Israel be remembered no more" (Ps. 83:3-4).' According to Kitson, as the nations gather against Jerusalem, 'Only one thing will stand between the Jewish nation and total annihilation: the covenants of the Lord and His promise to keep Israel.'[272] Just as God heard the cry of His people in Egypt, so the Son of God will hear the cry of His people in Israel, 'supernaturally strengthening'[273] them against their foes (Zech. 12:6-9). The Jewish nation will at that time look upon the One they have pierced, when 'the true Joseph discovers Himself to His brethren, and they are at once plunged into bitter sorrow and humiliation on account of their, and their nation's sin' (*cf.* Gen. 45:1-15; Zech. 12:10).[274]

This period of Great Tribulation has been portrayed by some as a second Holocaust, when Zechariah's prophecy of two thirds being cut down in the Land (Zech. 13:8) will be fulfilled during 'the fierce persecution of the Antichrist'.[275] As John Walvoord explains, 'Heart-rending as it may be to contemplate, the people of Israel who are returning to their ancient land are placing themselves within the vortex of this future whirlwind which will destroy the majority of those living in the land'.[276] However, as Zech. 14:3-16 makes clear, God will not forget His promises to Israel during these 'terrific convulsions',[277] for 'the time of her worst visitation is to be His opportunity.'[278]

Facing the Consequences

According to the word of the Lord through the prophet Zechariah,

'I am going to make Jerusalem a cup that sends all the surrounding peoples reeling...On that day, when all the nations of the earth are gathered against her, I

---

[270] Hitchcock, *Could the Rapture Happen Today?*, p. 93.

[271] Rosenberg, *Epicenter*, p. 163.

[272] Kitson, *Jerusalem*, p. 215.

[273] Dolan, *Israel in Crisis*, p. 56.

[274] Edward Dennett, *The Blessed Hope: Being Papers on the Lord's Coming and Connected Events* (London: G. Morrish, 1910), p. 89.

[275] Fruchtenbaum, *The Footsteps of the Messiah*, p. 197; *cf.* Charles C. Ryrie, *The Living End* (Old Tappan, NJ: Fleming H. Revell, 1976), p. 81.

[276] Walvoord, *Israel in Prophecy*, p. 113.

[277] Erich Sauer, *From Eternity to Eternity: An Outline of the Divine Purposes* (Carlisle: The Paternoster Press, 1994), p. 30.

[278] Sydney Watson, *The Mark of the Beast* (Edinburgh: B. McCall Barbour, 1977), p. 153.

will make Jerusalem an immovable rock for all the nations. All who try to move it will injure themselves' (Zech. 12:1-3).

Dave Hunt believes that the reason Jerusalem has remained 'the top news story in the world' is because of 'the fulfilment of multiple prophecies concerning this remarkable city and its unique place in God's will', which he maintains 'is absolute proof that God exists, that the Bible is His Word and that the Jews are His chosen people.'[279] Christian Zionists like Hunt believe that despite centuries of dispersion and persecution, and the establishment of the Church, the Jews remain the elect nation, God having declared: 'You only have I chosen of all the families of the earth' (Amos 3:2). As David Baron observes, 'they are not only the "ancient" nation, but the "everlasting" nation'.[280] Thus the Jewish people have been uniquely and irrevocably chosen to reveal the character and glory of God to the nations, and 'to test and expose the hearts of humanity.'[281] According to the parable of the sheep and the goats, the nations will be judged on the basis of how they treated Jesus' *Jewish* brethren (Matt. 25:31-46).

The consistent appeal Christian Zionists make to Gen. 12:2-3 has been described by one critic as 'a monotonous theme'.[282] Although it is somewhat reductionist to claim that 'Genesis 12:3 is Christian Zionism in a nutshell',[283] this text is a central tenet of Christian Zionist theology, God having promised Abraham that He would bless those who blessed him and curse those who cursed him. Christian Zionists take this scripture literally by applying it to the way the Gentile nations have treated the Jewish people, claiming that from Haman to Hitler, 'history shows how dangerous it is to hate [God's] chosen people.'[284] As Arnold Fruchtenbaum poignantly observes, 'The Jew "has stood at the graveside of all his enemies".'[285] In 1915, Sydney Watson declared that 'no nation can persistently persecute [the Jews] without eventually suffering,'[286] and in 1943 at a luncheon with his 'old friend'[287] Chaim Weizmann, Winston Churchill spoke of how 'God deals with the nations as they deal with the

---

[279] Dave Hunt, 'O Jerusalem, Jerusalem!', *The Berean Call*, September (2000), 1.

[280] David Baron, *Israel in the Plan of God* (Grand Rapids, MI: Kregel Publications, 1983), p. 214.

[281] Sandra Teplinsky, *Why Care About Israel? How the Jewish Nation is Key to Unleashing God's Blessings in the 21st Century* (Grand Rapids, MI: Chosen Books, 2004), p. 21.

[282] Dwight Wilson, *Armageddon Now! The Premillenarian Response to Russia and Israel since 1917* (Tyler, TX: Institute for Christian Economics, 1991), p. 28.

[283] Brog, *Standing with Israel*, p. 69.

[284] Allan A. MacRae, 'Hath God Cast Away His People?', in *Prophetic Truth Unfolding Today*, ed. by Charles L. Feinberg (Westwood, NJ: Fleming H. Revell, 1968), p. 95.

[285] Arnold G. Fruchtenbaum, *Israelology: The Missing Link in Systematic Theology* (Tustin, CA: Ariel Ministries Press, 1993), p. 838.

[286] Watson, *The New Europe*, p. 109.

[287] Jerusalem Post, *Front Page Israel*, p. 146.

Jews'.[288] As the Lord Himself solemnly declared, 'the nation or kingdom that will not serve you [Israel] will perish; it will be utterly ruined' (Isa. 60:12).

In his book, *Eye to Eye: Facing the Consequences of Dividing Israel* (2004), William Koenig warns of 'the dire consequences for those who have and will continue to attempt to divide Israel and touch the apple of God's eye'.[289] He is one of many who have made the link between natural and political disasters in the United States, and the way America has dealt with Israel. According to Derek Prince,

> In the eternal counsel of God He has determined to make Jerusalem the decisive issue by which He will deal with the nations. Those nations who align themselves with God's purposes for Jerusalem will receive His blessing. But those who follow a policy in opposition to God's purposes will be severely dealt with.[290]

Israel and Islam

Christian Zionists have accused the Church of being 'in a spiritual fog over the issue of Islam',[291] and believe that the Islamic nations are fulfilling a significant prophetic role in these days. Islamic opposition to Israel is traced back to the age-old conflict between Isaac and Ishmael, and Jacob and Esau (*cf.* Gen. 16:12; 25:23). According to Bennett, the Arab-Israeli conflict can be summed up in one word: 'Islam!' He writes,

> The advent of the recreated State of Israel in 1948 created the ultimate challenge to the Islamic world...A recreated Israel proves the Bible to be true and the teaching of the Koran to be false. Not only does a recreated Israel thrust a sword through the heart of Islamic belief, but it also adds insult to the injury by being recreated in the very centre of the Islamic heartland!...The honour of Allah has been sullied.[292]

In 1995, Hal Lindsey claimed that Iran was the 'key nation to watch'[293] in the build-up to the end-times. In response to Islamist President Mahmoud Ahmadinejad's repeated call for Israel's annihilation, a number of Christian Zionist books have been published highlighting the prophetic role of Iran/Persia in relation to Ezekiel 38-39. In *Jerusalem Countdown: A Warning to the World*

---

[288] Quoted in Eban, *My People*, p. 425.

[289] William R. Koenig, *Eye to Eye: Facing the Consequences of Dividing Israel* (Alexandria, VA: About Him, 2004), p. 170.

[290] Derek Prince, 'A Letter from Derek Prince', *Israel & Christians Today*, Autumn (2003), 3.

[291] Hagee, *Jerusalem Countdown*, p. 31.

[292] Ramon Bennett, *When Day and Night Cease*, Revised edn (Jerusalem: Arm of Salvation, 1996), p. 193.

[293] Lindsey, *The Final Battle*, p. 50.

(2006), John Hagee describes Iran as 'the command post for global Islamic terror',[294] and in his book, *Iran: The Coming Crisis* (2006), Mark Hitchcock charts the rise of the 'atomic ayatollah' and outlines 'God's prophetic program for Iran'.[295] In *The House Built on the Sand* (2006), Tony Pearce describes Israel's existence as 'a thorn in the flesh to the Islamic world', asserting that Islamic hostility towards Israel is based not upon the fallacy of Israel's occupation of 'Palestine', but on 'the fact that Israel exists.'[296]

Christian Zionists have increasingly likened Islam to Nazism. The alliance between Hitler and Haj Amin Effendi al-Husseini, the Grand Mufti of Jerusalem and relative of Yassir Arafat, has been well documented.[297] In 1942, al-Husseini declared on Berlin Radio: 'Kill the Jews – kill them with your hands, kill them with your teeth – this is well pleasing to Allah.'[298] Hunt argues that in the history of man's inhumanity to man, 'the Nazi Holocaust was a close second to Islam.'[299] With the emergence of what has been termed 'Islamofascism', Christian Zionists concur with Prager and Telushkin that we are living in 'the most frightening time for Jews since the Holocaust'.[300]

In 1936, Keith Brooks, founder of the American Prophetic League, stated that the Arab and Muslim world 'is not only anti-Semitic, but is out and out anti-Christ.'[301] Despite the astonishing claim of Riah Abu El-Assal, Anglican bishop of Jerusalem, that 'we do not have a history of "anti-Semitism" or anti-Jewish attitudes'[302] in the Middle East, *Mein Kampf* features regularly on Arab best-selling booklists, the *Protocols of the Elders of Zion* are frequently serialised on Arab television, and Holocaust denial continues unabated.

Christian Zionists believe that 'the interaction between Islam and the West' transcends what Samuel Huntington described as 'a clash of civilisations'.[303] According to Prince, 'The force that unites the so-called "Arab" nations is not genealogical, but spiritual. It is religion, not race. It is Islam…Thus the conflict in the Middle East has its real origin in opposing spiritual forces, not in

---

[294] Hagee, *Jerusalem Countdown*, p. vii.

[295] Hitchcock, *Iran*, p. 10.

[296] Pearce, *The House Built on the Sand*, pp. 32, 38.

[297] Joan Peters, *From Time Immemorial: The Origins of the Arab-Jewish Conflict over Palestine* (Chicago, IL: JKAP Publications, 2001), pp. 360-390.

[298] Quoted in Jan Willem van der Hoeven, *Babylon or Jerusalem?* (Shippensburg, PA: Destiny Image, 1993), p. 136.

[299] Hunt, *Judgment Day*, p. 37.

[300] Prager and Telushkin, *Why the Jews?*, p. xvii.

[301] Timothy P. Weber, *On the Road to Armageddon: How Evangelicals became Israel's Best Friend* (Grand Rapids, MI: Baker Academic, 2004), p. 170.

[302] Riah Abu El-Assal, *Caught in Between: The Extraordinary Story of an Arab Palestinian Christian Israeli* (London: SPCK, 1999), p. 143.

[303] Samuel P. Huntington, 'The Clash of Civilisations?', *Foreign Affairs*, Summer (1993), <http://www.alamut.com/subj/economics/misc/clash.html, 17 August 2006>.

nationalistic or economic factors.'[304] The 'Prince of Persia' in Daniel 10, for example, has been identified as 'the demonic principality which has masterminded Islam' and 'imprisoned millions of Arabs'.[305]

Commenting on the phenomenon of Islamic terrorism, Hunt notes that the 'bombings and murders come from a sincere religious motivation: the destruction of Israel and eventual subjugation of the entire world to Islamic law. And yet, somehow, it is all blamed upon Israel.' He dismisses any claim that Islam is a peaceful religion as a 'schizophrenic attempt to deny the truth'.[306] For example, in April 2002, trumped-up and unretracted allegations of a massacre in Jenin were brought against Israel, for which she was roundly condemned by the international community. Only after a careful investigation did the truth emerge.[307] Christian Zionists actively seek to redress what they perceive to be an anti-Israel agenda in the media. Refuting the argument of 'moral equivalence'[308] in biased media accounts, they consider the criticism consistently levelled against Israel to be a revival of the centuries-old Jew-hatred.[309] One notable opponent of Christian Zionism, Stephen Sizer, has been accused of introducing 'a variety of devastating misteachings' into the Church as he 'rewrites and manipulates' both history and the Bible, and in so doing 'fuels the Palestinian spiritual *intifada*'.[310] Sizer's theology was denounced as anti-Semitic in a 2002 cover article for *The Spectator* magazine.[311]

In closing, it is important to make two key points. Firstly, Christian Zionists believe that the enduring hatred of Islamic nations against the Jews can only be explained in terms of 'the age-abiding conflict between the God of Israel and His rebellious adversary, Satan'.[312] Addressing the United States Senate on the Israeli-Palestinian conflict in 2002, Senator James Inhofe declared: 'This is not a political battle at all. It is a contest over whether or not the word of God is

---

[304] Derek Prince, *The Last Word on the Middle East* (Eastbourne: Kingsway Publications, 1982), pp. 79-80.

[305] Kitson, *Jerusalem*, pp. 169-172.

[306] Dave Hunt, *A Cup of Trembling: Jerusalem and Bible Prophecy* (Eugene, OR: Harvest House Publishers, 1995), pp. 198-199.

[307] Richard Starr, 'The Big Jenin Lie', *The Daily Standard*, 8 May (2002), <http://www.weeklystandard.com/Content/Public/Articles/000/000/001/218vnicq.asp, 1 June 2006>.

[308] Geoffrey Smith, 'Christians, Israel and the Struggle for Peace', in *Israel: His People, His Land, His Story*, ed. by Fred Wright (Eastbourne: Thankful Books, 2005), p. 129.

[309] Michael L. Brown, *Our Hands are Stained with Blood: The Tragic Story of the 'Church' and the Jewish People* (Shippensburg, PA: Destiny Image Publishers, Inc., 1992), pp. 43-57.

[310] Gershon Nerel, 'Spiritual *Intifada* of Palestinian Christians and Messianic Jews', in Wright, *Israel*, pp. 216-217.

[311] Melanie Phillips, 'Christians who hate the Jews', *The Spectator*, 16 February (2002), <http://www.melaniephillips.com/articles/archives/000765.html, 6 June 2006>.

[312] David Noakes, 'The Restoration of all Things', in Wright, *Israel*, p. 272.

true.'[313] Secondly, in an age of growing suspicion, fear, and censorship, we must make a clear distinction between the individual Muslim, and the religion of Islam. As David Pawson cautions the readers of his book, *The Challenge of Islam to Christians* (2003), 'I would be grieved if this material caused or was used to stir up fear and hatred of Islamic followers...All Muslims are fellow human beings made in the image of God and for whom our Lord Jesus Christ laid down his own life. If divine love includes them, so must ours.'[314]

The Palestinian Hoax

Refuting Palestinian claims to the Land of Israel, Dave Hunt categorically states that there '*never* was a Palestinian people, nation, language, culture, or religion', and that the 'claim of descent from a Palestinian people who lived for thousands of years in a land called Palestine is a hoax'.[315] He describes as 'imposters'[316] those who have no historic connection to the Land, but who were drawn from neighbouring Arab countries by Israel's prosperity. A former Palestinian terrorist turned Christian describes the notion of a Palestinian people as '*a fiction of the Islamists*'[317] that was popularised after 1948, noting that when the Jews retook East Jerusalem in 1967, it became even more politically expedient for the Palestinian authorities to promote this fiction.

In their rebuttal of this Palestinian 'myth',[318] Christian Zionists cite as compelling evidence the renaming of Judaea as *Syria Palaestina* by Emperor Hadrian after Bar Kochba's defeat in AD135. Derived from Israel's ancient enemy the Philistines, *Palaestina*, which is 'a Latinised corruption of the Greek name "Philistia," the land of the Philistines',[319] was adopted by Hadrian in order to sever all Jewish connections with the Land. Thereafter, the Jewish homeland was referred to as 'Palestine', a name which continued to be used until Israel's re-establishment in 1948. It is important to note that in 1908 the World Zionist Organisation established a *Palestine* office in Jaffa, and that during World War II the British Army had a *Palestinian* Brigade comprised solely of Jewish volunteers, the *Palestinian* Symphony Orchestra was Jewish, and the *Palestine Post*, which today is known as the *Jerusalem Post*, was a Jewish newspaper. Postage stamps were also issued bearing the inscription 'Palestine-EI', where EI represented *Eretz Israel*.[320] As Wertheim asserts, the

---

[313] Quoted in Koenig, *Eye to Eye*, p. 18.

[314] David Pawson, *The Challenge of Islam to Christians* (London: Hodder & Stoughton, 2003), p. 8; *cf.* Hunt, *Judgment Day*, p. 319; Rosenberg, *Epicenter*, pp. 250-251.

[315] Hunt, 'O Jerusalem, Jerusalem!', 2.

[316] Hunt, *Judgment Day*, p. 7.

[317] Shoebat, *Why I Left Jihad*, p. 27.

[318] Peters, *From Time Immemorial*, pp. 14, 137-171.

[319] Neil Asher Silberman, *Digging for God and Country* (New York: Alfred A. Knopf, 1982), p. 5.

[320] Price, *Unholy War*, p. 136.

Jews would never have named their newspaper after another people or nation.[321] Consequently, references made by scholars to 'ancient Palestine'[322] or 'Iron Age Palestine'[323] are a contradiction in terms, while claims that Jews in the time of Jesus were 'living in Palestine'[324] are both unhistorical and spurious in origin.

According to a Christian Zionist reading of Middle Eastern history and politics, it 'took 20 years of propaganda to establish a myth that is now deeply embedded into the hearts and minds of both the Arab and non-Arab worlds...The mythical claim of Palestinian identity is simply another tactical manoeuvre in the Islamic war waged against Israel to effect her destruction.'[325]

The Jewish Roots of the Christian Faith

In a 1943 edition of *Our Hope* magazine, E. Schuyler English declared: 'The best friend that the Jew has is the Christian, who knows God's Word, His love for His Chosen People, and their place in the prophetic plan.'[326] In the nineteenth century, Anglican Bishop J.C. Ryle understood the centrality to the Christian faith of the Second Coming of Christ and Israel's restoration. In his sermon, 'Scattered Israel to be Gathered', he declared:

> I tell no man that these two truths are essential to salvation, and that he cannot be saved except he sees them with my eyes. But I tell any man that these truths appear to me distinctly set down in holy Scripture and that the denial of them is as astonishing and incomprehensible to my own mind as the denial of the divinity of Christ.[327]

The Church's theological betrayal of Israel can be traced back to the *adversus Judaeos* ('against the Jews') tradition, which spawned the doctrine that the Church had replaced Israel in the purposes and promises of God. Rooted in post-Apostolic writings such as the *Epistle of Barnabas* and the *Dialogue with Trypho, a Jew*, this tradition flourished in the allegorical school of Biblical

---

[321] Charlotte Wertheim, *War on God's People* (Chichester: New Wine Press, 2002), p. 48.

[322] Keith W. Whitelam, *The Invention of Ancient Israel: The Silencing of Palestinian History* (London: Routledge, 1996), p. 1.

[323] Philip R. Davies, *In Search of 'Ancient Israel'* (Sheffield: Sheffield Academic Press, 1992), p. 30.

[324] Naim Ateek, 'Jerusalem in Islam and for Palestinian Christians', in Walker, *Jerusalem*, p. 142.

[325] Ramon Bennett, *Philistine: The Great Deception* (Jerusalem: Arm of Salvation, 1995), p. 136.

[326] Quoted in Gaebelein, *The Conflict of the Ages*, p. xv.

[327] J.C. Ryle, *Are You Ready for the End of Time?* (Fearn: Christian Focus Publications, 2001), p. 112.

interpretation, which was championed by Origen (c. AD185-254) and Augustine (AD354-430). It is enshrined in the amillennial, Reformed, covenant theology[328] of the *Westminster Confession of Faith* (1646). By allegorising the Scriptures, Israel's promises were 'spiritually alchemised'[329] into Church blessings, thus paving the way for the denationalisation of Israel[330] and preparing the ground for much of the anti-Semitism of the Middle Ages. This overturned the premillennial eschatology of the early Church, which was its 'historic'[331] and 'orthodox'[332] faith. Amillennialism's 'devastating departure from true, literal belief in the Word of God'[333] spawned a theory of replacement which teaches that the Church has become 'God's *substituted Israel*'.[334] In the words of Nathaniel West, 'Israel was snuffed out...by Gentile hands'.[335]

In 2002, Knox Theological Seminary in Fort Lauderdale, Florida, issued 'An Open Letter to Evangelicals and Other Interested Parties', declaring that God's promises to Abraham and his descendants 'do not apply to any particular ethnic group, but to the church of Jesus Christ, the true Israel'; that the Third Temple is 'the church that Jesus promised to build'; that no New Testament writer foresaw 'a regathering of ethnic Israel in the land'; and that the 'promised Messianic kingdom of Jesus Christ has been inaugurated'.[336] Such replacementism is roundly condemned by Christian Zionists as a 'theology of supremacy',[337] a 'gross theological distortion' that is 'nothing short of anti-Semitism',[338] 'the mother of many heresies',[339] and 'a cancer in the Church'.[340]

---

[328] Covenant theology is essentially a philosophical system which teaches that there has only ever been *one* people of God, 'the Church', and that the Biblical covenants are all part of one, overarching 'covenant of grace', which God has entered into with the elect.

[329] R.A. Huebner, *The Truth of the Pre-Tribulation Rapture Recovered* (Millington, NJ: Present Truth Publishers, 1976), p. 29.

[330] Ronald E. Diprose, *Israel and the Church: The Origins and Effects of Replacement Theology* (Rome: Istituto Biblico Evangelico Italiano, 2000), pp. 69-98.

[331] Ryrie, *The Basis of the Premillennial Faith*, p. 17.

[332] Seiss, *The Last Times*, pp. 232-258.

[333] Don Hender, *The Nation of Israel: Its Foundation, Function, Failure, and Future* (Pearl Publishing Press, 2001), p. 29.

[334] E.B. Elliott, *Horae Apocalypticae, or A Commentary on the Apocalypse, Critical and Historical; Including also an Examination of the Chief Prophecies of Daniel: Vol. IV*, 2nd edn (London: Seeley, Burnside, and Seeley, 1846), p. 232.

[335] Nathaniel West, *The Thousand Year Reign of Christ* (Grand Rapids, MI: Kregel Publications, 1993), p. 420.

[336] Knox Theological Seminary, 'An Open Letter to Evangelicals and Other Interested Parties: The People of God, the Land of Israel, and the Impartiality of the Gospel', <http://www.knoxseminary.org/Prospective/Faculty/WittenbergDoor/, 3 June 2006>.

[337] Tim Price, 'The Restoration of Israel and the Kingdom of God', in Wright, *Israel*, p. 98.

[338] Kitson, *Jerusalem*, p. 226.

[339] Froese, *The Great Mystery of the Rapture*, p. 97.

˙ Christian Zionists point out that replacement theology also lies at the heart of Roman Catholicism. As Hunt explains,

> The Catholic Church has no comprehension of Bible prophecies concerning the return of Jews to Israel and of the Messiah returning to reign from the throne of His father David. Rome calls itself the New Jerusalem; old Jerusalem and the Jews are no longer part of God's plan.[341]

Over the centuries the persecution of the Jewish people has been seen by the Roman Catholic Church as evidence of her supremacy. According to Hunt, since Jesus was a Jew, Rome's treatment of the Jewish people 'testifies against Catholicism's claim to be Christian.'[342] He further maintains that this doctrine of replacement effectively 'laid the foundation for...the Nazi Holocaust',[343] a theology Holocaust historian Franklin Littell describes as 'the superseding or displacement myth', the 'logical extension'[344] of which was Hitler's 'Final Solution'. Christian Zionists draw a clear line of distinction between Christianity and Catholicism, between the true Church and the false, and despite acknowledging the 'tragic fact of history that the *outward, visible* Church is stained with the blood of the Jewish people',[345] deny that 'the Jew was ever persecuted by any *true* Christian'.[346]

The International Christian Embassy Jerusalem

In June 1971, a conference on Biblical prophecy was held in Jerusalem. Hosted by G. Douglas Young, it was the largest Christian gathering in Israel since independence was declared; David Ben Gurion gave the opening address. On 1 November that year, Young and fourteen other Christian leaders published a letter in the *New York Times* entitled, 'Evangelicals' Concern for Israel', in which they expressed alarm over the way American foreign policy in the Middle East was shifting in favour of the Palestinian Arabs. They called upon Evangelical Christians 'to affirm their belief in biblical prophecy and Israel's Divine Right to the Land by speaking now.'[347] On 31 January 1978, the

---

[340] Clarence H. Wagner, Jr, 'The Error of Replacement Theology', in Koenig, *Eye to Eye*, p. 323.

[341] Dave Hunt, *A Woman Rides the Beast* (Eugene, OR: Harvest House Publishers, 1994), p. 269.

[342] Hunt, *Judgment Day*, p. 288.

[343] Hunt, *A Woman Rides the Beast*, p. 272.

[344] Franklin H. Littell, *The Crucifixion of the Jews: The Failure of Christians to Understand the Jewish Experience* (Macon, GA: Mercer University Press, 1986), pp. 2, 30, 42.

[345] Brown, *Our Hands are Stained with Blood*, p. xiii.

[346] Scofield, *Prophecy made Plain*, p. 71.

[347] Hanson, *A Gentile*, pp. 343-347.

International Congress for the Peace of Jerusalem was convened. Hosted by Young and with Israeli Prime Minister Menahem Begin as guest speaker, a resolution was passed which established International Christians for Israel, and paved the way for the establishment of Bridges for Peace (BFP), Christian Friends of Israel (CFI), and the International Christian Embassy Jerusalem (ICEJ).

On 30 July 1980, the Israeli Knesset declared Jerusalem to be 'the Eternal and Indivisible Capital of Israel.' Fearing an Arab oil embargo, all thirteen embassies based in Jerusalem relocated to Tel Aviv. In response to the international outcry which followed Israel's declaration, Christians from twenty-three countries established their own embassy as a mark of solidarity with the Jewish people, adopting as their mission text Isa. 40:1-2. Under the leadership of Jan Willem van der Hoeven, the ICEJ officially opened its doors on 30 September 1980. It is perhaps best known for its annual hosting of Christian celebrations associated with the feast of Tabernacles, which have been attended by Israeli politicians and are said to anticipate the time when the nations will visit Jerusalem in the millennial kingdom (Zech. 14:16-19).[348]

On 27 August 1985, the ICEJ hosted the First International Christian Zionist Leadership Congress in the same concert hall where the First Zionist Congress was convened. Six hundred delegates gathered 'to pray and seek the Lord', to acknowledge their 'tremendous debt to Israel', and 'to show solidarity with her.' During three subsequent Congresses, held in 1988, 1996, and 2001, delegates condemned replacement theology, refuted Palestinian claims to the Land, and renewed their commitment 'to work with Israel and to encourage the Diaspora to fulfil the vision and goal of gathering to Israel the greater majority of the Jewish People from throughout the world.'[349] On 20 October 2005, the ICEJ launched an initiative to encourage Christian investment in Israel. This was in response to the anti-Israel divestment campaign spearheaded by the Palestinian Sabeel movement,[350] and backed by the Presbyterian Church (USA), the United Church of Christ (USA), the Episcopal Church (USA), and the Anglican Consultative Committee. As part of its initiative, the ICEJ secured a partnership with the Jerusalem Post, which launched a monthly *Christian* edition of its newspaper to bolster support for Israel in North America.

The ICEJ is not the only organisation within 'the great and boundless world of para-church' into which Christians have 'moved their efforts on behalf of

---

[348] van der Hoeven, *Babylon or Jerusalem?*, p. 175; Mitch and Zhava Glaser, *The Fall Feasts of Israel* (Chicago, IL: Moody Press, 1987), pp. 205-213.

[349] ICEJ, *Declaration of the International Christian Zionist Leadership Congress* (1985); *Proclamation of the Second International Christian Zionist Congress* (1988); *Proclamation of the Third International Christian Zionist Congress* (1996).

[350] Sabeel, 'A Call for Morally Responsible Investment', <http://www.sabeel.org/ documents/A%20nonviolence%20sabeel%20seco nd%20revision.pdf, 7 June 2006>.

Israel'.[351] Bridges for Peace was founded in 1976 as a ministry of reconciliation; Christian Friends of Israel was established in 1985 to minister Christ's love and teach the Church its Jewish heritage; and the International Christian Zionist Center (ICZC) was launched in 1997 to solicit Christian support on the basis of Zech. 8:23. On 5 January 2004, members of the Knesset launched the 'Christian Allies Caucus', with representatives of the ICEJ, CFI, and BFP attending the inaugural meeting. On 2 March 2004, these groups joined with Christians for Israel (CVI) to establish the European Coalition for Israel (ECI), which addresses the rising anti-Semitism in Europe.

In stark contrast to the ICEJ, the primary focus of organisations such as Jews for Jesus, Ariel Ministries, Chosen People Ministries, and Moriel is evangelisation. The ICEJ, Ebenezer Emergency Fund International, and Exobus have been criticised for adopting a non-evangelistic, love-never-fails approach towards the Jews. As Louis Goldberg explains,

> If all we share with Israelis is our love, then we have lost the basic meaning of true love. It is the love of Yeshua [Jesus] and only His atonement that changes people...A mere human love only loves people into a lost eternity! We have to be faithful to a God-honouring theology and missiology.[352]

The motto 'Love never fails',[353] which a number of organisations have adopted, is incompatible with Christian Zionism if it does not have an evangelistic focus. If preaching the Gospel is 'an article of faith'[354] for the Christian, then 'the Jewish people need to hear the gospel'. As Baruch Maoz insists, 'We Jews need Jesus because we are sinners as much as anyone else.'[355] According to fellow Jewish believer, Stan Telchin, 'the most anti-Semitic thing a Bible-believing Christian can do to the Jewish people is deny them access to the good news of Messiah Jesus', without whom 'the Jewish people are without hope'.[356]

In Conclusion

The *Encyclopaedia Judaica* incorrectly defines Christian Zionism as 'the active support of Christians' for Zionism.[357] As we have seen, Christian Zionism is not

---

[351] Paul C. Merkley, *Christian Attitudes towards the State of Israel* (London: McGill-Queen's University Press, 2001), p. 163.

[352] Louis Goldberg, 'Historical and Political Factors in the Twentieth Century affecting the Identity of Israel', in House, *Israel*, p. 136.

[353] Geoffrey Smith, 'Appendix: Love Never Fails', in Wright, *Israel*, pp. 313-315.

[354] Brog, *Standing with Israel*, p. 188.

[355] Baruch Maoz, *Judaism is not Jewish: A Friendly Critique of the Messianic Movement* (Fearn: Christian Focus Publications Ltd., 2003), pp. 43-44.

[356] Stan Telchin, *Abandoned: What is God's Will for the Jewish People and the Church?* (Grand Rapids, MI: Chosen Books, 2003), pp. 172, 177.

[357] *Encyclopaedia Judaica: Vol. XVI*, pp. 1152-1153.

the 'Christianisation' of Zionism, nor a reaction to it, but is firmly grounded in traditional Evangelicalism. A further critically important point is made by Merrill Simon, a Jewish Zionist, who observes that

> many Jews have been guilty of failing to make distinctions between Christian groups. To them, a non-Jew is a non-Jew; all Christians are to be lumped together. They tend to see no difference between Catholics, Evangelical Christians, and the liberal Protestant Church.[358]

It is not with Israel and the Jewish people that Christian Zionism is primarily concerned, but with the God of Israel and the Jewish Scriptures. As Walter Riggans explains, 'a biblical Zionism is about God before it is about Israel.'[359] Christian Zionists teach that the survival of the Jews and the re-establishment of the Jewish State authenticate the Bible and vindicate God's plan of salvation. They also assert that by detaching herself from her Jewish roots, the Church has been blinded to God's purposes, *and* love, for Israel. As Scofield wrote, 'It is the Jew's Bible I hold in my hand, and it is God's Bible back of that, and it is the Christian's Bible, because God has sent it to us through the Jew.'[360] In the words of Lewis Sperry Chafer,

> The love of God is toward Israel...So the Spirit-filled believer will learn to rejoice in the great prophecies and purposes of God for that people with whom He is in everlasting covenant, and for whom He has an everlasting love.[361]

Christian Zionism also ensures that the Lord Jesus Christ is seen as 'the crown and the shining star of all prophecy', and 'the King of Scripture'.[362]

---

[358] Merrill Simon, *Jerry Falwell and the Jews* (Middle Village, NY: Jonathan David Publishers, Inc., 1984), pp. 3-4.

[359] Riggans, *Israel and Zionism*, p. 30.

[360] Scofield, *Prophecy made Plain*, p. 67.

[361] Lewis Sperry Chafer, *He that is Spiritual: A Classic Study of the Biblical Doctrine of Spirituality*, Revised edn (Grand Rapids, MI: Zondervan, 1967), p. 50.

[362] Sauer, *The Dawn of World Redemption*, p. 155.

Chapter 2

Christian Palestinianism

Introduction

As Christian Zionism has gathered momentum, a relatively new, largely intellectual, professedly Christian, anti-Zionist movement has sprung up alongside, which I have classified as Christian Palestinianism. The following statements are representative of its ideology:

> It is…a total misunderstanding of the story of salvation and a perversion of God's plan for a Christian to want to re-establish a Jewish nation as an exclusive political entity…The Christian conscience should always discern what is the authentic vocation of the Jewish people and what is the other side of the coin, that is, the racist State of Israel (The Institute for Palestine Studies, 1970).[1]

> We categorically reject Christian Zionist doctrines as false teaching that corrupts the biblical message of love, justice and reconciliation…With urgency we warn that Christian Zionism and its alliances are justifying colonisation, apartheid and empire-building ('The Jerusalem Declaration on Christian Zionism', 22 August 2006).[2]

> Christian Zionism…seeks openly to use the Jewish Zionist cause in order to achieve its own theological and political reality, with dire consequences. The Christian Zionist worldview has cataclysmic consequences for a religiously integrated and lasting peace in Palestine/Israel…Christian Zionism portrays an unjust God, with an unjust people…[and]…seeks to exclude and expel and,

---

[1] Jean Corbon et al., 'What is Required of the Christian Faith concerning the Palestine Problem: A Memorandum by a Group of Middle Eastern Theologians', in *Christians, Zionism and Palestine: A Selection of Articles and Statements on the Religious and Political Aspects of the Palestine Problem*, ed. by The Institute for Palestine Studies (Beirut: The Institute for Palestine Studies, 1970), p. 74.
[2] Episcopal Diocese of Jerusalem, 'The Jerusalem Declaration on Christian Zionism', <http://www.j-diocese.com/DiocesanNews/view.asp?selected=238, 2 September 2006>.

arguably, eliminate whatever is perceived to be alien to its cause (General Assembly of the Church of Scotland, May 2007).[3]

Stephen Sizer's Conversion

Although Naim Ateek essentially founded Christian Palestinianism in 1994 when he launched the Palestinian Ecumenical Liberation Theology Center known as Sabeel, our survey begins with Stephen Sizer, an Evangelical vicar and former Christian Zionist who spearheads the pro-Palestinian propaganda campaign in Britain. Sizer is described by John Rackley, president of the Baptist Union of Great Britain, as 'the foremost authority on the phenomenon of Christian Zionism in Britain today', and by Naim Ateek as 'one of the most authoritative scholars in the world on the vital issue of Christian Zionism'.[4] Sizer's work was the basis for the Church of Scotland report denouncing Christian Zionism, which was approved by its General Assembly in May 2007.

Sizer describes Christian Zionism as 'a devious heresy' and 'an erroneous interpretation of the Bible which is subservient to the political agenda of the modern State of Israel'.[5] A signatory to the B.I.G. (Boycott Israeli Goods) Campaign, Sizer's involvement with groups such as Friends of Al-Aqsa,[6] the Islamic Human Rights Commission, Crescent International, and the Muslim Association of Britain is somewhat disturbing when we consider that his church is a member of the Evangelical Alliance.

According to his own testimony, Sizer once held dispensationalist beliefs before converting to the Palestinianist cause. He writes,

As a young Christian at Sussex University in the mid-1970's I was strongly influenced by Dispensational and Christian Zionist leaders such as David Pawson, Tim LaHaye and Hal Lindsey. Devouring Hal Lindsey's best-selling book, *The Late Great Planet Earth* (Lindsey 1970), and hearing in person his lectures on

---

[3] Church and Society Council, 'Christian Zionism: Hope or Despair?', <http://www.churchofscotland.org.uk/generalassembly/downloads/gareports07churchsociety.txt, 24 July 2007>.

[4] Christ Church Virginia Water, 'Published Writings of Stephen Sizer: Commendations', <http://www.christchurch-virginiawater.co.uk/articles/ivp.html, 7 June 2006>.

[5] Stephen R. Sizer, 'Christian Zionism: A British Perspective', in *Holy Land Hollow Jubilee: God, Justice and the Palestinians*, ed. by Naim Ateek and Michael Prior (London: Melisende, 1999), p. 196.

[6] Stephen R. Sizer, 'Christian Zionism and its Impact on Justice', *Al-Aqsa Journal*, 3.1 (October, 2000), 9.

ˈ eschatology and the Book of Revelation (Lindsey 1983), it seemed as if the Bible
was literally coming true in this generation...My 'conversion' came in two parts.[7]

The first stage of Sizer's conversion to Palestinianism occurred on the *Via
Dolorosa* during his first visit to Israel in 1990, when he was informed by his
Messianic tour guide that there was no such thing as a Palestinian people. The
second stage came when he heard a 'real-life Christian Palestinian',[8] Riah
Hanna Abu El-Assal (now Anglican bishop of Jerusalem) speak about an
indigenous 'Palestinian' Church. According to Sizer, it was then that he began
'to make sense'[9] of the Israeli-Palestinian conflict, prompting him to study
books written by leading Christian Palestinianists. In 1991, he accompanied
Garth Hewitt of Amos Trust on a concert tour of churches in Jerusalem and the
'West Bank'. This and subsequent tours helped to shape his new found
theology by 'deepening friendships'[10] with Naim Ateek (Sabeel), Jonathan
Kuttab (a Palestinian human-rights lawyer), Audeh Rantisi (Evangelical Boys
Home, Ramallah), Bishara Awad (Bethlehem Bible College), Elias Chacour
(Prophet Elias School, Ibillin), and Tom Getman (World Vision).

Sizer's experience of 'typical Palestinian hospitality', 'intrusive and rigorous
interrogations from Israeli security staff at Ben Gurion airport', and post-
graduate research into the impact of Holy Land tourism on the Palestinian
people, combined to deepen his affinity with the Palestinians and shatter his
'previously held naïve Zionist views'.[11] His new beliefs soon found expression
in his photographic history of the Holy Land, which was prefaced by Riah Abu
El-Assal.[12] His growing conviction that Palestinian Christians were 'threatened
with extinction'[13] prompted his doctoral thesis, which was published in 2004
under the title, *Christian Zionism: Road-map to Armageddon?* Reviewers of
Sizer's book, which they have hailed as the 'most important and comprehensive
on the subject to date', and the 'scholarly treatment to counteract the rabid
prophecy pack', have condemned Christian Zionism as 'pernicious', a 'totally
unbiblical menace', 'a powerful force that encourages the destruction of
millions of people', and 'one of the most dangerous and heretical movements in
the world which fuels the Arab-Israeli conflict'.[14]

---

[7] Stephen R. Sizer, 'The Premised Land: Palestine and Israel', in *They Came and They
Saw: Western Christian Experiences of the Holy Land*, ed. by Michael Prior (London:
Melisende: 2000), pp. 144-145.

[8] Stephen R. Sizer, *Christian Zionism: Road-map to Armageddon?* (Leicester: Inter-
Varsity Press, 2004), p. 10.

[9] Sizer, 'The Premised Land', p. 146.

[10] Sizer, *Christian Zionism*, p. 10.

[11] Sizer, 'The Premised Land', pp. 147-150, 159.

[12] Jon Arnold and Stephen R. Sizer, *A Panorama of the Holy Land* (Guildford: Eagle,
1998), p. 80.

[13] Sizer, *Christian Zionism*, p. 13.

[14] Christ Church Virginia Water, 'Published Writings', <7 June 2006>.

Sizer describes his own book, *Christian Zionism: Road-map to Armageddon?*, as 'a definitive critical rebuttal'[15] of Christian Zionist theology. However, his rebuttal fails on several counts:

1. His review of Zionism is inadequate and fails to account for the complexities of Jewish thought over the centuries.
2. His choice of 1800 as the starting date for his survey of Christian Zionism is too late, in that he pays scant attention to formative seventeenth-century writings and to key works published during the latter part of the eighteenth.
3. He relies heavily on secondary source material.
4. He fails to distinguish between the premillennial basis of Christian Zionism and postmillennialism, even portraying nineteenth-century Evangelical, Charles Simeon, as a premillennialist *and* a postmillennialist.
5. His definition of Christian Zionism as 'a political form of philo-Semitism' confuses benevolent acts towards the Jews with a specifically *Christian* outworking of Biblical theology.
6. His portrayal of Christian Zionism as 'Christian support for Zionism'[16] is both inaccurate and misleading.

Sizer's recently published book, *Zion's Christian Soldiers? The Bible, Israel and the Church* (2007), further attempts to discredit Christian Zionism. One of those he has called upon to endorse his book is Kenneth Cragg, former assistant Anglican bishop of Jerusalem. In his endorsement, Cragg suggests, rather crudely, that 'Zion's Christian Perverts might have been a wiser title'.[17]

Anxious for Armageddon

Donald Wagner, a Presbyterian minister and co-founder of Evangelicals for Middle East Understanding (EMEU), also experienced a radical, two-stage transformation from 'Zion to Palestine'. Claiming that he was once 'a Zionist' and 'a supporter of the State of Israel', he grew disillusioned with Christian Zionism after listening to an address by Ibrahim Abu-Lughod, a member of the Palestine Liberation Organisation's National Council. Wagner records how Abu-Lughod's speech 'stopped me in my tracks'. Subsequent meetings with 'top PLO officials'[18] sealed his conversion to Palestinianism.

Wagner has been described as 'probably the most outspoken and effective spokesman for Palestinian Christians'.[19] In his book, *Peace or Armageddon?*

---

[15] Sizer, 'The Premised Land', p. 160.

[16] Sizer, *Christian Zionism*, pp. 35-36, 41, 57, 152, 19.

[17] Friends of Al-Aqsa, <http://www.aqsa.org.uk/page_detail.aspx?id=357, 8 May 2007>.

[18] Donald Wagner, 'From Zion to Palestine: A Journey from Christian Zionism to Justice in the Holy Land', in Prior, *They Came and They Saw*, pp. 199, 203-205.

[19] Weber, *On the Road to Armageddon*, p. 248.

(1993), he claims that Christian Zionism 'thrives on war and conflict',[20] and in *Anxious for Armageddon* (1995) accuses Christian Zionists of harbouring an obsession with the end-time battle prophesied in the Bible. Wagner enlists the support of leading Evangelical scholar John Stott, who classifies prophecy 'among the so-called "matters indifferent"'[21] and describes Christian Zionism as 'biblically untenable'[22] and 'anathema to the Christian faith'.[23] Stephen Sizer, Munib Younan, Dan Cohn-Sherbok, Grace Halsell, and Irvine Anderson have all adopted Wagner's terminology, denouncing Christian Zionism as 'Armageddon theology'[24] and Christian Zionists as 'intrinsically and pathologically "anxious for Armageddon"'.[25] Likewise, Victoria Clark portrays Christian Zionism as a 'gun-slinging, Armageddon-fixated ideology',[26] while Barbara Rossing describes Armageddon as 'the event that dispensationalists crave above all else'.[27] Naim Ateek depicts Christian Zionism as 'the worst anti-semitism one can imagine', its goal being to 'bring the Jewish people to Israel in order to be annihilated or converted to the Christian Faith.'[28]

Jewish lawyer David Brog defends Christian Zionists against these venomous and unsustainable charges by arguing that they ignore the centrality to Christian Zionist theology of Gen. 12:1-3, which includes God's implicit command to *bless* the Jewish people. Brog dismisses the case against Christian Zionism as 'a caricature', an 'urban myth', and a 'smoking gun'.[29]

---

[20] Dan O'Neill and Don Wagner, *Peace or Armageddon? The Unfolding Drama of the Middle East Peace Accord* (London: Marshall Pickering, 1993), p. 97.

[21] John Stott, 'Foreword', in *The Land of Promise: Biblical, Theological and Contemporary Perspectives*, ed. by Philip Johnston and Peter Walker (Leicester: Apollos, 2000), p. 10.

[22] Quoted in Donald Wagner, 'Beyond Armageddon', *The Link*, 25.4 (Oct-Nov, 1992), 7, <http://www.ameu.org/uploads/vol25_issue4_1992.pdf, 7 June 2006>.

[23] Quoted in Wagner, *Anxious for Armageddon*, p. 80.

[24] Sizer, *Christian Zionism*, p. 23; Munib Younan, *Witnessing for Peace: In Jerusalem and the World* (Minneapolis, MN: Augsburg Fortress, 2003), pp. 92-93; Dan Cohn-Sherbok, *The Politics of Apocalypse: The History and Influence of Christian Zionism* (Oxford: Oneworld Publications Limited, 2006), p. xii; Grace Halsell, *Forcing God's Hand: Why Millions Pray for a Quick Rapture...and Destruction of Planet Earth* (Beltsville, MD: Amana Publications, 2003), p. viii; Irvine H. Anderson, *Biblical Interpretation and Middle East Policy: The Promised Land, America, and Israel, 1917-2002* (Gainesville, FL: University Press of Florida, 2005), p. 41.

[25] Sizer, *Christian Zionism*, p. 183.

[26] Victoria Clark, *Allies for Armageddon: The Rise of Christian Zionism* (New Haven, CT: Yale University Press, 2007), p. 256.

[27] Barbara R. Rossing, *The Rapture Exposed: The Message of Hope in the Book of Revelation* (New York: Basic Books, 2004), pp. 12, 138, 47.

[28] Naim Ateek, 'Introduction', in Naim Ateek, Cedar Duaybis, and Maurine Tobin, *Challenging Christian Zionism: Theology, Politics and the Israel-Palestine Conflict* (London: Melisende, 2005), p. 17.

[29] Brog, *Standing with Israel*, pp. 82, 183-184.

Zionist Apartheid

Christian Palestinianists are skilled in the propaganda art of 'labelling'. By attaching to Israel such emotive labels as 'apartheid', 'ethnic cleansing', 'genocide', 'massacre', and 'occupation', they have successfully turned the minds of many against the Jewish people. Such labelling is part and parcel of Palestinianist vocabulary, and is prevalent in the anti-Israel Arab media.[30] In his book, *Israel: An Apartheid State* (1987), Uri Davis eagerly anticipates 'the dismantlement of the state of Israel as a Jewish state'. He denounces Israel's treatment of the Palestinians as 'Zionist apartheid',[31] claiming that it is more radical and far-reaching than its South African predecessor. Rosemary Radford Ruether has followed suit, suggesting that in the signing of the Oslo Accords in 1993, Israel attempted 'to negotiate the terms of the surrender of the Palestinians to an Israeli scheme of colonial apartheid'.[32] Stephen Sizer has likewise accused Christian organisations which support the Jewish people of giving 'intransigent and partisan support for what remains *an apartheid state*'.[33] By equating Israeli policies with the repressive policy of racial segregation in South Africa, Donald Wagner has successfully solicited international support for the Palestinianist cause.[34] Desmond Tutu, patron of Sabeel, has helped to advance the cause still further by drawing the following comparisons:

> Now, alas, we see *apartheid* in Israel...Somehow, the Israeli government is placed on a pedestal in the US, and to criticise it is to be immediately dubbed antisemitic. People are scared in the US...because the pro-Israeli lobby is powerful – very powerful. Well, so what?...The apartheid government was very powerful, but today it no longer exists. Hitler, Mussolini, Stalin, Pinochet, Milosevic, and Idi Amin were all powerful, but, in the end, they bit the dust.[35]

Jean Zaru, a Palestinian theologian, tries to force a connection between the struggle of her people and the American civil rights movement, citing Martin Luther King's 'Letter from a Birmingham Jail' (16 April 1963).[36] According to Seymour Lipset, however, King expressed outrage on hearing an anti-Zionist

---

[30] Neill Lochery, *Why Blame Israel? The Facts behind the Headlines* (Cambridge: Icon Books, 2004), p. 3.

[31] Uri Davis, *Israel: An Apartheid State* (London: Zed Books Ltd., 1987), pp. xi, 26, 60.

[32] Rosemary Radford Ruether and Herman J. Ruether, *The Wrath of Jonah: The Crisis of Religious Nationalism in the Israeli-Palestinian Conflict*, 2nd edn (Minneapolis, MN: Fortress Press, 2002), p. xiv.

[33] Stephen R. Sizer, 'Christian Zionism, True Friends of Israel?', *Evangelicals Now*, December (2000), 14.

[34] Wagner, *Anxious for Armageddon*, pp. 178-179.

[35] Desmond Tutu, 'Foreword', in *Speaking the Truth: Zionism, Israel, and Occupation*, ed. by Michael Prior (Northampton, MA: Olive Branch Press, 2005), p. 12.

[36] Jean Zaru, 'Theologising, Truth and Peacemaking in the Palestinian Experience', in Prior, *Speaking the Truth*, p. 189.

remark at Harvard University in 1968, to which he responded: 'When people criticise Zionists, they mean Jews. You are talking anti-Semitism!'[37]

Such methods of paralleling are consistently employed by Christian Palestinianists to legitimise their cause and demonise the Jewish State. They are used to great effect by Elias Chacour, the undisputed godfather of the Christian Palestinianist movement.

The Nazification of the Jews

Elias Chacour is a Palestinian priest in the Greek Catholic (Melkite) Church, founder of the Mar Elias Educational Institutions in the Galilee, Vatican consultant for world Jewish relations, and the Vatican-approved bishop of Israel. Wagner claims that Chacour's autobiography, *Blood Brothers: A Palestinian's Struggle for Reconciliation in the Middle East* (1983), has 'touched the hearts and opened the minds of thousands of evangelicals concerning Christians in the Holy Land'.[38] By rewriting the history of the Israeli-Palestinian conflict, *Blood Brothers* paved the way for similar revisionist books by Audeh Rantisi, Mitri Raheb, and Riah Abu El-Assal.[39]

In his book, *We Belong to the Land* (1992), Chacour recalls being questioned by a member of the security staff at Ben Gurion Airport:

> The strident, arrogant tone of his voice chilled me to the bone...The tone implied 'dirty, dangerous Palestinian who does not count as a human being.' Today we Palestinians are considered dirty and dangerous, just as this policeman's father was called 'dirty Jew' only some forty years ago.[40]

Describing Chacour's statement as 'most poignant',[41] Stephen Sizer accuses Israel of ethnically cleansing the Palestinian people, claiming that 'Nazi treatment of the Jews illustrates how easily the denigration of an "inferior" people can lead to the denial of their human rights and the rationalisation for their removal or eradication.'[42] On 4 July 2006, in front of an audience of Christians and Jews which included Holocaust survivors, Sizer directly equated Israel with Nazi Germany when describing Prime Minister Olmert's policy as

---

[37] Seymour Martin Lipset, 'The Socialism of Fools: The Left, the Jews and Israel', *Encounter*, (December, 1969), 24, <http://www.wzo.org.il/en/resources/view.asp?id=1823, 7 June 2006>.
[38] O'Neill and Wagner, *Peace or Armageddon?*, p. 88.
[39] Audeh G. Rantisi, *Blessed are the Peacemakers: The Story of a Palestinian Christian* (Guildford: Eagle, 1990); Mitri Raheb, *I am a Palestinian Christian* (Minneapolis, MN: Fortress Press, 1995); Riah Abu El-Assal, *Caught in Between: The Extraordinary Story of an Arab Palestinian Christian Israeli* (London: SPCK, 1999).
[40] Elias Chacour, *We Belong to the Land* (London: Marshall Pickering, 1992), p. 3.
[41] Sizer, 'The Premised Land', p. 150.
[42] Sizer, *Christian Zionism*, p. 245.

his 'final solution'[43] to the Palestinian problem. Lynda Brayer similarly maintains that the policy of ethnic cleansing associated with the Nazi regime, and the more recent atrocities in Rwanda and the Balkans, 'is part and parcel of Zionist ideology' and 'an integral part of both its theory and its practice.'[44]

Precedent for this Nazification of the Jews is found in the work of British historian Arnold J. Toynbee (1889-1975), who accused the Zionists of driving Palestinian Arabs from their homes during Israel's War of Independence in 1948. Equating Zionism 'with Nazism', Toynbee declared how, 'in the Jewish Zionists I see disciples of the Nazis', suggesting that 'the spectacle of any Jews, however few, following in the Nazis' footsteps is enough to drive a sensitive gentile or Jewish spectator almost to despair.'[45]

Secular historian Regina Sharif, who is frequently cited by Christian Palestinianists, ranks Nazis in her list of non-Jewish Zionists. She asserts that on 'the theoretical as well as on the practical level, the Nazis and the Zionists saw eye to eye', and argues that the 'cornerstone of Zionist theory...found its ultimate justification in the Nazi theories of racial supremacy.' Sharif bases her historical survey of non-Jewish Zionism on UN Resolution 3379 (10 November 1975), which declared Zionism to be 'a form of racism and racial discrimination'. It should be noted that this was revoked by Resolution 4686 on 16 December 1991. Sharif also claims that 'Zionism, racism, and anti-Semitism are all part of one phenomena'.[46] Christian Palestinianists follow Sharif's example by appealing to the resolutions and charter of the United Nations to strengthen their position. Christian Zionists, on the other hand, portray the United Nations as 'a bastion of Jew hatred' for 'systematically singling out Israel for punitive treatment'.[47]

The Charge of Anti-Semitism

Grace Halsell, political journalist and former White House staff writer for President Lyndon B. Johnson, wheels out the Christian Zionist 'straw man' in her recently revised and much cited book, *Prophecy and Politics: Militant Evangelists on the Road to Nuclear War* (1987). Seeking to discredit Christian Zionists, Halsell targets Israel's relationship with the late Jerry Falwell and his

---

[43] Doreen Wachmann, 'Anti-Israel Man Cut Down to Sizer', *Jewish Telegraph*, 7 July (Manchester, 2006), 29.

[44] Lynda Brayer, 'The Separation of Jerusalem from the West Bank and Gaza', in *Jerusalem: What Makes for Peace! A Palestinian Christian Contribution to Peacemaking*, ed. by Naim Ateek, Cedar Duaybis, and Marla Schrader (London: Melisende, 1997), p. 146.

[45] Arnold J. Toynbee, *A Study of History, Vol. XII: Reconsiderations* (London: Oxford University Press, 1961), pp. 627-628.

[46] Regina S. Sharif, *Non-Jewish Zionism* (London: Zed Press, 1983), pp. 5, 1, 76.

[47] Hunt, *Judgment Day*, p. 31.

'political coalition'[48] known as the 'Moral Majority'. Having set Falwell up as the figurehead of Christian Zionism, she attempts to bolster her argument by tarring him with the same brush as disgraced television evangelists Jimmy Swaggert and Jim Bakker, cult leader Jim Jones, and apocalyptic suicide cults such as the Order of the Solar Temple, the Branch Davidians, and Heaven's Gate.[49] British journalist Victoria Clark has described the Branch Davidians, many of whom perished at Waco, Texas, in 1993, as 'a Christian Zionist sect'.[50]

Halsell accuses Christian Zionists of adopting 'the cult of a Chosen People',[51] of creating a 'cult worship of the Land of Israel', and of worshipping 'a tribal God'. She targets Dallas Theological Seminary as the 'fountainhead' of a doctrine which she claims teaches that 'God does not want us to work for peace, but rather *demands* that we wage a nuclear war that destroys planet earth'.[52] Seeking to bolster the pro-Palestinian cause, she accuses Christian Zionists of fueling 'a new anti-Semitism' in their support of Israel. By stretching the definition of anti-Semitism to cover 'other Semites',[53] whom she identifies as the indigenous Palestinian people, she has effectively torn it from its universally accepted connection with the Jewish people.

The Biblical Legend

Roman Catholic scholar Michael Prior holds high rank within the Christian Palestinianist movement. Despite claiming to have once held 'very favourable dispositions towards Israel and the Zionist enterprise',[54] Prior spent his latter years denouncing Zionism as 'one of the most pernicious ideologies of the 20th century'. Believing that the narrative of Israel's entry into Canaan ought to be read 'through the eyes of the Canaanites',[55] whom he describes as the 'innocent third party about to be exterminated',[56] Prior accuses modern-day Israel of 'ethnically cleansing Palestine of its indigenous non-Jewish population'.[57]

Prior not only takes issue with the way Christian Zionists interpret Scripture,

---

[48] Simon, *Jerry Falwell and the Jews*, p. 108.

[49] Halsell, *Forcing God's Hand*, pp. 9-10, 63.

[50] Clark, *Allies for Armageddon*, p. 263.

[51] Grace Halsell, *Prophecy and Politics: Militant Evangelists on the Road to Nuclear War* (Bullsbrook: Veritas Publishing Company Pty. Ltd., 1987), p. 54.

[52] Halsell, *Forcing God's Hand*, pp. 91, 113, 8, 114.

[53] Halsell, *Prophecy and Politics*, p. 55.

[54] Michael Prior, *Zionism and the State of Israel: A Moral Inquiry* (London: Routledge, 1999), p. xiii.

[55] Michael Prior, 'Studying the Bible in the Holy Land', in Prior, *They Came and They Saw*, pp. 121, 127.

[56] Michael Prior, 'Zionism and the Bible', in Ateek and Prior, *Holy Land Hollow Jubilee*, p. 84.

[57] Michael Prior, 'Zionism and the Challenge of Historical Truth and Morality', in Prior, *Speaking the Truth*, p. 39.

but launches a scathing attack on the Bible itself. Citing what he claims to be 'scandalous biblical texts'[58] full of 'menacing ideologies and racist, xenophobic and militaristic tendencies',[59] he argues that a 'straightforward reading'[60] of the Joshua narrative mandates ethnic cleansing and genocide. In his irreverent portrayal of the God of the Christian Zionist as 'the Great Ethnic-Cleanser, a militaristic and xenophobic genocidist, who is not sufficiently moral even to conform to the requirements of the Fourth Geneva Convention, or of any of the Human Rights Protocols which attempt to set limits to barbarism',[61] Prior reveals the full extent of his contempt for the authority of Scripture.

Such extreme statements serve to bridge the gap between the more mainstream Palestinianism of Sizer and Wagner, and the ultra minimalist school represented by Keith Whitelam and Philip Davies, who dismiss the value of theology and refute the veracity of Israel's Biblical history with rhetoric as offensive as Prior's. For example, in his book, *In Search of 'Ancient Israel'* (1992), Davies suggests that if Jeremiah and Ezekiel were not Biblical figures, we would be justified in portraying them as 'a quisling' and 'a pornographic or schizophrenic bigot'[62] respectively.

Prior acknowledges his debt to Whitelam's *The Invention of Ancient Israel* (1996),[63] and in so doing attempts to validate Christian Palestinianism by linking it with the academic world. Whitelam argues that no distinction should be made between 'Canaanites' and 'Israelites', and that 'Israel' represents 'but one thread in the rich tapestry of Palestinian history'.[64] The implication is clear: 'Palestine' predates 'Israel'. Christian Palestinianists exploit this Biblical revisionism by consistently portraying modern day Palestinians as 'Palestinian Canaanites' who were living in the Land 'long before the early Hebrews came',[65] and in so doing attempt to counter the Christian Zionist claim that the Palestinian people have no historical or Biblical right to the Land. In the words of Michael Prior, the 'biblical legend' of Israel's conquest of the Canaanites takes on new significance 'when one meets their modern counterparts, the Palestinians'.[66]

Shortly after many of his blasphemous statements were made at the 5th International Sabeel Conference in 2004, Michael Prior died.

---

[58] Prior, 'Zionism and the Bible', p. 83.

[59] Prior, *Zionism and the State of Israel*, pp. 162-165.

[60] Prior, 'Zionism and the Bible', p. 81.

[61] Michael Prior, 'The Holy Land and the Scandalous Performance of the Churches', *Cornerstone*, 30 (Winter, 2003), 6.

[62] Davies, *In Search of 'Ancient Israel'*, p. 45.

[63] Prior, *Zionism and the State of Israel*, p. 169.

[64] Whitelam, *The Invention of Ancient Israel*, pp. 66-67.

[65] Jad Isaac, Marla Schrader, and Suhail Khalilieh, 'The Colonisation of Palestine', in Ateek and Prior, *Holy Land Hollow Jubilee*, p. 122.

[66] Michael Prior, 'A Perspective on Pilgrimage to the Holy Land', in Ateek, Duaybis, and Schrader, *Jerusalem*, p. 129.

Hiding behind the Holocaust

Christian Palestinianists accuse Israel and her Christian Zionist allies of playing 'the Holocaust guilt-card'[67] by hiding behind 'Holocaust theology', exploiting Jewish 'victimhood', and 'wallowing in cheap guilt'.[68] Kenneth Cragg coldly denounces 'the awful authority of the Holocaust', which he claims 'unjustifies all Palestinian protest'[69] and gives Israel 'a warrant of innocence'.[70] Paul Eisen, a member of the executive committee of Friends of Sabeel UK, accuses Israel of adopting an 'eliminationist attitude'[71] towards the Palestinians. In his essay, *The Holocaust Wars*, he claims that Palestinians 'are not just facing the might of the Israeli state but also the power of organised world Jewry and its primary arm, the Holocaust.'[72] It is disturbing to find his essay posted on a web-site dedicated to neo-Nazi political prisoner and Holocaust denier, Ernst Zündel.

Rosemary Radford Ruether makes an illusionary connection between the Holocaust and 'a special Israeli psychological need to batter Palestinians',[73] while Zoughbi Elias Zoughbi accuses the Israeli government of giving its Jewish civilians license to commit 'dehumanising acts' against them, such as 'beating, maiming, killing, terrorising, and torturing'.[74] Stephen Sizer uses Norman Finkelstein's book, *The Holocaust Industry* (2000), to condemn the Jews for allegedly exploiting the Holocaust;[75] Michael Prior claims that Auschwitz has become for the Jewish people 'a place where they can hide their accountability in the present' and 'a symbol that makes them untouchable';[76] and Marc Ellis describes the Palestinians as 'the last victims of the

---

[67] Charles P. Lutz, 'What's So Special About This Space?', in Charles P. Lutz and Robert O. Smith, *Christians and a Land Called Holy: How We Can Foster Justice, Peace, and Hope* (Minneapolis, MN: Fortress Press, 2006), p. 31.

[68] Prior, 'Zionism and the Bible', p. 71.

[69] Kenneth Cragg, *This Year in Jerusalem* (London: Darton, Longman & Todd, 1982), pp. 129-131.

[70] Kenneth Cragg, *The Arab Christian: A History in the Middle East* (London: Mowbray, 1992), p. 28.

[71] Paul Eisen, 'Jewish Power', *RighteousJews.org*, 19 August (2004), <http://www.righteousjews.org/article10.html, 8 June 2006>.

[72] Paul Eisen, 'The Holocaust Wars', *The Zundelsite*, 30 May (2005), <http://www.zundelsite.org/zundel_persecuted/may20-05_eisen.html, 8 June 2006>; *cf.* Paul Eisen, 'Speaking the Truth to Jews', in Prior, *Speaking the Truth*, p. 202.

[73] Rosemary Radford Ruether, 'Western Christianity and Zionism', in *Faith and the Intifada: Palestinian Christian Voices*, ed. by Naim Ateek, Marc H. Ellis, and Rosemary Radford Ruether (Maryknoll, NY: Orbis Books, 1992), p. 154.

[74] Zoughbi Elias Zoughbi, 'Faith, Non-violence, and the Palestinian Struggle', in Ateek, Ellis, and Ruether, *Faith and the Intifada*, p. 102.

[75] Sizer, *Christian Zionism*, p. 21.

[76] Prior, *Zionism and the State of Israel*, p. 220.

Holocaust',[77] suggesting that it is time to move the Israeli-Palestinian conflict forward by bringing 'the era of Auschwitz'[78] to an end.

The Institutionalisation of Christian Palestinianism

In 1956, the Near East Christian Council (NECC) was established as a co-ordinating body for Protestant mission in the Middle East, changing its name in 1962 to the Near East Council of Churches. Subsequent alliances forged between Protestant and Orthodox churches in the region gave rise, in 1974, to a new Middle East Council of Churches (MECC), which is the oldest ecumenical organisation in the region. The MECC soon became affiliated to the World Council of Churches (WCC), which at that time was championing the cause of the PLO, enabling member churches in the East and West to unite around a common, pro-Palestinian policy.[79]

During the 1970s, many liberal Protestants began to embrace the liberation theology of the Roman Catholic theologian, Gustavo Gutiérrez, with its emphasis on social justice for the oppressed. In 1979, five thousand American church leaders formulated the La Grange Declaration, voicing their opposition to Christian Zionism and accusing Israel of occupation, land confiscation, and 'brutal torture'.[80] In 1982, following Israel's invasion of Lebanon, World Vision, a Christian humanitarian organisation, reversed its pro-Israel policy in what Wagner described as a 'remarkable shift'.[81] In the same year, Mercy Corps International launched a series of educational tours to the Middle East to encourage North American Christians to re-evaluate their support for Israel, a development Paul Merkley describes as a 'turning point for American evangelicals'.[82] In 1986, Evangelicals for Middle East Understanding (EMEU) was founded as a loose affiliation of North American churches and agencies which support Christians in the Middle East.[83] Also that year, Donald Wagner, who served as national director of the Palestine Human Rights Campaign during the 1980s, accompanied Ray Bakke of the Lausanne Committee for World Evangelisation on a 'listening tour'[84] of Israel and six neighbouring Arab

---

[77] Marc H. Ellis, 'The Boundaries of Our Destiny: A Jewish Reflection on the Biblical Jubilee on the Fiftieth Anniversary of Israel', in Ateek and Prior, *Holy Land Hollow Jubilee*, p. 236.

[78] Marc H. Ellis, *O, Jerusalem! The Contested Future of the Jewish Covenant* (Minneapolis, MN: Fortress Press, 1999), p. xviii.

[79] Merkley, *Christian Attitudes*, pp. 74-77.

[80] 'The La Grange Declaration', in Paul Nadim Tarazi, 'Covenant, Land and City: Finding God's Will in Palestine', *The Reformed Journal*, 29 (1979), 10-16.

[81] Wagner, 'Beyond Armageddon', 11.

[82] Merkley, *Christian Attitudes*, p. 86.

[83] Donald Wagner, 'Marching to Zion: Western Evangelicals and Jerusalem approaching the Year 2000', in Ateek, Duaybis, and Schrader, *Jerusalem*, p. 77.

[84] Merkley, *Christian Attitudes*, p. 85.

countries. In 1995, Wagner established the Center for Middle Eastern Studies at North Park University, Chicago. In 1999, the Holy Land Christian Ecumenical Foundation (HCEF) was launched to alert American Christians to the perceived plight of the Palestinian people.

Each of the groups cited above has contributed to the development of the Christian Palestinianist movement, but without question its leading architect is the former canon of St. George's Cathedral in Jerusalem, Naim Stifan Ateek.

The Palestinian Messiah

Naim Ateek was profoundly affected by the first *Intifada*, which broke out on 9 December 1987. In the aftermath of this Palestinian uprising, he published *Justice and Only Justice: A Palestinian Theology of Liberation* (1989), which was both the catalyst for, and subject of, the First International Symposium on Palestinian Liberation Theology, held at the Tantur Ecumenical Institute for Theological Studies near Jerusalem (10-17 March 1990). Ateek's objective was to set his new theology 'in the context of other Liberation Theologies from around the world'.[85] Seeking Biblical justification for this new school of thought, Geries Khoury describes Jesus as 'the first theologian in Palestine to teach liberation theology or Palestinian theology.'[86] Paul Merkley notes that at a time when liberation theology was on the wane, Palestinian Christians 'swiftly moved' to fill the vacuum, 'offering a fiery "Palestinian theology" that answered to all of the old enthusiasms.'[87] These views are epitomised by Elias Chacour, who believes it is time to 'set God free' from the Christian Zionist portrayal of Him as judge and executioner, and to 'proclaim to the whole world the simple naked reality: God is not a Christian!'[88]

In his article, *Christian Zionism: The Dark Side of the Bible*, Ateek describes Christian Zionist theology as 'one, if not the most dangerous, Biblical distortion that is challenging us today', and accuses its protagonists of 'unwittingly and unconsciously contributing to the oppression and killing of many innocent Palestinians by Israel'.[89] He believes that the New Testament 'de-territorialises the Gospel'[90] and 'de-Zionizes' the Old Testament, which he describes as a

---

[85] Sabeel, 'The Beginning of the Center', *Cornerstone*, 1 (Spring, 1994).

[86] Geries Khoury, 'The Palestinian Christian Identity', in Ateek, Ellis, and Ruether, *Faith and the Intifada*, pp. 73-74.

[87] Merkley, *Christian Attitudes*, p. 74.

[88] Elias Chacour, 'Empty Tomb and Risen Lord', in Ateek, Duaybis, and Schrader, *Jerusalem*, p. 14.

[89] Naim Ateek, 'Christian Zionism: The Dark Side of the Bible', *Cornerstone*, 30 (Winter, 2003), 1-2.

[90] Naim Ateek, 'A Palestinian Theology of Jerusalem', in Ateek, Duaybis, and Schrader, *Jerusalem*, p. 98.

'potentially dangerous document'.[91] Clothing supersessionism in the robes of liberation theology, Ateek paraded his newly fashioned doctrine in his 2001 Easter message, substituting 'Palestinians' for 'Jews' in the Passion narrative:

> Here in Palestine Jesus is again walking the via dolorosa. Jesus is the powerless Palestinian humiliated at a checkpoint, the woman trying to get through to the hospital for treatment, the young man whose dignity is trampled, the young student who cannot get to the university to study, the unemployed father who needs to find bread to feed his family...In this season of Lent, it seems to many of us that Jesus is on the cross again with thousands of crucified Palestinians around him. It only takes people of insight to see the hundreds of thousands of crosses throughout the land, Palestinian men, women, and children being crucified. Palestine has become one huge Golgotha. The Israeli government crucifixion system is operating daily. Palestine has become the place of the skull.[92]

Sabeel: The Nerve-Centre of Christian Palestinianism

In 1994, Ateek founded the Palestinian Ecumenical Liberation Theology Center in Jerusalem. More popularly known as *Sabeel* (the Arabic word for 'way' or 'spring'), this grassroots movement has greatly impacted theologians and peace activists around the world. The work of Sabeel, and the six international conferences it has hosted, has helped to define and solidify Christian Palestinianism. By drawing together churchmen, theologians, politicians, and peace activists from around the world, it has been able to solicit international support and broaden its appeal. According to its *Purpose Statement*, Sabeel 'strives to develop a spirituality based on love, justice, peace, non-violence, liberation and reconciliation for the different national and faith communities'.[93] Although it does not represent the Christian majority in Israel, Sabeel has been credited with playing 'no small part'[94] in forging links between western Christians and the Palestinian people.

Prior to its 5th International Conference in Jerusalem in 2004, Sabeel issued a statement condemning Christian Zionism for justifying 'empire, colonisation, apartheid, and oppression.'[95] Following the Conference, the *Jerusalem Sabeel Document* was published, outlining principles of non-violent resistance

---

[91] Naim Ateek, 'Zionism and the Land: a Palestinian Christian Perspective', in Johnston and Walker, *The Land of Promise*, pp. 212, 208.

[92] Naim Ateek, 'Jerusalem Easter Message', 10 April 2001, <http://www.hcef.org/hcef/index.cfm/mod/news/ID/16/SubMod/NewsView/NewsID/220.cfm, 9 June 2006>.

[93] Sabeel, 'Sabeel Purpose Statement', <http://www.sabeel.org/etemplate.php?id=2, 9 June 2006>.

[94] Prior, *Zionism and the State of Israel*, p. 155.

[95] Sabeel, 'The 5th International Sabeel Conference Statement: Challenging Christian Zionism', <http://www.sabeel.org/documents/5thConfStatementfinal.htm, 9 June 2006>.

énshrined in international law.[96] Sabeel has managed to establish itself within mainstream Christianity by networking with organisations such as Christian Aid and World Vision, and by drawing sponsorship for its conferences from the WCC, the Presbyterian Church (USA), and the Church of Scotland. Sabeel also operates through six international chapters, which constitute International Friends of Sabeel (IFOS). In the United Kingdom, the IFOS networks with organisations such as Amos Trust, Bible*Lands*, Christian Aid, and The Church Mission Society. Stephen Sizer is vice-chairman of Friends of Sabeel UK.

Through a series of workshops, lectures, conferences, youth camps, and its *Cornerstone* magazine, Sabeel has established itself as the very nerve-centre of the Palestinianist movement. It has also been the catalyst for the Institute for the Study of Christian Zionism (ISCZ), an inter-faith body of academics whose purpose is 'to promote the study of the history, theology, and politics of Christian Zionism while offering a biblical nonviolent vision about the conflicts surrounding Israel and Palestine, and their global impact.' The ISCZ claims that 'the ideology of Christian Zionism turns the good news of Jesus Christ into a militant, Crusader ideology that justifies violence in the name of God'.[97] Two of its founding members are Stephen Sizer and Donald Wagner.

Throwing Down the Gauntlet

Christian Palestinianism is theologically rooted in Reformed, covenant theology, which has 'redefined'[98] Israel. Consequently, the Church is said to be 'the real Israel, the Israel of God',[99] with Old Testament prophecies 'reinterpreted'[100] in favour of the Church. As Colin Chapman explains,

> When New Testament writers like John had seen the significance of the land and the nation in the context of the kingdom of God which had come into being in Jesus of Nazareth, they ceased to look forward to a literal fulfilment of Old Testament prophecies of a return to the land and a restored Jewish state. The one and only fulfilment of all the promises and prophecies was already there before their eyes in the person of Jesus. The way they interpreted the Old Testament must be the norm for the Christian interpretation of the Old Testament today.[101]

---

[96] Sabeel, 'The Jerusalem Sabeel Document: Principles for a Just Peace in Palestine-Israel', <http://www.sabeel.org/documents/Jerusalem%20Sabeel%20Document.pdf, 9 June 2006>.

[97] 'Evangelicals Challenge Christian Zionists: Contrary to Jesus' Life and Teaching', <http://www.christianzionism.org/News&CommentaryN.asp, 26 August 2006>.

[98] N.T. Wright, *The Climax of the Covenant* (Edinburgh: T.&T. Clark, 1991), p. 250.

[99] Rantisi and Beebe, *Blessed are the Peacemakers*, p. 107.

[100] Stephen R. Sizer, 'The Theological Basis of Christian Zionism: On the Road to Armageddon', in Ateek, Duaybis, and Tobin, *Challenging Christian Zionism*, p. 63.

[101] Colin Chapman, *Whose Promised Land?* (Oxford: Lion, 2002), p. 189.

Robert Smith claims that in the New Testament, the Land of Israel, Jerusalem, and the Temple 'are drained of their theological import.'[102] Gary Burge follows suit by claiming that the Land 'no longer has an intrinsic part to play in God's program for the world.'[103] Christian Palestinianists clamour for 'an inclusive theology of land'.[104] Claiming that the roots of Christianity are Palestinian, and not Jewish,[105] Elias Chacour calls for 'a new vision of election':

> We have been taught for centuries that the Jews are the Chosen People. We do not believe anymore that they are the Chosen People of God, since now we have a new understanding of that Choseness.[106]

Integral to this Palestinianist theology is a repudiation of the Christian Zionists' interpretation of Acts 1:6-8. Christian Palestinianists look to the French Reformer, John Calvin, as the theological champion of their replacementist theory. Calvin asserted that in Acts 1:6-8 there were 'as many errors...as words' in the disciples' question concerning Israel's restoration. This, he believed, showed 'how bad scholars they were under so good a Master', and therefore 'when he [Jesus] saith, *you shall receive power*, he admonisheth them of their imbecility.' Calvin further claimed that Jesus was attempting to 'lift up their minds' from 'the common error' of the Jewish nation, which believed that the Messiah would 'reign as a king in this world a thousand years'. This interpretation, he maintained, was the 'folly'[107] adopted by the early Church premillennialists. At the 5th International Sabeel Conference in 2004, Mitri Raheb denounced the disciples as 'very narrow-minded', 'nationalistic', and 'blinded'[108] for asking such a question. In his own exposition of these verses, Donald Wagner has contemporised Calvin's commentary:

> It was as if these disciples were saying, 'Well, Lord, we were truly impressed by the miracles you performed while we laboured with you. We were inspired as well by your great teachings. Then the resurrection was truly fantastic. But now, will

---

[102] Robert O. Smith, 'Politics, Faiths, and Fundamentalisms', in Lutz and Smith, *Christians and a Land Called Holy*, p. 44.

[103] Gary M. Burge, 'Theological and Biblical Assumptions of Christian Zionism', in Ateek, Duaybis, and Tobin, *Challenging Christian Zionism*, p. 54.

[104] Naim Ateek, 'Preface', in Ateek and Prior, *Holy Land Hollow Jubilee*, p. xiii.

[105] Elias Chacour, 'A Palestinian Christian Challenge to the West', in Ateek, Ellis, and Ruether, *Faith and the Intifada*, p. 87.

[106] Elias Chacour, 'Reconciliation and Justice: Living with the Memory', in Ateek and Prior, *Holy Land Hollow Jubilee*, p. 112.

[107] *Commentary Upon the Acts of the Apostles by John Calvin: Vol. I*, ed. by Henry Beveridge (Edinburgh: 1844), pp. 43-48.

[108] Mitri Raheb, 'The Third Kingdom', in Ateek, Duaybis, and Tobin, *Challenging Christian Zionism*, p. 265. As an observer at this conference, I challenged Mitri Raheb over the comments he had made, only to be shouted down by Stephen Sizer quoting Calvin's words at me.

you do the "big one"? Will you restore the kingdom to Israel now and drive the Romans from our land?' I think the Lord needed to employ every bit of his sense of humour at this point. I can see him saying, half in jest, and half seriously, 'I don't believe it! Where have you people been for the past three years? You've missed the point of everything!' Then Jesus became very harsh with the disciples...This is a clear word from the Lord to the futurist dispensationalists...Here Jesus was telling the disciples not to place their trust in nor devote their energy to end-time prophecy or the militant Zionist ideology of the Zealots.[109]

Naim Ateek claims that a Christian Zionist reading of the Bible offers Palestinians 'slavery rather than freedom, injustice rather than justice, and death to their national and political life.'[110] One of the goals of Christian Palestinianism is 'to seek new ways of interpreting Scripture',[111] which Ateek believes will enable the Palestinian church to reclaim the Bible. As he explains,

> When confronted with a difficult passage in the Bible or with a perplexing contemporary event one needs to ask such simple questions as: Is the way I am hearing this the way I have come to know God in Christ? Does this fit the picture I have of God that Jesus has revealed to me? Does it match the character of the God whom I have come to know through Christ? If it does, then that passage is valid and authoritative. If not, then I cannot accept its validity or authority.

In line with this reasoning, the destruction of Jericho is said to reflect 'a human understanding of God that is totally different from the God in Christ that Christians have experienced', while the dispossession of Naboth's vineyard is said to embody 'the tragedy of Palestine' and represent 'a central biblical paradigm for a Palestinian theology of liberation'.[112]

The persistent argument against Christian Zionism is that it has no academic authority. Throwing down the gauntlet, Colin Chapman claims that

> The case against Christian Zionists has been supported by new scholarship, as, for example, in the writings of N.T. Wright (1996) and Peter Walker (1994, 1996). Can work of this quality be matched by Christian Zionists, or are they simply, dare I say, repeating the same old arguments that have been put forward in the past?[113]

It is clear why N.T. Wright, the presiding bishop of Durham, has been used by

---

[109] Wagner, *Anxious for Armageddon*, p. 83.

[110] Naim Stifan Ateek, *Justice, and Only Justice: A Palestinian Theology of Liberation* (Maryknoll, NY: Orbis Books, 1990), pp. 74-75.

[111] Raheb, *I am a Palestinian Christian*, p. 59.

[112] Ateek, *Justice, and Only Justice*, pp. 81-88.

[113] Colin Chapman, 'Ten Questions for a Theology of the Land', in Johnston and Walker, *The Land of Promise*, p. 185.

Chapman to champion the Palestinianist cause. A notable academic, Wright believes that Jesus' response to His disciples in Acts 1:6-8 'reaffirms the expectation, but alters the interpretation' concerning Israel's restoration. He claims that in Jesus, 'Israel's god has restored his kingdom for his people',[114] so that any notion of the 'reconstitution of the land' must be discounted. Consequently, Jerusalem no longer has 'any spiritual significance'. Wright concludes that Christian Zionism represents 'the geographical equivalent of..."Christian" apartheid, and ought to be rejected as such.'[115]

Chapman has also chosen Stephen Sizer to champion the Palestinianist cause, claiming that *Christian Zionism: Road-map to Armageddon?* has 'thrown down the gauntlet in a way that demands a response from those who support the state of Israel for theological reasons.'[116]

In Conclusion

Christian Palestinianism is an inverted mirror image of Christian Zionism. All the basic elements of a Christian Zionist eschatology are reversed, so that the Bible is seen to be Christian, not Jewish, the land of the Bible is Palestine not Israel, the Son of God is a Palestinian not a Jew, the Holocaust is resented not remembered, 1948 is a catastrophe not a miracle, the Jewish people are illegal occupiers not rightful owners, and Biblical prophecy is a moral manifesto and not a signpost to the Second Coming. Despite enlisting support from the theological community and seeking validation through academia, the overriding thrust of Christian Palestinianism is political, not Biblical.

As we have seen, this reactionary movement, spearheaded by Sabeel, is a one-issue coalition of strange bedfellows whose diverse, ideological perspectives are held in tension as they unite against a common enemy. The above survey has not only charted the rise of Christian Palestinianism and identified its main protagonists, but by setting it alongside Christian Zionism has highlighted the fundamental differences which separate the two. In particular, the inherently Biblical and Evangelical nature of Christian Zionism has been contrasted with the inherently political and Liberal character of Christian Palestinianism. In the process, the reader has been alerted to the scale of this para-church movement which, by covering itself in a veneer of Biblical respectability, has gained a major foothold within the Evangelical Church.

Christian Zionism teaches that the God of the Bible is the God of history. Consequently, it cannot divorce itself from the political outworking of prophecies which relate to Israel's restoration and the return of Jesus Christ. Christian Zionists believe that God has always worked out His purposes

---

[114] N.T. Wright, *The New Testament and the People of God* (London: SPCK, 1992), pp. 374-375.

[115] N.T. Wright, 'Jerusalem in the New Testament', in Walker, *Jerusalem*, pp. 69, 75.

[116] Christ Church Virginia Water, 'Published Writings', <7 June 2006>.

through historical events, the fulfilment of prophecy being a sovereign work of God. As we shall see, these views are harmonious with the teachings of John Nelson Darby, who believed that the Christian 'has no business to mix himself up'[117] in politics, but who understood from the Scriptures that the Lord can 'make any nation minister to the deliverance of His favoured people, whatever their own objects and state may be?'[118] Pharaoh, Nebuchadnezzar, and Cyrus all bear testimony to the truth of this statement. Christian Zionists therefore reject the accusation that they are simply engineering political events in order to facilitate the fulfilment of prophecy.

As we have seen, Christian Zionism does not, as critics like Stephen Sizer maintain, subordinate Christ and the Church by elevating Israel. On the contrary, its focus on Israel is thoroughly Christ-centred, interpreting Israel's restoration in the light of Christ's return. In so doing, the Christian Zionist has uncovered the Jewish roots of the Christian faith, reclaimed Israel from the eschatological dustbin of Reformed theology, and unveiled the 'blessed hope', or Rapture, of the Church (Tit. 2:13).

As we now turn our attention to John Nelson Darby, the leading architect and patron of Christian Zionism, let us consider how supremely ironical it is that Darby's critics have elevated him to a position which Christian Zionists themselves have largely failed to recognise; I am grateful to them for this. This 'uncompromising champion for Christ's glory and God's truth'[119] is described by Stephen Sizer as 'the father of dispensationalism and its prodigy, Christian Zionism.'[120] Michael Prior acknowledges that more than anyone else, Darby 'laid the foundations for the development of Fundamentalist Evangelical Christian Zionism',[121] and Gary Burge maintains that if Herzl was the father of Jewish Zionism, then 'one could argue that Darby was the father of Christian Zionism, laying out many of its principal theological foundations.'[122]

John Nelson Darby 'is virtually unknown to the present generation of the church',[123] but in the light of such uplifting eulogy we must now ask: 'Who is this millenarian theologian who appears to be making such a comeback?'[124]

---

[117] Darby, *Letter to E. Maylan* (Montpellier, 24 March 1848), L1:130.

[118] Darby, *Reflections upon the Prophetic Inquiry and the Views advanced in it* (1829), CW2:16.

[119] William Kelly, *The Rapture of the Saints: Who Suggested it, or rather on what Scripture?* (London: T. Weston, 1903), p. 11.

[120] Stephen R. Sizer, 'Dispensational Approaches to the Land', in Johnston and Walker, *The Land of Promise*, p. 142.

[121] Prior, *Zionism and the State of Israel*, p. 139.

[122] Burge, 'Theological and Biblical Assumptions of Christian Zionism', p. 46.

[123] Floyd Saunders Elmore, *A Critical Examination of the Doctrine of the Two Peoples of God in John Nelson Darby* (ThD: Dallas Theological Seminary, 1991), p. 312.

[124] Kent Eaton, 'Beware the Trumpet of Judgement!: John Nelson Darby and the Nineteenth-Century Brethren', in *The Coming Deliverer: Millennial Themes in World Religions*, ed. by Fiona Bowie (Cardiff: University of Wales Press, 1997), p. 130.

Chapter 3

John Nelson Darby

According to Ernest Sandeen, 'John Nelson Darby deserves better treatment from historians than he has received either from those who have praised him or those who have reviled him. The assessment of his career has not been objectively written or the scope of his influence adequately appreciated.'[1] Joseph Canfield adds that the libraries of Evangelical schools 'have more than a shelf on D.L. Moody, and one can learn of Calvin, Luther, Wesley, Whitefield, Robert Murray McCheyne and even J. Gresham Machen. J.N. Darby's writings are always found on the shelf, but we really do not know the man himself.'[2]

Darby's Early Years

John Nelson Darby was born at 9 Great George Street, Westminster, London, on 18 November 1800. He was the youngest child of John Darby of Markley, East Sussex, and Leap Castle, Offaly (then King's County) in Ireland, and of Ann Vaughan, daughter of Samuel Vaughan, a sugar plantation owner from Philadelphia and an acquaintance of George Washington. The Vaughan family has been described as 'a galaxy of late eighteenth-century achievement'.[3] Darby was christened at St. Margaret's Church, Westminster, on 3 March 1801, and given the middle name Nelson 'in compliment to England's naval hero',[4] who was his godfather. His uncle, Admiral Sir Henry D'Esterre Darby, served under Admiral Lord Nelson as commander of the *Bellerophon* at the Battle of the Nile in 1798. On 17 February 1812, Darby enrolled at Westminster Public School, and three years later, on 3 July 1815, matriculated at Trinity College,

---

[1] Ernest R. Sandeen, *The Roots of Fundamentalism: British and American Millenarianism 1800-1930* (Chicago, IL: University of Chicago Press, 1970), p. 31.
[2] Joseph M. Canfield, *The Incredible Scofield and His Book* (Vallecito, CA: Ross House Books, 1988), p. ix.
[3] Timothy C.F. Stunt, 'Influences in the Early Development of J.N. Darby', in *Prisoners of Hope? Aspects of Evangelical Millennialism in Britain and Ireland, 1800-1880*, ed. by Crawford Gribben and Timothy C.F. Stunt (Carlisle: Paternoster Press, 2004), p. 50.
[4] W.G. Turner, *John Nelson Darby, A Biography* (London: C.A. Hammon, 1926), p. 14.

Dublin, as a *socius comitatus* (S.C.) or 'Fellow Commoner'.[5]

Darby graduated from Trinity as a Classical Gold Medallist on 10 July 1819, and in the same year was admitted to King's Inn in Dublin to study law. On 9 November he entered Lincoln's Inn in London and was called to the Irish Bar on 21 January 1822. Much to his father's displeasure, Darby forsook a career as a barrister, choosing instead the path to ordination; this decision cost him his inheritance. As he later explained,

> I was a lawyer; but feeling that, if the Son of God gave Himself for me I owed myself entirely to Him, and that the so-called Christian world was characterised by deep ingratitude towards Him, I longed for complete devotedness to the work of the Lord; my chief thought was to get round amongst the poor Catholics of Ireland.[6]

Although Darby was left a considerable fortune by his uncle, he was not the 'quintessential Anglo-Irish aristocrat'.[7] Leap Castle had been the ancestral family home since 1667, but of her three-times great uncle, Marigold Freeman-Attwood writes: 'John Nelson seems to have set little store by the gracious beauty of the home of his family, or by their worldly authority...He represents the Keep of the spirit; stout, foursquare, unadorned, the soul's bulwark against what Puritans such as he regarded as the vanities of materialism.'[8]

An Indefatigable Curate

Darby was ordained into the Church of Ireland as a deacon by William Bissett, bishop of Raphoe, on 7 August 1825, and as a priest by William Magee, archbishop of Dublin, on 19 February 1826. He was appointed curate over the large parish of Calary[9] in County Wicklow, one of the most impoverished regions in the Dublin diocese.[10] Nebeker suggests that Darby's preference for the poor made his message far more appealing than that of the affluent clergy,

---

[5] *Alumni Dublinenses: A Register of the Students, Graduates, Professors, and Provosts of Trinity College, in the University of Dublin*, ed. by G.D. Burtchaell and T.V. Sadler (London: Williams and Norgate, 1924), p. 210.

[6] Darby, *Letter to Prof. Tholuck* (185-), L3:297.

[7] Gary L. Nebeker, *The Hope of Heavenly Glory in John Nelson Darby (1800-1882)* (PhD: Dallas Theological Seminary, 1997), p. 268.

[8] Marigold Freeman-Attwood, *Leap Castle: A Place and its People* (Norwich: Michael Russell, 2001), p. 83.

[9] In *A Topographical Dictionary of Ireland* (1837), Calary is said to be 'situated in the rugged table lands which extend southward from the great Sugar Loaf mountain to the vicinity of Roundwood'. (Quoted in Max S. Weremchuk, *John Nelson Darby, A Biography* [Neptune, NJ: Loizeaux Brothers, 1992], p. 207.)

[10] Alexis de Tocqueville, *Journeys to England and Ireland* (New York: Arno Press, 1979), p. 158.

who believed that material prosperity and high social status were signs of God's blessing.[11] Darby made a peasant's hut his home, accusing his fellow clergymen of being 'worldly, covetous, eager for riches, honour, power – like the children of the age'.[12] In a letter to J.E. Batten in 1852 he wrote:

> Christ preferred the poor; ever since I have been converted so have I. Let those who like society better have it. If I ever get into it, and it has crossed my path in London, I return sick at heart. I go to the poor…That, unworthy as I am, is where I am at home and happy. I think I am intellectual enough, and my mind – though my education was in my judgment not well *directed*, save by God – cultivated enough to enjoy cultivated society. I have none of it, but I prefer the cross.[13]

Darby was an 'indefatigable curate' who laboured tirelessly in the harsh terrain of the Wicklow mountains. As Francis William Newman, brother of Cardinal John Henry Newman, recounts:

> Every evening he sallied forth to teach in the cabins, and roving far and wide over mountain and amid bogs, was seldom home before midnight. By such exertions his strength was undermined, and he so suffered in his limbs that not lameness only, but yet more serious results were feared. He did not fast on purpose, but his long walks through wild country…inflicted on him much severe deprivation: moreover, as he ate whatever food offered itself, – food unpalatable and often indigestible to him, his whole frame might have vied in emaciation with a monk of La Trappe. Such a phenomenon intensely excited the poor Romanists, who looked on him as a genuine 'saint' of the ancient breed…That a dozen such men would have done more to convert all Ireland to Protestantism, than the whole apparatus of the Church Establishment, was ere long my conviction.

Newman, who described Darby as 'a most remarkable man, – who rapidly gained an immense sway' over him, has left us with one of the most evocative portraits of the man he nicknamed 'the Irish clergyman':

> His 'bodily presence' was indeed 'weak!' A fallen cheek, a bloodshot eye, crippled limbs resting on crutches, a seldom shaven beard, a shabby suit of clothes and a generally neglected person, drew at first pity, with wonder to see such a figure in a drawing-room. It was currently reported that a person in Limerick offered him a halfpenny, mistaking him for a beggar…With keen logical powers, he had warm sympathies, solid judgment of character, thoughtful tenderness, and total self-abandonment.[14]

During the first quarter of the nineteenth century, Robert Daly, rector of

---

[11] Nebeker, *The Hope of Heavenly Glory*, pp. 118-119.
[12] Darby, *What is the Church, as it was at the Beginning? And what is its Present State?* (1866), CW14:85.
[13] Darby, *Letter to J.E. Batten* (London, rec'd 15 May 1852), L1:205.
[14] Francis W. Newman, *Phases of Faith* (London: Trübner & Co., 1881), p. 17.

Powerscourt in Dublin, contributed significantly to 'the injection of evangelical piety' into County Wicklow. In 1819, Daly invited Darby to attend the annual meeting of the Wicklow Auxiliary Bible Society, although Darby's involvement in the Evangelical fervour of that time was peripheral. From his graduation from Trinity until his riding accident in 1827, Darby's ecclesiastical position remained 'ambiguous'[15] as he underwent 'much spiritual exercise'.[16]

As a curate, Darby had gone 'from cabin to cabin to speak of Christ', even though he himself was 'not set free according to Romans viii.'[17] During what he described as his 'phases of faith', he had been influenced by the moral philosophy of Cicero's *De Officiis*.[18] Although he claimed to have trusted in Christ for salvation 'since June or July 1820 or 21', it would be several years before Darby experienced 'certain peace'. Recalling his 'occasional trials of unbelief, some of them painful',[19] he spoke of his bondage to the ritualism of the Roman Catholic Church at that time. In his critique of John Henry Newman's *Apologia Pro Vita Sua*, Darby recalled how his acquaintance with Romanism had been 'in theory and practice', and 'years before Dr. Newman' converted to Roman Catholicism. During this period he was 'much in Dr. Newman's state of mind', even sharing his 'horror of Protestantism'. He wrote:

> I fasted in Lent so as to be weak in body at the end of it; ate no meat on week days – nothing till evening on Wednesdays, Fridays, and Saturdays, then a little bread or nothing; observed strictly the weekly fasts, too. I went to my clergyman always if I wished to take the sacrament, that he might judge of the matter. I held apostolic succession fully, and the channels of grace to be there only. I held thus Luther and Calvin and their followers to be outside.[20]

In a letter to the Catholic newspaper, the *Français*, in 1878, Darby wrote about these 'six or seven years under the rod of the law'. Although he had believed in Jesus before he 'possessed Him'[21] as Saviour, his 'deliverance from bondage'[22] finally came while convalescing at his sister Susannah's home following a riding accident in October 1827. He recounted his experience:

---

[15] Timothy C.F. Stunt, *From Awakening to Secession: Radical Evangelicals in Switzerland and Britain 1815-35* (Edinburgh: T.&T. Clark, 2000), pp. 160, 164-165.

[16] *John Nelson Darby: Compiled from Reliable Resources chiefly by W.G. Turner*, ed. by E.N. Cross (London: Chapter Two, 1990), p. 16.

[17] Darby, *Letter* (Halifax, April 1877), L3:453-454.

[18] Darby, *The Irrationalism of Infidelity: being a Reply to 'Phases of Faith'* (1853), CW6:27-28.

[19] Darby, *Note to 2 Timothy 1:12 in Mr. Darby's Greek Testament ed. by Griesbach*, CBA 5540 (529).

[20] Darby, *Analysis of Dr. Newman's Apologia Pro Vita Sua: With a Glance at the History of Popes, Councils, and the Church* (1866), CW18:145-146, 156.

[21] Darby, *Letter* (1878), L2:433.

[22] Darby, *Letter to J.E. Batten* (Lausanne, rec'd 25 February 1851), L1:185.

An accident happened which laid me aside for a time; my horse was frightened and had thrown me against a doorpost. During my solitude, conflicting thoughts increased; but much exercise of soul had the effect of causing the scriptures to gain complete ascendancy over me. I had always owned them to be the word of God...At the same time, I saw that the Christian, having his place in Christ in heaven, has nothing to wait for save the coming of the Saviour, in order to be set, in fact, in the glory which is already his portion 'in Christ'...It seemed to me that the good hand of God had thus come to my help, hiding my spiritual weakness under physical incapacity.[23]

Once assured of salvation, Darby began to look for the true Church, but did not find it in Roman Catholicism. The conviction which kept him from 'turning in that direction'[24] was that 'the Roman Catholic church is ridiculous as a security for the soul'.[25] Darby also failed to find the true Church within Anglicanism, or in any of the dissenting churches which had emerged in the wake of the eighteenth-century Evangelical revival. In a pamphlet he wrote in 1827, he expressed his belief that the true Church was, in essence,

a congregation of souls redeemed out of 'this naughty world' by God manifest in the flesh, a people purified to Himself by Christ, purified in the heart by faith, knit together, by the bond of this common faith in Him, to Him their Head sitting at the right hand of the Father, having consequently their conversation...in heaven, from whence they look for the Saviour, the Lord of glory.[26]

The Catholic Millennium

Darby was convinced that 'the whole hope of the gospel' was 'denied by the doctrines of the Church of Rome',[27] but that did not stop him from exercising 'unwearied patience and love'[28] towards the Roman Catholic peasants of Ireland. Irish society was, at that time, 'a turbulent maelstrom'[29] of famine, disease, and poverty. The imposition of Protestant tithes, and the political impotence of the Roman Catholic Church, fueled an already inbred hatred towards Protestant England and the Anglo-Irish aristocracy. The failed

---

[23] Darby, *Letter to Prof. Tholuck* (185-), L3:298-299.

[24] Darby, *Letter* (1878), L2:434.

[25] Darby, *Analysis of Dr. Newman's Apologia Pro Vita Sua*, CW18:157.

[26] Darby, *Considerations addressed to the Archbishop of Dublin and the Clergy who signed the Petition to the House of Commons for Protection* (1827), CW1:5.

[27] Darby, *Second Address to his Roman Catholic Brethren, by A Minister of the Gospel,* CW18:15-16.

[28] Darby, *Address to his Roman Catholic Brethren, by A Minister of the Gospel,* CW18:1.

[29] Gary L. Nebeker, 'John Nelson Darby and Trinity College, Dublin: A Study in Eschatological Contrasts', *Fides et Historia,* 34.2 (2002), 98.

rebellions against the English of 1798 and 1803 and the demise of Napoleon Bonaparte, whom many Irish Catholics had hoped would liberate them from the English, led to great disillusionment. Hopes were rekindled, however, by the propagation of belief in the imminent, end-time restoration of Roman Catholic supremacy. This populist belief system, referred to by historians as 'folk apocalyptic', seemed to offer the Irish peasants hope for the future.

The Prophecies of Pastorini

In 1771, Charles Walmesley, Roman Catholic Vicar Apostolic of the Western District of England, wrote a book entitled, *The General History of the Christian Church from her Birth to her Final Triumphant State in Heaven, chiefly deduced from the Apocalypse of St. John the Apostle*. This book was later republished under the pseudonym 'Signor Pastorini', and entitled, *The Prophecies of Pastorini*, quickly becoming 'a popular Catholic manifesto of futurist postmillennialism'.[30] Circulated among Irish Catholic peasants in pamphlet and handbill form shortly after the outbreak of the French Revolution, it described Protestantism as 'a doomed edifice on the verge of annihilation',[31] and portrayed the Protestant Reformers as heretics who had united 'to destroy the ancient faith' of Rome. According to Walmesley, 1825 was to be the year when the fifth vial of God's wrath (Rev. 16:10) would be poured out upon the Protestant Church, ushering in the sixth age of millennial peace.[32] The 'cult of Pastorini' spread rapidly in Mayo, Westmeath, King's County, and Clare, becoming 'a religious focal point for agrarian, anti-English rebels like the Rockite movement and the Ribbonmen.'[33] One notable opponent of these apocalyptic groups was Daniel O'Connell, who campaigned for Catholic emancipation with the support of 'politically conscious Catholics'.[34]

The Prophecy Man

Just as influential as *The Prophecies of Pastorini* were itinerant millenarian 'prophets' such as Barney McHaighery, who roamed southern Ireland during

---

[30] Nebeker, *The Hope of Heavenly Glory*, pp. 124, 132.

[31] James S. Donnelly, Jr, 'Pastorini and Captain Rock: Millenarianism and Sectarianism in the Rockite Movement of 1821-4', in *Irish Peasants: Violence & Political Unrest 1780-1914*, ed. by Samuel Clark and James S. Donnelly, Jr (Manchester: Manchester University Press, 1983), p. 107.

[32] Charles Walmesley, *The General History of the Christian Church, from her Birth to her Final Triumphant State in Heaven, chiefly Deduced from the Apocalypse of St. John the Apostle* (London: 1771), pp. 204, 262.

[33] Robert Henry Krapohl, *A Search for Purity: The Controversial Life of John Nelson Darby* (PhD: Baylor University, Waco, 1988), pp. 40-41. Darby received a death threat from the Rockite movement while preaching in County Clare. (CBA 5540 [188].)

[34] Donnelly, 'Pastorini', p. 109.

the 1820s. Locals gathered to hear the 'prophecy man' interpret the signs of the times, particularly during the Napoleonic Wars 'when talk of the liberation of Ireland through foreign invasion and the revered name of Bonaparte were constantly on his lips.' Widespread illiteracy and a poor command of English amongst the Irish Catholic peasantry contributed to the popularity of these 'prophets', whose oracles were denounced by Protestants as 'a hotchpotch of Biblical imagery, native Irish folklore, Pastorini's prophecies, anti-Protestant invective, and ancient apocryphal oracles of St. Columkill and St. Bridget.'[35] The succession to the English throne of George IV in 1820, the death of Napoleon Bonaparte in 1821, and the passing of the prophetic year of 1825, all but quashed Catholic millenarian fervour. Although this folk apocalyptic was the complete antithesis of Darby's apolitical, otherworldly, and fundamentally Protestant millenarianism, it helps to contextualise Darby by painting the backdrop against which his pre-conversion ministry was conducted.

Trinity College, Dublin

According to Neatby, Trinity College was 'as much the academic parent of Plymouth Brethrenism, as Oxford of the Evangelical revival a hundred years earlier.'[36] Founded in 1592 as a divinity school, Trinity became 'a bulwark of English and Protestant influence'.[37] For much of its history the college was 'preponderantly Anglican', and from 1801 to 1921 'staunchly Unionist'.[38] During the late eighteenth and early nineteenth centuries, Trinity became 'a centre of millenarian ferment',[39] owing to its Protestant ethos and the conviction, strengthened in the wake of the American Revolution (1775), the French Revolution (1789), and the Irish Rebellion (1798), that 'the Church of Ireland still had before it an unfinished mission to make Ireland a Protestant nation'.[40]

Convinced that 'French enlightenment infidelity was making its presence known in Ireland',[41] particularly through the Society of the United Irishmen, Trinity lecturer Richard Graves urged students to uphold the established Protestant order. Graves was appointed dean of Trinity in 1814, the year before

---

[35] Nebeker, *The Hope of Heavenly Glory*, pp. 135-136.
[36] William Blair Neatby, *A History of the Plymouth Brethren*, 2nd edn (London: Hodder and Stoughton, 1902), p. 13.
[37] J.P. Mahaffy, *An Epoch in Irish History: Trinity College, Dublin, Its Foundation and Early Fortunes 1591-1660*, 2nd edn (London: T. Fisher Unwin, 1906), p. 58.
[38] R.B. McDowell and D.A. Webb, *Trinity College Dublin 1592-1952: An Academic History* (Cambridge: Cambridge University Press, 1982), p. xx.
[39] Nebeker, 'John Nelson Darby', 87.
[40] Joseph Liechty, *Irish Evangelicalism, Trinity College Dublin, and the Mission of the Church of Ireland at the End of the Eighteenth Century* (PhD: St. Patrick's College, Maynooth, 1987), p. 470.
[41] Nebeker, 'John Nelson Darby', 94.

Darby enrolled as a classics student, and tutored in classics and theology. Insisting on theological training for those seeking ordination, his recommended books included Thomas Newton's *Dissertations on the Prophecies* and Henry Kett's *History the Interpreter of Prophecy*.[42] According to his son, Graves was 'a favourite preacher in College', stirring within his students a 'seriousness and a spirit of religious inquiry but little felt before.'[43] Darby acknowledged the influence of 'Dean Graves',[44] commending him for upholding the Mosaic authorship of the Pentateuch; this is a notable tribute from one who infrequently credited people in his writings. Graves' interest in the study of Biblical prophecy relating to Israel's restoration, and his involvement with the Dublin auxiliary of the London Society for Promoting Christianity amongst the Jews (LSPCJ), may have had an influence on Darby.

Graves was described in 1811 as 'one of the few in this country, in late years, who turned his mind fully to the prophecies relating to the conversion and return of the Jews'.[45] In his sermons he spoke about the 'sacred', 'solemn', 'unprecedented', and 'singular' nature of the work of the LSPCJ, and about the 'lamentable neglect' of Christians who had failed the Jewish people. Preaching in Dublin on behalf of the Society in 1811, he declared:

> Alas! to this hour, I fear, the same principle, though somewhat softened and disguised, still acts with powerful opposition to the cause which now I plead; and though it may not impel to acts of positive cruelty, and direct persecution, it yet steels the heart against every impulse of sympathy, and every call of mercy.[46]

Although clearly familiar with the work of this 'prolific author',[47] the extent of Graves' influence on Darby is uncertain. Nevertheless, the fact that Darby graduated from Trinity in his time to become one of 'the earliest and most able defenders of futurism',[48] may be attributed, at least in part, to his influence.[49] The same can be said of Edward Hincks and Thomas Elrington, who also taught Darby at Trinity. Elmore notes Elrington's special interest in Biblical typology and the future restoration of the Jews, which, as we shall see, were

---

[42] Nebeker, *The Hope of Heavenly Glory*, p. 82.

[43] Elmore, *A Critical Examination*, p. 56.

[44] Darby, *The Irrationalism of Infidelity*, CW6:205.

[45] Elmore, *A Critical Examination*, p. 57.

[46] Richard Graves, *A Sermon Preached in St. Andrew's Church, Dublin, on Sunday, 21st April, 1811 in aid of the London Society, for Promoting Christianity amongst the Jews* (Dublin: 1811), pp. 1, 3, 18.

[47] John E.L. Oulton, *The Study of Divinity in Trinity College Dublin since the Foundation* (Dublin: Hodges, Figgis, & Co., 1941), p. 14.

[48] Sandeen, *The Roots of Fundamentalism*, p. 38.

[49] Although Graves *appears* to have advocated a form of postmillennialism, 'postmillennialists in Graves' day were known for their literalism with respect to prophecy.' (Elmore, *A Critical Examination*, p. 66.)

central to Darby's eschatology. It is therefore reasonable to conclude that the 'theological grist for Darby's later synthesis was certainly present at Trinity College in his student days', Darby having been trained 'in an atmosphere in which it was commonplace to refer to "the Church of Christ" and "the Jewish Nation" fulfilling different but related future roles.'[50]

'My Kingdom is not of this World'

On 10 October 1826, in a service at St. Patrick's Cathedral in Dublin, Archbishop Magee called upon the Established Church of Ireland to impose upon all Roman Catholic converts an oath of allegiance and supremacy to the Protestant faith and the British government. Convinced that Roman Catholicism in Ireland represented a serious threat to the State Church, a petition on behalf of the archbishop of Dublin, the bishop of Glandelagh, and the clergy under their jurisdiction, was submitted to the House of Commons on 1 February 1827, imploring the government to protect the Protestant faith 'against the machinations of its inveterate [Roman Catholic] adversaries'.[51] These developments had a profound effect on the course of Darby's life and ministry, as John Gifford Bellett later reminisced:

> All this had a very decided influence on his mind, for I remember him at one time as a very exact churchman, as I may speak, but it was evident that his mind had now received a shock, and it was never again what it had been.[52]

Recalling Jesus' words to Pilate, 'My kingdom is not of this world' (John 18:36), Darby was convinced that Magee's actions compromised the divine calling of the Church in a manner not dissimilar to those of Henry VIII, when he asserted civil authority over Rome. Since spiritual supremacy belonged to Christ, whose dominion was of a *heavenly* rather than earthly nature, Darby argued that Christ's ministers should not concern themselves with civil affairs.

According to Darby, before the oath was enforced, Roman Catholics had been converting to the true Christian faith 'at the rate of 600 to 800 a week'. When this harvest of souls came to an abrupt end, he held the archbishop and the Church of Ireland responsible. By appealing to the government for protection against Rome, Darby believed that the Church had subordinated itself to the authority of the State rather than Christ. In a private letter to the archbishop, he expressed concern that the Established Church was assuming an identity not dissimilar to that of the Church of Rome, which he described as a mere 'counterpart of the Christian scheme, set up by Satan on the decay of faith

---

[50] Elmore, *A Critical Examination*, pp. 58, 73-74.
[51] Quoted in Weremchuk, *John Nelson Darby*, pp. 212-213.
[52] John Gifford Bellett, *Interesting Reminiscences of the Early History of 'Brethren': with Letter from J.G. Bellett to J.N. Darby* (London: Alfred Holness, n.d.), pp. 2-3.

to hold its place, uniting men to an *earthly* head…instead of leading men to *heavenly* things' (*italics* mine).[53]

Although Darby was deeply disillusioned with the state of the Church, signs of spiritual life in Dublin soon rekindled his hope.

The Plymouth Brethren

In the late 1820s, a number of Christians who were discontented with the Established Church began to meet together in small groups in Dublin. This marked the beginning of Plymouth Brethrenism.

Although it is difficult to chart the precise chronology of events, we know that at that time Edward Wilson, assistant secretary of the Bible Society, took communion in his home in Upper Sackville Street with the converted Roman Catholic, Edward Cronin. In 1827, Cronin was also meeting in his own home at 13 Lower Pembroke Street with Mr Timms and his cousins, the Misses Drury. They were later joined by William Stokes and John Vesey Parnell, who became Lord Congleton. Around the same time, Anthony Norris Groves, who later pioneered Brethren missionary work, met with a small group every Sunday evening in the cottage of Miss Paget. This group included Francis Hutchinson and John Gifford Bellett, one of Darby's fellow undergraduates at Trinity.

In November 1829, these groups joined together in Hutchinson's home in Fitzwilliam Square, and all who 'truly loved the Lord' were made welcome. In May 1830, they relocated to 11 Aungier Street, from where 'the consolidating force'[54] of Plymouth Brethrenism was harnessed. In a letter to Bellett in 1864, Darby stated that 'it was not a small thing to me that you, with dear C. [Cronin] and H. [Hutchinson], were one of the first four, who with me, through God's grace the fourth, began to break bread in Dublin'.[55] In an undated letter from Boston, Massachusetts, Darby wrote: 'I was myself the beginning of what the world calls Plymouth brethren, though we began in Dublin.'[56]

Although Brethren historians suggest that Darby's involvement in the early Dublin meetings was infrequent, and probably confined to the period of his convalescence (Dec 1827 - Feb 1828), it was 'largely under his influence'[57] that the meetings developed. Groves, Bellett, Cronin, and Darby have all been cited by scholars as *the* founding father of Plymouth Brethrenism, but few have left a mark as indelible as that of John Nelson Darby, who has been described as the

---

[53] Darby, *Considerations addressed to the Archbishop of Dublin*, CW1:1, 12, 6.
[54] Neatby, *A History of the Plymouth Brethren*, p. 24.
[55] Darby, *Letter to J.G. Bellett* (September 1864), L1:383.
[56] Darby, *Letter* (Boston, n.d.), L2:208.
[57] Crawford Gribben, *The Irish Puritans: James Ussher and the Reformation of the Church* (Darlington: Evangelical Press, 2003), p. 122.

founder of 'Brethrenism as a system',[58] its 'leading architect'[59] ecclesiastically, the 'prime mover in co-ordinating and propagating its doctrines',[60] and the man who inspired 'the most influential of protestant millennial systems and one of the most significant Irish intellectual traditions.'[61] Even one of Darby's staunchest critics admitted that the movement's 'guiding and energising spirit throughout, was John Nelson Darby', and that in

> the grandeur of his conceptions, in the irresistible vehemence of his will, in his consummate strategical instinct, in his genius for administration, and most of all in his immense personal ascendancy, he stands unrivalled amongst the Brethren.[62]

In 1830, Francis William Newman, who had been employed as a private tutor in the Dublin home of Darby's brother-in-law, Sergeant Pennefather (later Lord Chief Justice of Ireland), invited Darby to Oxford University. As we noted earlier, Newman had been greatly impressed by Darby during his time in Dublin, and now wanted his colleagues and students at Oxford to meet this 'most remarkable man'. One of those Newman introduced him to during his stay at the university was Benjamin Wills Newton, a native of Plymouth who was to become one of Darby's close associates. Darby made a profound impression, instantaneously assuming 'the place of universal father-confessor, as if he had been a known and long-trusted friend'. Newman recorded how Darby's 'insight into character, and tenderness pervading his austerity, so opened young men's hearts, that day after day there was no end of secret closetings with him.'[63] One of the many young men who came to hear Darby speak at that time was the future Prime Minister, William E. Gladstone.[64]

On 6 February 1831, disillusioned Anglican, Henry Bellenden Bulteel, a fellow of Exeter College, Oxford, and curate of St. Ebbe's, preached the university sermon in which he castigated the Church of England and 'gave a most solemn and powerful warning from Romans 11:22, to apostate Christendom: "if thou continue not in His goodness, thou too shalt be cut

---

[58] Clarence B. Bass, *Backgrounds to Dispensationalism* (Grand Rapids, MI: Baker Book House, 1978), p. 64.

[59] Peter L. Embley, *The Origins and Early Development of the Plymouth Brethren* (PhD: St. Paul's College, Cheltenham, 1996), p. 36.

[60] Bass, *Backgrounds*, p. 48.

[61] Crawford Gribben, 'Introduction: Antichrist in Ireland – Protestant Millennialism and Irish Studies', in *Protestant Millennialism, Evangelicalism and Irish Society, 1790-2005*, ed. by Crawford Gribben and Andrew R. Holmes (Basingstoke: Palgrave Macmillan, 2006), p. 15.

[62] Neatby, *A History of the Plymouth Brethren*, p. 44.

[63] Newman, *Phases of Faith*, pp. 17, 28.

[64] William Kelly, *John Nelson Darby as I Knew Him* (Belfast: Words of Truth, 1986), p. 6.

off'.[65] The sermon caused a furore among the clergy, but drew the support of Darby, who circulated a pamphlet in Bulteel's defence. In the summer of 1831, Bulteel embarked on a preaching tour of the West Country, which resulted in many disillusioned Anglicans leaving the Church of England. In his response to the *Christian Journal*, which criticised those who had left the Church, Darby wrote:

> We leave it, because it is no company of believing disciples at all, but a very wicked and nefarious union between the Church and the world; because its essence and essential distinction is the chief of all iniquities, the mixing the Church in the world, the holding of apostate principles if not a ripened apostate state.

Darby believed that the Church of England was a 'modification of popery', the 'nursery of apostasy',[66] and 'a system of old bottles, which cannot bear the new wine of the kingdom'. He did, however, concede that there was 'truth in the hearts of many of her ministers, and in a feeble measure in her Articles'.[67]

The Plymouth Assembly

By the close of 1831, decisive steps had been taken to form the first 'Brethren' assembly in Plymouth. On 2 December, George Vicesimus Wigram, who became one of Darby's most loyal friends, purchased the disused Providence Chapel in Raleigh Street for £750. Referred to locally as the 'Providence People' and known for their open-air preaching and tract distribution, members of the assembly were nicknamed 'Plymouth Brethren' by critics. As Darby explained, 'The name Plymouth arose from the earliest publications which attracted attention issuing thence, and was so far harmless, as no human name was attached to them; one cannot help the world giving some.'[68] According to William Collingwood, their chief aim was 'to exhibit, in a Scriptural way, *the*

---

[65] *B.W. Newton and Dr S.P. Tregelles: Teachers of the Faith and the Future*, 2nd edn, ed. by George H. Fromow (Chelmsford: Sovereign Grace Advent Testimony, 1969), p. 3.

[66] Darby, *Reply to the Remarks in Two Leading Articles of the Christian Journal entitled 'Our Separating Brethren'* (1871), CW14:141, 143, 151.

[67] Darby, *The Claims of the Church of England Considered; being the close of a Correspondence between the Rev. James Kelly, of Stillogan, Ireland, and J.N. Darby*, CW14:195.

[68] Darby, *Letter* (Boston, n.d.), L2:208. Darby's followers were known as *Darbyites* (Ireland), *Darbysten* (Germany), *Darbystes* (France), and *Darbisti* (Italy). His doctrine has sometimes been labelled 'Darbyism', which he described as 'the offensive name'. (Darby, *What has been Acknowledged? or, the State of the Controversy about Elders, followed by a Short Answer to an Article of Mons. de Gasparin* [1852], CW4:293.)

common brotherhood of all believers',[69] hence all who truly belonged to Christ, and therefore to the family of God, were referred to as 'brother' or 'sister'. This explains how the name 'Brethren' came to be adopted.

Darby stressed the importance of the participation of the laity in church life, believing that if 'ever there was anything calculated to touch the heart of a Christian' it was the joining together of brothers and sisters in Christ around the Lord's Table. He added, 'For my own part I know of nothing, of what I may call the institutions of Christianity, connected with so much joy and fruitful influence to my soul.'[70] Darby also maintained that where there was an *ordained* priesthood 'there is the denial of Christianity',[71] and made the following distinction between Brethrenism and denominationalism:

> For a denominational body there is no room in the scriptural account of the Church or assembly, unless it be 'I am of Paul, and I of Apollos, and I of Cephas,' I of Luther, I of John Knox or Calvin. Churches are historic or ancestral (that is, not of God or scriptural). There is a great body which teaches beyond this – that of Rome, the abiding witness of the corruption and ruin of the Church or house of God placed in responsibility on earth, keeping its name and form, but in the hands of Satan and the seat of his power.[72]

Over the next few years the Brethren launched their own quarterly, the *Christian Witness*, and the Plymouth assembly grew significantly in numbers, relocating to larger premises in Ebrington Street in 1840. Although Darby's ministry took him far afield, he retained a close interest in, and affection for, his brothers and sisters in Plymouth. According to his letters, they were constantly in his thoughts and prayers, his desire being for them to flourish 'as the garden of the Lord'.[73] In a letter to Henry Borlase in 1834 he declared his great love for them,[74] and writing to Wigram in 1841 recalled that it was the love of Jesus, and not 'exact opinions on such or such a point', which had united the Brethren from the beginning. Darby wrote, 'I hold to love much more than to my views, or to those of others, or sustaining or destroying the views of others: hold fast by that, dear brother, for love is of God, and he that loveth is born of God.'[75]

---

[69] William Collingwood, *'The Brethren': A Historical Sketch* (Glasgow: Pickering & Inglis, 1899), p. 9.

[70] Darby, *The Gospel and the Church according to Scripture: being a Review of 'Church Doctrine, Bible Truth,' by the Rev M.S. Sadler* (1876), CW29:356-357.

[71] Darby, *Review of a Sermon Preached by the Rev. G.M. Innes, in the Quebec Cathedral, on Sunday, April 5th, 1868, and Published in the Quebec Mercury, April 9th,* CW14:271.

[72] Darby, *Presbyterianism: A Reply to 'The Church and the Pulpit'* (1868), CW14:334.

[73] Darby, *Letter to Miss Kingdom* (Limerick, 1832), L1:12.

[74] Darby, *Letter to Mr H. Borlase* (Dublin, 24 July 1834), L1:24.

[75] Darby, *Letter to G.V. Wigram* (Lausanne, 3 February 1841), L1:45-46.

Powerscourt

As the early house meetings were developing in Dublin, Theodosia Powerscourt, daughter of Colonel and Mrs Howard and second wife of Lord Powerscourt, was discoursing with students of Biblical prophecy at her nearby country estate. Described as 'a dear, humble saint'[76] who was 'pious and warm-hearted with more than a touch of the mystic',[77] Lady Powerscourt had previously attended the inaugural conference on Biblical prophecy at Albury Park, Surrey, in 1826. It is clear from his writings that Darby was well aware of the Albury conferences,[78] which, as we shall see later, brought together some of the most influential prophecy 'students' of his generation.

Informal gatherings at the home of Lady Powerscourt soon developed into a series of annual conferences, the first of which was held in October 1831 and presided over by Robert Daly. Powerscourt House soon became 'a centre of evangelical life and enquiry',[79] with thirty-five clergymen and fifteen laymen attending the inaugural conference. Those who gathered, including Darby and several of his Plymouth associates, were 'distressed at the condition of the Church', and came to the conference 'convinced that the hope of Christ's return should figure more prominently in the thinking of Christians.'[80] Topics under discussion included the state of the Established Church, the interpretation of prophecy, and the Second Coming of Christ.

It is interesting to note that Benjamin Newton, then 'Secretary at Oxford' for the LSPCJ, was 'conspicuous by his absence'[81] from its twelfth annual meeting on 26 September 1831, having elected instead to travel to Powerscourt. In the 1827 annual report of the Irish branch of the LSPCJ (also known as the Church of Ireland Jews Society),[82] Lady Powerscourt was listed as vice-patroness and John Gifford Bellett and Francis Hutchinson as subscribers.[83] Prior to his involvement with the Plymouth Brethren, George Müller, famed for his Bristol orphanages, arrived in Britain in March 1829 to train as a missionary with the LSPCJ. On 2 October 1830, the *Falmouth Packet and Cornish Herald* newspaper ran an article on the 'eleventh anniversary meeting of the Plymouth,

---

[76] W.E. Tayler, *Passages from the Diary and Letters of Henry Craik, of Bristol* (London: J.F. Shaw & Co., 1866), p. 168.
[77] Harold H. Rowdon, *The Origins of the Brethren 1825-1850* (London: Pickering & Inglis, 1967), p. 86.
[78] Darby, *The Irrationalism of Infidelity*, CW6:285.
[79] Stunt, *From Awakening to Secession*, p. 162.
[80] Rowdon, *The Origins of the Brethren*, p. 2.
[81] Embley, *The Origins and Early Development of the Plymouth Brethren*, p. 71.
[82] Kelvin Crombie, *A Jewish Bishop in Jerusalem: The Life Story of Michael Solomon Alexander* (Jerusalem: Nicolayson's Ltd., 2006), p. 27.
[83] Nicholas M. Railton, '"The Dreamy Mazes of Millenarianism": William Graham and the Irish Presbyterian Mission to German Jews', in Gribben and Holmes, *Protestant Millennialism*, p. 177.

Devonport, and Stonehouse Auxiliary' of the LSPCJ. In its report, it recorded that the meeting 'was addressed by the Revs. J.N. Darby, - Coffin, J. Lampen, J.B. Cartwright (of the parent society), - Harris, of Plympstock, and S. Nicholson, and Capt. [Percy] Hall, R.N.'[84] Although the extent of Darby's involvement with the LSPCJ is unclear, the fact that he addressed one of its meetings strongly indicates his practical support for Jewish evangelism.

At the second conference in September 1832, Lady Powerscourt 'threw in her lot'[85] with the Brethren after Darby called delegates to leave the Established Church. It is noteworthy that she understood the place of Israel in the prophetic scriptures, recording in her private study of Psalm 23 that this psalm,

> like most other promises and prophecies in the Old Testament, is to be applied literally to the Jewish people, still 'beloved for their fathers' sake;' and spiritually, to the Christian church.[86]

The topics discussed at this conference included the typology of the Jewish feasts and the return of the Jews to the Land. In between sessions, Darby wrote to the editor of the *Christian Herald*, reporting that delegates were particularly occupied with the question, 'By what covenant did the Jews, and shall the Jews, hold the land?'[87] This emphasis on the *future* restoration of Israel was to become a distinctive feature of Brethren eschatology. By the third conference in 1833, most of the participants, including Henry Craik and George Müller of Bristol, were members of the Plymouth Brethren. Subjects under discussion included the apostasy of the Church, the distinction between the Jewish and Christian dispensations, and 'the precious truth of the rapture'.[88]

Love for the Brethren

John Nelson Darby was tireless in calling true Christians to separate themselves from the apostate Church. As Coad explains, 'Heresy was to him a real and evil thing, working secretly and deviously beneath the surface, until it broke out in its full development, to the ruin of churches.'[89] Although he was tenacious and unyielding on matters of doctrine, and never shirked confrontation, Darby did not believe that he was above reproof. When faced with criticism of his work,

---

[84] 'London Society for Promoting Christianity among the Jews', *Falmouth Packet and Cornish Herald*, 2 October (1830), 320a.

[85] Rowdon, *The Origins of the Brethren*, p. 94.

[86] *Letters and Papers of the Late Theodosia A. Viscountess Powerscourt*, New edn, ed. by Robert Daly (London: G. Morrish, n.d.), p. 272.

[87] Darby, *Letter* (Granard, 15 October 1832), L1:7.

[88] H.A. Ironside, *A Historical Sketch of the Brethren Movement* (Neptune, NJ: Loizeaux Brothers, 1985), p. 23.

[89] F. Roy Coad, *A History of the Brethren Movement* (Exeter: The Paternoster Press Ltd., 1976), p. 112.

The Sufferings of Christ, he replied with typical humility:

> I have hitherto in my answers on questions of doctrine…dealt quietly and courteously with my adversaries. But I do see another hand and mind behind what is going on…As an attack on myself, I am glad not to answer it. If I have to take my adversaries up because they still carry on their warfare, and Satan is using them for mischief, I here declare I will not spare them, nor fail, with God's help, to make plain the tenets and doctrines which are at the bottom of all this. As regards myself, if I have one desire in my heart, it is that the blessed Lord may be glorified…If there be anything in these papers which dishonours Him – what I say is this: no explanation to defend myself…They are days in which His glory and the truth must be kept clear at all cost: I will put the match to burn all if there be anything which is against it.[90]

Writing to Mr Maylon from Geneva in 1840, Darby expressed how 'in all my weakness I have at least the good of the beloved church of my Saviour at heart'.[91] In a letter to Mr Spignio in 1877 he wrote: 'I hope that my love for the brethren with whom I cannot walk will be always increasing…Not to walk with them in a path that is not according to the word is not saying that one does not love them, but just the contrary.'[92] Perhaps the most striking example of Darby's ability to love the offender while condemning the offence is found in his response to Francis Newman's *Phases of Faith*. This was a work he 'had no thought' of sparing, but which drew from him 'somewhat different' feelings because of his close acquaintance with the author. As Darby explained,

> If the book is a guilty one, its author is guilty of it. But there is another feeling arises as to the author, which does not as to the book. To the book I can measure out, without a pang, unmingled feelings of disgust and contempt; to the author I could not. The thought of him awakens sorrow, regret, pain, a thousand feelings which the evil I find in his work…contribute to produce. I do mourn…But I write that you may at least feel that my attacking your book is as far as possible from bitterness toward you…May the Lord, who alone has power to blot out and overcome our wretchedness, and new-create the heart, make you – as in other ways He has me – a monument of His almighty and infinite grace![93]

Darby always desired 'the fullest liberty for the Spirit, but not the least for the flesh',[94] and could not countenance 'sentimental mercy'. In an exchange of letters about a brother he believed was in error, he wrote: 'What we need to know then is, whether affection for an individual should lead us to renounce the

---

[90] Darby, *The Sufferings of Christ*, CW7:140-141.
[91] Darby, *Letter to Mr Maylon* (Geneva, 2 January 1840), L1:35.
[92] Darby, *Letter to Mr Spignio* (New York, 5 March 1877), L2:386.
[93] Darby, *The Irrationalism of Infidelity*, CW6:1-2.
[94] Darby, *Letter to G.V. Wigram* (Stafford, 31 January 1839), L1:29.

truth of the word of God.'[95] Darby 'unfeignedly' desired the restoration of those in error, provided there was true repentance and a sincere desire to be freed 'from the deceiving or blinding power of the enemy in habits of thinking'.[96] As far as he was concerned, unity was never to be made 'a cover for evil'.[97] To those who questioned his approach to church discipline, Darby replied:

> People say, we have been *too narrow*, we must mix up a little. No, never, I cannot go back...I have nothing to go back from. The one desire of my heart is the beauty and blessing of the church – the bride of Christ. That will make me earnestly love all saints for they are of it. I desire its entire separation to Christ to whom she belongs – espoused as a chaste virgin. My feet in the narrow way – my heart as large as Christ's.[98]

In a letter to his friend, J.G. Bellett, Darby declared that, 'while specially happy in evangelising, my heart ever turns to the church's being fit for Christ. My heart turns there.'[99] These statements not only help to refute Stephen Sizer's accusation that Darby subordinated the Church and Christ to Israel, but provide us with an important personal insight into Darby's approach to conflict. This leads us to consider the much-chronicled rift between Darby and Newton, which not only split the Brethren into its 'Open' and 'Exclusive' camps, but also stigmatised a man who found the whole episode 'very painful.'[100]

Darby and Newton

Darby's relationship with Benjamin Newton has been likened to 'a thermometer which registered the health'[101] of the Plymouth Brethren. While itinerating in Switzerland, Darby was informed that Newton had assumed a more authoritative position within the Plymouth assembly. A charge of clericalism was subsequently brought against him by Darby, and was heard by thirteen leading members of the Brethren in April 1845. However, the root of the ensuing rift between Newton and Darby lay not in their ecclesiastical differences, but in the interpretation of Biblical prophecy.

As early as 1834, Newton had absented himself from the Powerscourt conference in protest against Darby's teaching on the *imminent* Rapture of the Church. Although his eschatology, like Darby's, highlighted the importance of the Abrahamic Covenant, and a restored Israel at 'the centre of the earth's

---

[95] Darby, *Letter* (New York, February 1877), L3:452-453.

[96] Darby, *Letter to J.G. Deck* (rec'd 29 August 1851), L1:193-195.

[97] Darby, *A Letter on Separation*, CW1:351.

[98] Darby, *What is the Church and in what sense is it now in Ruin? On the Epistle to the Ephesians*, M4:166-167.

[99] Darby, *Letter to J.G. Bellett* (September 1864), L1:384.

[100] Darby, *Letter to G.V. Wigram* (Plymouth, 21 April 1845), L1:79.

[101] Rowdon, *The Origins of the Brethren*, p. 58.

government for blessing',[102] the two men differed over the timing and nature of the Rapture. Following Darby's criticism of Newton's eschatology, which Newton had outlined in his *Thoughts on the Apocalypse*, a pamphlet war ensued, and when attempts at arbitration failed, Darby severed his connection with the Plymouth assembly. Newton was acquitted of the charge of clericalism, but his position became untenable after a manuscript of his lecture notes on the sufferings of Christ was circulated by James Lampen Harris and Christopher McAdam. Harris and McAdam were among those who charged Newton with 'serious heresy'[103] in relation to his doctrine of the humanity of Christ, and, failing to convince his fellow Brethren that his doctrine was not heretical, Newton withdrew from the Plymouth assembly on 8 December 1847 and moved away from the area.

The Bethesda Circular

The shock waves from the Darby-Newton rift were so far reaching that they caused irreparable damage to the Brethren movement as a whole. When the Woodfall brothers, who followed Newton's doctrine, left Plymouth to join the Bethesda assembly in Bristol, Darby called upon its leaders, Müller and Craik, to publicly condemn Newton's teaching. Following a meeting of the church elders, a statement known as *The Letter of the Ten*[104] was issued, rejecting his request. Darby responded by ending his association with the Bristol assembly, and on 26 August 1848 issued the 'Bethesda Circular', which not only excommunicated Bethesda but split Plymouth Brethrenism down the middle. Although Müller later denounced Newton's teaching,[105] he refused to be reconciled to Darby when he was approached by him in the summer of 1849. Those who allied themselves with Darby soon became known as 'Exclusive Brethren', while those who sided with Müller and Craik were referred to as 'Open Brethren'. In a letter to J.E. Batten in 1852, Darby distanced himself from such labels, explaining that

> no one has less sought to make a party than I have: I trust my heart is too much in heaven to find such a thing supportable...But I shall pursue the course I believe to

---

[102] Benjamin Wills Newton, *Prophecies Respecting the Jews and Jerusalem Considered. In the Form of a Catechism*, 4th edn (London: Houlston and Sons, 1888), p. 28.
[103] *Newton and Tregelles*, ed. by Fromow, p. 6.
[104] The 'Ten' were Henry Craik, George Müller, Jacob Henry Hale, Charles Brown, Elijah Stanley, Edmund Feltham, John Withy, Samuel Butler, John Meredith, and Robert Aitcheson. (Henry Groves, *Darbyism: Its Rise and Development, and a Review of 'The Bethesda Question'* [London: n.d.], p. 44.)
[105] Coad, *A History of the Brethren Movement*, p. 159.

be of God, and He who judges the secrets of men's hearts will judge all things and all men. The cry of party does not move me. It is evidently the enemy's cry.[106]

Darby's Response to the Rift

As we have seen, differences in approach to the interpretation of Biblical prophecy, particularly over the Rapture of the Church, undoubtedly contributed to the split between Darby and Newton. As far as Darby was concerned, his conscience was 'as clear as the day', believing that he had 'avoided the smallest act approaching to hostile or party feeling – quite the contrary.'[107] As he expressed in a letter to Bellett in 1863, 'I think you will find, and it has been my comfort when I have recurred to them, that in all my controversies, French and English, some great fundamental or practical truth has been in question...For disputation I have no taste.'[108] Although he was never one for personal vendettas, Darby was not prepared, as in the case of *The Letter of the Ten*, to submit to a church body which did not bear the authority of Christ. As he explained in a letter written in 1867,

> God knows I have never sought to have dominion over the faith of any one whatsoever, whilst seeking to help their joy, and I think I have this testimony in the conscience of all the brethren: I am heartily their servant for the love of Christ, but I do not accept that they should have dominion over mine.[109]

Many have blamed Darby for the rift with Newton and Bethesda, portraying him as a 'dictator with plenary powers'[110] who acted in a 'vindictive and violent'[111] manner. We must let Darby speak for himself. Writing to J.E. Batten in 1852, he expressed how he felt when he left the Plymouth assembly:

> I thought myself alone. I think the brethren behaved very badly, but I recognise my own failing enough to leave all that, and walk straight now through grace; if others will not, I mourn, but do not change my path...I endeavour, and earnestly desire, to show grace and largeness of heart to those I think even wrong. I do not deny that in the conduct of the affair, the failure of judgment as I think of others, has made my own path much more difficult, but I cast all this on God, and go on looking to Him. The result is in His hands. If alone, alone; if He grant union, it

---

[106] Darby, *Letter to J.E. Batten* (London, rec'd 15 May 1852), L1:204.

[107] Darby, *Letter to G.V. Wigram* (Plymouth, 21 April 1845), L1:79.

[108] Darby, *Letter to J.G. Bellett* (Toronto, March 1863), L1:348.

[109] Darby, *Letter* (1867), L3:382.

[110] Henry W. Clark, *History of English Nonconformity: Vol. II* (London: Chapman and Hall Limited, 1913), p. 391.

[111] Sandeen, *The Roots of Fundamentalism*, p. 61.

· will be my heart's joy, but at any rate faithfulness, and His favour and approbation. This is my answer to these things.[112]

Robert Cameron, a leading figure in the American Bible and Prophecy Conference Movement, provides further insight into the mind of the much-maligned Darby. In an article written for the magazine, *Perilous Times*, in April 1917, he recalled his meeting with Darby towards the end of his life:

> Over forty years ago, at my own table in New York City, Mr Darby called Mr Newton 'dear brother Newton'. I expressed my deep surprise at the use of such an endearing term concerning the one who had been freely called 'that dangerous man', 'the arch enemy', 'the fearful blasphemer', and other equally harsh terms. At once Mr Darby replied: 'Mr Newton is the most godly man I ever knew.' I said, 'Well, then, what was all this trouble and condemnation about, if Mr Newton is such a godly man?' He answered promptly, 'Oh, but Mr Newton had taught blasphemous doctrines about the person of our blessed Lord, and these had to be dealt with.'[113]

It is true that Darby was 'relentless' in his pursuit of the Newton heresy, but he was convinced that he had acted in the best interests not only of the Brethren as a whole, but of Newton himself. When Newton finally acknowledged his error, Darby notified the Brethren and gave a typically warm response: 'If Mr. N were restored, it would be the joy of my heart.'[114]

Whatever the rights and wrongs of the split, it is difficult to remain impartial. People were hurt, relationships were fractured, and an entire movement rent asunder. The whole episode makes for compelling reading. However, it is unfortunate that historians have, in the main, tended to sympathise with Newton and Bethesda, and have cast Darby as the villain of the peace.

The Man behind the Message

Darby has been described by critics as the man who 'helped to deceive by many means',[115] a 'tortured and confused man' whose humility gave way to 'vindictiveness',[116] one who was unable 'to coexist with anyone who opposed

---

[112] Darby, *Letter to J.E. Batten* (London, rec'd 15 May 1852), L1:206.

[113] Coad, *A History of the Brethren Movement*, p. 163.

[114] Darby, *Notice of the Statement and Acknowledgement of Error circulated by Mr. Newton*, CW15:117, 123.

[115] H.A. Baker, 'A "Pre-Tribulation Rapture" is a New Theory', *Watching and Waiting*, July-August (1956), 242.

[116] Bass, *Backgrounds*, pp. 98, 144.

his views',[117] 'the leader of an extravagant class of schismatics',[118] a 'prophet of doom',[119] the 'black sheep'[120] of the Plymouth Brethren, 'a maze of contradictions',[121] one who 'could not resist playing Witchfinder General', a man 'capable of cruelty and unpleasantness towards his enemies',[122] one 'apt to jump half informed into violent partisanship',[123] 'a petty tyrant, for he was most tyrannical about petty things',[124] a 'Goliath of dissent'[125] who 'displayed a wonderful power of bending other minds to his own',[126] one whose doctrine was 'incendiary'[127] and whose discipline 'anti-christian',[128] a man who 'relished the role of the disgruntled teacher',[129] one whose teachings displayed 'an arrogant spiritualism, most subversive of all peace and brotherhood among Christians',[130] a man whose doctrine has 'shaken Christianity's foundations',[131] a man of 'breathtaking dogmatism'[132] who 'ruthlessly destroyed churches'[133] by 'trampling in the dust the rights of every conscience', one who elevated himself to the 'high pinnacle of infallibility',[134] a man of 'distinct egocentricity'[135]

---

[117] Jonathan D. Burnham, *A Story of Conflict: The Controversial Relationship between Benjamin Wills Newton and John Nelson Darby* (Milton Keynes: Paternoster, 2004), p. xviii.

[118] James Kelly, 'Letter to the Rev. J. Darby (Stillorgan Glebe, Dublin, 28 January 1842)', in Darby, *The Claims of the Church of England*, CW14:177.

[119] Ben Witherington III, *The Problem with Evangelical Theology: Testing the Exegetical Foundations of Calvinism, Dispensationalism and Wesleyanism* (Waco, TX: Baylor University Press, 2005), p. 167.

[120] Eaton, 'Beware the Trumpet', p. 136.

[121] Krapohl, *A Search for Purity*, p. 159.

[122] Andrew Walker, *Restoring the Kingdom: The Radical Christianity of the House Church Movement* (Guildford: Eagle, 1998), pp. 243, 246.

[123] F. Roy Coad, *Prophetic Developments with Particular Reference to the early Brethren Movement* (Pinner: CBRF Publications, 1966), p. 28.

[124] Sandeen, *The Roots of Fundamentalism*, p. 31.

[125] Joseph D'Arcy Sirr, *A Memoir of the Honourable and Most Reverend Power Le Poer Trench, Last Archbishop of Tuam* (Dublin: William Curry Jr & Company, 1845), p. 344.

[126] Newman, *Phases of Faith*, p. 21.

[127] Krapohl, *A Search for Purity*, p. 190.

[128] Groves, *Darbyism*, p. 41.

[129] Burnham, *A Story of Conflict*, p. 172.

[130] Thomas Croskery, *A Catechism on the Doctrines of the Plymouth Brethren*, 5th edn (London: James Nisbet & Co., 1866), preface.

[131] Ronald M. Henzel, *Darby, Dualism and the Decline of Dispensationalism* (Tucson, AZ: Fenestra Books, 2003), p. 53.

[132] Iain H. Murray, *The Puritan Hope: A Study in Revival and the Interpretation of Prophecy* (London: The Banner of Truth Trust, 1971), p. 200.

[133] Coad, *A History of the Brethren Movement*, p. 164.

[134] Groves, *Darbyism*, pp. 47, 84.

[135] Larry E. Dixon, 'The Importance of J.N. Darby and the Brethren Movement in the History of Conservative Theology', *Christian Brethren Review*, 41 (1990), 43.

whose style was about 'the most uncouth, irrelevant, obscure, of any author',[136] and one whose 'increasingly tyrannical domination of the Brethren weakened their witness and relegated them to the outer fringes of nineteenth century Protestantism.'[137] In the light of such vitriol, we must ask: Is this a faithful portrait of John Nelson Darby, or a grotesque caricature?

A Man of One Aim

In 1867, John Jewell Penstone published a response to 'the course of animosity against Mr. Darby' which he felt was being 'so unrelentingly pursued' by some, and which had led 'some otherwise excellent and honourable men into a path of misrepresentation which has been coolly persevered in even after such evidence as any candid enquirer would require at their hands had entirely broken down.'[138] In spite of all the accusations made against him, Darby holds a place of affection in the hearts of many.

Darby has been described as 'a great and good man, an uncompromising champion for Christ's glory and God's truth',[139] 'one of the most remarkable servants of Christ that this country has produced',[140] 'a great man and ever greater servant of God'[141] whose 'greatness...gave prominence to his weaknesses',[142] 'a really good man' whose 'largeness of heart...showed itself in many ways',[143] 'a man of commanding intellect'[144] who was 'tireless in his missionary zeal to teach the Bible',[145] 'the Tertullian of these last days',[146] a man of 'simple and unaffected piety; combined with the ripest scholarship and unequalled ability in expounding the Word of God',[147] 'a man of one aim – the glory of God' who was 'always maintaining that close communion with the

---

[136] William Reid, *Plymouth Brethrenism Unveiled and Refuted*, 2nd edn (Edinburgh: William Oliphant and Company, 1876), p. 17.

[137] Krapohl, *A Search for Purity*, p. vi.

[138] John Jewell Penstone, *A Caution to the Readers of 'A Caution Against the Darbyites' [by John Eliot Howard]. With a few words on 'The Close of Twenty-Eight Years' Association with J.N.D.'* (London: G. Morrish, 1867), p. 3.

[139] Kelly, *The Rapture of the Saints*, pp. 11-12.

[140] 'An Extract from "The Christian Commonwealth," 11th May, 1882', in *The Last Days of J.N.D. (John Nelson Darby) From March 3rd to April 29th, 1882, With Portrait*, 2nd edn (Christchurch: N.C.M. Turner, 1925), p. 26.

[141] Julius Anton von Poseck, Darby's co-worker on his German translation of the New Testament, quoted in Weremchuk, *John Nelson Darby*, p. 140.

[142] Weremchuk, *John Nelson Darby*, p. 139.

[143] Kelly, *John Nelson Darby*, pp. 22, 19.

[144] Collingwood, *'The Brethren': A Historical Sketch*, p. 19.

[145] LaHaye, *Rapture under Attack*, pp. 159-160.

[146] Henry Pickering, *Chief Men among the Brethren*, 2nd edn (London: Pickering & Inglis, 1961), p. 11.

[147] Walter Scott, *John Nelson Darby* (Hamilton: n.d.), p. 8.

Lord that gave lustre to his testimony and fragrance to his life',[148] 'a man of overwhelming devotion, whose charismatic personality galvanised disciples throughout his long life',[149] one who was 'generous to the wasting of his substance, and possessed of more than martyr courage',[150] a man capable of 'remarkable humility' who demonstrated 'an especial sympathy'[151] with children, a man used by God 'to bring cosmos out of chaos for the church of God',[152] the founder of a movement which 'attempted a more thoroughgoing revival of primitive Christianity than either the Puritan or Wesleyan movements',[153] and 'a leader of matchless sagacity' whose life resembled 'a landscape with its towering rocks and solitudes; its verdant meads and meandering streams; its rushing torrents and calm lakes; each of which stand upon the canvas as the arresting feature of the picture.'[154] Even Max Weremchuk, 'a most ardent Darby follower'[155] turned critic, remains impressed by Darby's 'devotion to Christ and his high level of personal holiness'.[156]

The Heart of Darby

It is impossible to engage with Darby doctrinally without first engaging with the man behind the message. Coad, Neatby, and Burnham are among those who have paid scant attention to the more 'pastoral' episodes in his life, and in so doing have unwittingly left us with an incomplete, and often distorted, picture.

John Nelson Darby put his Christian faith into practice. As Francis Newman observed, 'For the first time in my life I saw a man earnestly turning into reality the principles which others confessed with their lips only.'[157] The following cameos open up a window into the heart of a man who, like his Master, 'preferred the poor'.[158] During one of Darby's many visits to the United States,

---

[148] Carron, *The Christian Testimony*, pp. 346-347.
[149] Ian S. Rennie, 'Nineteenth-Century Roots of Contemporary Prophetic Interpretation', in *A Guide to Biblical Prophecy*, ed. by Carl E. Armerding and W. Ward Gasque (Peabody, MA: Hendrickson Publishers, 1989), p. 56.
[150] J.C. Philpot, quoted in *John Nelson Darby*, ed. by Cross, p. 30.
[151] Coad, *A History of the Brethren Movement*, pp. 107-108.
[152] Napoleon Noel, *The History of the Brethren 1826-1936: Vol. I* (Denver, CO: W.F. Knapp, 1936), p. 54.
[153] J. Gordon Melton, *The Encyclopedia of American Religions: Vol. I* (Detroit, MI: Gale Research Company, 1978), p. 411.
[154] *John Nelson Darby*, ed. by Cross, pp. 75-76.
[155] Weremchuk, *John Nelson Darby*, p. 11.
[156] Max S. Weremchuk, 'John Nelson Darby: Bicentennial Reflections - Is Darby still Relevant?', *Brethren Archivists & Historians Network Review*, 2.2 (Autumn, 2003), 69.
[157] Newman, *Phases of Faith*, p. 18.
[158] Darby, *Letter to J.E. Batten* (London, rec'd 15 May 1852), L1:205.

A poor brother whose children kept tame rabbits was extremely anxious to entertain the great man to dinner...The household were all on the tiptoe of expectation...with the sole exception of one downcast little fellow, whose tame rabbit had been requisitioned as the principal dish for the honoured guest's refection. Whilst the dinner was in process of serving, Mr. Darby, noticing the little lad's downcast demeanour, enquired the reason; and the little fellow (contrary to previous instructions) blurted out the whole truth, with the result that J.N.D. expressed his sympathy with him in a practical manner. Declining to eat any of the little fellow's pet, as soon as the meal was over he took him to where there was a large tank of water, and producing some mechanical toy ducks from his pocket, the great man played with the little boy for an hour or so.[159]

Other stories are recorded of Darby 'playing *bear* with little folks, running after them on all fours, and growling to their delight and terror.'[160]

Turning the clock back to his days as a curate in the remote hills of County Wicklow, Darby recalled a visit he made to a boy in the last stages of consumption. The young lad, who was illiterate and had never read the Bible, told Darby how he had become sick after searching the mountains in inclement weather for one of his father's flock. Having found the sheep, the boy carried it on his shoulders back to his father. Darby used the boy's own story to teach him about the parable of the lost sheep, and recorded what followed:

He accepted Christ as his Saviour, he earnestly prayed to be carried home like the lost sheep in the heavenly Shepherd's arms. He died humbly, peacefully, almost exulting, with the name of Jesus, my Saviour and my Shepherd, the last upon his lips.[161]

In his discourse, *On Discipline* (1841), Darby wrote:

One thing I would pray for, because I love the Lord's sheep, is that there might be shepherds. I know nothing next to personal communion with the Lord, so blessed as the pastor feeding the Lord's sheep, the Lord's flock; but it is the *Lord's* flock...I know nothing like it on earth – the core of a true-hearted pastor, one who can bear the whole burden of grief and care of any soul and deal with God about it. I believe it is the happiest, most blessed relationship that can subsist in this world.[162]

One notable weakness in Darby scholarship is that researchers have not allowed the man to speak for himself. Darby's private correspondence is full of honest self-appraisal, revealing servant-hearted humility and an acute awareness of his

---

[159] *John Nelson Darby*, ed. by Cross, p. 42.
[160] Weremchuk, *John Nelson Darby*, p. 157.
[161] John Nelson Darby, *How the Lost Sheep was Found: An Incident in the Life of the Late J.N. Darby* (Kingston-on-Thames: Stow Hill Bible & Tract Depot, n.d.), pp. 14-15.
[162] Darby, *On Discipline* (1841), CW1:348-349.

own human failings and inadequacy. This is borne out in a letter to William Kelly, the editor of his *Collected Writings*, to whom Darby expressed the following concern:

> MY DEAR BROTHER, – I have got frightened on seeing the title page of what you are publishing of my old papers…It has a kind of pretentious look, making a kind of author of me who attaches himself to his works and his works to himself, which is not really the case. I feel as little as it is possible to feel I believe of authorship, save in the first place that what God does not give is useless in the church, or worse; and, not having naturally *that* kind of pride, sometimes I do not like what I have written, sometimes I do.[163]

Darby longed for 'a deeper well of Christ'[164] in his life from which others could draw, and rejoiced at seeing men 'raised up to continue the work' he had begun. In a letter to Timothy Loizeaux, he described himself as a 'hewer of wood' and a 'drawer of water' for those with 'more courage'.[165] Never interested in 'mere academic pursuits',[166] Darby wrote for the benefit of the Brethren,[167] his *Synopsis of the Books of the Bible* having been published 'to help the reader'[168] study God's word. Writing to J.B. Stoney in 1866, he stated that he had not written more than God had given him for others to use.[169]

Darby had an acute sense of his own weakness, and frequently acknowledged God's 'great and sweet and precious patience with His poor servant'.[170] He considered himself to be 'feeble at intercession',[171] confessed to a 'lack of courage',[172] and ran the Christian race with 'sadly feeble failing steps'.[173] He also considered himself to be 'too bad to be worth thinking about',[174] 'no wise master-builder',[175] 'a poor workman',[176] 'a poor worm',[177] and 'a poor unworthy creature'.[178] Looking back on his life in 1852, Darby recorded what he saw in a letter to J.E. Batten:

---

[163] Darby, *Letter to W. Kelly* (Milwaukee, 8 August 1867), L3:389.
[164] Darby, *Letter* (10 November 1860), L3:326.
[165] Darby, *Letter to Timothy Loizeaux*, L2:244.
[166] Elmore, *A Critical Examination*, p. 19.
[167] Darby, *Letter to G.V. Wigram* (Montpellier, 1 June 1847), L1:118.
[168] Darby, *Preface*, S1:vii.
[169] Darby, *Letter to J.B. Stoney* (New York, 29 November 1866), L1:468.
[170] Darby, *Letter to Timothy Loizeaux*, L2:244.
[171] Darby, *Letter to A.B. Pollock* (Toronto, October 1866), L1:461.
[172] Darby, *Letter to Timothy Loizeaux*, L2:243.
[173] Darby, *Letter to J.G. Deck* (rec'd 29 August 1851), L1:230.
[174] Darby, *Why Do I Groan?*, CW12:197.
[175] Darby, *Letter to G. Wolston* (Elberfeld, 3 January 1870), L2:60.
[176] Darby, *Letter to R.T. Grant* (Montreal, 1868), L1:524.
[177] Darby, *Letter to Mr. Mahoney* (Dublin, 28 May 1880), L3:90.
[178] Darby, *Letter to C. McAdam* (Chicago, June 1875), L2:348.

I have seen many swerve and seek ease, I have seen my own failure and feebleness in it, but the path is Christ's, and I desire to walk there still. I did not enter into this path for its success, but for its truth, because I believed it Christ's. I walk in it still for the same reason. I did not enter into it for brethren, or brethrenism: there were none to join. I did so because the Spirit and the word showed me it, and that it was following Christ.[179]

In an age when death came suddenly, Darby was always ready to offer the bereaved his 'entire sympathy'.[180] In 1864, he lost John Gifford Bellett, one of his closest friends. Bellett had written to Darby shortly before his death with the tenderest recollection of their friendship:

I came to know you, not slightly as before, but in an apprehension that instinctively bound me to you, and this now for forty years has never abated. What do I owe the God of my eternal life for feeding and strengthening that life, and enlarging its capacities through your ministry, in secret and in public! I have loved you as I suppose, in a certain sense, I have loved no other, and now, after so long a time, we are found together, still in the dear fellowship of the same confession.[181]

Bellett's daughter recalled how frequently Darby visited the family home, and how her father regarded him as one of his 'dearest friends'.[182] In his last letter to Bellett, Darby expressed the depth of his love for his brother in Christ:

I have ever found in you, dear brother, everything that was kind; nor be assured was it lost upon me, though I am not demonstrative...It is to you, dear brother, my heart turns now, to say how much I own and value your love, and to return it; I rejoice that while I have been the object of many kindnesses on your part down here, it is one which will never cease, which has had Jesus our Master for its bond, though with many human kindnesses. But oh, what joy to know oneself united to Him! It adds a joy untold to every sweetness: it is the source of it too. Surely He is all. For me, I work on till He call me, and though it would be a strange Dublin without you, yet I go on my way, serve others, say little and pass on. Not that I do not deeply love others, but this will all come out in its truth in heaven, perhaps on one's death-bed; but I have committed my all to Him till that day. My hope is still to see you, my beloved brother; should I not, be assured there is none who has loved you more truly and thankfully than myself; it can hardly be unknown to you, though with me it is more within than without. Peace be with you. May you find the blessed One ever near you; that is everything.[183]

---

[179] Darby, *Letter to J.E. Batten* (London, rec'd 15 May 1852), L1:205.
[180] Darby, *Letter to Mrs Monthenez* (Montpellier, 15 March 1844), L1:71-72.
[181] Bellett, *Interesting Reminiscences*, p. 22.
[182] L.M. Bellett, *Recollections of the Late J.G. Bellett by his Daughter* (London: A.S. Rouse, 1895), p. 27.
[183] Darby, *Letter to J.G. Bellett* (September 1864), L1:383-384.

Darby did see his friend shortly before he died. As Bellett's daughter recorded, 'Dear John held him in his arms, and expressed in ardent terms his great affection for him.' Speaking of her father's love for Darby, she wrote: 'My father used to say, "If I deserve any credit it is that I early discerned what there was in John Darby!"'[184] What was in Darby was also in Bellett – a deep longing for the Saviour, which Bellett expressed in prayer shortly before he died:

> My precious Lord Jesus, Thou knowest how fully I can say with Paul, 'To depart and to be with Thee is far better.' Oh, how far better! I do long for it! They come and talk to me of a crown of glory, I bid them cease; of the glories of heaven, I bid them stop. I am not wanting crowns, I have *Himself* – Himself! I am going to be with *Himself!*'[185]

Darby's Farewell

In February 1881, after a 'bad fall' at Dundee, Darby described how his 'heart and lungs' had become 'a feeble spring'[186] to his body. A 'paralytic stroke'[187] soon followed, leaving him unable to walk 'without an arm and a stick'.[188] During his final days many Brethren, whose hearts were 'crushed' with sorrow, gathered by his bedside. One 'sister' recalled how everything she heard about Darby was 'lovely, and in keeping with his life of devotedness and service'.

John Nelson Darby died on 29 April 1882 at Sundridge House in Bournemouth, the home of his friend, Mr Hammond. He was 81 years old. At the prayer meeting before the funeral, Darby's farewell letter was read out:

> My Beloved Brethren: After years of communion in weakness, I have only bodily strength to write a few lines, more of affection than ought else. I bear witness to the love not only in the Lord ever faithful but in my beloved brethren in all patience towards me; and how much more, then, from God, unfeignedly do I bear witness to it. Yet I can say, Christ has been my only object; thank God, my righteousness too. I am not aware of anything to recall, little now to add. Hold fast to Him; count on abundant grace in Him to reproduce Him in the power of the Father's love; and be watching and waiting for Christ. I have no more to add, but my unfeigned and thankful affection in Him.[189]

At the funeral, attended by upwards of a thousand people, C. Stanley read from John 14:1-3 and 1 Thess. 4:14-17, 'and in a few words referred to our departed

---

[184] Bellett, *Recollections*, pp. 119, 28.
[185] J.M.H., *Last Words of Five Hundred Remarkable Persons*, 2nd edn (London: Gospel Publication Depot, n.d.), pp. 21-22.
[186] Darby, *Letter* (February 1881), L3:482.
[187] Darby, *Letter to W.H. Kelly* (Ventnor, 31 October 1881), L3:190.
[188] Darby, *Letter to J.G. Deck* (February 1882), L3:213-215.
[189] *The Last Days of J.N.D.*, pp. 2, 17.

brother as having been the means of reviving the truth as to the Lord's coming.'[190] The epitaph on Darby's Bournemouth gravestone reads as follows:

JOHN NELSON DARBY

'As unknown and well known'
Departed to be with Christ
29th April 1882
Aged 81
II COR. V. 21.

Lord let me wait for Thee alone
My life be only this
To serve Thee here on earth unknown
Then share Thy heavenly bliss.[191]
J.N.D

In Conclusion

When Darby died 'he left behind him some fifteen hundred churches – in Britain and on the Continent, in North America and the West Indies, in New Zealand and Australia – who looked to him as their founder or their guide.'[192] Darby's legacy also includes his Bible translations in English, French, and German, and his Italian translation of the New Testament, all of which 'reflect serious scholarship.'[193] What is little known outside the Brethren movement, however, is that Darby also wrote a great number of hymns, spiritual songs, and poems. As one member of the present-day Brethren recently informed me,

I feel, and every darbyite would, that the man cannot be understood without his poetry...His hymns are above all why Darby brethren who did not know him personally have loved his memory through the generations, as opposed to just respecting his command of Scripture...As well as bringing out the inner import to him of heavenly-mindedness and of the hope of the Lord's coming, they are marked by something else that belongs to his conviction of the believer's union with Christ in glory – his sense of the Father's love.[194]

---

[190] Scott, *John Nelson Darby*, pp. 10-11; *cf. The Last Days of J.N.D.*, pp. 22-23.

[191] J.N. Darby, *Spiritual Songs* (Lancing: Kingston Bible Trust, 1974), p. 5. Darby's obituary appeared in *The Times* on 3 May 1882, and the centenary of his death was marked by the newspaper on 11 January 1982 and on 29 April 1982.

[192] Coad, *A History of the Brethren Movement*, p. 107.

[193] Harold H. Rowdon, 'John Nelson Darby', in *New Dictionary of Theology*, ed. by Sinclair B. Ferguson and David F. Wright (Leicester: Inter-Varsity Press, 1994), p. 187.

[194] Private email received from Dr Theodore Balderston, dated 10 March 2007.

Chapter 4

Darby's Eschatology

Reading Darby

To those who rely on secondary sources to appraise his theology, John Nelson Darby issued the following warning:

> If they fall into the snare of taking other people's representations of my doctrine, or read my words under the effect of them, they will have to deal with God about it, and see why.[1]

Decades of misrepresentation, shabby scholarship, and over dependence on secondary material have combined to create 'the Darby myth'. By looking carefully at his actual writings, we will explode this myth and debunk the critics who have maligned Darby and misrepresented his doctrines.

Scholars generally agree that Darby is difficult to read. His writing style has been described as 'turgid',[2] while poor sentence construction and repetition often blunt the edge of his argument. This is not surprising given the age in which he lived. According to his close friend William Kelly, Darby was 'deliberate and prayerful in weighing a Scripture', but as an 'early riser and indefatigable worker' he 'wrote rapidly, as thoughts arose in his spirit', having little time 'to express his mind as briefly and clearly as he could wish.'[3] Scholars of Ernest Sandeen's calibre have dismissed Darby's writings as 'almost uniformly unintelligible',[4] while others have suggested that his eschatology was 'ingeniously cobbled together from apocalyptic passages throughout the Bible'.[5] These statements do Darby a great disservice.

Walter Scott described Darby as possibly 'the most voluminous theological

---

[1] Darby, *Letter* (New York, 21 November 1866), L3:376.
[2] Rowdon, 'John Nelson Darby', p. 186.
[3] Kelly, *John Nelson Darby*, pp. 10-11.
[4] Sandeen, *The Roots of Fundamentalism*, p. 31.
[5] Paul S. Boyer, 'John Darby meets Saddam Hussein: Foreign Policy and Bible Prophecy', *The Chronicle of Higher Education: The Chronicle Review*, 14 February (2003), <http://chronicle.com/weekly/v49/i23/23b01001.htm, 5 June 2006>.

writer of the nineteenth century'.[6] His life's work comprises private letters and meditations, jottings and essays, commentaries and Biblical synopses, Gospel tracts and pamphlets, and hymns and poetry. Such diversity demands thorough research if Darby is to be faithfully represented.

Darby's writings reveal a surprising degree of consistency in his thinking, with very little evidence of any substantial change after 1829. This must be attributed in large measure to his conversion to Christ and his convalescence in Dublin, when he applied himself to a serious and protracted study of the Scriptures. As Darby himself testified, his life, ministry, and beliefs were transformed at this time, which explains why much of his theology was quickly formulated and why so few sources appear in his writings.

Critics of Darby have dismissed his theology as 'new doctrine',[7] 'among the sorriest in the whole history of freak exegesis',[8] 'a feat of the imagination',[9] 'cunning craftiness',[10] the 'theological equivalent of comfort food and escapist entertainment',[11] 'a Zionism of the worst sort',[12] 'deep anti-evangelical heresy',[13] and 'the root from which many of the present-day heresies and vagaries have sprung'.[14] One of the most vitriolic onslaughts comes from the pen of the radical Old Testament scholar, James Barr, who writes:

> If dispensationalism is not heresy, then nothing is heresy. In comparison with it, many of the traditional deviations commonly branded as heretical, such as Pelagianism, Monophysitism, Nestorianism and the like, are no more than minor disturbances in the flow of the entire doctrinal current of Christianity. Dispensationalism is more like Gnosticism among the traditional heresies, in that it creates almost an entire new mythology of its own, though this mythology takes the outward form of Biblical interpretation.[15]

Former dispensationalist Stephen Sizer has a more conspicuous axe to grind when claiming that Darby's eschatology is rooted in the theology of the second-century heretic, Marcion.[16] Such outlandish statements have seriously hindered critical research of Darby's writings, and the Evangelical Church needs to raise more than just its eyebrows. One notable critic of

---

[6] Scott, *John Nelson Darby*, p. 4.
[7] Baker, 'A "Pre-Tribulation Rapture" is a New Theory', 241-244.
[8] Alexander Reese, *The Approaching Advent of Christ: An Examination of the Teaching of J.N. Darby and his Followers* (London: Marshall, Morgan & Scott Ltd., n.d.), p. 146.
[9] James Barr, *Fundamentalism* (London: SCM Press Ltd., 1981), p. 195.
[10] Samuel P. Tregelles, *Pastoral Relations* (London: Houlston & Sons, n.d.), pp. 40-41.
[11] Witherington III, *The Problem with Evangelical Theology*, p. 96.
[12] Bahnsen and Gentry, *House Divided*, p. 165.
[13] John H. Gerstner, *Wrongly Dividing the Word of Truth: A Critique of Dispensationalism*, 2nd edn (Morgan, PA: Soli Deo Gloria Publications, 2000), p. v.
[14] John A. Anderson, *Heralds of the Dawn* (Aberdeen: 1933), p. 30.
[15] Barr, *Fundamentalism*, p. 196.
[16] Sizer, *Christian Zionism*, p. 137.

dispensationalism, George Eldon Ladd, at least acknowledged that Darby's eschatology was eagerly adopted 'because its basic futurism seemed to be a recovery of a sound Biblical prophetic interpretation – which in fact it was', a recovery which gave to the doctrine of the Lord's return 'the importance it deserved'. According to Ladd, 'Darbyism in fact restored something precious which had long been lost.'[17] Christian Zionists agree.

Jerusalem in Focus

Darby began a series of lectures in Geneva in 1840 with the following appeal: 'It should be the endeavour of the Christian, not only to be assured of his salvation in Christ, but also of all the results of this salvation.'[18] Darby believed that one of the 'results', or outworkings, of salvation was a clear understanding of Israel's place in the purposes of God, since salvation in Christ was 'from the Jews' (John 4:22) and had come to the Gentiles 'to make Israel envious' (Rom. 11:11). Darby took Paul's metaphor of the olive tree, into which Gentile believers in Christ had been grafted, to show that the root of the tree was 'not Gentile, but Abrahamic and Jewish'; since 'the root bore the branches',[19] there was no ground for Gentile-Christian pride (Rom. 11:20-22). He also maintained that despite God's judgment of Israel, on account of her apostasy and rejection of the Messiah, 'that which God had once chosen and called He never casts off. He does not repent of His counsels, nor of the call which gives them effect.'[20] According to Darby, it was incumbent upon the Church, therefore, to understand God's continuing purposes for Israel, especially in relation to the Messiah's *Second* Coming. He also emphasised the relationship between Israel and the Church as two *distinct* people groups in God's purposes.

As we saw earlier, Christian Zionists believe that the re-establishment of the State of Israel in 1948 is the fulfilment of Biblical prophecy and the premier sign of Christ's return. Darby understood the prophetic scriptures relating to Israel's restoration, and in his day observed with great anticipation how world attention was focussing once again on the Holy Land. Precisely one hundred years before Israel's rebirth he wrote:

> As far as the world is concerned, Jerusalem is nothing; it is a city trodden down, with neither commerce nor riches nor aught else. Superstition is established there on the sepulchre of the Lord. It is true, indeed, that the kings of the earth are beginning to look that way, because providence is leading in that direction, but as

---

[17] George Eldon Ladd, *The Blessed Hope* (Grand Rapids, MI: William B. Eerdmans Publishing Company, 1978), p. 43.

[18] Darby, *The Hopes of the Church of God, in Connection with the Destiny of the Jews and the Nations as Revealed in Prophecy* (1840), CW2:278.

[19] Darby, *Notes on Romans* (1870), CW26:110.

[20] Darby, *Romans*, S4:222-223.

· for God, He ever thinks of it; it is always His house, His city. His eyes and His heart are there continually. Now faith understands this.[21]

In *The Hopes of the Church of God, in Connection with the Destiny of the Jews and the Nations as Revealed in Prophecy* (1840), Darby wrote about what he perceived to be the beginning of the build up to a future gathering of nations against Jerusalem:

> All nations have their attention occupied about Jerusalem (Zech.12:3), and know not what to do about it...We do not mean that all this yet comes out plain...But the principles which are found in the word of God are acting in the midst of the kingdoms where the ten horns are to appear: that is, we find all western Europe occupied about Jerusalem, and preparing for war; and Russia, on her side, preparing herself, and exercising influence over the countries given to her in the word [of God]; and all the thoughts of the politicians of this world concentrate themselves on the scene where their final gathering in the presence of the judgment of God will take place.[22]

Darby's observations could have been made by any number of twenty-first century Christian Zionist writers.

Darby's Dispensations

John Nelson Darby's eschatology laid the foundations for a system of theology known as dispensationalism. As we shall see later, 'dispensational concepts'[23] predate Darby, while the word 'dispensation' has been used by theologians of opposing viewpoints ever since the Protestant Reformation.[24] However, as a recognised and distinct *system* of theology, dispensationalism is properly traced back to Darby, who understood God's dealings with mankind in terms of clearly defined time periods, which he termed 'dispensations' or 'economies'. Sadly for many Christians the word 'dispensationalism' 'usually evokes an immediate reaction'[25] which is less than favourable. This can be attributed, in large measure, to those who have stigmatised the term and veiled its true meaning because of their replacementist beliefs, and their opposition to the doctrine of the pretribulation Rapture. The stigma and confusion surrounding dispensationalism is easily dispelled.

Darby identified three distinct groups in the Bible: Israel, the Church, and the nations. While emphasising the importance of their interrelationship in

---

[21] Darby, *Studies on the Book of Daniel* (1848), CW5:151.

[22] Darby, *The Hopes of the Church*, CW2:342.

[23] Charles C. Ryrie, *Dispensationalism Today* (Chicago, IL: Moody Press, 1965), p. 83.

[24] Arnold D. Ehlert, 'A Bibliography of Dispensationalism', *Bibliotheca Sacra*, 101-103 (1944-1946); Ryrie, *Dispensationalism Today*, pp. 71-74.

[25] Ryrie, *Dispensationalism Today*, p. 9.

God's purposes, he stressed the distinctive way in which God has dealt, is dealing, and will continue to deal with each of them individually. Although, as we shall see, Darby identified a number of dispensations to help the Christian understand God's sovereign reign over history, this was not his main focus. Instead, as he expressed in a letter to Mr Maylon from Neuchâtel in 1839,

> the near coming of the Saviour, the gathering together of His own, and the sanctification and joy of those who are manifested, are always the thoughts predominant in my soul.[26]

Defining Terms

Although Darby used the term 'dispensation', he was not enamoured with it. As he wrote in 1841, 'I do not hold to the word dispensation, although it is generally used to specify a certain state of things, established by the authority of God, during a given period.'[27] Based on his understanding of the Greek word *oikonomia* in Eph. 1:10, Darby used the word dispensation to describe God's 'active administration'[28] of human affairs on earth. He noted how *oikonomia* had been commonly used in the days of the Apostle Paul to refer to 'the *administration of a house*',[29] and applied this to Eph. 1:10, believing that Paul was speaking of God's active administration, or management, of the world. This application can be seen in Luke 12:42, where Jesus speaks of 'the faithful and wise manager [*oikonomos*], whom the master puts in charge of his servants'. As Charles Ryrie explains,

> In this household-world God is dispensing or administering its affairs according to His own will and in various stages of revelation in the process of time.[30]

Although Bible translators have disagreed on the precise rendering of *oikonomia*, using words like 'order', 'government', and 'manage' to convey its meaning, it is noteworthy that *oikonomia* in Eph. 1:10 is rendered 'dispensation' in the King James Bible. Theologians have also used this word to speak of God's 'economy of salvation', which the early Christian apologist, Irenaeus, defined as 'the way in which God has ordered the salvation of

---

[26] Darby, *Letter to Mr Maylon* (Neuchâtel, 22 November 1839), L1:31-32.

[27] Darby, *Some further Developments of the Principles set forth in the Pamphlet, entitled 'On the Formation of Churches' and Reply to some Objections made to those Principles* (1841), CW1:169.

[28] Darby, *The Apostasy of the Successive Dispensations* (1836), CW1:124.

[29] Darby, *Remarks on the Pamphlet of Mr. F. Olivier entitled, 'An Essay on the Kingdom of God; followed by a Rapid Examination of the Views of Mr. John Darby'*, CW1:288.

[30] Ryrie, *Dispensationalism Today*, p. 31.

humanity in history.'[31] Seen in this light, the term 'dispensation' can be firmly grounded within traditional Evangelical theology, and rescued from those who have irresponsibly dismissed dispensationalism as an unorthodox doctrinal system.

God's Dealings with Man

Darby's dispensational scheme is not easily extracted from his writings. References to the dispensations he identified are relatively scarce, principally because his emphasis lay not in the dispensations themselves, but in the fundamental distinction between Israel and the Church. As Darby explained in *Elements of Prophecy* (1850), 'though Jerusalem, or Israel, or even the church, may be that in connection with which Christ may be glorified, it is only as connected with Him that they [the dispensations] acquire this importance.'[32]

Darby believed that dispensations had been ordained by God to prove to man, in his *fallen* state, how helpless he was without His intervention, and that the dispensations properly began with Noah, after God had given him responsibility to be fruitful and govern the new earth. Darby's dispensational scheme can be summarised as follows:

I.   **Noah**: 'conscience'
II.   **Abraham**: 'promise'
III. **Israel**: 'Jewish dispensation'
      - *Moses*: 'age of the law', 'Mosaic dispensation'
      - *Aaron*: 'dispensation of priesthood', 'Levitical dispensation'
      - *Kings*: 'kingly dispensation'
IV.   **Gentiles**: 'times of the Gentiles'
V.   **Church**: 'dispensation of the Spirit', 'dispensation of the Holy Ghost's power', 'dispensation of the gospel', 'church dispensation', 'dispensation of the profession of Christianity', 'Christian dispensation', 'New Testament dispensation'
VI.   **Millennium**: 'dispensation of the fulness of times'.[33]

---

[31] Quoted in Alister E. McGrath, *Christian Theology: An Introduction* (Oxford: Blackwell Publishers, 1994), p. 251.

[32] Darby, *Elements of Prophecy, in Connection with the Church, the Jews, and the Gentiles* (1850), CW11:41.

[33] Darby, *The Apostasy of the Successive Dispensations* (1836), CW1:125-127; *Connection of the Cross with the Entire Development of God's Ways with Man* (1854), CW22:370; *The Dispensation of the Kingdom of Heaven*, CW2:53-63; *The Testimony of God; or The Trial of Man, the Grace and the Government of God* (1861), CW22:337; *The Hopes of the Church*, CW2:374-376; *Some Further Developments of the Principles*, CW1:169-186; *An Appeal to the Conscience of those who take the Title of 'Elders of the Evangelical Church at Geneva'; and a Reply to one of them*, CW4:328-329; *Notes on the Apocalypse, Gleaned at Lectures in 1842*, CW5:15; *Evidence from Scripture of the*

In *The Apostasy of the Successive Dispensations* (1836), Darby spoke of the communion with God which is now possible through Christ, stating that only when sinners are born again and see the excellence of the Lord Jesus do they recognise the full extent of man's sinful condition. As he explained,

> This...we have to learn in its details, in the various dispensations which led to or have followed the revelation of the incarnate Son in whom all the fulness was pleased to dwell – the obedient man, God manifested, the suffering Saviour, the exalted Righteous One...The detail of the history connected with these dispensations brings out...the principles and patience of God's dealings with the evil and failure of man.

Darby explained how, in every dispensation, there was 'total and immediate failure' from the outset on man's part, and although 'the patience of God' allowed a dispensation to continue for a time, 'there is no instance of the restoration of a dispensation' once man has failed, despite there being 'partial revivals of it through faith.'[34] He believed that one such revival, through repentance, had occurred in the days of Ezra and Nehemiah. As Darby summed up in *The Hopes of the Church of God* (1840),

> The whole state of man, before and after the deluge, under the law, under the prophets, only served as a clearer attestation that man was lost. He had failed throughout, under every possible circumstance, until, God having sent His Son, the servants said, 'This is the heir; let us kill him.' The measure of sin was then at its height; the grace of God then did also much more abound, and gave us the inheritance – us poor sinners, the inheritance with Christ in the heavenly glory, of which we possess the earnest, having Christ in spirit here below.[35]

Israel and the Church

Darby differentiated between the Jewish dispensation under Moses, and the present dispensation, or 'church dispensation',[36] under Christ. He conceded that

---

Passing Away of the Present Dispensation, CW2:89-121; *Remarks on the Pamphlet of Mr. F. Olivier,* CW1:289; *On the Apostasy, What is Succession a Succession of?* (1840), CW1:114-115; *Lectures on the Second Coming,* CW11:229, 253; *The Character of Office in the Present Dispensation* (1838), CW1:94; *The Dispensation of the Fulness of Times,* CW13:152-166; *Studies on the Book of Daniel,* CW5:128-138; *Divine Mercy in the Church and Towards Israel,* CW2:149-154; *On the Gospel according to John* (1871), CW25:244; *Elements of Prophecy, in Connection with the Church, the Jews, and the Gentiles* (1850), CW11:48.

[34] Darby, *The Apostasy of the Successive Dispensations* (1836), CW1:124-125.

[35] Darby, *The Hopes of the Church,* p. 374.

[36] Darby, *Remarks on the Pamphlet of Mr. F. Olivier,* CW1:289.

the latter was not a 'very exact'[37] expression, since the Church was to be taken *from* the earth, and the dispensations properly related to God's dealings with man *upon* the earth. Darby therefore preferred the word 'parenthesis'[38] when describing the Church age. Whereas the Jewish dispensation had been designed 'to exhibit the government of God [on the earth] by means of an elect nation',[39] the dispensation of the Church had been designed to gather *from* the earth 'a heavenly people' made up of Jews *and* Gentiles. Through the atoning sacrifice of Jesus, 'a new and living way' had been opened up for the individual Jew and Gentile (Heb. 10:19-20). Darby believed, however, that this way had been closed to Israel as a *nation*, until 'the true Aaron [Christ] comes out of the tabernacle'[40] to turn godlessness away from those who are 'ever and unchangeably loved as a people' (*cf.* Rom. 11:26).[41] According to Darby, Israel would then be recognised by the nations as favoured by God, 'an impossible thing', he argued, 'as long as the present dispensation lasts'.[42]

Further light on the distinction Darby made between Israel and the Church is found in his correspondence with Church of England minister James Kelly, to whom Darby explained his rationale for leaving the Established Church:

> In the first place, we are not Jews but Christians. Judaism [Israel] was an elect nation; there could be no such thing as leaving it: Christianity is not, but a gathering of saints. God has not recorded His name in the English nation; but wherever two or three are gathered together in His name, there is Jesus in the midst of them. What the temple was to a Jew, the gathering of the saints is to me. My complaint of the Establishment is that it is not, and never was, a gathering of saints…Israel, I repeat, was a national election; Christianity is not.[43]

This distinction between Israel as the earthly people of God, and the Church as the heavenly people of God, is foundational to Darby's eschatology and was, in his mind, 'the hinge upon which the subject and the understanding of Scripture turns'.[44] It would prove to be 'the mainspring'[45] of his thought.

---

[37] Darby, *Some further Developments of the Principles*, CW1:158.

[38] Darby, *The Dispensation of the Fulness of Times*, CW13:155.

[39] Darby, *On the Formation of Churches*, CW1:139.

[40] Darby, *The Day of Atonement*, CW19:253.

[41] Darby, *Exposition of the Epistle to the Romans* (1871), CW26:186; *cf. Thoughts on Romans 11, and on the Responsibility of the Church in reference to a Pamphlet of Mr. F. Olivier, entitled 'Defence of the Principles laid down in the Pamphlet, "Essay on the Kingdom of God," etc.'* (1844), CW1:298-337.

[42] Darby, *Some further Developments of the Principles*, CW1:173.

[43] Darby, *The Claims of the Church of England*, CW14:197.

[44] Darby, *Reflections upon the Prophetic Inquiry*, CW2:18.

[45] Rowdon, *The Origins of the Brethren*, p. 51.

The Apostasy of the Church

Integral to Darby's eschatology was his belief that a 'general falling away',[46] or apostasy, would take place in the Church prior to Christ's return. As he declared in 1852,

> If I could cry with a voice which should resound through all the world, and make itself heard by all Christians, I would warn them of this solemn truth...The principle of the apostasy, of the open revolt of the last day...has produced a system which is in opposition to God. The result of it will be the cutting off of all that calls itself Christian (always excepting the true children of God, who will be taken away).[47]

Darby noted how, in the early days of the Church, there were those who had begun in the Spirit, but had turned to the observance of the law (Gal. 3:1-5), while others had given heed 'to seducing spirits, and doctrines of devils' (1 Tim. 4:1). He described this as the 'moral departure from God in the bosom of Christianity',[48] and in this sense believed that the Church had failed dispensationally. As early as 1827, when he first perceived that the Church had lost its 'primitive form',[49] Darby claimed that the latter-day apostasy had 'set in',[50] but that it would not reach its full height until immediately prior to Christ's return.[51] In spite of the apostasy, however, he maintained that Christ would 'present to Himself a glorious church',[52] describing the Rapture as the day when 'God taketh the beggar from the dung-hill to set him among princes.'[53]

In his tract, *The Notion of a Clergyman, Dispensationally the Sin against the Holy Ghost*, Darby denounced the Established Church 'system' for substituting 'man for God'. He argued that the human principles on which the institutional Church had been established had replaced the power and presence of the Holy Spirit, describing the institution of the clergy as 'the sin against the Holy Ghost in this dispensation'; only the Holy Spirit could exercise 'the vicarship of Christ in the world'.[54] According to Darby, the Established Church, with its 'clerical principle',[55] had failed in the same way that 'the Jewish system' had;

---

[46] Darby, *Remarks on the State of the Church*, CW1:240.

[47] Darby, *What has been acknowledged? or, the State of the Controversy about Elders, followed by a short answer to an article of Mons. de Gasparin* (1852), CW4:300.

[48] Darby, *On the Apostasy*, CW1:120.

[49] Darby, *What has been acknowledged?*, CW4:294.

[50] Darby, *On the Apostasy*, CW1:119.

[51] Darby, *Some further Developments of the Principles*, CW1:160.

[52] Darby, *Christianity not Christendom*, CW18:252.

[53] Darby, *The Closing Days of Christendom* (London: C.A. Hammond, n.d.), p. 15.

[54] Darby, *The Notion of a Clergyman, Dispensationally the Sin against the Holy Ghost* (1868), CW1:38.

[55] Darby, *Christianity not Christendom*, CW18:275.

all that remained was the 'sorest judgment'.[56] Although the true Church would be raptured to be with Christ, Darby taught that the nominal or professing Church, 'which had the name of Christianity',[57] would be 'spued out of His mouth' (Rev. 3:16).[58] As he exclaimed, 'We want Christianity, not Christendom; we have had enough of this.'[59]

Darby was convinced that only 'a remnant'[60] of professing Christians were truly born-again, and that although this faithful remnant was now 'lost in the midst of the multitude', it would be preserved, 'for God has no thought of failing in His faithfulness'. Consequently, Darby believed that 'all true Christians' will be 'preserved and caught up to heaven'.[61]

As far as Darby was concerned, one of the underlying reasons why the Church, as the visible 'pillar and foundation of the truth' (1 Tim. 3:15), had fallen into ruin was that she had confused her own *raison d'être* with that of Israel. As he explained,

> Deny Israel's place and glory with Messiah, and the church will become earthly, rise in its own conceits, and finally, as a system down here, [be] cut off.[62]

Darby argued that as long as the Church believed that she had replaced Israel in the purposes of God, she would remain blind to the 'blessed hope' (Tit. 2:13).

Darby and the Bible

Darby's eschatology was rooted in his devotion to Jesus Christ and his study of the Bible. He was thankful that he had been 'brought up to know the Scriptures',[63] and despite being well read,[64] was *homo unius libri* ('a man of

---

[56] Darby, *The Notion of a Clergyman*, CW1:38-39.

[57] Darby, *Enquiry as to the Antichrist of Prophecy* (1849), CW5:220.

[58] Darby, *Letter to Miss Cottrell*, L2:362.

[59] Darby, *Christianity not Christendom*, CW18:251.

[60] Darby, *Letter to H.C. Anstey* (London, March 1880), L3:69.

[61] Darby, *What is the Church, as it was at the beginning?*, CW14:85-86.

[62] Darby, *An Examination of the Statements made in the 'Thoughts on the Apocalypse,' by B.W. Newton; and An Enquiry how far they accord with Scripture*, CW8:112.

[63] Darby, *Readings on Numbers*, N&J:379.

[64] 406 items are listed in the catalogue of Darby's library. (*Catalogue of the Library of the late John Nelson Darby, Esq. Comprising Important Works relating to Theology, History, Geography, Archaeology, Voyages and Travels, & c. Benedictine and Best Editions of the Fathers of the Church, Rare Editions of the Scriptures, Bibliography, Dictionaries, & c. Which will be sold by auction, by Messrs Sotheby, Wilkinson & Hodge...On Monday, 25th November, 1889, and following day* [London: J. Davy & Sons, 1889; CBA 12002].) The auction was advertised in *The Times* on 5 November 1889. On 9 December, the newspaper recorded that the sale had realised £834 10s. Darby had once considered parting with his library, but 'it was the care of [the Apostle] Paul for his books that had restrained him.' (Sauer, *From Eternity to Eternity*, p. 121.)

one book'). His *Synopsis of the Books of the Bible*, first published in 1857, has been cited as 'evidence that his mind was saturated with the word of God'.[65] Darby described the Bible as 'the only secure resting-place for man amid the darkness of this world',[66] and as that which commanded 'absolute authority'[67] for his soul. As he wrote to Mr Spignio towards the end of his life, 'when I left the Episcopal church, there was no one with whom I could walk; I was led on and guided simply by the word of God.'[68] One who was well placed to corroborate Darby's testimony was Francis William Newman, who in 1830 described Darby as 'a devoted person' who 'has got many books but doesn't use them, only his Bible'.[69] In *Phases of Faith*, Newman recalled his early impressions after meeting Darby in Dublin:

> He had practically given up all reading except that of the Bible...I remember once saying to him, in defence of worldly station,- 'To desire to be rich is unchristian and absurd; but if I were the father of children, I should wish to be rich enough to secure them a good education.' He replied: 'If I had children, I would as soon see them break stones on the road, as do any thing else, if only I could secure to them the Gospel and the grace of God.' I was unable to say Amen, but I admired his unflinching consistency;- for now, as always, all he said was based on texts aptly quoted and logically enforced.[70]

As Timothy Stunt has noted, the search for sources in Darby's writings other than the Bible is 'a fruitless task.'[71] In his response to Newman's *Phases of Faith*, Darby insisted that the Bible had been his sole guide:

> I have, through grace, been by it converted, enlightened, quickened, saved. I have received the knowledge of God by it to adore His perfections – of Jesus, the Saviour, joy, strength, comfort of my soul. Many have been indebted to others as the means of their being brought to God...This was not my case. That work, which is ever God's, was wrought in me through the means of the written word.[72]

However, as Darby expressed in a letter to T.K. Rossier in 1850, it was not only the *study* of God's word which was important, but the manner in which it was studied:

> I think, indeed, dear brother, that, as you say, you have studied too much, and read the Bible too little. I always find that I have to be on my guard on this point. It is

---

[65] Elmore, *A Critical Examination*, p. 9.

[66] Darby, *Evidence from Scripture*, CW2:89.

[67] Darby, *The Irrationalism of Infidelity*, CW6:5.

[68] Darby, *Letter to Mr Spignio* (New York, 5 March 1877), L2:386.

[69] Alfred C. Fry, *The Fry MS* (Manchester: John Rylands University Library), p. 235.

[70] Newman, *Phases of Faith*, p. 18.

[71] Stunt, 'Influences', p. 56.

[72] Darby, *The Irrationalism of Infidelity*, CW6:3.

the teaching of God and not the labour of man that makes us enter into the thoughts and the purpose of God in the Bible. We search it without doubt, but the cream is not found through much labour of the mind of man. I do not think that any one will believe that I do not wish that it should be much read, but I do wish that it should be read with God.

It was Darby's habit 'scarcely to put one foot before the other in the study of the word' until he was able to say, 'This is *the* mind of God.' Seldom did he have to retrace his steps, even when he was influenced by 'a few details' that he had 'adopted from others'. Darby believed it was important for a diversity of opinion to exist among Christians on matters that were not fundamental to the Christian faith, for therein lay a safeguard. As he expressed to Rossier in 1850,

> In general, I like better reading what is not according to my own thought, because one always gains (if there is piety, and the foundations are solid) something by reading it...So that it does not trouble me to find in your own work ideas different from my own. Besides, if the foundations are well maintained, I like that there should be great breadth amongst brethren, and not a party formed upon certain views, provided also that devotedness and separation from the world, and the truths that leads us to this, be also maintained in all their energy, because the blessing of souls is in question in this.[73]

William Kelly later recalled of Darby that 'it was very touching to observe that one, to whose richly suggestive help so many were indebted, was himself so frank to own any fresh thought of value in another'.[74]

Darby's Convalescence

During Darby's convalescence in Dublin, certain scriptures gained 'complete ascendancy' over him. As he explained in a letter to Professor Tholuck,

> In my retreat [convalescence], the 32nd chapter of Isaiah taught me clearly, on God's behalf, that there was still an economy [dispensation] to come, of His ordering; a state of things in no way established as yet. The consciousness of my union with Christ had given me the present heavenly portion of the glory, whereas this chapter clearly sets forth the corresponding earthly part. I was not able to put these things in their respective places or arrange them in order, as I can now; but the truths themselves were then revealed of God, through the action of His Spirit, by reading His word.[75]

Here we locate the point at which Darby began to understand the purposes of God in terms of distinct dispensations. According to Henzel, it was his study of

---

[73] Darby, *Letter to T.K. Rossier* (Pau, 25 March 1850), L3:255-259.
[74] Kelly, *The Rapture of the Saints*, pp. 8-9.
[75] Darby, *Letter to Prof. Tholuck* (185-), L3:298-299.

Isaiah 32 which 'set off the chain reaction that led to Dispensationalism'.[76] As Darby told McAdam in 1863,

> I am daily more struck with the connection of the great principles on which my mind was exercised by and with God, when I found salvation and peace, and the questions agitated and agitating the world at the present day: the absolute, divine authority and certainty of the Word...personal assurance of salvation in a new condition by being in Christ; the church as His body; Christ coming to receive us to Himself; and collaterally with that, the setting up of a new earthly dispensation, from Isaiah xxxii. (more particularly the end); all this was when laid aside at E.P.'s [Edward Pennefather's] in 1827.[77]

Church Tradition

Darby believed that the Israel-Church distinction had been obscured by the Church 'fathers', whom he considered 'untrustworthy on every fundamental subject'.[78] The Reformers did not fair much better in his estimation:

> I avow, I could not tie myself to any of the ancients, nor own their authority in any way. I may *learn* from them (I would, I trust, gladly from any one), and own thankfully, what was given them of God. I see in Luther an energy of faith for which millions of souls ought to be thankful to God, and I can certainly say I am. I may see a clearness and recognition of the authority of scripture in Calvin, which delivered him and those he taught...from the corruptions and superstitions which had overwhelmed Christendom...But present these to me as a standard of truth – I reject them with indignation. They were not inspired. Their teachings are not the word of God.[79]

Darby described the *Thirty-nine Articles* and the *Westminster Confession of Faith* as 'poor protection for the faith of God's elect', being 'elastic enough to admit many novel doctrines and all manner of evil ones'.[80] He also claimed that many of his contemporaries had 'borrowed enormously from Millenarians' in developing systems of Biblical interpretation 'founded on tradition, not on the word'.[81] Darby's first major work on prophecy reveals not only his familiarity with the writings of his day, but more importantly how little influenced he was

---

[76] Henzel, *Darby*, p. 112.

[77] Darby, *Letter to C. McAdam* (Guelph, 10 February 1863), L1:344-345.

[78] Darby, *The House of God; the Body of Christ; and the Baptism of the Holy Ghost* (1860), CW14:68; *cf. Have we a Revelation from God? A Review of Professor Smith's Article 'Bible,' in the 'Encyclopaedia Britannica,' ninth edition* (1877), CW29:60.

[79] Darby, *The Sufferings of Christ*, CW7:205. Darby described Luther's New Testament as 'the most unfaithful translation I know'. (*The Sufferings of Christ*, CW7:208.)

[80] Darby, *The 'Notes on Leviticus' and the 'Quarterly Journal of Prophecy'*, CW10:32.

[81] Darby, *Brief Remarks on the Work of the Rev. David Brown*, CW11:342, 386.

by them. He wrote, 'For my own part, if I were bound to receive all that has been said by the Millenarians, I would reject the whole system; but their views and statements weigh with me not one feather.' Every modern writer on prophecy whose writings he had read, with one anonymous exception, was 'far too much removed from the control of Scripture'. Darby encouraged his fellow Brethren not to trust the mind of any man, believing that it had been all too easy for Christians to engage in 'the presumptuous and hasty pursuit' of their own ideas, which had been 'given out to a greedy public, glad of novelty...and ready to neglect their own souls for unfounded and idle speculations.'[82]

Darby and Prophecy

In 1828, John Gifford Bellett informed Darby that he had met a group of men in London 'who were warm and alive on prophetic truth, having had their minds freshly illuminated by it'. As Bellett later recalled, Darby's mind had already 'travelled rapidly'[83] in the area of Biblical prophecy. Certainly, Darby's *Reflections upon the Prophetic Inquiry and the Views advanced in it* (1829) reveal the extent to which his mind had travelled since his convalescence. Although his understanding of 'prophetic truth' deepened over time, little of any substance changed after 1829. As he expressed in a letter to G.V. Wigram in 1866, 'Of the truth of my teaching in general, I have never had a question. That many things have been more clearly defined in my mind since all the questioning is but natural.'[84] In 1865, Darby communicated the following instruction to William Kelly, who was editing his work: '*Some* of the earlier publications would require a note or two, where clearer light was acquired, but had better not be altered.'[85]

Darby viewed Scripture as 'a harmonius whole',[86] believing that the authority of the Old Testament was 'so interwoven with the whole text and substance of the New Testament that if it goes the New goes with it'.[87] The New Testament was 'in every thought' based on the Old, and unintelligible without it. Although 'a new foundation' for man's relationship with God had been laid in Christ, there yet remained a continuity in God's purposes, which Darby likened to 'a thread by which another state of things, the millennial state, is connected with the whole of God's dealings' with Israel. God, in Christ, had not instituted 'a wholly new system', for the One who had spoken through His prophets had now spoken, without contradiction, in the Person of His Son (Heb.

---

[82] Darby, *Reflections upon the Prophetic Inquiry*, CW2:2-5.

[83] Bellett, *Interesting Reminiscences*, p. 3.

[84] Darby, *Letter to G.V. Wigram* (New York, 22 November 1866), L1:464-465.

[85] Darby, *Letter to W. Kelly* (Toronto, 1865), L1:397.

[86] Darby, 'Inspiration and Interpretation', in *Dialogues on the Essays and Reviews* (1862), CW9:344.

[87] Darby, 'Remarks on Rationalist Views', in *Dialogues*, CW9:363.

1:1-2).[88] Although Calvary had made 'an impassable gulf between the Old and New', the New Testament 'confirmed and adopted' the Old just as the Old had 'predicted and prepared the way'[89] for the New. According to Darby, one of the most significant ways in which the New Testament had confirmed and adopted the Old was in relation to God's promises to Israel.

Three Principles of Prophecy

Darby was never preoccupied with prophecy in the way that many Christian Zionists are today. He believed that prophecy, like the rest of the Bible, was intended to have 'a sanctifying, strengthening and directing influence' on Christians through their 'sober and holy study of the word of God'.[90] Darby applied three basic principles to the study of Biblical prophecy:

1. Whenever the Jews are addressed, we must look for 'a plain, common-sense, literal statement, as to a people with whom God had *direct* dealings upon earth'. Whenever the Gentiles are addressed, 'the system of revelation must to them be symbolical'.[91] Although figurative language was used in prophecy, 'the subject of the prophecy is never a figure'.[92]
2. 'The history of the Bible is the history of the Jews', and since history is factual, historical references must be taken literally.
3. In God's sight, 'the desolation of the Jewish people...[is]...but for a moment'.[93] Since prophecy concerned Israel in the first instance, her restoration is integral to the manifestation of God's glory upon the earth.

As Darby declared in his *Studies on the Book of Daniel*,

> First, the thoughts of God are upon the glory of Christ, who, on His re-appearance, will reign over the earth...Secondly...the Jews are the habitual object of the thoughts of God; for, although He cannot recognise them for the moment, as being under His chastening hand, they are nevertheless still His people...and... will by and by be re-established in all their privileges...He was and is always the God of the Jews.[94]

Darby believed that if the Jewish people and the city of Jerusalem were viewed together as the great subject and centre of prophecy, then most prophecies

---

[88] Darby, *Hebrews*, S5:281-283.
[89] Darby, 'Inspiration and Interpretation', CW9:340.
[90] Darby, *Reflections upon the Prophetic Inquiry*, CW2:2-3.
[91] Darby, *On 'Days' Signifying 'Years' in Prophetic Language* (1830), CW2:35.
[92] Darby, *The Prophets*, S2:328.
[93] Darby, *On 'Days' Signifying 'Years'*, CW2:36.
[94] Darby, *Studies on the Book of Daniel*, CW5:151-153.

would appear 'more distinct and more simple'[95] to the Christian. He used the expression 'prophetic earth'[96] as a way of describing the sphere of God's dealings with Israel, the Church being 'a collateral subject of prophetic revelation'.[97] As Darby summarised,

> There are two great subjects which occupy the sphere of millennial prophecy and testimony: the church and its glory in Christ; and the Jews and their glory as a redeemed nation in Christ: the heavenly people and the earthly people; the habitation and scene of the glory of the one being the heavens; of the other, the earth. Christ shall display His glory in the one according to that which is celestial; in the other, according to that which is terrestrial…When all this is accomplished, God shall be all in all…Though the church and Israel be, in connection with Christ, the centres respectively of the heavenly and the earthly glory, mutually enhancing the blessing and joy of each other, yet each has its respective sphere…angels, principalities, and powers in the one; the nations of the earth in the other.[98]

Darby and Politics

As far as Darby was concerned, Christians were not to 'meddle' in politics, but were to rest in the knowledge that 'God governs, and governs with a view to the glory of Christ, and that He will infallibly bring about His purposes.'[99] Writing to E. Maylan from Montpelier in 1848, he voiced concern over Christian involvement in forthcoming elections, believing that one who is united to the *heavenly* Christ 'has no business to mix himself up with the most declared activity of the world', and with the system 'the Lord is about to judge'.[100] In a letter to the *Français* newspaper in 1878 he wrote: 'We do not mix in politics; we are not of the world; we do not vote.'[101] Francis Newman noted how Darby was 'opposed to *all* political action'.[102] Darby explained that it was his 'business' simply to walk right with God: 'If I am to set the world right I must join with the world, and I cannot have any principles but theirs…Let the world go on its own way, and you go yours – that is Christ's.'[103]

Darby's apolitical stance was not inconsistent, however, with his conviction that God governed history using political processes. Responding to a pamphlet

---

[95] Darby, *Scope of Prophecy*, CW2:51.
[96] Darby, *Notes on the Apocalypse*, CW5:41, 93.
[97] Darby, *Elements of Prophecy*, CW11:43.
[98] Darby, *Divine Mercy*, CW2:122-123.
[99] Darby, *Progress of Democratic Power, and its Effect on the Moral State of England*, CW32:333.
[100] Darby, *Letter to E. Maylan* (Montpellier, 24 March 1848), L1:130.
[101] Darby, *Letter* (1878), L2:439.
[102] Newman, *Phases of Faith*, p. 20.
[103] Darby, *The Christian's Attitude towards the World* (London: G. Morrish, n.d.).

which claimed that God could not use 'wicked Gentiles' to gather the Jews back to their land, Darby asked:

> Cannot the Lord make any nation minister to the deliverance of His favoured people, whatever their own objects and state may be? And such seems to be the very tenor of prophecy.[104]

The Scriptural Mirror

Darby believed that a Christian's primary calling was to prepare for Christ's return. As he expressed in his synopsis of 1 Thessalonians, 'We are converted in order to wait for Him.'[105] Waiting did not imply inactivity, however, for the Gospel needed to be proclaimed to the sinner. As Rowdon observes, the most distinctive feature of missionary work among the early Brethren was that 'it arose largely from the conviction that the Scriptural prophecies concerning the Second Advent of Christ would shortly be fulfilled.'[106] The premillennialism Darby espoused was 'an energising hope.'

Darby sought to rouse the Church from the 'taunting dream'[107] of postmillennialism, which anticipated a world 'blessed with a millennium without the presence of Jesus'. The postmillennialists of his day viewed the millennial reign of Christ in spiritual terms, believing that it would be ushered in through the preaching of the Gospel. They rejected any notion of Christ's physical return to Jerusalem. Citing the Thessalonians, who had been 'penetrated to such a degree with the hope of the return of Christ, that they did not think of dying before that event', Darby dismissed the notion of a spiritual millennium without Christ as mere abstraction. In his *Brief Remarks on the Work of the Rev. David Brown*, he wrote:

> The post-millennial Christian may, nay must, love His appearing as an abstract idea; but it is no present hope: he looks to the gospel spreading and filling the whole earth...He can therefore love the appearing though it has no practical reality for him...A present hope it cannot be. It is not that he cannot morally love it...but he must look for it across at least a thousand years, and hence...we constantly see death take the place, as an equivalent, of the Lord's coming – a thing unknown to Scripture, blessed as death is for the saint. But this catching up of the saints to meet the Lord in the air and be forever with Him, and His appearing, and the day of the Lord, are all confounded by these theologians.[108]

---

[104] Darby, *Reflections upon the Prophetic Inquiry*, CW2:16.

[105] Darby, *1 Thessalonians*, S5:69.

[106] Rowdon, *The Origins*, p. 187.

[107] Scroggie, *The Lord's Return*, p. 122.

[108] Darby, *Brief Remarks on the Work of the Rev. David Brown*, CW11:335.

According to Darby, Christians were to expect a continual progress of evil. This, he believed, would herald the reign of Antichrist, which only 'the glorious appearing of Christ',[109] and not the preaching of the Gospel,[110] would overthrow.

Darby also took issue with the historicist school of Biblical interpretation, which interpreted the prophetic 'days', 'weeks', 'months', and 'years' in Daniel and Revelation figuratively, and applied apocalyptic events recorded in these books to the pre-Rapture period of the Church. Darby maintained that these events would be fulfilled *after* the Rapture, and criticised the historicist school for being 'most injurious' to the 'real meaning'[111] of prophecy. As he wrote in his *Notes on the Apocalypse*, 'The faithful are called to believe in the prophecy before it is fulfilled.'[112] Darby thus defined prophecy as 'the history which God has given us of futurity', or 'the scriptural mirror, wherein future events are seen'.[113] He denounced historicism as nothing more than 'a morbid disposition to apply all things to our own times'.[114]

Covenant

Darby believed that although the word *covenant* was 'common in the language of a large class of professors' in the Church, 'much obscurity' had arisen with regards to understanding the development and unfolding of God's covenants. This was due to 'a want of simple attention to Scripture',[115] the covenant theology of the Reformed Protestant tradition bearing witness to this fact. According to Darby, failure to distinguish between the conditional and the unconditional had obscured not only Israel's place in the purposes of God, but also that of the Church itself.

Darby's understanding of covenant was rooted in the promises of God to Abraham, which he believed were '*without* condition'.[116] These promises were confirmed to Isaac and Jacob, 'renewed in David', and always 'confined to Israel'.[117] By contrast, the promises given to Israel through Moses at Sinai were given 'on condition of obedience'.[118] Darby further differentiated between Israel's *ownership* and *occupation* of the Land, the former having been guaranteed by God's oath, the latter requiring Israel's obedience. Although individuals could disqualify themselves from experiencing God's blessings,

---

[109] Darby, *The Hopes of the Church*, CW2:298.
[110] Darby, *Notes on the Apocalypse*, CW5:79.
[111] Darby, *Notes on the Revelation* (1839), CW2:179.
[112] Darby, *Notes on the Apocalypse*, CW5:60.
[113] Darby, *The Hopes of the Church*, CW2:362, 371.
[114] Darby, *On 'Days' Signifying 'Years'*, CW2:40.
[115] Darby, *The Covenants*, CW3:44.
[116] Darby, *The Hopes of the Church*, CW2:361; *cf. Genesis*, S1:46.
[117] Darby, *Have we a Revelation from God?*, CW29:97.
[118] Darby, *Connection of the Cross*, CW22:369.

God's ultimate purpose for the nation itself could never fail. Darby concluded that 'God's word never confounds'[119] His covenants.

In his *Thoughts on Isaiah the Prophet*, Darby wrote: 'During winter the tree seems dead; but in spring, when the grace of God renews its shining on the people, the tree recovers.'[120] Owing to her protracted exile, many in the Church of his day believed that Israel's tree was dead. Darby, on the other hand, insisted that God's unconditional promises would be 'fulfilled to the letter',[121] since God was faithful. Rather than abrogating God's promises, Calvary had enabled Christ to 'secure the sure mercies of David (Acts 13:34), that is to say, confirm in His own name all the promises made to Israel.'[122] Darby believed that it was critical for the Church to understand this, 'for when has God failed in His promises?'[123] If God could fail in His promises to Israel, could He not also fail in His promises to the Church?[124]

The New Covenant

Darby taught that 'all the essential privileges of the New Covenant'[125] applied not only to individual Jews and Gentiles who were 'born again'[126] in the present age, but also to national Israel 'in the last days, when Messiah reigns over them'.[127] As he stated in his synopsis of Hebrews,

> God has established and revealed the Mediator, who has accomplished the work on which the fulfilment of the promises can be founded in a way that is durable in principle, eternal, because [it is] connected with the nature of God Himself...The Mediator has paid the ransom. Sin has no more right over us...Thus the Christian position, and the hope of the world to come, founded on the blood and on the Mediator of the New Covenant, are both given here. The one is the present position of the believer, the other is secured as the hope of Israel.[128]

The Parenthesis of the Church

Critics of Darby have consistently targeted his phrase, 'the parenthesis of the

---

[119] Darby, *An Introduction to the Bible (trans. from the French)*, CW34:4.

[120] Darby, *Thoughts on Isaiah the Prophet*, CW30:177.

[121] Darby, *Divine Mercy*, CW2:162.

[122] Darby, *The Purpose of God*, CW2:273.

[123] Darby, *Divine Mercy*, CW2:162.

[124] Darby, *The Hopes of the Church*, CW2:348, 353.

[125] Darby, *Hebrews*, S5:341.

[126] Darby, *The Gospel and the Church according to Scripture*, CW29:336.

[127] Darby, *Letter* (1860), L3:324-325.

[128] Darby, *Hebrews*, S5:352-353, 360.

church',[129] claiming that according to Darby's eschatology, the Church is 'on the sidelines' and 'a non-factor'.[130] Such claims are completely unfounded. Darby described the period from Pentecost to the Rapture as a 'lapse of time' or 'parenthesis'[131] in God's purposes for Israel, those purposes being centred around the re-establishment of David's throne in Jerusalem. In his reading of Rev. 3:21, he noted that there were two distinct thrones in view in the letter to the Laodicean church: the Father's heavenly throne on which Jesus is seated, exercising authority *over* the earth, and an earthly throne on which He will one day sit, exercising authority *upon* the earth (*cf.* 2 Sam. 7:12-16; Isa. 9:6-7). With this in mind, Darby believed that the Church 'fills up, in detailed exercise of grace, the gap in the regular earthly order of God's counsels', until Israel's 'reception again under the New Covenant',[132] when Christ is installed as King in Zion (Ps. 2:6).

In a letter to Major Lancey in 1848, Darby explained how Israel and the nations were the subject of Old Testament prophecy, and not the Church:

> I distinguish entirely between the *church* and prophecy. I do not believe the church is the subject, though it is the recipient and depository of prophecy, as Abraham was of what should happen to Lot...Prophecy gives the career of *earthly* events, the wickedness of man, or the dealings of God. But the church is not earthly; its life is hid with Christ in God...Hence it was hid in God from the foundation of the world (Eph. iii.), and the prophets do not speak of it...We are properly nowhere, save in the extraordinary suspension of prophetic testimony, or period, which comes in between the sixty-ninth and seventieth week of Daniel.[133]

Referring to Daniel's prophecy of the seventy 'sevens' or 'weeks' (Dan. 9:24-27), Darby explained: 'You get the sixty-nine weeks, and then a long parenthesis in which Christ is set aside and the Jews on the earth...until the time of the Gentiles is fulfilled. During this period the church, the heavenly thing, is called.'[134] He believed that only when the Church was raptured would God re-establish His seat of government in Jerusalem.

An important clarification needs to be made at this point. Darby believed that if the Jews had repented as a nation and received the Messiah at His *first* advent, then 'all was ready for [Jerusalem's] re-establishment in glory'. The kingdom would then have been restored to Israel. However, in the foreknowledge of God, Christ knew that He would be rejected and that the kingdom would not be restored at that time. As Darby wrote in his synopsis of Daniel, 'Through grace we know' that God had yet more excellent thoughts and

---

[129] Darby, *On the Gospel according to John* (1871), CW25:244.

[130] Wagner, 'Marching to Zion', pp. 80-81.

[131] Darby, *Lectures on the Second Coming*, CW11:243, 253.

[132] Darby, *The Character of Office*, CW1:94.

[133] Darby, *Letter to Major Lancey* (Plymouth, 1 May 1848), L1:131-132.

[134] Darby, *Lectures on the Second Coming*, CW11:320.

purposes, and that man's state was such that this could not have been, as the event proved.'[135] Given such clear distinctions, it is evident that Darby *did not* subordinate the Church to Israel. In fact, it was to the Church that he attached 'the greatest possible importance'.[136]

The Greater Inheritance of the Church

Darby stressed time and again that the Church had inherited *better* promises than Israel by virtue of her *spiritual* status, having been seated with Christ in heavenly, not earthly, realms (Eph. 2:6).[137] He wrote about 'a special place of glory', 'far superior blessings', 'higher and distinctive and proper privileges',[138] 'better privileges',[139] 'a higher and far higher blessing',[140] a 'better place',[141] 'a yet better portion',[142] and 'a higher and new glorious title' that had been reserved for the Church. Although Israel was 'the favoured glorious nation'[143] on earth and the future seat of Christ's millennial kingdom, Darby believed that the Church, and not Israel, would *govern* the earth with Christ during this period. In a letter from Lausanne in 1844, he stressed the difference between *union with* the risen Christ now (the privilege of the Church), and *belonging to* Christ when He reigns in Jerusalem (the privilege of Israel). He recognised that 'union with the Son of God one with the Father' was not part of the Old Testament promises given to Israel, but was 'a mystery hidden from ages and generations'.[144] Henzel suggests that the Church's heavenly union with Christ 'became the lens through which [Darby] viewed all Biblical doctrine, colouring all of it in either the blue shades of heaven or the brown shades of earth.'[145]

Restoration to the Land of Israel

According to William Kelly, 'Maintain simply and firmly the literal restoration of Israel as wholly distinct from Christianity, and you have a bulwark against pseudo-spiritualism, and a groundwork, if rightly used, for seeing our special

---

[135] Darby, *Daniel*, S2:531.

[136] Darby, *The Gospel and the Church*, CW29:337.

[137] Darby, *Numbers*, S1:294.

[138] Darby, *An Examination of the Statements*, CW8:220, 228, 109.

[139] Darby, *1 Thessalonians*, S5:88.

[140] Darby, *Brief Analysis of the Epistle to the Hebrews in Connection with the Priesthood of Christ: with Reply to Some Tracts on the Latter Subject*, CW15:232.

[141] Darby, *Reply to Judge Marshall's Tract on the Tenets of the Plymouth Brethren, so called* (1877), CW31:347.

[142] Darby, *The Melchisedec Priesthood of Christ* (1834), CW2:68.

[143] Darby, *An Examination of the Statements*, CW8:112, 223.

[144] Darby, *Letter* (Lausanne, 14 November 1844), L3:241.

[145] Henzel, *Darby*, p. 87.

and heavenly privileges.'[146] By 1829, Darby was already reflecting on 'the restoration of the Jews to their own land', a restoration he saw 'scattered through all Scripture' and one which rested 'on the whole plan of God's dispensed purposes.'[147] He identified the inextricable bond which existed between the Jewish people and the Land of Israel, asserting that only in their ancient homeland would a Jewish remnant be 'blessed with Israel's blessings, according to promise',[148] regenerated by the Holy Spirit,[149] and delivered from the nations which would besiege Jerusalem before Messiah's return.[150] Darby pointed out that

> even the geography of Scripture is always considered according to the position of the Holy Land. If we have a king of the south, it is a king to the south of Palestine; for Palestine is the centre of all God's thoughts as to the government of this world. Jerusalem is His chosen city.[151]

Darby noted how, in his command to Joseph to leave Egypt with the infant Jesus (Matt. 2:20), the angel Gabriel had mentioned the land they were to return to 'by the name that recalls the privileges bestowed by God. It is neither Judea nor Galilee; it is "the land of Israel".'[152] He believed that this land had been 'entrusted to Israel', and that the Gentiles had 'no right'[153] to it even when occupying the Land during her exile. In an article published in the *Christian Witness* in 1834, Darby not only described the Land of Israel as 'the great centre of divine providence', but also as 'the Jewish land'.[154]

Not my People, Always my People

On account of her spiritual adultery, God declared Israel *Lo-ammi* ('not my people'; Hos. 1:9). At that moment, Israel 'ceased to be the scene in which God displayed His character',[155] the Babylonian destruction of Jerusalem having signalled the beginning of the times of the Gentiles 'by separating the *government* from the *calling* of God – two things which had long been united in

---

[146] William Kelly, *Lectures Introductory to the Study of the Minor Prophets* (London: W.H. Broom, 1871), p. 526.
[147] Darby, *Reflections upon the Prophetic Inquiry*, CW2:26.
[148] Darby, *The Rapture of the Saints and the Character of the Jewish Remnant* (1857), CW11:121.
[149] Darby, *Joel*, N&C4:199.
[150] Darby, *The Hopes of the Church*, CW2:336-339.
[151] Darby, *Studies on the Book of Daniel*, CW5:150.
[152] Darby, *Matthew*, S3:34.
[153] Darby, *Joel*, N&C4:196.
[154] Darby, *On the Extended Scope of Prophecy*, CW2:43.
[155] Darby, *Scope of Prophecy*, CW2:46.

the Jewish people'.[156] In other words, on the basis of God's 'everlasting love' (Jer. 31:3), Israel would never cease to be His people (*ammi*),[157] even though their seat of government would be suspended for a season. Even *after* the Babylonian exile, Zechariah had described the Jewish nation as the apple of God's eye (Zech. 2:8). Paraphrasing the words of the Apostle Paul in Rom. 11:1, Darby exclaimed: 'He did not change His mind; no, *never!*'[158] He believed it was critically important for the Church to realise that

> Israel is always the people of God...Israel cannot cease to be the people of God. 'The gifts and calling of God are without repentance', and it is of Israel that this is said. God never ceases to consider Israel as His people; but He *has* ceased *to govern* them as His people, and to have His throne in the midst of them upon the earth...In all times, Israel is His people, according to His counsels, and the thoughts of His love. This does not prevent their being called 'Lo-ammi' (not my people) as to the government of God.[159]

Since the mystery of the Church had not been revealed until the time of the Apostles (Eph. 3:1-13), and since Jesus Himself had only ever spoken of the *ekklesia* ('assembly') in a *future* context (Matt. 16:18), Darby insisted that the Church had never previously existed 'in fact', but was an entirely 'new thing'.[160] Consequently, 'it is not in Zion that we are to look for the church.' As he wrote in 1840,

> It has been asserted, that in these chapters [Isaiah 33, 49, 62, 65], Zion means the church; but when all the joy is come, 'Zion said, The Lord hath forsaken me.' Impossible, if Zion be the church. What! the church forsaken in the midst of its joy?

The promises of judgment *and* blessing, consistently coupled together in the prophetic writings, were, in Darby's mind, given to one and the same people, the Jews. It was unreasonable, therefore, 'to apply all the judgments to Israel, and all the blessings which concern the same persons to the church.'[161] Darby accused the emerging school of modern philosophy and theology, which was applying *Jewish* prophecies to the Church, of making a nonsense of God's prophetic word. He wrote:

---

[156] Darby, *Divine Mercy*, CW2:149.

[157] Darby, *Scope of Prophecy*, CW2:47.

[158] Darby, *What is the Church and in what Sense is it Now in Ruin?*, M4:163.

[159] Darby, *Examination of a few Passages of Scripture, the Force of which has been Questioned in the Discussion on the New Churches; with Remarks on Certain Principles alleged in Support of their Establishment* (1850), CW4:254-255.

[160] Darby, *What is the Church?* (1849), CW3:386-387.

[161] Darby, *The Hopes of the Church*, CW2:343, 357-359.

> If Jeremiah says, God had plucked them down, and He would build them up; and the plucking down is applied to Jews, and the building up to Christians, nonsense is made of it at once...But if we take them as they are delivered, they are comparatively speaking perfectly simple. Yet it is into this very error this new school falls.[162]

In his critique of Benjamin Jowett's essay, *On the Interpretation of Scripture*, Darby denounced the use of *temporal Israel* (the nation of Israel) and *spiritual Israel* (the Church) as 'a mere abuse of words'. He insisted that 'Zion means Zion when she is prophesied about', since any prophecy given to Israel 'speaks to her on the moral ground she is on',[163] and cannot be arbitrarily applied to the Church, which stands in a different relationship with God.

The Feasts of Israel

Darby's *Synopsis* is replete with detailed, typological analysis of the Scriptures. He believed that just as Christ's atonement had been foreshadowed in the Levitical system (*cf.* Heb. 8:5; 10:1), so the restoration of Israel and the Rapture of the Church had been foreshadowed throughout the Old Testament. He maintained that there was 'peculiar grace',[164] or blessing, for Christians who understood the types, shadows, and patterns found in the Scriptures.

In his synopsis of Genesis, Darby saw Jacob as a 'type' of the earthly nation of Israel, being the 'heir of the promises according to the flesh' who had been 'driven out of the land of promise' but 'kept by God to enjoy it afterwards'. He saw in Jacob's marriages to Rachel and Leah 'the Lord, who, while loving Israel (Rachel), has yet first received the Gentiles or the church, and then the Jews.'[165] He perceived in the departure of Enoch a 'type' of the pretribulation Rapture of the Church,[166] and believed that the deliverance of Noah and Lot foreshadowed the future deliverance of a Jewish remnant through the Great Tribulation. Darby also noted the typological importance of the Joseph narrative (*cf.* Genesis 45; Zech. 12:10; Matt. 23:39), where

> Joseph takes the position (as put to death) of Jesus raised to the right hand of the supreme throne over the Gentiles, in the end receiving his brethren from whom he had been separated.[167]

Darby stressed the typological importance of the feasts of Passover, Pentecost,

---

[162] Darby, 'Modern Philosophy and Modern Theology, both Compared with Scripture', in *Dialogues*, CW9:184.

[163] Darby, 'Inspiration and Interpretation', CW9:305.

[164] Darby, *Leviticus*, S1:153-154.

[165] Darby, *Genesis*, S1:65, 59.

[166] Darby, *Lectures on the Second Coming*, CW11:242; *Hebrews*, S5:388-390.

[167] Darby, *Exodus*, S1:83.

and Tabernacles. He explained that the spring feasts of Passover and Pentecost had had their fulfilment, or 'antitypes', in the crucifixion of Jesus (1 Cor. 5:7) and in the outpouring of the Holy Spirit (Acts 2). The autumn feast of Tabernacles, or Ingathering, would have its 'antitype' when the Jewish exiles were gathered to the Land and then to Christ.[168] Darby believed that the 'large gap, a characteristic gap' between the spring and autumn feasts represented, in typology, the parenthesis of the Church, with the final feast of Tabernacles pointing prophetically to a supernatural harvest of souls.[169] He described this feast as 'the joy of the millennium',[170] when surviving nations will celebrate the feast in Jerusalem (Zech. 14:16-19). He also noted how, unlike the preceding feasts, Tabernacles had an *eighth* day. This, he believed, typologically represented the beginning of Christ's millennial reign upon the earth, a period which would be marked by the outpouring of 'exhaustless boundless sources of heaven-caught supplies'[171] upon Israel *and* the nations.

The Second Coming and the Rapture

In 1828, Darby declared: 'Let the almighty doctrine of the cross be testified to all men, and let the eye of the believer be directed to the coming of the Lord.'[172] The following year he remarked how his mind had been struck, 'long before the detail of millennial views opened themselves to it', with the realisation that in every New Testament letter 'the coming of the Lord Jesus is…made the prominent object of the faith and hope of believers'.[173] When asked about this during a Bible reading meeting in Rochdale, Darby explained:

> A man may not know much about the rapture of the church, and yet be waiting for someone to come and take him out of this scene. Before ever I knew about the Lord's coming, I think I loved His appearing. I knew nothing about the doctrine, but the principle of loving His appearing was in my mind…What I delight in, is Christ's coming and setting aside the whole thing I am in.[174]

This personal longing for Christ's return remains a distinctive feature of Christian Zionism, and is conspicuous by its absence from premillennial eschatologies which advocate a midtribulation, post-tribulation, or pre-wrath Rapture.

Headed by Robert Van Kampen and Marvin Rosenthal, the more recent pre-

---

[168] Darby, *Leviticus*, S1:268; *Deuteronomy*, S1:359.

[169] Darby, *The Feasts* (1836), CW19:262, 271-272.

[170] Darby, *Leviticus*, S1:267.

[171] Darby, *The Feasts* (1836), CW19:273-274.

[172] Darby, *Considerations on the Nature and Unity of the Church of Christ* (1828), CW1:30.

[173] Darby, *Reflections upon the Prophetic Inquiry*, CW2:25.

[174] Darby, *Reading at Rochdale (Colossians 1)*, N&J:100.

wrath school has some 'unusual features'.[175] These centre around the division of Daniel's seventieth week into three distinct periods: the beginning of sorrows, the Great Tribulation, and the Day of the Lord. The Great Tribulation is said to be the time of *Satan's* wrath, and the Day of the Lord the time of *God's* wrath, both of which occur during the second half of this final seven-year period. The Church is said to be raptured *after* the Great Tribulation but *before* the Day of the Lord and consequently *before* the wrath of God.

This redefinition of *tribulation* and *wrath* has been described as 'the most confusing interpretation of end-time events ever put together', which 'blasts the hope out of the Rapture'[176] by making the Church wait anxiously for Antichrist, and not expectantly for the Lord. In stark contrast, Darby's life and ministry was characterised by a joyful expectation and personal longing for his Saviour. This longing had characterised the early Thessalonian believers who had 'turned to God from idols to serve the living and true God, and to wait for His Son from heaven, whom He raised from the dead – Jesus, who rescues us from the coming wrath (1 Thess. 1:9-10).' In *The Freshness of Faith*, Darby offered the following insights into these verses:

> A most extraordinary thing to do! Waiting for God's Son! that is, all our hopes are clean out of this world. Do not expect anything from earth, but look for something from heaven, and this God's Son Himself, 'even Jesus which delivered us from the wrath to come'…Those who were looking for Christ were entirely delivered 'from the wrath to come.' This gives a very distinct position to the Christian…Here is the historical fact of wrath passed. At Christ's first coming He had taken up the whole question of wrath…All the question is totally and finally settled: sin is borne once, and He who bore it is raised from the dead…This sets me in perfect freedom; and it does more, because it links me up with Christ in heaven. I know He is coming. Why? Because I know Him there. This divine Person before my soul – this Christ – the Man who, infinitely interested about my sins, died for me, He is waiting in heaven…We are waiting, our bodies to be raised, when we are to see Him and be like Him…We are really waiting for something: for what? For the Person who has so loved us…Government under Christ is going to be set up. All things are to be put under His feet…I shall be happy long before that…We love His appearing, but we love Himself better. Therefore we wait for Him to take us to Himself…I cannot be waiting for God's Son from heaven if I am expecting wrath…Suppose God said, 'Tonight,' etc., would you say, This is what I want? If not, there is something between your affections and Christ.[177]

Darby did not believe that Christians could be 'scripturally right'[178] if their hearts were not longing for Jesus to catch them up to heaven; where the Church

---

[175] Benware, *Understanding End Times Prophecy*, p. 221.
[176] Tim LaHaye, *Rapture under Attack* (Sisters, OR: Multnomah, 1998), pp. 101, 69-70.
[177] Darby, *The Freshness of Faith*, CW21:359-363.
[178] Darby, *Joying in God*, p. 3.

had lost this, it had lost its 'true character'.[179]

Darby has been described as the man who formulated the pretribulation Rapture 'in its modern form',[180] who 'originated the Rapture as a stock part of Evangelical theology',[181] and who did 'more than any other man to organise and popularise' this doctrine 'in the United States and Great Britain.'[182] However, many Christians who support the State of Israel and understand the Jewish roots of the Christian faith as Darby did, delay the Rapture, believing that both Israel *and* the Church will go through the Great Tribulation. This is inconsistent with Christian Zionism, in that it fails to appreciate the inherent *Jewishness* of scriptures such as the Olivet Discourse (Matthew 24-25). It was Darby's understanding that the expectation of Christ's imminent return 'had ruled the intelligence, sustained the hope, [and] inspired the conduct, of the apostles,'[183] and that the spiritual decline of the Church owed much to the loss of this expectation.[184] As he expressed in a Bible reading meeting on Numbers,

> People accept the Lord's coming as a doctrine that He will appear, but not as coming at any moment to take up the church. The Rapture and the church are identified in Scripture, but the coming of the Lord is in the Old Testament, as well as in the New...I remember when brethren were very much exercised about the truth of the Rapture...It is a truth that will sift Christians amazingly.[185]

Darby contended that whenever the Second Coming was referred to in Scripture it applied 'not only to the day of the Lord, but also to what precedes that day, that is, to the Rapture of the church'.[186] He believed that the Bible spoke of a definite time lapse between the catching up of the saints and their subsequent return with Christ, and could not agree with B.W. Newton that 'Christ visibly concludes the age when He receives the saints'. According to Darby's reading of the New Testament,

> when He appears, we appear with Him...that this His epiphany destroys Antichrist (2 Thess. 2), and that He comes at the close of the three years and a half

---

[179] Darby, *Address, delivered at Manchester, June 19, 1873* (N.pl., n.d.), p. 3.

[180] Benware, *Understanding End Times Prophecy*, p. 196.

[181] Robert K. Whalen, 'Dispensationalism', in *Encyclopedia of Fundamentalism*, ed. by Brenda E. Brasher (London: Routledge, 2001), p. 134.

[182] LaHaye, *Rapture under Attack*, p. 159.

[183] Darby, *The Hopes of the Church*, CW2:291.

[184] Darby, *The Rapture*, CW11:157; cf. *Is the Coming of Christ for His Saints the Proper Hope of the Church?*, CW10:262.

[185] Darby, *Readings on Numbers*, N&J:390.

[186] Darby, *Notes on the Apocalypse*, CW5:23.

of tribulation as lightning, and then His sign is seen in heaven, and that ends the age.[187]

Darby also drew attention to the opening verses of Revelation, and the reference to Jesus 'coming with the clouds', to 'every eye' seeing Him, and to 'all the peoples of the earth' mourning because of Him (Rev. 1:7). As he exclaimed, 'What an entire difference between the two aspects of the coming of the Lord!'[188] Since the coming of Jesus was 'the blessed hope' of the Church, Christians could not possibly be among 'all the peoples of the earth' found *wailing* at His return. As Darby stated, true believers possessed the 'inestimable privilege of exemption from going through these evil days'.[189] A clear distinction had to be made, then, between Christ's *parousia* ('coming') and His *epiphaneia* ('appearing'). As he explained,

> 'Coming' is a general word; you get the 'appearing of his coming' in 2 Thessalonians 2. First He comes, and does not appear, and takes us up to be with Himself. But 'when he shall appear', we shall appear with Him in glory.[190]

To lose sight of the Rapture was, in Darby's estimation, 'to lose our essential portion',[191] and to become like the servant who said in his heart, 'My Lord delays to come' (Matt. 24:48). Christians were to be 'always expecting' the Rapture 'as a present thing, and wishing for it as a present thing…uncertain when it will come.'[192] Since there was no event to be fulfilled 'between us and heaven',[193] the Church 'should always expect it'.[194]

Darby also noted how the Second Coming 'presents itself' to the Christian 'in almost every page' of the Bible, being 'a substantive part of the faith of the church of God'. To those who believed that it was only in death that Christ came to them, he remarked:

> Do you make death the same as Christ? If this were the case, we should have Him coming hundreds and hundreds of times; whereas we only read of His coming twice…Shall I tell you what will happen when Christ comes? Resurrection!

Living in the constant expectation and hope of Christ's return is conducive to holy living and faithful service, the Apostle Paul having prayed that the Thessalonians would be 'kept blameless at the coming of our Lord Jesus

---

[187] Darby, *Answer to a 'Letter to the Brethren and Sisters who meet for Communion in Ebrington Street'*, CW8:333.

[188] Darby, *Seven Lectures on the Prophetical Address to the Seven Churches*, CW5:265.

[189] Darby, *Notes on the Epistles to the Thessalonians* (1869), CW27:304.

[190] Darby, *Reading at Rochdale*, N&J:101.

[191] Darby, *1 Thessalonians*, S5:107.

[192] Darby, *A Few Brief Remarks on 'A Letter on Revelation 12'*, CW11:25-26.

[193] Darby, *The Rapture*, CW11:157; *cf. Lecture (Luke 12:35-53)*, N&J:180.

[194] Darby, *Notes on the Revelation*, CW2:213.

Christ' (1 Thess. 5:23). As Darby concluded, 'Conversion, joy in service, holiness, a believer's death, the goal of blamelessness, all are connected with the coming of the Lord.' Such was the lesson of the wise and faithful steward (Luke 12:35-48), the talents (Matt. 25:14-30), and the ten virgins (Matt. 25:1-13), about which Darby made one final, and *critical*, observation:

> If the bride has got the sense of being the bride of Christ, she must desire to be with the Bridegroom; there is no proper love to Christ unless she wants to be with Him.[195]

A Secret Rapture?

Darby was somewhat ambivalent as to whether the Rapture would occur without the world knowing. He believed that the question of *secrecy* had been used against him by 'adversaries of the truth', and had obscured 'the great and vital truth of the Rapture',[196] namely the distinction between Israel and the Church. One such adversary was B.W. Newton, who urged Christians to be suspicious of a doctrine he claimed was 'so truly new as the *secret* coming of the Lord'.[197] One of Darby's associates, William Trotter, responded to Newton's charge of 'newness' by insisting that

> a doctrine cannot be proved true by the number of its adherents, or by the length of time during which it has been generally received. Much less is a doctrine true because it is soothing to ourselves, or palatable to men in general. The one, only, infallible test of the truth of any doctrine is, What saith the word of God?[198]

Darby claimed that the Church had placed too much emphasis on its canons, creeds, and articles of faith, and not enough on God's written word and 'the grace and teaching of the Spirit of God', which he believed offered 'the only security of the saints in these dark and evil days'.[199]

One of the most outspoken critics of Darby and the Brethren was Alexander Reese, who claimed that around 1830

---

[195] Darby, *The Coming of the Lord that which Characterises the Christian Life*, CW32:246-252.

[196] Darby, *The Rapture*, CW11:120.

[197] Benjamin Wills Newton, *The Second Advent of our Lord not Secret but in Manifested Glory* (London: Houlston and Wright, 1862), p. 4; *cf. Five Letters on Events Predicted in Scripture as Antecedent to the Coming of the Lord*, 3rd edn (London: Houlston and Sons, 1877), pp. 1-23.

[198] William Trotter, *Plain Papers on Prophetic and Other Subjects*, Revised edn (London: G. Morrish, n.d.), p. 195.

[199] Darby, *Remarks on Three Tracts entitled 'Signs of the Coming of the Lord: For whom are they given?'*, CW11:22-23.

a new school arose within the fold of Pre-millennialism that *sought to overthrow* what, since the Apostolic Age, have been considered by *all pre-millennialists* as established results, and to institute in their place a series of doctrines that had *never been heard of before.* The school I refer to is that of 'The Brethren' or 'Plymouth Brethren,' founded by J.N. Darby (*italics* mine).[200]

Such sweeping and unsubstantiated allegations do not stand up to scrutiny. It was never Darby's intention to 'overthrow' established truth, but to 'rescue plain Scripture statements from the garbage of theology',[201] statements which the Church had discarded. Critics like Reese have sought to discredit Darby by attributing his doctrine of the pretribulation Rapture to sources other than the Bible. As Stanton summarises, 'Pretribulationism has been variously attributed to the writings of Edward Irving, to the utterances of a woman-prophet in a trance, to the writings of Darby and his associates, to a godly clergyman named Tweedy, and ultimately to the Devil himself.'[202] The alleged connection between Darby, Irving, and the 'woman-prophet' will be examined later.

The Great Tribulation

One of the most distinctive features of Darby's eschatology is his emphasis on the *Jewishness* of certain scriptures. Darby believed that as 'the full confidante of God'[203] and 'vessel of divine testimony',[204] the Church was responsible for correctly identifying the intended recipients, or subjects, of prophecy. One of the legacies of replacementism had been the Church's failure to understand the continuity between the Testaments. Darby believed that this continuity could be plainly seen in the opening verses of Matthew, when the genealogy of Jesus

> sets Christ before us in the character of the Son of David and of Abraham, that is to say, in connection with the promises made to Israel.[205]

Darby noted how the Spirit-inspired songs of Mary and Zechariah focused on 'the hopes and promises given to Israel' and 'all the blessing of the millennium'[206] which awaited her, and how the sending out of the disciples 'to the lost sheep of Israel' (Matt. 10:6) proved 'how much the ways of God with Israel form the subject of this Gospel'.[207] He further noted how, at the close of

---

[200] Reese, *The Approaching Advent of Christ*, p. 19.
[201] Darby, *Brief Remarks on the Work of the Rev. David Brown*, CW11:353.
[202] Gerald B. Stanton, *Kept from the Hour: A Systematic Study of the Rapture in Bible Prophecy* (Grand Rapids, MI: Zondervan Publishing House, 1956), p. 217.
[203] Darby, *Notes on the Revelation*, CW2:167.
[204] Darby, *The Coming of the Lord and the Translation of the Church*, CW11:179.
[205] Darby, *Matthew*, S3:27.
[206] Darby, *Luke*, S3:322-323.
[207] Darby, *Matthew*, S3:83.

the New Testament, 'the position and imagery of the Revelation are all Jewish in character', identifying the woman clothed with the sun in Rev. 12:1-6 as 'the Jewish people owned of God'[208] who are sheltered from Satan for three-and-a-half years. Equating this period with the time of distress 'unequalled from the beginning of the world until now – and never to be equalled again' (Matt. 24:21), Darby believed that the Great Tribulation centred around Israel and the Jewish people,[209] and would be 'cut short' for the sake of the *Jewish* elect (Matt. 24:22). As he wrote in a letter to Mr Ulrich, 'The great tribulation is either Jewish as in Matthew xxiv., or over the whole world after the church is gone (Rev.vii.); with neither of these has the church to do.'[210]

Darby believed that Christ's discourse on the Mount of Olives, 'at least to verse 31', had been addressed to the disciples 'as Jews, as believing Jews no doubt, but as Jews', and not to the Church, 'because the church did not yet exist to be addressed'.[211] As he explained,

> There will be at the close a tribulation, a time such as there has never been, till the Lord's coming brings deliverance...Shall we, who compose the church, be in this tribulation? The answer to this question must be sought in the passages which speak of the tribulation itself. The first of them, Jeremiah 30:7, is as clear as possible in announcing those to whom it applies: 'It is the time of Jacob's trouble, but he shall be delivered out of it.' This time, then, of trouble, such as never was nor will be (so that there cannot be two), is the time of Jacob's trouble. Nothing can be clearer or more distinct...The next is Daniel 12:1. This is also positively declared to be of Daniel's people. The whole prophecy is the description of what is to happen to Daniel's people in the last days...Michael, also...will then stand up for that people, and, as Jeremiah had said, they will be delivered (that is, the elect remnant – those written in the book). Daniel's testimony then is also quite clear. The tribulation is the tribulation of Daniel's people. But this is rather important because it carries us at once to Matthew, the Lord Himself declaring that He speaks of this same time and same event, using the terms of Daniel, and referring to him by name as well as to the statements of the passage...But all the language of the passage in *Matthew* confirms this. Those who are in Judea are to flee to the mountains...The abomination which causes desolation stands in the holy place. They are to pray that their flight may not be on the sabbath. False Christs and false prophets are to seduce...the Jewish people. All is local and Jewish – has no application to hopes which rest on going to meet Christ in the air...*Mark* relates evidently to the same event and almost exactly in the same

---

[208] Darby, *Notes on the Revelation*, CW2:168-169, 211.

[209] Darby, *Letter to J.A. Von Poseck* (1861), L3:335; *Notes on the Epistles to the Thessalonians*, CW27:304.

[210] Darby, *Letter to Mr Ulrich*, L2:231.

[211] Darby, *Remarks on Three Tracts*, CW11:3.

terms. Thus these four passages, which speak of the unequalled tribulation, apply it distinctly to Jacob, Jerusalem, and Judea, and the Jews, not to the church.[212]

Did this mean that Darby viewed these scriptures as being of no value to the Church? 'No, to be sure we do not. But we may consider them as not relating to the church at large, though given to it, as all the Scriptures are.' The issue was one of application, and those to whom the Lord's word applied in these passages were 'located in Judea'. As Darby asked, 'Is the church, in its church standing, located in Judea? Are not all the subjects Jewish, as well as the facts, save the one of the gospel of the kingdom going to all nations, and that before the end?'[213]

Citing Christ's promise to the church in Philadelphia that it would be kept 'from the hour of trial' (Rev. 3:10), Darby stated that whenever the Church is addressed 'it is with a declaration that she will be kept from that hour which shall come to try others'.[214] From 'a multitude of passages' [including Matt. 13:41-43; 1 Cor. 15:51-52; Col. 3:4; 2 Thess. 1:8-10; Rev. 3:10; 19:14] he insisted that 'the saints are caught away',[215] or raptured, before the seventieth week begins, when the Antichrist attempts to deceive and destroy Israel. A remnant of Jews would, however, escape, as Darby explained:

> At the end Antichrist is owned by the nation [Israel], rejected by the remnant. The beast makes a covenant with the Jews for that week, but breaks it in the midst of the week…You get then three and a half years that remain to be accomplished, when abominations (i.e., idolatry) will overspread the Jewish people, the times and laws will be changed. At that very time Satan is come down (in chapter 12 of Revelation), and the woman, the true remnant in Jerusalem, flees into the wilderness for a time, times, and half a time. This is Daniel's half-week.[216]

In other words, Darby taught that Antichrist would assume his 'proper distinctive character in Jerusalem'[217] during the second three-and-a-half years of Daniel's seventieth 'week', establishing 'a kind of suzerainty' to make the Jews 'worship a strange God'.[218] In the process, he would seek to install himself not only as 'a royal power in Palestine',[219] but as God himself. Darby stated that the *first* half-week was not the primary concern of Daniel 9, Matthew 24, or Revelation 11, the second half-week being 'the great subject of testimony'

---

[212] Darby, *What Saints will be in the Tribulation?*, CW11:110-111.
[213] Darby, *Remarks on Three Tracts*, CW11:13.
[214] Darby, *What Saints will be in the Tribulation?*, CW11:112.
[215] Darby, *Letter to J.A. Von Poseck* (1861), L3:334.
[216] Darby, *Lectures on the Second Coming*, CW11:320.
[217] Darby, *Notes on the Revelation*, CW2:199.
[218] Darby, *Questions of Interest as to Prophecy*, CW5:228-229.
[219] Darby, *Enquiry as to the Antichrist*, CW5:220-221.

which 'alone is referred to by the Lord'.[220]

In his *Notes and Comments* on Daniel, Darby noted how the 'people of the ruler who will come (Dan. 9:26)' referred, in the first instance, to the Roman armies under Titus who sacked Jerusalem and the Temple in AD70. However, he believed that this merely foreshadowed the time when Antichrist, as 'the head of the [reconstituted] Roman power', would beguile the Jewish people, 'make all their forms cease – the sacrifice of the restored temple and city', and 'persecute the Jews bitterly'.[221]

Darby identified the first beast of Revelation 13 as 'the great imperial Gentile power'[222] centred in Rome[223] which is given *civil* authority by Satan 'during the time, times, and half a time'.[224] Contrary to mainstream Christian Zionism, he believed that the *second* beast was the Antichrist, a false Messiah wielding the power of the first beast through a policy of 'religious seduction'. Resembling a lamb but speaking like a dragon, the Antichrist opposes 'the person and glory of Christ and the essential doctrines of truth'[225] by 'religious energies of evil in connection with Christianity and Judaism'. These two beasts, Darby believed, would be 'coexistent',[226] exercising civil *and* religious authority concurrently on behalf of an unholy trinity.[227] As he explained,

> The dragon gives the throne to the beast, as the Father to Christ; and the second beast exercises in spiritual energy the power of the first beast in his presence, as the Holy Ghost with Christ.[228]

According to Darby, the Rapture would 'give room'[229] for the manifestation of this unholy trinity, whose attention would be focussed on Jerusalem, the place God had chosen as a dwelling for His Name (*cf.* Deut. 12:5; 2 Sam. 7:13).

Israel Renewed in Heart

Citing Ezekiel 37, which he described as 'a detailed history of the re-establishment of Israel',[230] Darby believed that the Jewish people would be restored *physically* to their land before being restored *spiritually* through the Messiah. He understood, however, that before the nation finally looked upon

---

[220] Darby, *Are there Two Half-Weeks in the Apocalypse?* (1857), CW11:172.

[221] Darby, *Daniel*, N&C4:182.

[222] Darby, *Enquiry as to the Antichrist*, CW5:218.

[223] Darby, *Notes on the Revelation*, CW2:218.

[224] Darby, *Lectures on the Second Coming*, CW11:319.

[225] Darby, *Enquiry as to the Antichrist*, CW5:216; *cf. Signs of Antichrist*, CW5:226.

[226] Darby, *Questions of Interest as to Prophecy*, CW5:227.

[227] Darby, *Notes on the Revelation*, CW2:241-244.

[228] Darby, *Lectures on the Second Coming*, CW11:323.

[229] Darby, *Enquiry as to the Antichrist*, CW5:219.

[230] Darby, *The Hopes of the Church*, CW2:360-361.

the One they had pierced (Zech. 12:10), a false shepherd would arise (Zech. 11:15-17)[231] who would 'put himself in direct opposition to Christ'. As head of the reconstituted Roman Empire (Dan. 2:41), this false Messiah, or Antichrist, would 'arrogate to himself His [Christ's] rights as King of the Jews' before being destroyed by Christ at His Second Coming. The true Shepherd of Israel would then gather to Himself the surviving remnant of Jews as 'His earthly people'.[232] On the basis of Ezek. 36:22-32, Darby believed that the Jewish nation would have to be 'renewed in heart' before receiving what he termed 'the earthly blessings' or 'promises of Canaan'.[233] In a series of lectures given in Geneva in 1840, he outlined the chronology of events as he understood it:

What has happened to the nations by their having had government given over to them? They have become 'beasts': so the four great monarchies are called. Once the government is transferred to the Gentiles, they become the oppressors of the people of God: first, the Babylonians; secondly, the Medes and Persians; thirdly, the Greeks; then, the Romans. The fourth monarchy consummated its crime at the same instant that the Jews consummated theirs, in being accessory, in the person of Pontius Pilate, to the will of a rebellious nation, by killing Him who was at once the Son of God and King of Israel...In the meantime, what happens? First, the salvation of the church. The iniquity of Jacob, the crime of the nations, the judgment of the world, and that of the Jews – all this becomes salvation to the church. It was accomplished all in the death of Jesus. Secondly, all that has passed since that stupendous event has no other object than the gathering together of the children of God...Then what takes place?

The church goes to join the Lord in the heavenly places...and the marriage of the Lamb will take place...Where will the nations be? The government of the fourth monarchy will be still in existence, but under the influence and direction of Antichrist; and the Jews will unite themselves to him...Dear friends, as soon as the church shall be received to Christ, there will follow the battle in heaven...Satan will be expelled from heaven, without being yet bound; but he will be cast down to earth...and will raise up in particular the apostate part of it, which has revolted against the power of Christ coming from heaven...Under the conduct of Antichrist, the fourth monarchy will become the sphere upon which the activity of Satan will then be displayed, who will unite the Jews with this apostate prince against heaven...This wicked one, having joined himself to the Jews, and having placed himself at Jerusalem, as the centre of government of the earth, will be destroyed by the coming of the Lord of lords and King of kings; and Christ will anew occupy this chief seat of government, which will become the place of the throne of God on the earth...The remnant of the Jews is delivered, and Antichrist destroyed...The first thing, then, which the Lord will do will be to purify His land (the land which belongs to the Jews)...of all the wicked, in short, from the Nile to

---

[231] Darby, *Zechariah*, S2:671-672.
[232] Darby, *The Hopes of the Church*, CW2:324.
[233] Darby, *Notes from Lectures on the Epistle to the Hebrews*, CW27:335.

the Euphrates. It will be done by the power of Christ in favour of His people re-established by His goodness.

When the people are living thus in peace, another enemy will come up, namely, Gog; but he will come only for his destruction. It would seem that in those times...there will be a discovery much more calm, much more intimate, of the Lord Jesus to the Jews. This is what will take place when He will descend on the Mount of Olives, where 'his feet shall stand,' according to the expression of Zechariah 14:3,4...Blessing to the Gentiles will be the consequence of the restoration of the Jews, and of the presence of the Lord...Those who shall have seen the glory manifested in Jerusalem will go and announce its arrival to the other nations. These will submit themselves to Christ; they will confess the Jews to be the people blessed of their Anointed, will bring the rest of them back into their land, and will themselves become the theatre of glory, which, with Jerusalem as its centre, will extend itself in blessing wherever there is man to enjoy its effects...Instead of the adversary in the heavenly places...Christ and His church will be there, the source and instrument of blessing ever new. The glorified church...will fill the heavenly places with its own joy; and in its service will constitute the happiness of the world...Behold the heavenly Jerusalem, witness in glory of the grace which has placed her so high![234]

Two Kinds of Christianity?

Drawing from the work of Coad and Fromow, Stephen Sizer wrongly asserts that B.W. Newton 'eventually came to recognise Darby's elevation of Israel above the Church as heresy'. As Sizer continues, 'to affirm that in some way the Jews could be blessed apart from faith in Jesus Christ was in the words of one of Newton's biographers, "virtually to say there are two kinds of Christianity, two Gospels, two ways, and two ends of salvation."'[235] As can be clearly seen from the above survey, Sizer has grossly misrepresented and maligned Darby. He is not alone. Gerstner's claim that the 'dispensational

---

[234] Darby, *The Hopes of the Church*, CW2:378-382. Based on Isa. 10:5 and Mic. 5:5, Darby identified another end-time figure, namely 'the Assyrian'. This represents a rather unique aspect of his eschatology. Based on Dan. 2:29-45 and Ezekiel 38-39, Darby believed that when Christ returns, the world will be divided between 'Babylon', or the reconstituted Roman Empire centred in Western Europe and headed by Antichrist, and 'the Assyrian', a Russian confederation of nations headed by its chief power, Gog. He argued that after Antichrist's destruction, the Assyrian will attack Israel before being defeated by Christ. The Assyrian is said to represent the final instrument of God's judgment towards Israel. (*The Assyrian*, N&C4:64-75; *Notes on the Revelation*, CW2:222-226; *Review of 'Lectures on the Second Advent,' and 'The Apocalypse Unfulfilled'*, CW33:12; *Ezekiel*, S2:476; *Thoughts on Isaiah the Prophet*, CW30:196; *Lectures on the Second Coming*, CW11:329; *Divine Mercy*, CW2:152-153.)
[235] Sizer, *The Promised Land*, p. 50.

distinction between Israel and the Church' not only 'denies grace completely' but implies 'more than one way of salvation', and therefore 'no salvation at all',[236] is equally scurrilous. Darby insisted that there had only ever been one way of salvation for Jew, Gentile, *and* Israel. In a private letter written in 1860, he declared that 'Jesus died for that nation', and that 'all the efficacious value for Israel then, as for us now, is in the blood of the Lamb.'[237] Darby emphatically asserted that

> if anyone doubts, after twenty years that I have been preaching, whether I teach the necessity of redemption through the blood [of Christ] for all and every redeemed soul, I could hardly expect to disabuse him by telling him the contrary twenty times over.[238]

In the light of the above accusations, it is important to note that the restoration of Israel lay at the heart of Newton's *own* eschatology, a point conveniently omitted by critics like Sizer. In *Babylon, Its Future History and Doom*, Newton records how '*manifested* and *completed* fulfilments of prophecy are always connected' with the Jewish people, whom he believed were 'likely soon to re-occupy Palestine'. He added that 'the disposition of many in Israel to return to Jerusalem' was a clear sign of 'the last days', and that 'the great event of the now near future, is the return of unregenerate, unrepentant, unforgiven Israel to "Immanuel's land."' Newton claimed that Romans 9-11 had been 'neglected' and '*despised*' by a Church which had 'coveted converted Israel's future position in the Earth'. He also believed that many in the Church had been 'bewitched' and 'befooled', having become 'more blind than Samson' for believing that Israel's promises had been transferred to the Church. Newton castigated Evangelicals for not condemning this theology of replacement, which he described as one of the 'deadly heresies'[239] ruining the Church.

The Third Temple

In the section on Christian Zionism, we noted that Christ's pre-Ascension discourse with His disciples has been described as its 'Magna Carta'. In his own exposition of Acts 1:6-8, Darby suggested that even a child would understand that the Lord 'explicitly sanctions'[240] the expectation of His disciples regarding the restoration of the kingdom to Israel. As he wrote in *The Hopes of the Church*, 'Jesus did not say that this was never to happen; He only

---

[236] Gerstner, *Wrongly Dividing the Word of Truth*, pp. 302-303.

[237] Darby, *Letter* (1860), L3:325.

[238] Darby, *Answer to 'A Second Letter to the Brethren'*, CW8:369.

[239] Benjamin Wills Newton, *Babylon, Its Future History and Doom: With Remarks on the Future of Egypt and other Eastern Countries*, 3rd edn (London: Houlston & Sons, 1890), pp. 161-162, 523, 381, 434-435, 495.

[240] Darby, *Brief Remarks on the Work of the Rev. David Brown*, CW11:355.

said, that the time of this restoration is not revealed.'[241] The focus of the Church was to be on the proclamation of the Gospel, until the time came when God would 'again take up His counsels and dealings with the Jewish nation'.[242]

Darby believed that Israel's complete restoration would coincide with the inauguration of Christ's millennial reign on earth, which he described as 'a restoration of Paradise under the second Adam, the restoration of communion between earth and heaven so long interrupted'.[243] This period would also witness the fulfilment of Acts 3:21, namely the restitution of all things as 'promised long ago' by the prophets,[244] when God's promises to Israel 'shall be accomplished in favour of that people', and when the Gentile nations 'will be subordinate to Israel, the supreme people on the earth.'[245] Although there is only one specific reference in the Bible to a thousand-year reign (Rev. 20:4-5), Darby believed that the doctrine of the millennium was 'uniformly taught in the New Testament',[246] and explicitly evident in the Old (*cf.* Isa. 11:6-9; 65:17-25).

One of the major bones of contention within Christian Zionist circles relates to the rebuilding of the Temple and the reinstitution of the sacrificial system (*cf.* Ezekiel 40-48; Zech. 14:21). As we have previously noted, Darby reconciled the restoration of the sacrificial system in the millennium with the New Covenant: 'If Israel will have sacrifices, as well as an earthly temple and priesthood, they will be only commemorative signs of the one great offering of Christ.'[247] In 1832, Darby wrote a letter to the editor of the *Christian Herald* reviewing William Burgh's *Lectures on the Second Advent* and *The Apocalypse Unfulfilled*. Darby found much of Burgh's views 'exceedingly consistent' with his own, and suggested that 'on all prophecy that is properly Jewish', Burgh had been 'favoured' with 'great clearness of apprehension'. Darby described his claim that Antichrist would one day 'place his abomination' in a literal Temple in Jerusalem as 'a very important truth'.[248] Without diminishing the role of the Roman Catholic Church in the coming Antichrist deception, Darby effectively repositioned the eschatological satellite to face eastward in the direction of Jerusalem, rather than westward in the direction of Rome.

The Jewish Remnant

Darby believed that although the Psalms offered Christians comfort and assurance in times of trial, many of them prophetically anticipated the suffering

---

[241] Darby, *The Hopes of the Church*, CW2:291.

[242] Darby, *Some further Developments of the Principles*, CW1:181.

[243] Darby, *Reflections upon the Prophetic Inquiry*, CW2:24.

[244] Darby, *II Peter*, S5:502.

[245] Darby, *The Testimony of God*, CW22:363.

[246] Darby, *Brief Remarks on the Work of the Rev. David Brown*, CW11:364.

[247] Darby, *Letter* (1860), L3:325.

[248] Darby, *Review of 'Lectures on the Second Advent'*, CW33:1-3.

of the Jews during the Great Tribulation.[249] Through his personal study of the Psalms, Darby had acquired a deeper sense of Christ's love for the Jews 'as God's people!',[250] and taught that in order to understand this prophetic aspect 'we must see the Jewish remnant faithful in trial, and the Spirit of Christ taking up this position to link them with the strength of Jehovah'.[251] As he explained,

> They will see before them the anger of God and will be in anguish, feeling how much they have deserved it; the power of Satan will be there in an entirely special manner; the mass of the people will be upraised against this remnant. Christ has passed through these troubles, although He did not deserve to do so...He has accomplished atonement for Israel in such a manner that, finally, the wrath of God will not burst forth against the remnant of this people.[252]

Despite lamenting in a letter to G.V. Wigram that 'few apprehend [Christ's] interest in the remnant of Israel',[253] Darby was mindful of those who struggled to follow his exposition of the Psalms, not wanting to 'turn the Christian away'[254] from Christ's atoning sacrifice on the cross.

The Faithfulness of God

In 1857, Darby expressed his delight that the doctrines of the Rapture and Israel's restoration were captivating many in the Church:

> The Rapture of the saints to meet the Lord in the air, before His manifestation to the earth, and the existence of a Jewish remnant, in whom the Spirit of God is graciously working before the Lord manifests Himself to them for their deliverance, is happily attracting the attention of Christians. It has made sufficient way to be the occasion of a renewed opposition, which can only do good by urging serious Christians to examine the scriptures on the subject – an examination which will, under grace, spiritually enlarge their apprehensions on many most important points, full of blessing and interest for their souls.[255]

Darby's close attention to these twin themes stemmed from his personal

---

[249] Darby, *Letter published in 1859 as an 'Extract from a Letter written long ago,' probably occasioned by 'Observations on a Tract, entitled, Remarks on the Sufferings of the Lord Jesus,' etc.*, L1:122.

[250] Darby, *The Psalms*, N&C3:276.

[251] Darby, *Observations on a Tract entitled 'Remarks on the Sufferings of the Lord Jesus: A Letter addressed to certain Brethren and Sisters in Christ, by B.W. Newton'* (1847), CW15:71.

[252] J.N. Darby, *The Non-Atoning Sufferings of Christ, 1864. Translated from the French of J.N.D.* (London: G. Morrish, n.d.), pp. 4-5.

[253] Darby, *Letter to G.V. Wigram* (New York, 22 November 1866), L1:464.

[254] Darby, *Letter* (1864), L2:69.

[255] Darby, *The Rapture*, CW11:118.

devotion to God and his study of the Scriptures, which convinced him that the Jewish people 'are very dear to our God and Father, if they be not to us'.[256] He believed that the Bible demonstrated in the clearest of terms the sovereign grace and faithfulness of God towards the Jews,[257] and in so doing revealed what God is 'in Himself.'[258] Supersessionism was not only repugnant to Darby, but a blasphemous slur on God's character. However, it must be stated that whenever Darby spoke about Israel's restoration, he was anxious to help the Church understand its *own* position and responsibility. As he explained,

> The one desire of my heart is the beauty and blessing of the church – the bride of Christ. That will make me earnestly love all saints for they are of it. I desire its entire separation to Christ to whom she belongs – espoused as a chaste virgin.[259]

One reason why Darby believed that the Church had fallen into apostasy was because it had 'looked on the Jews as entirely set aside', forgetting that 'the gifts and calling of God are without repentance'. Since God 'never changes His mind' and 'never sets aside His own design and purpose', He could never reverse His election of Israel. Darby lamented the fact that many of his fellow Christians had been 'wise in their own conceit, thinking that the Jews are set aside, and that the church never can be.'[260] As we have seen, this unshakeable conviction can be traced back to his convalescence in Dublin, when he began to understand the distinction between Israel and the Church. The remarkable degree of consistency in Darby's writings owes much to this period of his life, his eschatology being the fruit not of any formal theological training or academic pursuit, but of a search that was 'deeply personal', and one which 'just happened to coincide with a period of church history in which public interest in prophecy had reached a fever pitch.'[261]

In Conclusion

One of the most remarkable outworkings of Darby's eschatology is found in Philip Hallie's book, *Lest Innocent Blood be Shed*. Hallie, a Jewish writer, visited Le Chambon-sur-Lignon in south-eastern 'Vichy' France, where he interviewed villagers who had survived World War II. He records that, during the War, there were, among the three thousand Chambonnais villagers, a large number of 'Darbystes', and that many Jewish refugees had found shelter on their farms 'because of the special sympathy the Darbystes had for Jews.' As Hallie explains, 'Believing that every word of the Bible was inspired by God,

---

[256] Darby, *The Hopes of the Church*, CW2:363.
[257] Darby, *On the Epistle to the Romans*, CW33:367.
[258] Darby, *Fragments*, N&C2:164.
[259] Darby, *What is the Church and in what Sense is it Now in Ruin?*, M4:166-167.
[260] Darby, *Lectures on the Second Coming*, CW11:285.
[261] Henzel, *Darby*, pp. 53-54.

the Darbystes had a thorough knowledge of the history of the Jews as that history is told in the Old Testament.' He relates how, on one occasion, a German Jewish refugee came to a Darbyste farm to buy eggs, only to be asked by the farmer's wife if she was Jewish. The terrified woman revealed her identity, and to her astonishment, the farmer's wife called her family, introduced the lady as 'a representative of the Chosen People!',[262] and gave her refuge. In his book, *Standing with Israel: Why Christians Support the Jewish State* (2006), David Brog explains why this villager and her family were prepared to put their lives at risk to help this victim of the Nazi Holocaust:

> This Jewish refugee had stumbled upon a village of Plymouth Brethren, known in French as 'Darbyites' after the movement's founder, John Nelson Darby. Here, in the heart of Vichy France, was a settlement of religious Protestants who rejected replacement theology and believed instead that the Jews were the chosen people of God. In the midst of a genocide, the theology of the Plymouth Brethren led this Christian family to quite literally embrace the Jewish people.

The fact that Hallie, a Jewish ethicist, and Brog, a Jewish politician and lawyer, have recognised Darby's legacy in the response of these Chambonnais is truly remarkable. Citing the distinction Darby made between Israel and the Church, and his condemnation of replacement theory, Brog asserts that 'Darby's view of the Jewish people' was not only 'revolutionary',[263] but is foundational to Christian Zionism. As the atrocities of the Holocaust were being perpetrated, and while much of the Protestant Church either cowered in silence or looked on with cold indifference, the villagers of Le Chambon put Darby's theology into practice. The pastor and 'soul'[264] of this 'city of refuge' was André Trocmé, who was posthumously awarded the 'Medal of Righteousness' by Israel in 1972 for helping to 'transform the region into a vast haven for fleeing Jews, numbering into the thousands.'[265] It is a fitting tribute not only to the villagers of Le Chambon, but also to John Nelson Darby, that these 'righteous' acts have been recognised by the Department for the Righteous among the Nations at Yad Vashem in Jerusalem, and described by the Department's director, Mordecai Paldiel, as 'probably the most celebrated case of Christian charity'[266] in the history of the Holocaust. The Bible 'knows nothing of abstract truth'.[267]

---

[262] Philip Hallie, *Lest Innocent Blood be Shed: The Story of the Village of Le Chambon and how Goodness happened there* (London: Harper Torchbooks, 1985), pp. 48, 183.

[263] Brog, *Standing with Israel*, pp. 41, 46.

[264] Hallie, *Lest Innocent Blood be Shed*, p. 45.

[265] Mordecai Paldiel, *Sheltering the Jews: Stories of Holocaust Rescuers* (Minneapolis, MN: Fortress Press, 1996), p. 36; *cf.* Donald Lowrie, 'Chambon-sur-Lignon', in *Anthology of Holocaust Literature*, ed. by Jacob Glatstein, Israel Knox, and Samuel Margoshes (New York: Atheneum, 1968), pp. 375-381.

[266] Paldiel, *Sheltering the Jews*, p. 36.

[267] Scroggie, *The Lord's Return*, p. 131.

Chapter 5

The Puritans

In his book, *Israel's Good News* (1688), Anders Pedersen Kempe brought the following indictment against the Church: 'You heathen Christians, you let yourselves be persuaded by false teachers...to believe that the Jews were forever disinherited and rejected by God, and that you were now the rightful Christian Israel to possess the land of Canaan forever.'[1] In the light of this charge, we will now examine the extent to which Christian Zionism can be traced back through the post-Reformation history of the Protestant Church.

The Post-Apostolic Church

Although the Church was 'far from settled'[2] on matters of eschatology during the period which followed the Apostles, there is a general consensus among scholars that early Christian interpretations of Biblical prophecy were predominantly premillennial. Historicist E.B. Elliott concedes that during the first four centuries of the Church, the 1260 'days' of Daniel's prophecy were interpreted literally.[3] However, with the rise of the second-century allegorical school of Clement in Alexandria, the influence of third and fourth-century allegorists *par excellence*, Origen and Augustine, and the legalisation of Christianity under Constantine, premillennialism was supplanted by amillennial and, later, postmillennial eschatologies. As Kromminga summarises, 'Since Origen chiliasm [premillennialism] had no first-rate advocate in the ancient Church; since Constantine the Great it had no literary representation; since Augustine its hold upon the common people waned.' This departure from the faith of the early Church was made 'complete'[4] during the Middle Ages, when amillennialism underpinned not only the dogma of the Roman Catholic Church, but the theology of the early Protestant catechisms, canons, and confessions. It was not until the late sixteenth century that belief in the premillennial return of

---

[1] Quoted in Brearley, 'Jerusalem in Judaism', p. 109.

[2] John F. Walvoord, *The Rapture Question*, 2nd edn (Grand Rapids, MI: Zondervan, 1979), p. 156.

[3] Elliott, *Horae Apocalypticae: Vol. III*, pp. 229-230.

[4] Diedrich H. Kromminga, *The Millennium in the Church: Studies in the History of Christian Chiliasm* (Grand Rapids, MI: William B. Eerdmans Publishing Company, 1945), pp. 102, 164.

Christ, along with an eschatological interest in 'Zion', underwent a revival.

Apocalypticism in the Middle Ages

Described as 'the most outstanding figure among the medieval expositors of prophecy', the twelfth-century Cistercian abbot, Joachim of Fiore (c.1130-1202), stemmed the allegorical tide of the Donatist, Tichonius, whose *Book of Rules* had been popularised by Augustine of Hippo and had underpinned Roman Catholic dogma for centuries. Tichonius believed that a *spiritual* millennium had been inaugurated at Christ's first advent, and that it would expire on His return in AD381. There would be no literal thousand-year reign of Christ, however, since the Church of Rome was God's kingdom on earth.[5]

Although the trend towards a more literal and historical interpretation of prophecy began in the ninth century with the Benedictine monk, Berengaud,[6] it developed in the twelfth and thirteenth-century writings of Anselm of Havelberg and Albertus Magnus, and in the fourteenth-century writings of Nicholas of Lyra. Joachim's influence, however, was by far the most enduring, particularly his Trinitarian division of history into the dispensations of the Father (beginning with Adam), the Son (beginning with John the Baptist), and the Holy Spirit (to begin in the year 1260). Joachim equated the dispensation of the Son with the 1260 'days' of Daniel. His most noted followers, known as the Spiritual Franciscans,[7] circulated authentic *and* spurious Joachian manuscripts throughout Europe during the Middle Ages. One 'avid prophecy student', who 'called on the apocalyptic scriptures and Joachian sources'[8] to give prophetic meaning to his voyages of discovery, was Christopher Columbus (1451-1506).[9]

Joachim's belief that historical events were recorded in Revelation 'raised history to a supreme place of importance',[10] paving the way for the 'year-day' theory which was to predominate among Protestant scholars until the nineteenth century. He also believed that the coming age of the Spirit would witness the reconciliation of Jews and Christians, the Jewish people being

---

[5] Le Roy Edwin Froom, *The Prophetic Faith of our Fathers: Vol. I* (Washington, D.C.: Review and Herald, 1950), pp. 683, 893.

[6] Elliott, *Horae Apocalypticae: Vol. III*, pp. 232-233.

[7] Marjorie Reeves, *Joachim of Fiore and the Prophetic Future* (London: SPCK, 1976), pp. 29-30.

[8] Paul Boyer, *When Time Shall Be No More: Prophecy Belief in Modern American Culture* (Cambridge, MA: Belknap Press, 1999), pp. 225, 56.

[9] Columbus sought to acquire sufficient gold from the New World to restore Jerusalem to Christ, and thereby usher in the millennium. (*The Oxford Companion to the Bible*, ed. by Bruce M. Metzger and Michael D. Coogan [Oxford: Oxford University Press, 1993], p. 355.) Three centuries earlier, Richard the Lionheart had conferred with Joachim in Messina before attempting to drive Saladin out of Jerusalem, Saladin having been identified as the Antichrist. (Boyer, *When Time Shall Be No More*, p. 51.)

[10] Froom, *The Prophetic Faith: Vol. I*, p. 695.

'integral'[11] to his theological system. The dignity he afforded the Jews, coupled with his quasi-postmillennialism, contrasted sharply with Augustinian amillennialism, which had injected anti-Semitism into the Church.

Richard Bauckham has suggested that English apocalypticism 'was eclectic in its use of many medieval traditions and interacted closely with Continental Protestant thinking.'[12] By the end of the sixteenth century, four medieval apocalyptic traditions had been revised, namely (i) the Antichrist legend,[13] (ii) spiritualising commentaries on the Apocalypse based largely on Tichonius, (iii) the Joachimist tradition, and (iv) the apocalypticism of John Wyclif and the Lollards. The majority of sixteenth-century Reformers identified Antichrist either with the Pope or the Papal institution. This belief was central to the theology of the Protestant Reformers,[14] although it did not gain confessional status until 1615, when the Irish Articles, drawn up by James Ussher (1580-1656), were ratified by the Convocation of the Church of Ireland.[15]

Historian, playwright, and bishop of Ossory, John Bale (1495-1563), was 'one of the most vigorous and prolific writers of Protestant propaganda in the first generation of Reform',[16] and set the pattern for sixteenth-century apocalyptic study in England with his book, *The Image of bothe Churches* (c.1545). Bale's delineation of a false and true Church set the tone for Protestant exegesis, while his amillennial eschatology, rooted in the Augustinian tradition of the Reformers, remained 'virtually unchallenged' until 1640. His work prepared the way for apocalypticists such as the inventor of logarithms, John Napier (1550-1617), whose mathematical approach to the Bible injected a more predictive element into the Puritan exposition of prophecy.[17] In his book, *A Plaine Discovery of the Whole Revelation of Saint John* (1593), Napier not only distinguished between a false and true Church, but outlined seven dispensations which he believed would culminate in a future age of peace.

On the Continent, the sixteenth century was characterised by 'a theology of persecution and a theology of history'.[18] Norman Cohn suggests that between

---

[11] Robert E. Lerner, *The Feast of Saint Abraham: Medieval Millenarians and the Jews* (Philadelphia, PA: University of Pennsylvania Press, 2001), pp. 120, 3.

[12] Richard Bauckham, *Tudor Apocalypse* (Oxford: The Sutton Courtenay Press, 1978), pp. 49-50.

[13] Based on the tenth-century 'biography' of Antichrist by the French Abbot Adso, entitled *Libellus de Antichristo* ('Little Work on Antichrist'). Adso believed that the Antichrist would be a Jew of the tribe of Dan who would one day rule from Jerusalem.

[14] Christopher Hill, *Antichrist in Seventeenth-Century England* (London: Oxford University Press, 1971), pp. 7-31.

[15] Gribben, 'Introduction: Antichrist in Ireland', p. 6.

[16] Bauckham, *Tudor Apocalypse*, p. 21.

[17] Crawford Gribben, *The Puritan Millennium: Literature and Theology 1550-1682* (Dublin: Four Courts Press Ltd., 2000), pp. 38, 42.

[18] Bauckham, *Tudor Apocalypse*, pp. 31, 13.

the close of the eleventh century and the first half of the sixteenth,

> it repeatedly happened in Europe that the desire of the poor to improve the
> material conditions of their lives became transfused with phantasies of a new
> Paradise on earth, a world purged of suffering and sin, a Kingdom of the Saints.[19]

Charismatic leaders well versed in apocalyptic literature were able to rally the
disenchanted peasantry to their cause, during an age when 'economic misery
and political oppression'[20] prevailed. According to Garrett, one of the reasons
why millenarian beliefs have endured is that they have served as 'a comforting
explanation of events and conditions that would otherwise be threatening and
incomprehensible.'[21] The more radical charismatics, influenced by the writings
of John Wyclif, Jan Hus, and Jerome of Prague, believed that they had been
commissioned by God to usher in a new age.

Wyclif's translation of the Bible into English (c.1382) paved the way for
William Tyndale's translation of the New Testament into English in 1525/6 and
Myles Coverdale's English translation of the Bible in 1535. A new era had
dawned, the Bible having been 'exhumed from the neglect of centuries'[22] and,
through the printing revolution, made affordable and accessible to the common
people. The Scriptures soon occupied a central place in English society,
instructing the Church and influencing astronomers, astrologers, politicians,
economists, scientists, and historians alike.[23]

England and the Bible

The seventeenth century has been described as 'the great age of prophetical
commentary',[24] when 'religion touches life at every level and leaves its mark in
some way on every individual'.[25] This century witnessed the rise to prominence
of English Puritanism, which was rooted in the theology of Wyclif, Tyndale,
Knox, and Hooper. Characterised by simple worship, high morals, and
scholarly excellence, the central tenet of Puritanism was the authority of the

---

[19] Norman Cohn, *The Pursuit of the Millennium* (London: Secker & Warburg, 1957), p.
xiii.

[20] P.G. Rogers, *The Fifth Monarchy Men* (London: Oxford University Press, 1966), p. 5.

[21] Clarke Garrett, *Respectable Folly: Millenarians and the French Revolution in France
and England* (London: The John Hopkins University Press, 1975), p. 13.

[22] William Bramley-Moore, *The Church's Forgotten Hope, or Scriptural Studies on the
Translation of the Saints*, 2nd edn (London: George J.W. Pitman, 1903), p. 165.

[23] Christopher Hill, *The English Bible and the Seventeenth-Century Revolution* (London:
The Penguin Press, 1993).

[24] W.H. Oliver, *Prophets and Millennialists: The Uses of Biblical Prophecy in England
from the 1790s to the 1840s* (Auckland: Auckland University Press, 1978), p. 31.

[25] Bryan W. Ball, *A Great Expectation: Eschatological Thought in English
Protestantism to 1660* (Leiden: E.J. Brill, 1975), p. 5.

Bible,[26] which, for centuries, had been subordinated to the authority of the Roman Catholic Church. It is not possible, however, to identify 'an orthodox [Puritan] perspective'[27] with regards to eschatology.

Gribben notes how amillennial, premillennial, and postmillennial eschatologies 'each found expression within the puritan movement', while apocalyptic beliefs in general 'remained in a state of flux'. The same can be said in relation to Israel. William Pynchon, Richard Baxter, and Alexander Petrie were among those who dismissed any suggestion of a future conversion and national restoration of Israel, while William Perkins, Richard Sibbes, and Thomas Parker upheld the more 'staple component'[28] of Puritan eschatology, namely that the Jews would turn to Christ *without* being restored nationally.[29] As the seventeenth century progressed it became increasingly common for Puritans to discourse on the conversion of the Jews, not only in Biblical commentaries, but in Parliamentary sermons as well. The same theme was expressed more devotionally in the *Directory for the Public Worship of God* (1645), the *Larger Catechism of the Westminster Assembly* (1648), and in various Puritan diaries and biographies.[30]

Commentaries on Daniel and Revelation abounded during the first half of the seventeenth century; even King James I took a personal interest in prophecy before his accession to the throne. As Ball writes,

> By the time the crown had passed from Tudors to Stuarts there had developed within English Protestantism a marked awareness of those doctrines which concerned the end of time and the final consummation of history. The last age had come. These days were the last days.

Although economic depression, academic study, and a revolutionary climate were contributory factors, the main reason why eschatological convictions reached their high point between 1640 and 1660 was 'the inherent religious feeling of the age, built on the twin foundations of the great historical tradition of Reformation theology and the complete contemporary reliance upon the Bible as the source of revealed truth.'[31]

---

[26] Douglas J. Culver, *Albion and Ariel: British Puritanism and the Birth of Political Zionism* (New York: Peter Lang, 1995), p. 57.

[27] Richard W. Cogley, 'The Fall of the Ottoman Empire and the Restoration of Israel in the "Judeo-centric" Strand of Puritan Millenarianism', *Church History*, 72.2 (June, 2003), 305.

[28] Gribben, *The Puritan Millennium*, pp. 16, 32, 39.

[29] Cogley, 'The Fall of the Ottoman Empire', 306-307.

[30] Murray, *The Puritan Hope*, pp. 100-103.

[31] Ball, *A Great Expectation*, pp. 23, 7.

All 'Israel' shall be Saved

Despite breaking free from Rome, early sixteenth-century Reformers failed to remove the shackles of Augustinian amillennialism from their Protestant theology. Belief in a future reign of Christ on earth had been condemned by Calvin as 'too childish either to need or to be worth a refutation'; in his opinion, 'even a blind man' could see 'what stupid nonsense these people talk'.[32] However, Paul's reference to all 'Israel' being saved (Rom. 11:26), which Luther and Calvin had interpreted in relation to the Church, was taken by Theodore Beza, Calvin's successor in Geneva, to mean 'non-Christian Jews whose religion was Judaism'.[33]

The Marian exiles, who had fled Britain for the Continent during the reign of 'Bloody' Queen Mary (1553-1558), not only injected 'an exegetical shock into conventional Augustinian amillennialism'[34] with their more optimistic eschatology, but provided annotations to the Biblical text which changed the thinking of many Protestants concerning Israel. It is interesting to note that in the original 1560 edition of the Geneva Bible, the marginal note appended to Rom. 11:26, where the Apostle Paul declares, 'And so all Israel shall be saved', defines 'Israel' as 'the whole nation of the Jews'. This emphasis on Israel's *national* salvation was a notable departure from conventional amillennialism.[35]

The English God

In his study of seventeenth-century English millenarianism, Bernard Capp states that apocalyptic and millenarian ideas 'blended with the intense nationalism of the period and with the Calvinist concept that only the predestined few, the elect, would be saved.' As the only major Protestant country in Europe, England was seen by many of its people as 'an elect nation destined by God to play a great part in destroying Rome to hasten the world's end, or in setting up the millennium.'[36] Although this belief was 'absent from Tudor apocalyptic exegesis in general', it quickly gained impetus following the coronation of Elizabeth I in 1558 and the return of the Marian exiles.

Following the defeat of the Spanish Armada in 1588, Queen Elizabeth was hailed as 'a noble conqueror of Antichrist'.[37] Thomas Rogers' book, *An*

---

[32] *Institutes of the Christian Religion, by Jean Calvin: Vol. III*, ed. by John T. McNeill (London: SCM Press, 1961), XXV:5.

[33] Peter Toon, 'The Latter-Day Glory', in *Puritans, The Millennium and the Future of Israel: Puritan Eschatology 1600-1660*, ed. by Peter Toon (Cambridge: James Clarke & Co. Ltd., 1970), p. 24.

[34] Gribben, *The Puritan Millennium*, pp. 57-58.

[35] See also Toon, 'The Latter-Day Glory', p. 24.

[36] Bernard S. Capp, *The Fifth Monarchy Men: A Study in Seventeenth-century English Millenarianism* (London: Faber and Faber, 1972), pp. 33-34.

[37] Bauckham, *Tudor Apocalypse*, pp. 87, 128.

Historical Dialogue touching Antichrist and Poperie (1589), was one of many which expounded this belief, as 'the horizons of England's national anticipations and aspirations became global.'[38] Second only to the Bible in popularity, and treated as a kind of appendix to it,[39] was John Foxe's *Actes and Monuments* (or the *Book of Martyrs*), which depicted the enduring struggle between the false and true Church. Dedicated to Queen Elizabeth I, it was 'the most elaborate expression of the apocalyptical expectancy with which the returned exiles and their party greeted Elizabeth at her accession.'[40] John Aylmer, one of the Marian exiles and later bishop of London, wrote a tract on the eve of his return rallying support for the queen under the banner, 'God is English'.[41] The Protestant Reformation and the defeat of the Armada 'intensified the religious sense of English nationhood', with many believing that England was now the new 'Israel'. As Collinson notes, 'every biblical type and figure of God's people was now applied to England, *ad nauseum*', as if those who held such a view 'were living, in a sense, in the pages of the Bible.'[42] No one expounded this belief more eloquently than Aylmer, who wrote:

England says to her children, 'God hath brought forth in me the greatest and excellentest treasure that He hath for your comfort and all the worlds. He would that out of my womb should come that servant of Christ John Wyclif, who begat Huss, who begat Luther, who begat the truth. What greater honour could you or I have than that it pleased Christ as it were in a second birth to be born again of me among you?'[43]

For English millenarians like Aylmer, Foxe, Hackluyt, and Jewel, 'Zion' became 'the symbol of their own national future'.[44]

Restorationism in Puritan Literature

Although Kobler traces an embryonic form of Restorationism back to Duns Scotus, William of Occam, and John Wyclif, the return of the Jews to the Land

---

[38] J.A. de Jong, *As the Waters Cover the Sea: Millennial Expectations in the Rise of Anglo-American Missions 1640-1810* (Kampen: J.H. Kok, 1970), p. 15.
[39] Patrick Collinson, *The Birthpangs of Protestant England: Religious and Cultural Change in the Sixteenth and Seventeenth Centuries* (Basingstoke: Macmillan Press, 1988), p. 12.
[40] William Haller, *Foxe's Book of Martyrs and the Elect Nation* (London: Jonathan Cape, 1963), p. 124.
[41] Quoted in Haller, *Foxe's Book of Martyrs*, p. 245.
[42] Collinson, *The Birthpangs*, pp. 6-7, 10.
[43] Quoted in Haller, *Foxe's Book of Martyrs*, pp. 87-88.
[44] Franz Kobler, *The Vision was There: A History of the British Movement for the Restoration of the Jews to Palestine* (London: Lincolns-Prayer Publishers, 1956), p. 13.

only emerged as the subject of *serious*[45] theological debate towards the close of the sixteenth century, with the publication of works by Andrew Willet (1590) and Thomas Draxe (1608).[46] However, the man many have wrongly labelled 'the father of the British Doctrine of the Restoration of the Jews'[47] was 'the leading English Presbyterian',[48] Thomas Brightman (1562-1607).

Thomas Brightman: Muddying the Waters

Thomas Brightman has been described as 'the first Puritan Judeo-centrist',[49] based on his belief that the millennium would be inaugurated by the conversion of the Jews. Culver suggests that the 'systematic treatment *par excellence* of the idea of Jewish restoration' was Brightman's *Apocalypsis Apocalypseos* (1609), published in English as *A Revelation of the Apocalyps* (1611) and *A Revelation of the Revelation* (1615). He further claims that Brightman's commentary contains 'the single strongest impulse in Great Britain in support of the doctrine of Jewish national restoration'.[50]

Brightman's eschatology, like Puritan eschatology in general, was largely transitional in that it departed from the amillennialism of the Reformers while anticipating the postmillennialism of the English Unitarian, Daniel Whitby (1638-1726). Brightman's commentary on Revelation, in which he warned of a calamity about to befall Christendom, is a blend of pre- and postmillennial concepts. From a premillennial perspective, Brightman confined the Great Tribulation to the Jews and to the period immediately prior to 'their receiving again into grace'. He also connected the drying up of the river Euphrates in Rev. 16:12 to the return of the Jews to the Land, linking their conversion to the overthrow of Roman Catholic idolatry; only then, he believed, would the Church 'provoke their brethren the Jews to the faith, that impediment being taken away, which most of all hindered their conversion'. From a postmillennial perspective, Brightman spoke of 'the elect Jews being chosen

---

[45] In 1586, Ralph Durden proposed to lead the Jews back to the Land and rebuild Jerusalem. Francis Kett claimed that Jesus was already in Jerusalem, and urged God's people to hasten there; he was convicted of heresy and burned alive in 1589. Richard Farnham and John Bull allegedly set sail in a boat made of bulrushes to convert the 'lost tribes', while Thomas Tany proclaimed himself 'King of the Jews' before endeavouring to lead them back to their homeland. (J.F.C. Harrison, *The Second Coming: Popular Millenarianism 1780-1850* [London: Routledge & Kegan Paul Ltd., 1979], pp. 11-38.)

[46] Christopher Hill, 'Till the Conversion of the Jews', in *Millenarianism and Messianism in English Literature and Thought 1650-1800*, ed. by Richard H. Popkin (Leiden: E.J. Brill, 1988), pp. 15-16.

[47] Kobler, *The Vision was There*, p. 16.

[48] Kenneth G.C. Newport, *Apocalypse and Millennium: Studies in Biblical Eisegesis* (Cambridge: Cambridge University Press, 2000), p. 24.

[49] Cogley, 'The Fall of the Ottoman Empire', 304-308.

[50] Culver, *Albion and Ariel*, p. 79.

into one Christian people', and portrayed Christ returning in person *at the close* of the millennial age. Speaking of the Rider on the white horse (Rev. 19:11-21) he wrote,

> We may not suppose that Christ shall come forth in any visible shape; these things are far from his last coming...but he will shew forth openly and evidently such a force in the administration of things, as this figure represents.

Brightman also claimed that Satan had been bound when Constantine became emperor,[51] and that Constantine was the 'manchild' referred to in Rev. 12:5. Gribben suggests that Brightman made 'a breathtaking advance'[52] in Puritan eschatology by claiming that a millennial period had already been inaugurated with the preaching of John Wyclif. Brightman believed that from that time onwards the saints had begun to reign with Christ, a reign which would end in the year 2300. He further asserted that the 1260 'days' of Daniel's prophecy were to be understood as years, that Antichrist was manifest in the Papal institution, and that the destruction of the 'lawless one' at Christ's Second Coming would be the time when 'Christ shall take the Jews into the fellowship of his holy Church'.[53]

Such beliefs are completely inconsistent with the premillennial eschatology of John Nelson Darby and Christian Zionism, and are best labelled 'embryonic postmillennialism'.[54] Donald Wagner's depiction of Brightman as 'the first futurist premillennial dispensationalist' and 'the British forerunner of Christian Zionism, a type of John the Baptist in this field', is therefore historically and theologically untenable. Wagner's claim that he experienced 'a sense of timelessness' when reading Brightman, feeling that, 'aside from the archaic language and style, I could be reading a volume written by Hal Lindsey, Pat Robertson, or Jerry Falwell,'[55] is astonishing.

Hugh Broughton

In 1548, Archbishop Thomas Cranmer appointed Martin Bucer to the position of regius professor of divinity at Cambridge, and Peter Martyr to the same position at Oxford. Bucer and Martyr, German and Italian Reformation theologians respectively, helped to inspire a long tradition of Biblical scholarship which interpreted 'Israel' in Romans 11 to mean ethnic Israel, and not the Church. The translation of Peter Martyr's *Commentary upon Romans*, published in London in 1568, has been described as the first volume in English

---

[51] Thomas Brightman, *A Revelation of the Apocalyps* (Amsterdam: 1611), pp. 212, 633, 624, 634, 652.

[52] Gribben, *The Puritan Millennium*, p. 43.

[53] Brightman, *A Revelation*, pp. 657, 644.

[54] Gribben, *The Puritan Millennium*, p. 103.

[55] Wagner, *Anxious for Armageddon*, pp. 86-87.

to expound the restorationist theme at any length. One Cambridge student who was influenced by Martyr's commentary was Hugh Broughton (1549-1612), 'the first Englishman to propose going as a missionary to the Jews in the Near East', and one of the first 'to propose the idea of translating the New Testament into Hebrew for the sake of the Jews.'[56] A graduate of Magdalene College and a renowned rabbinic and Hebrew scholar, Broughton believed that the book of Revelation was the Gentile counterpart to Daniel, whose prophecies, he maintained, were confined to the Jews. His commentaries on Daniel (1596) and Revelation (1610) were 'departures from past Protestant tradition'.[57]

Broughton had called on his countrymen to trust God for deliverance from the Spanish Armada in 1588. He also appealed to Elizabeth I, and later to James I, when Rabbi Abraham Ruben of Constantinople called for help in translating the New Testament into Hebrew. Broughton was undoubtedly one of the leading forerunners of the Restorationist movement, believing that God's blessing would rest upon the nation which answered such a noble call.[58] In his supplication to James I, he wrote:

> Duty to God and the King binds me, written to of old and often, to stir the sincere conscience of the King, who is *the able* to afford help, and so *should be readiest* to show pity towards the Nation that taught us salvation.[59]

Sir Henry Finch

Henry Finch (c.1558-1625) was legal officer to King James I and a Member of Parliament for Canterbury; he was made a knight of the realm in 1616. Described as 'a man of extraordinary personality and accomplishments',[60] he was the 'most conspicuous seer of the Restoration movement', and 'a veritable precursor of Zionism'.[61] Along with his publisher, William Gouge, Finch was charged and arrested for publishing what is arguably the most important Restorationist work of the Puritan era, *The Worlds Great Restauration, or The Calling of the Jewes, and with them of all the Nations and Kingdomes of the*

---

[56] Murray, *The Puritan Hope*, p. 42.
[57] Katherine R. Firth, *The Apocalyptic Tradition in Reformation Britain 1530-1645* (Oxford: Oxford University Press, 1979), p. 158.
[58] Hugh Broughton, 'To the Right Honorable, the Temporal Lords of the Queen of Englands most Excellent Privy Councell (29 July 1599)', in Hugh Broughton, *The Works of the Great Albionean Divine* (London: 1662), p. 673.
[59] Hugh Broughton, 'A Supplication to the Kings Majesty, concerning Piety towards the Jews of our Constantines Town', in Broughton, *The Works*, p. 696.
[60] Culver, *Albion and Ariel*, p. 101.
[61] Michael J. Pragai, *Faith and Fulfilment: Christians and the Return to the Promised Land* (London: Vallentine, Mitchell and Company Ltd., 1985), p. 13.

Earth, to the Faith of Christ (1621).[62]

Appealing to the Jews of the Diaspora, Finch declared: 'Out of all the places of thy dispersion, East, West, North, and South, his [God's] purpose is to bring thee home again, and to marry thee to himself by faith for evermore.' A man of prayer, Finch expressed how his heart would 'never fail to pray' for their prosperity:

> Bowing my knees to the Father of our Lord Jesus Christ, the God of glory, that he would hasten that which he hath spoken concerning thee by the Prophets of old, and by the Apostles sent by his son. Whose counsels are without repentance, his love never changes.[63]

Finch made a clear distinction between Israel and the Church, countering the inherent supersessionism of Reformed, amillennial, covenant theology (rooted in Augustine's *City of God*), which had made 'little or no change in the disposition of Christians'[64] towards the Jews. As he explained,

> Where *Israel, Judah, Zion, Jerusalem,* & c. are named in this argument, the Holy Ghost means…Israel properly descended out of *Jacobs* loins. The same judgment is to be made of their returning to their land and ancient seats, the conquest of their foes, the fruitfulness of their soil, the glorious Church they shall erect in the land itself of Judah, their bearing rule far and near. These and such like are not Allegories, setting forth in terrene similarities or deliverance through Christ (whereof those were types and figures) but meant really and literally of the Jews.[65]

Much to the displeasure of James I, Finch predicted that all nations, and kings, would one day be subject to a restored Jewish kingdom. According to Kobler, 'the persecution he had to suffer for his belief in the revival of the Jewish people gave a dramatic colouring and brought the rising Christian theory of the return of the Jews into the limelight of history.'[66]

---

[62] Lucien Wolf describes it as an 'early manifestation of Zionism'. (*Menasseh ben Israel's Mission to Oliver Cromwell. Being a reprint of the Pamphlets published by Menasseh ben Israel to promote the Re-admission of the Jews to England 1649-1656,* ed. by Lucien Wolf [London: Macmillan & Co., Limited, 1901], p. xxi.)

[63] Henry Finch, 'To all the seed of Jacob, far and wide dispersed. Peace and Truth be multiplied unto you', in Henry Finch, *The Worlds Great Restauration, or The Calling of the Jewes, and with them of all the Nations and Kingdomes of the Earth, to the Faith of Christ* (London: William Gouge, 1621), preface.

[64] Isaac Da Costa, *Israel and the Gentiles: Contributions to the History of the Jews from the Earliest Times to the Present Day* (London: James Nisbet and Co., 1850), p. 467.

[65] Henry Finch, 'A Briefe and Summarie Declaration of the Prophecies of the Old and New Testament, so far as they concerne the calling of the Jewes', in Finch, *The Worlds Great Restauration,* p. 6.

[66] Franz Kobler, 'Sir Henry Finch (1558-1625) and the first English Advocates of the Restoration of the Jews to Palestine', in *The Jewish Historical Society of England:*

The Popularisation of Puritan Restorationism

Two of the leading Puritans who propagated belief in the restoration of the Jews were Henry Archer and Robert Maton. Archer co-pastored a church in Arnhem, Holland, with Thomas Goodwin, who later served as chaplain to Oliver Cromwell. Central to Archer's eschatology were Christ's words in Acts 1:6-8, which he believed had confirmed the disciples 'in their opinion of a Kingdom' but had corrected them 'in the thoughts of the times, when it should be'.[67] Archer maintained that Christ had already established what he called His *providential* and *spiritual* reign *over* the earth, and was now preparing to inaugurate His *monarchical* reign *upon* the earth. He also believed that once this latter reign on David's throne had been established, Christ would return to heaven, entrusting His earthly government to the saints.

In 1642, Robert Maton's book, *Israel's Redemption*, was published. Widely read, it drew concerted opposition from Alexander Petrie, the minister of the Scots Kirk in Rotterdam. Petrie, in the spirit of Augustine, Calvin, and the Augsburg Confession,[68] branded the Restorationism of men like Maton as 'silly and ridiculous', 'heresy', and 'an old Jewish fancy and Cerinthian fable'.[69] Maton, and the Bible expositors he related to, believed that the truth concerning Israel's restoration had been suppressed by the Antichrist system operating in the Church since the time of the Apostles. Commenting on Acts 1:6-8 he wrote:

So evidently do these words express an earthly kingdom…that no expositor which I have met with does deny it, and therefore seeing they could not but embrace the sense, me thinks they should not so rashly have rejected the consequence.

Maton not only attacked the 'strange language' of Roman Catholicism, but also the 'strange interpretation' of Protestant theologians who had applied the names Israel, Zion, and Jerusalem to the Church. He believed that there was 'not one text in all the Scripture, wherein a Gentile is called a Jew, or an Israelite; or wherein the Church of the Gentiles is called Israel, Zion, or Jerusalem.'[70]

Transactions - Sessions 1945-1951: Vol. XVI (London: The Jewish Historical Society of England, 1952), p. 110.

[67] Henry Archer, *The Personall Raigne of Christ upon Earth* (London: 1642), p. 10.

[68] The Augsburg Confession (1530) was the first major Protestant confession. Drafted by Philip Melancthon, it became definitive for Lutherans. Article XVII condemns the premillennial eschatology of those 'who are now spreading certain Jewish opinions, that before the resurrection of the dead the godly shall take possession of the kingdom of the world, the ungodly being everywhere suppressed.'

[69] Alexander Petrie, *Chiliasto-mastix, or, The Prophecies in the Old and New Testament concerning the Kingdome of our Saviour Jesus Christ, vindicated from the misinterpretationes of the Millenaries and specially of Mr. Maton in his book called Israels Redemption* (Roterdame, 1644), pp. 5-6.

[70] Robert Maton, *Israel's Redemption, or the Propheticall History of our Saviours Kingdome on Earth* (London: 1642), pp. 3, preface. Maton's response to Petrie was

Froom suggests that with the American Puritan, Increase Mather (1639-1723), 'we reach the high-water mark in seventeenth-century prophetic interpretation'.[71] A graduate of Trinity College, Dublin, Mather served as ambassador for the Massachusetts Bay Colony. In a series of lecture-sermons entitled, *The Mystery of Israel's Salvation, Explained and Applied* (1669), he spoke of a three-fold kingdom in which Christ was already ruling *providentially* and *spiritually*, and would one day rule *Davidically* when the Jews had been restored to the Land. According to Mather,

> when God is about to accomplish this great and glorious design of his grace and providence, he will have much prayer to be made for it, and therefore will he discover it unto his servants, that so they may be stirred up to cry mightily unto the Lord, that he would perform the intents of his heart.

He gave six reasons why Israel would be saved as a nation: (i) God's mercy and grace, (ii) Israel's national election, (iii) God's power, (iv) the fulfilment of prophecy, (v) God's everlasting covenant with Abraham, and (vi) the prayers of the saints. Although Acts 1:6-8 was pivotal to his eschatology,[72] his denial of a future, visible reign of Christ on earth was a significant departure from seventeenth-century Restorationism.

An equally popular work in Britain was *The Accomplishment of the Scripture Prophecies* by Pierre Jurieu (1637-1713), minister of the French Church in Rotterdam. This 'notable Huguenot controversialist'[73] believed that the Sabbath day's rest foreshadowed a seventh dispensation for the earth, which would be characterised by Christ's visible reign. It was inconceivable to Jurieu's mind that the Church could have fulfilled prophecies which had been given specifically to Israel. As he exclaimed,

> If this be so, certainly all these *Prophecies* are cheats; the Holy Spirit hath deceived this Nation, all their Oracles are false, and God hath born them up with vain hopes; for this is trifling with God and men, to say, that these promises were accomplished in that small number of *Jews*, who were converted to *Christianity*...Besides, we must observe, that the *Messiah* belongs to the *Jews*, he was promised to the *Jews*; this Nation from its very original hath been fed with the hopes of the *Messiah's coming*...In a word, let all these *Oracles* be viewed, and it will be seen that the *people of Israel* must be the *ruling*, the *chosen*, the

---

entitled, *Israel's Redemption Redeemed* (1646), and was later republished as *Christ's Personall Reigne on Earth One Thousand Yeares* (1652), and *A Treatise of the Fifth Monarchy* (1655).

[71] Froom, *The Prophetic Faith: Vol. III*, p. 127.

[72] Increase Mather, *The Mystery of Israel's Salvation, Explained and Applied: or, A Discourse Concerning the General Conversion of the Israelitish Nation* (London: 1669), pp. 21, 130-131.

[73] Oliver, *Prophets and Millennialists*, p. 39.

Holy people, and that the *Gentiles* must be made happy, because they shall be incorporated into this *Israel*.[74]

One of the most notable and respected Bible scholars of the Puritan era was Joseph Mede, the 'dean'[75] of English Millenarianism and 'doyen of seventeenth-century commentators'.[76] His writings were among those banned by the anti-Puritan and anti-Restorationist archbishop of Canterbury, William Laud. In a sermon preached before James I on 19 June 1621, Laud condemned belief in the future restoration of Israel as the 'error of the Jews' and 'monstrous opinions', naming Sir Henry Finch as the man who could 'out-dream the Jews'.[77] The Long Parliament lifted Laud's ban in 1640, imprisoning and later beheading the disgraced archbishop and calling for Mede's commentary, *Clavis Apocalyptica* (1627), to be translated into English. This work was undertaken by Richard More, and published as *The Key to the Apocalypse* or *The Key of the Revelation* in 1643.

In his essay, *The Mystery of S. Paul's Conversion; or The Type of the Calling of the Jews*, Mede expounded his historicist brand of premillennialism, which set the pattern for generations to come.[78] He was inspired by the German theologian and encyclopedist, Johann Heinrich Alsted (1588-1638), whose *Tractatus de mille annis* (1618), later published as *Diatribe de mille annis apocalypticis* (1627), was translated into English as *The Beloved City: or, the Saints Reign on Earth a Thousand Yeares* (1643). Although Mede was more cautious on eschatological matters than many of his contemporaries, the restoration of the Jews *was* conspicuous in his writings. He believed, for example, that Saul's conversion on the road to Damascus foreshadowed the return of the Jews to the Land and their subsequent conversion to Christ.

In a fascinating letter to Sir Henry Stuteville, dated 7 April 1621, Mede defended Sir Henry Finch's book, *The World's Great Restauration*, in the wake of the controversy surrounding its publication. He insisted that England's monarch 'need not be afraid to aver and maintain, that one day they [the Jews] shall come to Jerusalem again; be Kings & chief Monarchs of the Earth; sway & govern all, for the glory of Xt [Christ]; that shall shine amongst them'.[79] In stark contrast to the futurist eschatology of Christian Zionism, however, Mede

---

[74] Pierre Jurieu, *The Accomplishment of the Scripture Prophecies, or the Approaching Deliverance of the Church*, 2nd edn (London: 1687), pp. 298-299.

[75] Richard H. Popkin, 'Introduction', in Popkin, *Millenarianism*, p. 5.

[76] Oliver, *Prophets and Millennialists*, p. 35.

[77] *The Works of the Most Reverend Father in God, William Laud, D.D., Vol. I: Sermons*, ed. by William Scott (Oxford: John Henry Parker, 1847), pp. 19-20.

[78] de Jong, *As the Waters Cover the Sea*, p. 25.

[79] *The Court and Times of James the First: Vol. II*, ed. by Robert Folkestone Williams (London: Henry Colburn, 1848), p. 250; *cf.* Joseph Mede, *A Paraphrase and Exposition of the Prophecie of Saint Peter, concerning the Day of Christ's Second Comming; described in the Third Chapter of his Second Epistle* (London: 1642), p. 9.

believed that the 'temple' of 2 Thess. 2:4 referred to the Church, and not the Jerusalem Temple.[80] Nevertheless, the works of Alsted and Mede 'suggested to Puritan preachers that sound Biblical exegesis demanded that the millennium of Revelation 20 be viewed as in the future, not in the past or present'.[81]

Oliver Cromwell and the Readmission of the Jews

What makes the Puritan form of Restorationism so fascinating is that it developed in the absence of any official Jewish presence in England. In fact, the lot of the Jews had been a 'peculiarly miserable'[82] one since they landed on English shores with William the Conqueror in 1066. The prosperity they achieved as moneylenders, coupled with the anti-Semitic climate of the Crusades, aroused strong feelings of envy, suspicion, and hatred towards them. The Jewish communities of Norwich and Lincoln, for example, were subjected to the notorious 'blood libel' in 1144 and 1255, following the deaths of young William of Norwich and Hugh of Lincoln respectively. The exile of the Jews from England in 1290 did not prevent Geoffrey Chaucer (c.1343-1400) from tainting English literature with the mark of anti-Semitism in his *Prioress's Tale*.[83] Similarly, Christopher Marlowe's *The Jew of Malta* and William Shakespeare's *The Merchant of Venice* helped foment anti-Jewish sentiment by creating a grotesque Jewish caricature which ensured that the Jews remained an 'incessantly victimised'[84] people.

After Richard I embarked on his crusade to the Holy Land in 1190, Jewish communities in England were subjected to mob riots, culminating in the massacre of Jews in York on 16 March 1190. Throughout the Middle Ages the English not only helped to propagate the *adversus Judaeos* ('against the Jews') theology of replacement, but formulated ecclesiastical legislation which kept the Jewish people in *servitus Judeorum* ('perpetual servitude'). During the Fourth Lateran Council in 1215, Pope Innocent III decreed that all Jews under

---

[80] Joseph Mede, *Daniels Weekes: An Interpretation of Part of the Prophecy of Daniel* (London: 1643), p. 33. In contrast, William Twisse, the renowned prolocutor for the Westminster Assembly of Divines and author of the preface to *The Key of the Revelation*, believed that once the Jews had been restored by God to the Land, the Antichrist, or '*Grand Seignior*', would 'raise all his power gathered together out of all Nations under him to oppose them, and at first shall prevail'. (William Twisse, 'A Preface Written by Doctor Twisse, Showing the Method and Excellency of Mr Mede's Interpretation of this Mysterious Book of the Revelation of Saint John', in Joseph Mede, *The Key of the Revelation*, trans. by Richard More [London: 1643], p. 9.)

[81] Toon, *Puritans*, p. 7.

[82] H. Grattan Guinness, *Light for the Last Days: A Study in Chronological Prophecy*, Revised edn (London: Morgan & Scott Ltd., 1917), p. 134.

[83] Geoffrey Chaucer, *The Canterbury Tales* (London: Marshall Cavendish Partworks Ltd., 1988), p. 179.

[84] Guinness, *Light for the Last Days*, p. 134.

his jurisdiction were to wear a linen patch over their outer garments as a badge of identification. This decree was enforced in England in 1218 by the Papal-appointed archbishop of Canterbury, Stephen Langton, who, at the Council of Oxford in 1222, forbade Jews from building new synagogues. With the emergence of the Italian bankers, or 'pope's usurers', Jewish moneylenders were no longer indispensable, and in 1275, Edward I passed the Statute of Judaism forbidding Jews from engaging in such business. In 1290, the fate of English Jewry was sealed when a royal edict was issued calling for the immediate expulsion of all Jews from British shores. Although Portuguese Sephardic merchants such as Antonio Fernandez Carvajal (c.1590-1659) were granted rights of residency in London during the exile, there was no *official* Jewish presence in England until the edict was repealed by Charles II in 1660.

Captivated by Hebrew

As sixteenth-century life in England became increasingly centred around the Bible, 'the Old Testament regained a place of honour next to the New, and the "language of Canaan" spoken by God to the Israelites became a tool of Biblical scholarship much in demand.'[85] As early as 1530, Henry VIII had secured the services of Italian Hebraist Marco Raphael to aid him in his dispute with the Pope over his divorce proceedings against Catherine of Aragon.[86] Other Hebraists, such as John Immanuel Tremellius, were soon employed in English universities and 'familiarised the Englishman, for the first time for three centuries, with the existence and the appearance of the authentic Jew'.[87] By the time Puritan scholars began travelling to the Continent to sit at the feet of the rabbis, 'most Englishmen agreed that God spoke Hebrew',[88] which they described as the language of Eden[89] and of Heaven itself.[90] Even the Act of Uniformity in 1549, which required all public worship to be conducted in English rather than Latin and established the Book of Common Prayer as the only legal form of worship, effectively authorised the *private* use of Hebrew in this country. These developments did not escape the attention of the Jewish communities of Europe, which had been largely supportive of the English during Queen Elizabeth's struggle with the Spanish.

---

[85] David S. Katz, *The Jews in the History of England 1485-1850* (Oxford: Clarendon Press, 1994), p. 110.
[86] David S. Katz, *Philo-Semitism and the Readmission of the Jews to England 1603-1655* (Oxford: Clarendon Press, 1982), p. 10.
[87] Cecil Roth, *A History of the Jews in England*, 3rd edn (Oxford: Clarendon Press, 1964), p. 148.
[88] Katz, *Philo-Semitism*, p. 44.
[89] Nigel Smith, 'The Uses of Hebrew in the English Revolution', in *Language, Self and Society: A Social History of Language*, ed. by Peter Burke and Roy Porter (Cambridge: Polity Press, 1991), p. 56.
[90] Wilson, *Our Father Abraham*, p. 128.

English poetry proved a popular medium for expressing the growing concern for the plight of the Jews. George Herbert and Henry Vaughan produced 'the most extensive Anglican verse on the Jews in that period',[91] and in so doing reflected the predominantly *conversionist* theology of early seventeenth-century Anglicanism. Herbert, for example, poetically prayed 'that some Angel might a trumpet sound; at which the Church falling upon her face should cry so loud, until the trump were drowned, and by that cry of her dear Lord obtain, that your sweet sap might come again!'[92] Alluding to Romans 11, Vaughan wrote of his desire to 'see the Olive bear her proper branches', convinced that

> He who loved the world so, as to give His only Son to make it free, whose spirit too does mourn and grieve to see man lost, will for old love from your dark heart this veil remove.[93]

However, it was the controversy fuelled by Sabbatarian extremists such as John Traske (c.1585-1636), who believed that Christians were obliged to keep some of the laws of Moses, which proved the catalyst for the first public debate in England since 1290 on the relationship between Christians and Jews.[94]

As the seventeenth century progressed, the call for religious tolerance, as set forth in Leonard Busher's tract, *Religious Peace or a Plea for Liberty of Conscience* (1614), grew louder. During the Interregnum years (1649-1660), the study of Biblical Hebrew was stimulated by the expectation 'that the Jews might return to England, as a prelude to the second coming of Christ.'[95] In his pamphlet, *An Apology for the Honourable Nation of the Jews, and all the Sons of Israel* (1648), Edward Nicholas indicted the English for their crimes against 'the most honourable Nation of the world'. Citing Jeremiah's prophecy that 'all who devour you will be devoured' (Jer. 30:16), Nicholas claimed that many of the calamities which had befallen England were due to 'the transcendency of this sin'.[96] He warned that without national repentance, God would withdraw His favour and protection. In his pamphlet he also outlined 'the many promises made by God by the mouths of his Prophets' concerning the return of the Jews to 'their own country'. Ezekiel 37 was proof, he believed, that the Land of Israel was 'lawfully theirs, by the donation of God Himself', but that 'their restoration and inhabitation of their country here on Earth' was 'yet to be

---

[91] Nabil I. Matar, 'George Herbert, Henry Vaughan, and the Conversion of the Jews', *Studies in English Literature 1500-1900*, 30.1 (Winter, 1990), 79.

[92] George Herbert, 'The Jews', in *The Works of George Herbert*, ed. by F.E. Hutchinson (Oxford: Clarendon Press, 1978), p. 152.

[93] Henry Vaughan, 'The Jews', in *The Works of Henry Vaughan*, 2nd edn, ed. by L.C. Martin (Oxford: The Clarendon Press, 1957), pp. 499-500.

[94] Katz, *The Jews*, p. 112.

[95] Smith, 'The Uses of Hebrew', p. 52.

[96] Edward Nicholas, *An Apology for the Honourable Nation of the Jews, and all the Sons of Israel* (London: 1648), pp. 4-5.

fulfilled'.[97]

In 1649, English Puritans Joanna Cartwright and her son Ebenezer called upon England to readmit the Jews by presenting to Lord Fairfax *The Petition of the Jewes for the Repealing of the Act of Parliament for their Banishment out of England*. This first petition for Jewish readmission encouraged England to be 'the first and the readiest to transport Israel's sons and daughters in their ships to the Land promised to their forefathers, Abraham, Isaac and Jacob for an everlasting Inheritance.'[98]

Menasseh ben Israel

According to Lucien Wolf, Menasseh ben Israel (1604-1657) 'must always hold the chief place on the first page of the history of the present Anglo-Jewish community.' Following the slaughter of Jews in Eastern Europe in the aftermath of the Thirty Years' War (1618-1648), Ben Israel, the chief rabbi of Amsterdam, petitioned Oliver Cromwell for help. In his appeal he spoke of the Jewish hope of restoration to their ancient homeland:

> For I conceived that our universal dispersion was a necessary circumstance, to be fulfilled before all that shall be accomplished which the Lord hath promised to the people of the *Jews*, concerning their restoration, and their returning again into their own land, according to those words, *Dan.12,7*…And I knew not, but that the Lord who often works by natural means, might have designed and made choice of me for the bringing about this work. With these proposals therefore, I applied myself, in all zealous affection to the *English Nation*, congratulating their glorious liberty which at this day they enjoy.[99]

Ben Israel's most famous work, *The Hope of Israel* (1650), was inspired by the explorer, Antonius Montezinus, who, in 1644, persuaded him that the first inhabitants of America were descended from the so-called 'lost tribes' of Israel, and that many other descendants had been located in other parts of the world, particularly in South America.[100] Translated by Moses Wall for the benefit of those who were waiting for the redemption of Israel,[101] *The Hope of Israel* was

---

[97] Nicholas, *An Apology*, pp. 7-9.

[98] Tuchman, *Bible and Sword*, p. 121.

[99] *Menasseh ben Israel's Mission*, ed. by Wolf, pp. vii, xvi.

[100] Shalom Goldman, 'Introduction', in *Hebrew and the Bible in America: The First Two Centuries*, ed. by Shalom Goldman (London: University Press of New England, 1993), pp. xiv-xv. Puritan interest in the 'lost tribes' can be traced back to an essay by Queen Elizabeth's ambassador to Russia, Giles Fletcher, which was printed in Samuel Lee's book, *Israel Redux: or, the Restauration of Israel* (1677).

[101] Menasseh ben Israel, *The Hope of Israel*, 2nd edn, trans. by Moses Wall (London: 1651), preface; cf. Moses Wall, 'Considerations upon the Point of the Conversion of the Jews', in Ben Israel, *The Hope of Israel*, p. 50.

dedicated 'to the Parliament, the Supreme Court of England, and to the Right Honourable the Council of State'. Ben Israel had been encouraged by the correspondence he had exchanged for several years with the eminent Englishman, John Dury, who assured him that the readmission of the Jews had been favourably considered. He also corresponded with German Protestant Henry Oldenburg, later secretary of the Royal Society and Dury's son-in-law. In a letter to Ben Israel, dated 4 August 1657, Oldenburg expressed 'the love' which he bore 'for the well-being' of the Jewish people. Having discovered an unpublished work in France entitled, *They that Arouse the Dawn*, which spoke tenderly of Israel's restoration, he wrote:

> I for my part, most honoured Sir, am convinced that those prophecies which were made to you in the books of Moses and of the Prophets concerning your return to the land of Judah and your perennial happiness therein were by no means fulfilled on your return from the Babylonian captivity. Indeed, although the Holy Land was recovered at that time, nevertheless you never enjoyed then that liberty and that flourishing state which the prophecies announced...It is hence to be concluded that they will come to pass in the future.

Not wishing to arouse opposition from the Orthodox community in Amsterdam, which opposed any human agency involved in Israel's restoration, Ben Israel sent his son Samuel and brother-in-law David Dormido to England in 1654 with his petition for the readmission of the Jews. Despite Cromwell's support, the petition was rejected. Ben Israel decided to travel to England in person, and writing to his kinsmen on 2 September 1655 reassured them that England was 'no longer our ancient enemy, but has changed the papistical religion and become excellently affected to our nation'.[102] On 31 October 1655, he presented his *Humble Address...in Behalf of the Jewish Nation* to the Lord Protector, hoping to secure for his people the liberty to pray in their own synagogue, 'and besides to sue also for a blessing upon this Nation, and People of England, for receiving us into their bosoms, and comforting Zion in her distress.'

Ben Israel observed how 'the opinion of many Christians and mine do concur herein, that we both believe that the restoring time of our Nation into their Native Country, is very near at hand'. He knew that, according to Biblical prophecy, the Jews had to be dispersed to every nation before Messiah would come and re-establish them in the Land, and therefore believed that it was imperative for the Jews to return to England.[103] Cromwell welcomed the petition, sharing many of the rabbi's convictions,[104] and on 4 December 1655

---

[102] *Anglo-Jewish Letters (1158-1917)*, ed. by Cecil Roth (London: The Soncino Press, 1938), pp. 48-51.

[103] *Menasseh ben Israel's Mission*, ed. by Wolf, pp. 78-79.

[104] In his speech at Whitehall to the Nominated Parliament on 4 July 1653, Cromwell referred to Psalm 68 and declared that 'it may be, as some think, God will bring the Jews home to their station from the isles of the sea'. (Wilbur Cortez Abbott, *The Writings and*

convened a conference in Whitehall to consider the readmission of the Jews. This gathering of statesmen, lawyers, merchants, and theologians has been described as 'the culmination of the English philo-semitic movement'.[105]

Athough no decision was reached at Whitehall, Cromwell had shown 'a favourable inclination towards our harbouring the afflicted Jews, (professing he had no engagements but upon scriptural grounds) in several Speeches that he made.'[106] Despite *unofficially* rescinding the expulsion edict of 1290, significant opposition arose in the form of a pamphlet war, which was orchestrated by William Prynne.[107] In his own narrative of the Whitehall proceedings, Henry Jesse expressed grave concerns that if the Jewish people were not readmitted at once, 'the Lord may show his displeasure to be great against England'.[108] Finally, after the restoration of the monarchy in 1660, Jews were *officially* welcomed back to England and granted the protection of the King.

The Fifth Monarchists

For those who became known as the Fifth Monarchy Men,[109] the millennial reign of Christ was their rallying cry and the Law of Moses their banner.[110] Opposing the monarchy of Charles I and later the Protectorate of Oliver Cromwell, they sought to establish a Sanhedrin of saints which would bring England into full subjection to Christ, the only true monarch. Mostly Baptists and Independents, they pronounced God's judgment on the world while assuring themselves of a special role in the coming kingdom.[111]

The Fifth Monarchists believed that they were fulfilling Nebuchadnezzar's dream of the rock, which destroys the statue of empires and fills the earth (Dan. 2:29-45). In *The Little Horn's Doom & Downfall; or, a Scripture prophesie of King James, and King Charles, and of this present parliament unfolded* (1651), Mary Cary perceived the restoration of the twelve tribes of Israel to be an integral part of the establishment of Christ's reign upon the earth. Nathaniel Homes insisted that the 'most distinguishable' nation of the Jews

---

Speeches of Oliver Cromwell: Vol. III [Cambridge, MA: Harvard University Press, 1945], p. 65.)

[105] Katz, *Philo-Semitism*, p. 196.

[106] Henry Jesse, *A Narrative of the Late Proceeds at Whitehall, concerning the Jews* (London: 1656), p. 10.

[107] *Menasseh ben Israel's Mission*, ed. by Wolf, pp. 107-147.

[108] Jesse, *A Narrative*, p. 7.

[109] They included Mary Cary, John Carew, John Tillinghast, Thomas Harrison, Robert Overton, Christopher Feake, John Canne, Vavasor Powell, John Rogers, Thomas Venner, John Spittlehouse, and William Aspinwall.

[110] Capp, *The Fifth Monarchy Men*, p. 14.

[111] Harrison, *The Second Coming*, p. 183.

shall not pass away to be changed into another people, or mixedly drowned, as an ingredient among many others to extinguish their name and Genealogies.

Homes believed, however, that the future of the Jewish people lay ultimately within a universal and glorified Church on earth, maintaining that their conversion and restoration would prepare the way for the 'fifth Monarchy of the Saints reigning on earth under Christ'.[112]

Welsh itinerant preacher and Fifth Monarchist, Vavasor Powell (1617-1670), concluded his *Useful Concordance to the Holy Bible* with a section entitled, 'A Collection of the Prophecies which Concern the Calling of the Jews, and the Glory that shall be in the Latter Days'. Citing numerous prophecies, Powell declared that the Jewish nation 'shall be gathered from all parts of the Earth where they are now scattered, and brought home into their own land', that Jesus Christ 'shall appear at the head of them', and that, having been restored and 'converted to the Faith of Christ', the Jews 'shall be formed into a state, and have Judges and Counsellors over them as formerly'. He believed that the Land itself 'shall be made eminently fruitful', that 'Jerusalem shall be rebuilt, and after the full Restoration of the Jews, shall never be destroyed nor infested with Enemies anymore', and that shortly before their conversion 'there shall be great Wars, Confusion and Desolation throughout all the Earth.'[113] Powell viewed the restoration and conversion of God's people as a precursor to Christ's millennial reign. His *Concordance* was recommended by Puritan theologian, chaplain, and 'favourite preacher'[114] of Cromwell, John Owen (1616-1683).

More than any other movement during this period, the Fifth Monarchists represented 'the total fusion of millenarian theology and political extremism'.[115] Thomas Harrison and Robert Overton had served under Cromwell in the New Model Army, and were among the first to enlist in the battle to establish Christ's millennial rule on earth. As Ball writes, 'It was the sword that set the

---

[112] Nathaniel Homes, *The Resurrection Revealed: or The Dawning of the Day-Star, about to rise, and radiate a visible incomparable glory, far beyond any, since the Creation, upon the Universal Church on Earth, for a Thousand Years yet to come, before the ultimate Day, of the General Judgment: To the raising of the Jews, and the ruin of all Antichristian, and secular powers, that do not love the Members of Christ, submit to his Laws, and advance his interest in this Design* (London: 1654), pp. 83-84, 505.

[113] Vavasor Powell, *An Useful Concordance to the Holy Bible, with the various Acceptations contained in the Scriptures, and Marks to distinguish Commands, Promises, and Threatenings. Also a Curious Collection of Similies, Synonymous Phrases, and Prophecies, relating to the Call of the Jews, and the Glory that shall be in the Latter Days*, 2nd edn (London: n.d.), p. 543.

[114] Gribben, *The Puritan Millennium*, p. 151.

[115] *Puritans*, ed. by Toon, p. 66.

Fifth Monarchists apart. Militancy was their hallmark.'[116] This 'amorphous'[117] band of millenarians, with their over-realised eschatology, sent shock waves throughout England. Millenarianism was no longer the property of the nation but of a party, having fallen into the hands of those 'who rejected the mediation of king, bishop or prince.'[118] Despite the writings of philo-Semites like Henry Archer and Robert Maton, 'the Jews fell into the background'[119] as the *spiritual* reign of Christ was emphasised and the future restoration of Israel downplayed. By 1661, however, 'Fifth Monarchism as a revolutionary creed was dead.'[120]

Sabbatai Zevi

Many Puritans were gripped with excitement after rumours came out of Constantinople in 1648 that the Jewish mystic, Sabbatai Zevi (1626-1676), had publicly pronounced the ineffable Name of God, thereby declaring himself to be the Messiah. Responding to these rumours, Henry Oldenburg wrote to the Dutch philosopher, Baruch Spinoza, on 8 December 1665:

> Everyone here talks of the rumour that the Israelites, who had been scattered more than two thousand years, are about to return to their native land. Only few here believe it, but many desire it…As for me, I cannot believe it so long as the news is not confirmed by trustworthy men in Constantinople…which, if confirmed, should cause all things in the world to be changed.[121]

Having declared his intention to lead the Jews back to their ancient homeland, Zevi set 1666 as the year of restoration. Renowned diarist, Samuel Pepys, was among those caught up in the excitement. However, a second war with Holland (1665-1667), the Black Death (1665), and the Great Fire of London (1666) diverted England's attention away from this pseudo-messiah. The messianic fervour finally fizzled out in 1666 when Zevi was arrested by the Ottomans and converted to Islam.[122] For the next hundred years little interest was shown in the restoration of the Jews, and few books written on the subject, as the 'minimal creed'[123] of the Enlightenment trespassed on the authority and inspiration of the

---

[116] Ball, *A Great Expectation*, p. 185.

[117] Gribben, *The Puritan Millennium*, p. 50.

[118] William M. Lamont, *Godly Rule: Politics and Religion, 1603-60* (London: Macmillan and Co. Ltd., 1969), p. 107.

[119] Hill, 'Till the Conversion of the Jews', p. 21.

[120] Christopher Hill, *The Experience of Defeat* (London: Faber & Faber, 1984), p. 66.

[121] Kobler, *The Vision was There*, pp. 33-34; *cf.* Gershom Scholem, *Sabbatai Sevi: The Mystical Messiah 1626-1676*, trans. by R.J. Zwi Werblowsky (Princeton, NJ: Princeton University Press, 1973), pp. 101-102, 333-336.

[122] Da Costa, *Israel and the Gentiles*, pp. 474-484.

[123] John Arthur Oddy, *Eschatological Prophecy in the English Theological Tradition c.1700 - c.1840* (PhD: University of London, 1982), p. 35.

Bible. Although eschatology 'fell upon hard times'[124] during this period, there were still those who faithfully kept the premillennial torch burning.

The Eighteenth-Century Awakening

One of the chief torchbearers of the eighteenth century was Bishop Thomas Newton (1704-1782). In the seventh of his twenty-six *Dissertations on the Prophecies* (1754), Newton marvelled at the uniqueness of the Jewish nation which, 'like the bush of Moses, hath been always burning, but is never consumed'. He insisted that if God's *judgments* had been poured out upon Israel to the letter, then so too would His promised *blessings*; God was faithful and true. Noting how the Jews had been 'most cruelly used and persecuted' in 'the worst of popish countries', he believed that it was the responsibility of the *true* Church to 'choose rather to be the dispensers of God's mercies than the executioners of his judgments.'[125] It is interesting to note that an article written by Newton was included in a series of extracts published for the instruction and improvement of young people. Believing that the fulfilment of prophecies relating to Israel was an 'unanswerable argument for the truth of the Bible', he wrote:

> And what a marvellous thing is it, that after so many wars, battles, and sieges, after so many fires, famines, and pestilences, after so many rebellions, massacres, and persecutions, after so many years of captivity, slavery, and misery, they are not destroyed utterly, and though scattered among all people, yet subsist as a distinct people by themselves? Where is any thing comparable to this to be found in all the histories, and in all the nations under the sun?[126]

In 1721, Joseph Perry published his book on the millennial reign of Christ, highlighting the imminency of the Second Coming and the preceding time of Jacob's trouble. He also stressed the importance of Acts 1:6-8, insisting that there was 'nothing in the answer' given to the disciples 'that Christ reprehends them for'.[127] Samuel Collet dedicated his own *Treatise of the Future Restoration of the Jews and Israelites to their own Land* (1747) to the Jews,

---

[124] Gribben, 'Introduction: Antichrist in Ireland', p. 8.

[125] Thomas Newton, *Dissertations on the Prophecies, which have remarkably been fulfilled, and at this time are fulfilling in the world: Vol. I* (London: 1754), pp. 191, 242.

[126] Thomas Newton, 'The Fulfilment of the Mosaical Prophecies concerning the Jews as Unanswerable Argument for the Truth of the Bible', in Vicesimus Knox, *Elegant Extracts: or, Useful and Entertaining Passages in Prose, Selected for the Improvement of Young Persons*, 8th edn (London: [1803]), p. 234.

[127] Joseph Perry, *The Glory of Christ's Visible Kingdom in this World, asserted, proved, and explained, in its two-fold branches; first spiritual, secondly personal* (Northampton: 1721), p. 157.

> to show, that you, who are now dispersed among the Nations, will, in a short time, with the rest of the *Israelites*, be restored to your own Land, and enjoy there the greatest Prosperity, and that, through you, all the Nations will be blessed.[128]

Arguably the most significant work of this period was Joseph Eyre's *Observations upon the Prophecies relating to the Restoration of the Jews* (1771). Written in response to Bishop William Warburton's allegorical approach to Scripture, which denied Israel's future restoration, Eyre's work was listed in Joshua Brooks' *Dictionary of Writers on the Prophecies* (1835). In the aftermath of the Evangelical Awakening, Eyre reminded the Church that the new dawn spoken of by the prophets

> appears to me to be no way applicable to any state of Christianity that has ever yet existed, but to relate to the conversion and restoration of the *literal Israel*, the *Jews* and ten tribes, in the latter times, and to that reign of Christ when the church shall be *triumphant*; before which period I apprehend it to be only a church *militant*, either suffering persecution, or struggling with heresy, error, and superstition. That the kingdom of HEAVEN, of CHRIST, or of GOD, (all which are synonymous terms) is already come, tho' asserted by most of our theological writers, is in my judgment a position by no means agreeable to Scripture.

In his book, Eyre cited numerous prophecies 'to confute the opinion of those who deny any future Restoration of *Israel*'. He described Ezekiel 36-39 as 'the longest and most entire Prophecy in the whole Bible, concerning the future restoration of both *Judah* and *Israel*', and expressed indignation towards 'metaphorical commentators' who, if allowed, would 'render the whole of the sacred writings unintelligible and uncertain'. Identifying 'the elect' in Matt. 24:22 as Jewish, he stressed the importance of Acts 1:6-8 with these words:

> Now can it be imagined, that if the Apostles had been in an error of such consequence, our Lord would not have endeavoured to set them right, and have answered in some such manner as he did to the Sadducees, *Ye do err, not knowing the Scripture*…If therefore the kingdom is never to be restored to *Israel*, our Lord here informed his Apostles, that God had put in his own power the times and seasons of that which was never to happen; but this is a manner of speaking that is inconsistent with common sense: how much more so with divine wisdom![129]

In his *Dissertation on the Prophecies relating to the Final Restoration of the*

---

[128] Samuel Collet, *A Treatise of the Future Restoration of the Jews and Israelites to their own Land. With some Account of the Goodness of the Country, and their Happy Condition there, till they shall be Invaded by the Turks: With their Deliverance from all their Enemies, when the Messiah will establish his Kingdom at Jerusalem, and bring in the last Glorious Ages. Addressed to the Jews* (London: 1747), p. iii.

[129] Joseph Eyre, *Observations upon the Prophecies relating to the Restoration of the Jews* (London: 1771), pp. viii-ix, 48, 53, 121-122.

Jews (1784), Church of England rector and historian, Edward W. Whitaker (1752-1818), suggested that the key to understanding Biblical prophecy lay in distinguishing between the Abrahamic and Sinaitic Covenants, the former containing 'an absolute assurance of everlasting possession, and a grant, never to be defeated, of the promised land to Abraham and his seed'.[130] In his *Remarks on the Signs of the Times* (1798), Edward King argued that the Christian world was 'too backward to believe, and apprehend, what is really written' about Christ's return, having been 'blinded by their constant habit of contending against the Jews'. He accused theologians of making a 'presumptuous mystical application' of Israel's promises to the Church, and of failing to understand that the Jews were to be restored to the Land *before* their conversion and '*in a time of great trouble*'. He added: 'We approach unto the latter days! – I tremble whilst I write!'[131] Although Whitaker and King should not be squeezed into a Christian Zionist mould, their inclusion serves to emphasise a shift in eighteenth-century Evangelical theology, which paved the way for a more developed form of Restorationism in the nineteenth century.

Missionary-minded Evangelicals like William Cooper, Henry Hunter,[132] and Claudius Buchanan, the 'leading Anglican apologist for missions among Jews',[133] did much to stimulate interest in the Jewish people. Cooper, a London bookbinder's apprentice, frequently addressed congregations of Jews and Gentiles in Whitechapel, London, and was regularly featured in the Scottish *Missionary Magazine*. He acknowledged Israel's priority in salvation, numbered himself among the 'Gentile dogs', and reminded his fellow Christians to view 'the ancient Israel of God' with 'rapturous delight and veneration'. In his sermon, *The Promised Seed* (1796), he declared:

> It is evident from their present condition, which is nothing less than a standing miracle, that they are preserved for some very extraordinary event...Look at a Jew, and you see a miracle; - his nation is stamped on his countenance; and it is an honourable nation...Look at a Jew, and you are a witness of the accomplishment of all the threatenings of Moses and the prophets. Behold a Jew, and you see an expectant of the fulfilment of the Scriptures, and a monument of their veracity; for the time will come, I hope it is near, when all Israel shall be saved.[134]

---

[130] Edward Whitaker, *A Dissertation on the Prophecies relating to the Final Restoration of the Jews* (London: 1784), p. 32.

[131] Edward King, *Remarks on the Signs of the Times* (London: 1798), pp. 23-27.

[132] Henry Hunter, *The Rise, Fall, and Future Restoration of the Jews* (London: 1806).

[133] de Jong, *As the Waters Cover the Sea*, p. 195.

[134] William Cooper, *The Promised Seed: A Sermon, Preached to God's Ancient Israel, the Jews, at Sion-Chapel, Whitechapel, on Sunday afternoon, August 28, 1796*, 3rd edn (London: 1796), pp. 14, 9, 34; *cf. Christ the True Messiah: A Sermon, Preached, at Sion-Chapel, Whitechapel, to God's Ancient Israel, the Jews, on Sunday, August 28,*

Frequently cited in eighteenth and nineteenth-century millenarian writings is the work of esteemed Bible scholar and bishop, Samuel Horsley (1733-1806). Described as 'the leading exponent of orthodoxy' and 'the most distinguished spokesman for the Church in the decade of the French Revolution',[135] he is perhaps best remembered for his controversy with the Unitarian minister, Joseph Priestley. In his exposition of Hosea, Horsley sought to correct the 'great mistake' of 'the most learned expositors', namely their long-standing 'prejudice' against 'the future exaltation of the Jewish nation'. He believed that by applying prophecies 'unnaturally' to the Church, scholars had 'wrapt the writings of all the prophets in tenfold obscurity, and those of Hosea more than the rest'. Horsley claimed that the spiritualisation of Biblical prophecy 'had obtained a general currency in the world...supported by the authority of great names', although within his own circles it had

> long been the persuasion of our best Biblical scholars and ablest divines, that the restoration of the Jews is a principal article of the prophecy, being, indeed, a principal branch of the great scheme of general redemption.[136]

In Conclusion

Franz Kobler has aptly described the Puritan era as 'the cradle'[137] of Restorationism. The Christian revival of interest in the Jewish people, and in Biblical prophecies pertaining to their return to *Eretz Yisrael*, owed much to the restoration of Biblical authority in the Church after centuries of Roman Catholic oppression. However, the dispensational premillennialism which John Nelson Darby espoused was *not* anticipated by the English Puritans. Certain *strands* of his eschatology were clearly evident in the writings of men like Sir Henry Finch and Hugh Broughton, but Christian Zionism as a composite whole did not appear until Darby's convalescence in Dublin, when the fundamental distinction between Israel and the Church, along with a *futurist* interpretation of the last days, came into sharp focus. As the eighteenth century drew to a close, events in France and the Middle East conspired to transform the political landscape of Europe, convincing many in the Church that Biblical prophecy was the only basis for correctly interpreting the signs of the times.

1796 (London: 1796); *Daniel's Seventy Weeks: A Sermon Preached at Sion-Chapel, on Sunday afternoon, September 18, 1796, to the Jews*, 3rd edn (London: 1796).

[135] Sheridan Gilley, 'The Church of England in the Nineteenth Century', in *A History of Religion in Britain*, ed. by Sheridan Gilley and W.J. Sheils (Oxford: Blackwell, 1994), p. 294.

[136] Samuel Horsley, *Biblical Criticism on the first fourteen Historical Books of the Old Testament; also, on the first nine Prophetical Books: Vol. II*, 2nd edn (London: Longman, Brown, Green, & Longmans, 1844), pp. 135, 153.

[137] Kobler, 'Sir Henry Finch', p. 119.

This section would be incomplete without the mention of two brothers who were raised up by God in the eighteenth century to revive a dying nation and pierce the conscience of a slumbering Church. Without John Wesley (1703-1791) and his brother Charles (1707-1788), there would almost certainly have been no Evangelical Awakening in Britain. One of the legacies of the Wesley brothers was a renewed love for the Scriptures, which paved the way for nineteenth-century Evangelical interest in Biblical prophecy, and in the promised restoration of the Jews. Although the eschatology of the Wesley brothers is unclear, the following extract from one of their hymns, which John Wesley included in his *Collection of Hymns, For the Use of the People called Methodists* in 1779, suggests that they had more than a passing interest in the Jewish nation. The hymn appears in a section headed, 'For the Jews':

We know it must be done,
For God hath spoke the word:
All Israel shall the Saviour own,
To their first state restored:
Rebuilt by his command,
Jerusalem shall rise;
Her temple on *Moriah* stand
Again, and touch the skies.

Send then thy servants forth,
To call the Hebrews home;
From East, and West, and South, and North,
Let all the wanderers come:
Where'er in lands unknown
The fugitives remain,
Bid every creature help them on,
The Holy Mount to gain.

An offering to their Lord,
There let them all be seen,
Sprinkled with water and with blood,
In soul and body clean:
With Israel's myriads seal'd,
Let all the nations meet,
And show the mystery fulfill'd,
The family complete![138]

---

[138] John Wesley, *A Collection of Hymns, For the Use of the People called Methodists* (London: Wesleyan Conference Office, n.d.), pp. 423-424.

Chapter 6

Nineteenth-Century Restorationism

On 10 November 1790, Richard Beere, Anglican rector of Sudbrooke in Lincolnshire, wrote a letter to William Pitt, the Younger, which has been described as 'a memorable attempt – the first of its kind – to influence English foreign policy in favour of the restoration of the Jews'.[1] Convinced that restoration was imminent, Beere believed that the British Prime Minister had been raised up by God to effect the return of the Jewish exiles, just as Cyrus king of Persia had been during the Babylonian exile. He wrote:

> I hope you will endeavour to make a powerful exertion to effect this great purpose…And perhaps no man that ever trod the Stage of the Theatre of this World, ever had such an opportunity of doing this and acting so great a part, as you have on the present occasion.[2]

Beere hoped that Britain would 'comply with the will of God', not just from religious motives but 'from motives of sound policy'.[3]

This convergence of theology and politics was to be a consistent feature of nineteenth-century Restorationism, with the notable exception of Darby and the Brethren. When appraising nineteenth-century premillennialists who believed in the promised restoration of the Jews, it is imperative that we differentiate between the underlying *historicism* of men like Bickersteth, Drummond, Irving, and Hechler, and the underlying *futurism* of Darby, the Witherbys, and Burgh. I will therefore continue to classify *historicists* as Christian Restorationists, and *futurists* as Christian Zionists, a distinction which must be maintained in order to correctly identify and chart the course of Christian Zionism. Unfortunately, historians have typically been unwilling to engage in the complexities of Christian eschatology, and have overlooked the theological intricacies involved. This has led to misleading classifications and artificial genealogies which have served only to muddy the eschatological waters.

---

[1] Franz Kobler, *Napoleon and the Jews* (Jerusalem: Massada Press Ltd., 1975), p. 26.

[2] *Anglo-Jewish Letters*, ed. by Roth, p. 203.

[3] Richard Beere, *A Dissertation on the 13ᵗʰ and 14ᵗʰ verses of the 8ᵗʰ chapter of Daniel; containing strong and cogent arguments, to prove that the commencement of the final restoration of the Jews, to the Holy Land, is to take place in the ensuing year, A.D. 1791* (London: 1790), pp. 42-43.

The French Revolution

The rise of republicanism and the demise of the *ancien régime* in France prompted many Evangelicals to re-evaluate their approach to Biblical interpretation. The French Revolution was viewed by many as 'Prophecy's Rosetta Stone',[4] and the key which would 'unlock the treasure chest of Biblical prophecy.'[5] This was the age of the historicist, who interpreted Daniel's 1260 'days' as years, and typically dated the start of this period in AD529, when Byzantine Emperor Justinian codified Roman law in his *Codex Justinianus*. Four years later, Justinian issued a decretal epistle to the bishop of Rome, which effectively gave primacy to Rome on ecclesiastical matters, and in 534 reissued his codex in expanded form, thus bringing into effect the *Corpus Juris Civilis*. This formed the basis of civil law throughout the Roman Empire, and served to unite Church and state, confirm Papal supremacy, and ensure that Jews throughout the empire were kept in perpetual servitude. Historicists, who identified Antichrist with the Pope, believed that the 1260 'days' of 'Papal domination'[6] had ended with the outbreak of the French Revolution in 1789, the abolition of the French monarchy, the rise of Napoleon Bonaparte, and the exile of Pope Pius VI in 1798.

James Bicheno

In 1793, Baptist minister James Bicheno (1752-1831) expressed his belief that the French Revolution was a precursor to the Second Coming,[7] and that a chain of events had been set in motion which would lead to the overthrow of the papal Antichrist system. In 1800, he published *The Restoration of the Jews the Crisis of all Nations*, marvelling at how God had faithfully preserved His ancient covenant people:

> For the preservation of this people through such a sea of miseries, and through so many centuries, and for such purposes as the scriptures assert, is a long-continued miracle, more stupendous than all others which God has wrought in proof of divine revelation, and that which is admirably calculated, at the present crisis particularly, to excite our faith and confidence in the overruling providence of God, and to soothe and stay the mind, amidst the agitation of all the elements of human society, and under the expectation of calamities the most awful.

---

[4] Mark Rayburn Patterson, *Designing the Last Days: Edward Irving, the Albury Circle, and the Theology of The Morning Watch* (PhD: University of London, 2001), p. 44.
[5] David Hempton, *Religion and Political Culture in Britain and Ireland* (Cambridge: Cambridge University Press, 1996), p. 98.
[6] Elliott, *Horae Apocalypticae: Vol. III*, p. 244.
[7] James Bicheno, *The Signs of the Times: or, The Overthrow of the Papal Tyranny in France, the Prelude of Destruction to Popery and Despotism; but of Peace to Mankind* (London: 1793).

According to Bicheno, belief in Israel's restoration was not confined to 'a few obscure individuals of the present day', but had been 'the fixed opinion of the brightest luminaries of the Christian church in all ages'. He suggested that if the promised return of the Jews had been fulfilled when 42,360 exiles returned from Babylon (Ezra 2:64), or was to be applied spiritually to the Church, then the Bible was 'a mere nose of wax, which may be twisted to any thing'. Believing that God was about to raise up a European nation to facilitate restoration, Bicheno conceded that faith and politics were inseparable:

> I am weary of politics, and, in ordinary cases, above all things dislike their mixture with the subjects of religion; but here it is impossible to separate them, they are so originally, and necessarily, interwoven with the subject.[8]

Religion and politics were inextricably linked in the policies of Napoleon Bonaparte, a young French officer who emerged from Corsican obscurity to elevate the Jewish people to a position of unprecedented importance. In so doing, he transformed both the political *and* theological landscape of early nineteenth-century Europe. As Kobler explains,

> The encounter of the Jewish people with Napoleon was a turning point of Jewish history. For the first time, a modern statesman had envisaged the Jewish problem as a fundamental issue of international politics…Whether he fancied himself to be another Solomon who would rebuild the Temple of Jerusalem or a new Herod wielding authority over the dispersed nation, Napoleon considered the Jewish people as a partner in his world-wide plans.[9]

Napoleon's Proclamation

Despite the absence of a Jewish presence in Corsica during his childhood, Napoleon was fascinated with the Old Testament and the history of the Jews. After assuming command of the French Army in 1796, he liberated Jewish communities in Italy and Malta. Many Jews hailed him as *chelek tov* (Hebrew for Bona-parte, meaning 'Good Portion') and *ohev Israel* ('Lover of Israel'). According to Kobler, 'The elements of freedom and national revival which were inherent in Bonaparte's victories and reflected in his proclamations became manifest in the treatment of the Jews.'[10] Seeking to 'strike a blow'[11] at

---

[8] James Bicheno, *The Restoration of the Jews the Crisis of all Nations; to which is now prefixed, A Brief History of the Jews, from their First Dispersion, to the Calling of their Grand Sanhedrin at Paris, October 6th, 1806. And An Address on the Present State of Affairs, in Europe in General, and in this Country in Particular*, 2nd edn (London: 1807), pp. 2-3, 86, 127, 233.

[9] Kobler, *Napoleon and the Jews*, p. 213.

[10] Kobler, *Napoleon and the Jews*, p. 18.

England's Eastern Empire, Napoleon landed at Alexandria on 1 July 1798, and within a few months had shifted his focus to the Holy Land.

On the first day of Passover 1799, Napoleon issued a proclamation calling upon the Jews to rally under his banner '*pour rétablir l'ancienne Jérusalem*' (to restore old Jerusalem). Published in the French government newspaper, *Moniteur Universal de Paris*, the proclamation was intended to harness the support of world Jewry for his imperial cause by dangling before them the carrot of a restored homeland. Adopting the language of revolution and nationalism, Napoleon 'made free use of the fashionable dialect and called the Jews a nation',[12] an unprecedented step for a world leader to take. Despite his political aspirations and the ultimate failure of his 'Palestine' campaign, which 'radically altered the geo-political situation'[13] in the Middle East, Napoleon's appeal to the Jews 'indicated an awareness of the special connection between the Jewish people and the Land of Israel',[14] a connection he sought to destroy upon his return to France. Perceiving French Jews to be 'a nation within a nation',[15] Napoleon embarked on a new campaign to strip away their distinctiveness by persuading them to surrender autonomy, 'Become Frenchmen',[16] and thus 'find Jerusalem in France'.[17] For many Evangelicals in Britain, events had taken a sinister turn.

George Stanley Faber

Anglican theologian George Stanley Faber (1773-1854), an admirer of James Bicheno's work, believed that one of the 'many signs of the times' was the demise of the Ottoman Empire, which he claimed would 'prepare the way for the Return of the Ten Tribes' and 'synchronise with the Return of the Two Tribes.'[18] Diverging from mainstream historicism, he predicted that the 1260 'days' of the 'Papal and Mohammedan apostasies' would conclude in 1866, when the Jews would begin to return to their homeland. This, he believed,

---

[11] James Parkes, *Whose Land? A History of the Peoples of Palestine*, Revised edn (Harmondsworth: Penguin Books Ltd., 1970), p. 177.

[12] Philip Guedalla, *Napoleon and Palestine* (London: George Allen & Unwin Ltd., 1925), pp. 31-36.

[13] Crombie, *A Jewish Bishop in Jerusalem*, p. 8.

[14] Kelvin Crombie, *Anzacs, Empires and Israel's Restoration 1798-1948* (Osborne Park: Vocational Education & Training Publications, 1998), p. 41.

[15] Simon Schwarzfuchs, *Napoleon, the Jews and the Sanhedrin* (London: Routledge & Kegan Paul, 1979), p. 49.

[16] Alan Edelstein, *An Unacknowledged Harmony: Philo-Semitism and the Survival of European Jewry* (London: Greenwood Press, 1982), p. 138.

[17] Guedalla, *Napoleon and Palestine*, p. 35.

[18] George Stanley Faber, *The Predicted Downfall of the Turkish Power the Preparation for the Return of the Ten Tribes* (London: Thomas Bosworth, 1853), pp. 36, vii.

would signal a period of 'unexampled trouble'[19] for Jacob. Remarkably, in the light of Britain's future role, Faber was convinced that a maritime power would be raised up by God to aid Israel's restoration. As he wrote in *A General and Connected View of the Prophecies* (1808),

> I may add, that *we* of this great protestant maritime nation are *peculiarly* interested; for it certainly is not impossible, that we may be *the messenger-people* described by Isaiah as destined to take a very conspicuous part in the conversion and restoration of *Judah*. Hitherto we have been preserved, a column in the midst of surrounding ruins. While mighty empires totter to their base, and while *Antichrist* advances with rapid strides to his predicted sovereignty over the enslaved kings of the Roman earth; *we*, through the blessing of divine Providence, have attained to a pitch of naval pre-eminence unknown and unexampled in former ages. Such being our present circumstances, it is no less our interest as politicians, than our duty as Christians, to endeavour, each according to our opportunity and measure, to promote the conversion of *the house of Judah*.[20]

In a sermon preached on behalf of the LSPCJ in 1822, Faber asserted that *Jewish* believers were destined to become God's final, and most successful, missionaries on earth. He denounced those who, 'by the process of spiritualisation', had 'perverted' prophecies which spoke of 'the glory of the Lord' rising upon Zion (Isa. 60:1) by applying them to 'the Christian Church'.[21] Faber's underlying historicism was a departure from Darby's eschatology, although it is interesting to note that Darby possessed a copy of his book, *On the Mysteries of the Cabiri* (1803).

Signs of the Times

In 1840, a little known author by the name of J.B. Webb wrote *Naomi*, a novel set in the days of the Second Temple's destruction. It was written to attract 'the attention of the young and thoughtless to the wonderful fulfilment of the prophetic word of God'. In her preface, Webb made the following observation:

> The signs of the present times point strongly towards the Holy Land and the once glorious city of Jerusalem; and the eyes of many (both Jews and Gentiles) are

---

[19] George Stanley Faber, *A General and Connected View of the Prophecies, relative to the Conversion, Restoration, Union, and Future Glory, of the Houses of Judah and Israel; the Progress, and Final Overthrow, of the Antichristian Confederacy in the Land of Palestine; and the Ultimate General Diffusion of Christianity: Vol. I*, 2nd edn (London: 1809), pp. 20, 365.

[20] Faber, *A General and Connected View: Vol. II*, p. 340.

[21] George Stanley Faber, *The Conversion of the Jews to the Faith of Christ, the true Medium of the Conversion of the Gentile World. A Sermon [on Isa. 60:1-5] Preached before the London Society for Promoting Christianity amongst the Jews, 18 Ap. 1822, Covent Garden, Parish Church of St. Paul* (London: 1822), p. 17.

turned thither in anxious expectation of the approaching fulfilment of those promises of favour and restoration which are so strikingly set forth in Scripture, with reference to that land and her scattered and degraded people...Let us pray earnestly for their conversion and preparation to meet their expected Messiah; thus shall we be exercising the highest duties of Christian charity, and (if we may so express it) 'preparing the way of the Lord'.[22]

We recall how Darby himself made a similar observation that year when he wrote about the nations being 'occupied about Jerusalem'.[23] Some years later, Bishop J.C. Ryle proclaimed in a sermon on behalf of the LSPCJ that a

man must be blind who does not observe how much the attention of politicians and statesmen in these days is concentrating on the countries around Palestine...But I think I hear the voice of God saying, 'Remember the Jews, look to Jerusalem.'[24]

Although Evangelicals were not alone in taking 'an unusual interest...in Zion's stones and dust',[25] Darby, Webb, and Ryle believed that in the return of the Jews to the Land they were witnessing one of the most important 'signs' that Jesus had spoken about concerning His return (Luke 21:5-36; Matt. 24:1-35).

According to Robert Whalen, the tone of those who studied Biblical prophecy during 'the greatest century which Christianity had thus far known'[26] was 'sober and scholarly' and 'eminently respectable'.[27] With the founding of the LSPCJ, 'a new dimension was added to the relationship between the millennialists in England and the Jewish people.'[28]

The London Society for Promoting Christianity amongst the Jews

In his preface to *The Jews and their Evangelisation* (1899), a text-book written for the Student Volunteer Missionary Union, W.T. Gidney stated that the purpose of the LSPCJ was 'to interest Christians generally, and Missionary Students in particular, in the Evangelisation of God's ancient people Israel.'[29]

---

[22] J.B. Webb, *Naomi; or The Last Days of Jerusalem* (Edinburgh: W.P. Nimmo, Hay, & Mitchell, 1887), pp. 5-8.

[23] Darby, *The Hopes of the Church*, CW2:342.

[24] Ryle, *Are You Ready for the End of Time?*, p. 158.

[25] Wilkinson, *God's Plan for the Jew*, p. 92.

[26] Kenneth Scott Latourette, *A History of Christianity* (London: Eyre and Spottiswoode Limited, 1954), p. 1063.

[27] Robert K. Whalen, '"Christians Love the Jews!" The Development of American Philo-Semitism, 1790-1860,' *Religion and American Culture*, 6.2 (Summer, 1996), 240.

[28] Jonathan Frankel, *The Damascus Affair: 'Ritual Murder,' Politics and the Jews in 1840* (Cambridge: Cambridge University Press, 1997), p. 288.

[29] W.T. Gidney, *The Jews and their Evangelisation* (London: Student Volunteer Missionary Union, 1899), p. vii.

By the close of the nineteenth century, twenty-three missionary societies had been established in England and Scotland,[30] the LSPCJ being 'the oldest, as well as the most extensive',[31] in the world. This society became 'a major rallying point'[32] for Christians who believed in the promised return of the Jews.

On 4 August 1808, the London Society (for the Purpose of Visiting and Relieving the Sick and Distressed, and Instructing the Ignorant, especially such as are of the Jewish Nation) was established under the leadership of Joseph Frey, the son of a German rabbi.[33] On 1 March 1809, the Society changed its name to the London Society for Promoting Christianity amongst the Jews,[34] issuing its first report on 23 May 1809.[35] Annual reports reveal how widespread support for the LSPCJ was, its fourth report in 1812 including a letter from the Baptist missionary to India, William Carey. As Kelvin Crombie writes, 'The list of supporters reads like an evangelical and social *Who's Who*.'[36] Early vice-presidents included the Duke of Devonshire, along with seven earls, five viscounts, and several members of Parliament. In 1813, Queen Victoria's father, the Duke of Kent, was appointed patron.[37] After incurring considerable debts, the Society was brought under the jurisdiction of the Church of England in 1815. By 1829, the number of provincial auxiliary committees of the LSPCJ had risen to thirty-six.[38] From 1841, successive archbishops of Canterbury served as patron of the Society, now known as the Church's Ministry among Jewish People (CMJ), until 1992, when George Carey declined the office.[39]

Underlying Historicism

With so many Evangelicals associated with the LSPCJ, the question of how to

---

[30] Mel Scult, *Millennial Expectations and Jewish Liberties: A Study of the Efforts to Convert the Jews in Britain, up to the Mid Nineteenth Century* (Leiden: E.J. Brill, 1978), p. 90.

[31] W.T. Gidney, *The History of the London Society for Promoting Christianity amongst the Jews, from 1809-1908* (London: LSPCJ, 1908), p. 12.

[32] Frankel, *The Damascus Affair*, p. 288.

[33] Frey had initially arrived in London in 1801 to train as a missionary to Africa with the London Missionary Society (LMS).

[34] Lewis Way, *Reviewers Reviewed; or, Observations on Article II of the British Critic for January 1819, New Series, entitled, 'On the London Society for Converting the Jews'*, 2nd edn (London: 1819), p. 25.

[35] LSPCJ, *The First Report of the Committee of the London Society for Promoting Christianity amongst the Jews*, 2nd edn (London: 1819), p. 7.

[36] Kelvin Crombie, *For the Love of Zion* (London: Hodder & Stoughton, 1991), p. 13.

[37] Crombie, *ANZACS*, p. 45.

[38] Todd M. Endelman, *The Jews of Georgian England, 1714-1830* (Philadelphia, PA: Jewish Publication Society of America, 1979), pp. 72-73.

[39] Yaron Perry, *British Mission to the Jews in Nineteenth-Century Palestine* (London: Frank Cass, 2003), p. 199.

interpret Biblical prophecy became an issue. As Gidney explains,

> Some dissatisfaction was caused by certain prophetical views attributed to the Society, and, on a remonstrance from the Patrons, the Committee, on October 27th, 1823, disclaimed all intention of promulgating any particular views as to the nature of the Millennium, their object being the conversion of the Jews to vital Christianity, and they undertook that in the *Jewish Expositor*, a neutrality should be maintained on disputed prophetical points.[40]

The first, and most notable, casualty of this disclaimer was the vice-president, Lewis Way, whose unswerving premillennialism and insistence that the Jews would be restored to the Land *before* coming to faith in Christ led to his 'broken-hearted'[41] resignation. Patterson notes how ironic it was that 'the very issue that had brought the cause of the Jews to prominence'[42] separated Way from the Society in which he had played such a formative role. Although, as we shall see, the main thrust of the LSPCJ shifted towards evangelism, the outbreak of the Russian pogroms in 1881/2 prompted the Society to issue a statement expressing not only its 'deep sympathy' with the Jewish refugees, but its conviction that their 'trials' signalled 'the beginning of a fulfilment of the prophetic Scriptures foretelling the return of the Jews to their own land'. The Society saw events in Russia as 'a preparatory movement towards their complete uprooting in the lands of their adoption, leading them to turn their eyes to the land promised to their fathers for an everlasting inheritance.'[43]

Owing to the underlying historicism of the LSPCJ, or London Jews Society as it was more commonly known, Stephen Sizer's claim that 'Christian Zionism as a movement can be dated precisely to the founding of the London Jews Society'[44] is misleading. The LSPCJ was the spearhead of the Christian *Restorationist* movement, which was premillennial *and* political in essence but which failed to make the same clear, Biblical distinction between Israel and the Church which Darby and the Brethren made. Nevertheless, as we shall see, there were many areas of doctrinal agreement between them.

Edward Bickersteth

The name of Edward Bickersteth (1786-1850) is synonymous with the Church Missionary Society (CMS) and the Evangelical Alliance he helped to found. In

---

[40] Gidney, *The History of the London Society*, p. 71.

[41] A.M.W. Stirling, *The Ways of Yesterday: Being the Chronicles of the Way Family from 1307 to 1885* (London: Thornton Butterworth, Limited, 1930), p. 270.

[42] Patterson, *Designing the Last Days*, p. 50.

[43] Quoted in Crombie, *For the Love of Zion*, p. 109.

[44] Stephen R. Sizer, 'The Historical Roots of Christian Zionism from Irving to Balfour: Christian Zionism in the United Kingdom (1820-1918)', in Ateek, Duaybis, and Tobin, *Challenging Christian Zionism*, p. 21.

the light of what he described as the 'present very peculiar situation of the land of Judea, and of the Jewish nation', Bickersteth published a series of discourses on the restoration of the Jews which were designed to encourage the sober and earnest study of the Scriptures. He believed that the Bible was 'so full of large and rich hope, as to the future condition of this remarkable people,' and that a true understanding of Israel's restoration was necessary for 'the completeness of Christian faith'. He also prayed that England 'might be favoured among the nations of the earth in aiding the restoration of Israel!' Bickersteth was convinced that the promised return of the Jews to their land would serve as 'an ensign to all the inhabitants of the earth, of the return of the Lord', Jesus' response in Acts 1:6-8 having been phrased in such a way as 'to keep alive the attention of the church to this future glory of Israel'.[45]

Bickersteth was adamant that 'in their plain and obvious meaning' the promises of God spoke of Israel's 'perpetual possession' of the Land, and that it was necessary to 'freely restore to our brethren the Jews their own promises...without impoverishing our own stores of blessings'. For centuries the Church had done what was 'most hateful to God' by robbing the Jews of their inheritance 'under the assumption of superior spiritual discernment'.[46] This, he believed, owed much to the Church's persistent 'selfishness, unbelief and high-mindedness', which had made many Christians deaf to 'the warning note' of prophetic fulfilment being struck by the 'clock of Providence'. As he addressed the LSPCJ in 1834, 'The church has greatly lost the hope of Christ's speedy coming, and of the recovery of his people Israel.' Bickersteth claimed that only 'faithful Christians' who were taking a 'special and peculiar interest' in the Jewish people understood the signs of the times, and the need to proclaim 'a King returning to Zion, as well as a Redeemer crucified on Calvary'.[47]

Charles Simeon

Charles Simeon (1759-1836) was one of the most respected Evangelical leaders of the late eighteenth and early nineteenth centuries. He served as vicar of Holy Trinity, Cambridge, for fifty-four years, and helped found the CMS. Although his eschatology does not fit easily into a Darbyist mould, the sermons he preached on behalf of the LSPCJ, to which he was 'pre-eminently attached',[48] and the remarks he made in private towards the end of his life, reveal a deep-

---

[45] Edward Bickersteth, *The Restoration of the Jews to their own Land, in Connection with their Future Conversion and the Final Blessedness of our Earth*, 2nd edn (London: R.B. Seeley and W. Burnside, 1841), pp. ii, lxviii, xci, cxi, 111.

[46] Bickersteth, *The Restoration of the Jews*, pp. ix, xxiii, 34, 46.

[47] Bickersteth, *The Restoration of the Jews*, pp. xxxv, 148, xli, 82-83, lxxx, 65.

[48] Daniel Wilson, 'Recollections of the Rev Charles Simeon (1837)', in *Memoirs of the Life of the Rev. Charles Simeon*, 2nd edn, ed. by William Carus (London: J. Hatchard & Son, 1847), p. 844.

seated and Biblically-rooted interest not only in the *conversion* of the Jews, but in their *national restoration*. For this 'watchman'[49] on the walls of Jerusalem (*cf.* Isa. 62:6), the Jews were 'perhaps the warmest interest of his life'.[50]

Charles Simeon was a 'Bible Christian'.[51] In 1785, he acquired a copy of John Brown's *Self-Interpreting Bible*, which became 'the favourite companion of his devotional hours'. It is noteworthy that Brown included a section in his Bible entitled, *A Collection of the Prophecies which concern the Calling of the Jews, and the Glory which shall be in the Latter Days.* Simeon wrote to Brown on 19 January 1787 to express his appreciation:

> Your Self-interpreting Bible seems to stand in lieu of all other comments; and I am daily receiving so much edification from it, that I would wish it in the hands of all serious ministers. I have conceived a thought of purchasing a few to give to those godly ministers, who would find it very inconvenient to purchase it for themselves.[52]

Simeon's involvement with the Jews was primarily channelled through the LSPCJ, which he served for many years as 'a kind of one-man general staff, preaching for the Society, recruiting workers, spreading propaganda, collecting funds, advising on overall strategy'.[53] Along with Lewis Way and Alexander McCaul, he has been described as one of the 'three fathers of the Society'.[54]

Preaching on his 'favourite theme'[55] to as many as five thousand on one occasion,[56] Simeon consistently called for the Jews to be made a priority in prayer and proclamation.[57] He spoke of the Church's 'criminal'[58] indifference and prejudice towards the Jewish people, and suggested that if Christians were

---

[49] Bickersteth, *The Restoration of the Jews*, p. 52.

[50] H.C.G. Moule, *Charles Simeon* (London: Methuen & Co., 1892), p. 122.

[51] Robert S. Dell, 'Simeon and the Bible', in *Charles Simeon (1759-1836): Essays written in Commemoration of his Bi-Centenary by Members of the Evangelical Fellowship for Theological Literature*, ed. by Arthur Pollard and Michael Hennell (London: SPCK, 1959), p. 32.

[52] *Memoirs*, ed. by Carus, pp. 67-68; *cf.* John Brown, *The Self-Interpreting Bible* (Glasgow: Blackie & Son, 1845), p. xi.

[53] Arthur Pollard, 'The Influence and Significance of Simeon's Work', in Pollard and Hennell, *Charles Simeon*, p. 180.

[54] Gidney, *The History of the London Society*, p. 159.

[55] *Memoirs*, ed. by Carus, p. 819.

[56] Gidney, *The History of the London Society*, p. 61.

[57] Charles Simeon, *The Jews Provoked to Jealousy. A Sermon preached on Wednesday, June 5, 1811, at the Church of the United Parishes of St. Antholin and St. John Baptist, Watling Street* (London: 1811), p. 28.

[58] Charles Simeon, *The Conversion of the Jews; or, Our Duty and Encouragement to Promote it. Two Discourses, preached before the university of Cambridge, on February 18th and 25th, 1821* (London: 1821), p. 8.

more earnest in prayer then 'God would arise and have mercy upon Zion'.[59] He accused Britain of 'as universal and disgraceful an opposition to the Jews, as could well be expected from any civilised community', and the Church for being so 'altogether asleep' that 'to bring the subject before a Christian audience seems almost to require an apology'. He also accused ministers of being ignorant about Old Testament prophecy and the 'mystery' of Israel in Rom. 11:25, and admonished Christians in general for failing to understand God's mercy towards the Jewish people.[60] At Cambridge University in 1822, Simeon suggested that the sight of a Jew ought to 'cause our bowels to yearn over him'.[61] One of those who may have heard him preach that day was John Gifford Bellett, Darby's closest friend. In a letter to his brother George, Bellett wrote:

> I have lately heard two delightful sermons from Mr. Simeon, for the Jews, and indeed, he convicted me of having impiously and inhumanly disregarded them. He showed from Scripture that God appeared to have always sympathised with the sufferings of Jerusalem, even while denouncing vengeance against their sins, which is particularly exhibited in our Lord's lamentation over her while predicting her ruin.[62]

Stephen Sizer's claims that the 'growth of Christian Zionism within Anglican evangelical circles was undoubtedly shaped to a large degree by the initiatives of Charles Simeon', and that Simeon 'remained a postmillennialist and believed the millennium had already begun', confuses the issue on two counts. Firstly, Sizer incorporates a postmillennial eschatology into his definition of Christian Zionism. Secondly, having identified Simeon as a *post*millennialist, he then refers to his 'literal reading of the Bible and premillennial eschatology'.[63] Such confusion demands correction.

Although Simeon distanced himself from prophetic speculation,[64] 'to the last the thought of the recovery of Israel to the divine Messiah was on Simeon's heart.'[65] Regrettably, scholars have paid scant attention to the period of his protracted and final illness, during which he spent considerable time in the

---

[59] Charles Simeon, *A Sermon, Preached before the Society on May 8, 1818, at the Parish Church of St. Paul, Covent Garden, prefixed to The Tenth Report of the London Society for Promoting Christianity amongst the Jews* (London: 1818), p. 15.

[60] Simeon, *The Conversion of the Jews*, pp. 46, 7, 26.

[61] Charles Simeon, *Sovereignty and Equity Combined: or The Dispensations of God towards Jews and Gentiles Illustrated. A Sermon preached before the University of Cambridge, May 5, 1822* (Cambridge: 1822), p. 19.

[62] Bellett, *Recollections*, p. 16. Darby met Simeon in Cambridge in 1830. (Darby, *Further Remarks upon Righteousness and Law*, CW10:133-134.)

[63] Sizer, *Christian Zionism*, pp. 36, 41.

[64] *Memoirs*, ed. by Carus, p. 659.

[65] Moule, *Charles Simeon*, p. 124.

Scriptures, as Darby had done during his Dublin convalescence. In his address to the annual meeting of the LSPCJ in 1835, Simeon made the following confession: 'Though I have studied the subject of the Jewish question for many years, and written upon it not a little, I have never understood it *until within the last few months*'[66] (*italics* mine). In 'his dying testimony' concerning the Jews, which was delivered on his behalf to the Undergraduates' Missionary Association on 31 October 1836, Simeon drew attention to those scriptures which relate both to the spiritual *and* physical restoration of the Jewish nation; he described them as '*gold, every one of them*'.[67] His biographer, William Carus, president of the Undergraduates' Missionary Association and senior dean at Trinity College, Cambridge, records how Simeon 'begged' him to

> observe the strong expressions which God had been pleased to use when describing *His* intense and unalterable regard for His ancient people. 'See,' said he, 'how wonderfully He speaks; He calls them, 1. The dearly beloved of my soul:- and then He says, 2. I will plant them in their own land assuredly with my whole heart, and with my whole soul:- and then again, 3. He will rejoice over them with joy; He will rest in his love; He will joy over thee with singing:- nay, more, 4. They shall be a name and a praise among all the people of the earth.'[68]

Simeon's address to the Undergraduates' Missionary Association is important not only for *what* he expressed, but *how* he expressed it. As he explained,

> The thing which I wish to bring before you is this:- Ought we, or ought we not, to resemble Almighty God in the things most near and dear to God himself?...Have we no cause for shame, and sorrow, and contrition, that we have resembled him so little in past times?...Can we hope for God's blessing on our own souls, when we have so little regard for the souls of his most dear people, and so little resemblance in ourselves to him respecting them? I say no more. May God speak to all of you with thunder and with love. And may my *dying* hour be a source of *life* to God's interest among you all, both in this place and throughout the world![69]

The Keystone of Prophecy

Other Restorationists laid considerable stress on the ingathering of the Jews. According to Charles Jerram (1770-1853), one of Simeon's students at Cambridge, there was perhaps 'no *one* subject, upon which so many prophecies have been delivered as the future restoration of the Jews.' He believed that if God's promised judgments had been fulfilled to the letter, so too would His

---

[66] Gidney, *The History of the London Society*, p. 148.
[67] *Memoirs*, ed. by Carus, p. 815. The 'golden' scriptures Simeon referred to were Jer. 12:7; Rom. 11:28; Ezek. 36:22; Jer. 32:41; and Zeph. 3:17-20.
[68] *Memoirs*, ed. by Carus, p. 818.
[69] Quoted in Bickersteth, *The Restoration of the Jews*, pp. 291-293.

promised blessings; if not, God's word was 'totally unintelligible and useless'. Jerram appealed to the Abrahamic Covenant when distinguishing between Israel's occupation and possession of the Land, claiming that 'if the grant of the Almighty Maker and Governor of the universe can constitute a legal title to an everlasting possession, the claim of the Jews to the land of Palestine will always be reasonable and just.'[70]

John Aquila Brown, a self-confessed 'Philo-Judaean', insisted that 'unless the Jew be made the Keystone of every prophetic structure', then much of the Bible was incomprehensible. Like Darby, he criticised Bible commentators who had appropriated to the Church Israel's promised blessings, while leaving 'the inheritance of the curses...to that afflicted people'. In *The Jew, the Master-Key of the Apocalypse* (1827), Brown wrote:

> The unfounded glosses of our English Bibles have...prevented men from judging for themselves of the Divine record; and the air of authority with which they are invested, as if they were a part of the text itself, leaves an insensible impression on the mind from childhood to old age, which is productive of evil, and has done injury to the cause of Israel...Such, indeed, is the extraordinary state of the present day, that a bible is not to be obtained without these same unfounded notes and comments...These things ought not so to be.[71]

In 1822, John Fry, the rector of Desford in Leicestershire, published his book, *The Second Advent*, which was 'much discussed'[72] by early nineteenth-century students of Biblical prophecy. Like Darby, Fry made the same connections in the Psalms between 'the sufferings of the rejected Saviour' and 'Israel's desolation'.[73] He also noted how, in Acts 1:6-8, Jesus 'admits the justness'[74] of His disciples' expectation concerning Israel's restoration.

In 1829, John Hooper, rector of Albury in Surrey and a delegate at the Albury Park conferences (see below), published his address on *The Doctrine of the Second Advent*, which he had given to members of the Church of England in the parish of Westbury in Wiltshire. Hooper deplored the spiritualisation of Scripture, which had blighted the Church for centuries, and wrote indignantly:

> It is easy, very easy to spiritualise away any passage of Scripture, but it is not so easy to compensate for the loss we sustain in so doing. I doubt not, that this

---

[70] Charles Jerram, *An Essay Tending to Shew the Grounds Contained in Scripture for Expecting a Future Restoration of the Jews* (Cambridge: 1796), pp. 40, 21, 9.

[71] John Aquila Brown, *The Jew, the Master-Key of the Apocalypse; in answer to Mr. Frere's 'General Structure,' and the Dissertations of the Rev. Edw. Irving, and Other Commentators* (London: 1827), pp. 9, v, 1, xiii-xiv.

[72] Kobler, *The Vision was There*, p. 49.

[73] John Fry, *The Second Advent; or, the Glorious Epiphany of our Lord Jesus Christ. Being an attempt to elucidate, in chronological order, the Prophecies both of the Old and New Testaments: Vol. I* (London: 1822), p. 98.

[74] Fry, *The Second Advent: Vol. II*, p. 204.

system of spiritualising, which is now alas, so universally adopted, is the stronghold of Satan, in these last and degenerate days…Happy is the man, who in reading his Bible needs no other reason to believe what he reads, than that he finds it there. Happy the man who knows and believes, that not one jot or tittle of it shall pass till all be fulfilled![75]

Despite his underlying historicism, Hooper's observations on the Rapture of the true Church resemble those of J.N. Darby. In *The Translation*, Hooper spoke of earthly and heavenly dispensations, of an end-time apostasy within the Church, of the preservation of a faithful Christian remnant, and of the 'Jewishness' of Matthew 24 and the Great Tribulation passages. He also referred to a time *subsequent* to the Rapture when Christ will be seen *with* His saints by the rest of the world.[76] In an article for *The Morning Watch*, Hooper seemed to locate the Rapture *before* the commencement of Daniel's seventieth week, when speaking of 'our deliverance from the impending judgments'.[77]

The Clapham Sect

Between 1780 and 1850, 'Britain changed more than she had done for many hundreds of years'.[78] The first half of the nineteenth century was characterised by social and economic upheaval as the nation adjusted to the transition from agriculture to industry. The middle and upper classes also reacted against the ideology of the French Revolution, which threatened the stability of the nation. As Charles Breunig comments,

the 'revolutionary virus'…could not be confined to France indefinitely. Despite the efforts of European rulers to quarantine the 'disease', many individuals were infected by it and became its carriers in the Restoration era following the defeat of the revolutionary and Napoleonic armies.[79]

The transition from a wartime to a peacetime economy during the reign of George III was accompanied by economic depression, largely due to the passing of the Corn Laws in 1815. The campaign for Roman Catholic Emancipation, led by Daniel O'Connell and the Catholic Association, added to the maelstrom and drove many Protestants 'to an unusually close study of the

---

[75] John Hooper, *The Doctrine of the Second Advent, briefly stated in an address to the Members of the Church of England, in the Parish of Westbury, Wilts* (London: James Nisbet, 1829), p. 6.

[76] John Hooper, *The Translation: or, The Changing of the Living Saints, and their Deliverance from the Judgments which are coming on the earth* (London: William Edward Painter, 1846), p. 18.

[77] John Hooper, 'The Church's Expectation', *The Morning Watch*, 4 (1832), 321.

[78] Harrison, *The Second Coming*, p. 219.

[79] Charles Breunig, *The Age of Revolution and Reaction 1789-1850* (London: Weidenfeld and Nicolson, 1970), p. 61.

"signs of the times".[80] Dimont has aptly described this period as one of 'contagious revolutions'.[81]

Although they were 'never organised solely under one banner',[82] Evangelicals were extremely influential during the nineteenth century. With the death of many of the fathers of the Evangelical Revival, the mantle was taken up, in part, by a group of laymen who 'made a permanent difference to the history not only of England but of the modern world.'[83] This group included William Wilberforce, Granville Sharp, Lord Teignmouth, Henry Thornton, Charles Grant, and Zachary Macaulay, who were collectively known as the Clapham Sect, since 'most of the schemes of piety and benevolence which distinguished the second generation of Evangelicals either originated from Clapham, or found their strongest supporters there.' Characterised by an 'exceedingly comfortable'[84] lifestyle and a 'distinctive middle-class piety',[85] the Claphamites founded and promoted societies such as the Religious Tract Society (1799), the Church Missionary Society (1799), and the British and Foreign Bible Society (1804). They engaged in various philanthropic causes and disseminated their views through the *Christian Observer* magazine.

In the second report of the LSPCJ (27 December 1809), William Wilberforce is listed as one of its vice-presidents, while subsequent reports indicate that Robert Grant, the younger son of Charles Grant, and Zachary Macaulay were also closely associated with the Society. Macaulay's son, Thomas Babington Macaulay, led the campaign for Jewish emancipation in Britain,[86] and in an address to the committee of the House of Commons on 17 April 1833, responded to those who opposed the removal of Jewish civil disabilities, with skillful oratory and compelling reason:

> Another objection which has been made to this motion is that the Jews look forward to the coming of a great deliverer, to their return to Palestine, to the rebuilding of their Temple, to the revival of their ancient worship, and that therefore they will always consider England, not their country, but merely as their place of exile...Indeed Christians, as well as Jews, believe that the existing order

---

[80] Grayson Carter, *Anglican Evangelicals: Protestant Secessions from the Via Media, c.1800-1850* (Oxford: Oxford University Press, 2001), p. 196.

[81] Dimont, *Jews*, p. 318.

[82] Peter Toon, *Evangelical Theology 1833-1856: A Response to Tractarianism* (London: Marshall, Morgan & Scott, 1979), p. 204.

[83] Ernest Marshall Howse, *Saints in Politics: The 'Clapham Sect' and the Growth of Freedom* (London: George Allen & Unwin Ltd., 1976), p. v.

[84] John H. Overton, *The English Church in the Nineteenth Century, 1800-1833* (London: Longmans, Green, & Co. 1894), pp. 66, 94.

[85] Boyd Hilton, *The Age of Atonement: The Influence of Evangelicalism on Social and Economic Thought, 1795-1865* (Oxford: Clarendon Press, 1988), p. 7.

[86] Israel Finestein, *Jewish Society in Victorian England* (London: Vallentine Mitchell & Co., 1993), pp. 78-103.

of things will come to an end. Many Christians believe that Jesus will visibly reign on earth during a thousand years. Expositors of prophecy have gone so far as to fix the year when the Millennial period is to commence. The prevailing opinion is...in favour of...1866; but, according to some commentators, the time is close at hand. Are we to exclude all millenarians from Parliament and office, on the ground that they are impatiently looking forward to the miraculous monarchy which is to supersede the present dynasty and the present constitution of England, and that therefore they cannot be heartily loyal to King William?[87]

Although the Claphamites identified with the philanthropic and evangelistic thrust of the LSPCJ, the extent of their concern for the promised *restoration* of the Jews is uncertain. It is clear, however, that historians have either underestimated or downplayed their concern for the Jewish people, perhaps due to the eschatological complexities involved. Claphamite preoccupation with improving society contrasts starkly, however, with the 'other-worldliness' of Darby, who believed that *all* hope lay in Christ's return. Even so, the Claphamites represent an important branch of the Christian Restorationist network which was developing in the nineteenth century, and which brought to the fore both the historical plight, and future prospect, of the Jewish people.

The Albury Park Conference

In his *Narrative of the Circumstances which led to the setting up of the Church of Christ at Albury* (1833), wealthy landowner, banker, and Member of Parliament, Henry Drummond (1786-1860) recalls how, in 1826,

> the majority of what was called the Religious World disbelieved that the Jews were to be restored to their own land, and that the Lord Jesus Christ was to return and reign in person on this earth.

Describing himself as 'a Bible Christian', Drummond believed 'every word' of Scripture 'in its plain literal meaning',[88] and sought to counter 'the mass of infidelity which lurked under the guise of what was called evangelical religion'.[89] In 1826, he joined Lewis Way, James Hatley Frere, James Stratton, and Thomas White in London to establish *The Society for the Investigation of Prophecy*. A decision was then taken to inaugurate a conference at Albury Park Mansion in Surrey in November that year. Albury Park had been Drummond's

---

[87] Thomas Babington Macaulay, *The Miscellaneous Writings and Speeches of Lord Macaulay*, New edn (London: Longmans, Green, Reader, & Dyer, 1873), pp. 547-548.

[88] Henry Drummond, *Narrative of the Circumstances which led to the setting up of the Church of Christ at Albury* (1834), p. 7.

[89] Andrew Landale Drummond, *Edward Irving and His Circle: Including some Consideration of the 'Tongues' Movement in the Light of Modern Psychology* (London: James Clarke & Co. Ltd., n.d.), p. 7.

residence since 1819, and was to be the home of 'responsible and reasonable premillennialism'[90] for the next four years. With the support of the parish rector, Hugh McNeile, Drummond invited thirty of the most notable millenarians of the day who had 'preserved their faith' in Israel's restoration and Christ's return. Without 'any distinction of sect or party',[91] they included 'that matchless pioneer missionary'[92] and man of 'erratic genius',[93] Joseph Wolff, and 'the fanatical anti-liberal William Cuninghame'.[94]

Albury Historicism

The first Albury conference deliberated upon 'the great prophetic questions which...most instantly concern Christendom'. These included 'the times of the Gentiles', 'the present and future condition of the Jews', and 'the future advent of the Lord.' According to one delegate, Edward Irving, there was 'harmony and coincidence' on all the main issues:

> We believed in common that the present form of the dispensation of the gospel was for a time commensurate with the times of the Gentiles, which again are commensurate with the period of Jerusalem's being trodden under foot, and of the Jews' dispersion; that the restoration of the Jews would introduce altogether a new era into the church and the world, which might be called the universal dispensation of the benefits of Christ's death, while this is the dispensation to the church only...That the conclusion of the latter in great judgments, and the commencement of the former in great mercies, was hard at hand, yea even at the very door; all being agreed that the 1260 and 1290 days of Daniel were accomplished, and the remaining 45 begun, at the conclusion of which the blessedness will be fully arrived. And that during the judgment, which may open upon us any day, we are to look for the second advent of the Lord in person, to raise the dead bodies of his saints, and with them to reign upon the earth.[95]

Irving's statement that the 'days of Daniel were accomplished' reveals the historicist, and therefore Christian *Restorationist* nature of Albury Park eschatology. Patterson's claim that 'Albury took up a futurist interest in the prophecies' is inaccurate, since delegates interpreted the prophetic days of Daniel and Revelation *symbolically*, not literally. Patterson is therefore wide of

---

[90] Stunt, 'Influences', p. 46.
[91] Drummond, *Narrative*, p. 7.
[92] G.R. Balleine, *A History of the Evangelical Party in the Church of England* (London: Church Book Room Press Ltd., 1951), p. 203.
[93] Stirling, *The Ways of Yesterday*, p. 205.
[94] Oliver, *Prophets and Millennialists*, p. 107.
[95] Edward Irving, 'Preliminary Discourse', in *The Coming of Messiah in Glory and Majesty, by Juan Josafat Ben-Ezra, a Converted Jew, translated from the Spanish, with a Preliminary Discourse, by the Rev. Edward Irving, A.M: Vol. I* (London: L.B. Seeley and Son, 1827), pp. clxxxviii, clxxxix-cxc.

the mark in claiming that 'the perspective held by the Albury Circle is essentially identical to that found in contemporary dispensationalism and known today as pretribulational premillennialism'.[96]

Henry Drummond

According to Drummond's *Tracts for the Last Days*, the departure of the Church from 'the perfect model' in the New Testament was 'remidiless'. All hope lay in Christ's return, and not in 'the gradual and progressive enlargement of the preaching of the Gospel'. In Tract XXII, entitled, *The Restoration of the Jews*, Drummond lamented the neglect of prophecy which was 'very generally and most mischievously prevalent'[97] in the Church. He believed that the 'present Christian dispensation' would not pass 'insensibly' into the millennial state through the preaching of the Gospel, but would be 'terminated by judgments' falling 'principally, if not exclusively, upon Christendom'. The Jews would be restored, but in 'a time of great trouble'.[98]

Drummond maintained that the doctrine of Israel's restoration 'ought to have been one of the standing traditions and one of the abiding points of faith in the Church',[99] and feared for those who denied 'so plain a testimony'. In his *Defence of the Students of Prophecy* (1828), he summarised his position:

> 1. That the Jews are to be restored as a nation to their own land. 2. That at the same time the Gentiles are to be visited with judgments. 3. That the time of the restoration of the Jews is to be a season of increased happiness…4. That a long period of time is to elapse, during which this season of happiness is to be enjoyed. 5. That Christ is to be ruler of this restored Jewish nation.[100]

In his *Dialogues on Prophecy* (1827),[101] Drummond described the Rapture, or 'raising of the saints', as the *first* phase of the Second Coming, which would incorporate 'the appearances of the Lord to raise his saints, and again in order to save his national Israel'.[102] He argued that there was much 'unsanctified benevolence' in the Church, and that many had lost sight of this 'grand truth'

---

[96] Patterson, *Designing the Last Days*, pp. 38, 26.

[97] Henry Drummond, *Tracts for the Last Days: Vol. I* (London: William Edward Painter, 1844), pp. iii, 364, 343-344.

[98] Henry Drummond, *Dialogues on Prophecy: Vol. I* (London: James Nisbet, 1827), p. 100.

[99] Drummond, *Tracts: Vol. I*, p. 344.

[100] Henry Drummond, *A Defence of the Students of Prophecy, in Answer to the Attack of the Rev Dr Hamilton, of Strathblane* (London: James Nisbet, 1828), pp. 26, 22-23.

[101] Based on conversations with fellow delegates, to whom he gave pseudonyms. (See *A Dictionary of Writers on the Prophecies, with the Titles and Occasional Description of their Works*, ed. by Joshua W. Brooks [London: Simpkin, Marshall and Co., 1835].)

[102] Drummond, *Dialogues: Vol. II*, pp. 47, 22.

by devoting their energies 'in one continued bustle for the circulation of Bibles and Tracts, sending out missionaries, and emancipating the oppressed of mankind'. This was, in his estimation, 'a tremendous delusion: the last, and therefore the highest finished of all Satan's devices'.[103] Believing that postmillennialism had lulled the Church into 'a fatal security', Drummond denounced as 'absolute nonsense'[104] the teaching that Israel's promised restoration had been fulfilled at Christ's first advent.

The Catholic Apostolic Church

Before leaving Drummond, it is important to note that he was one of the founding members of the Catholic Apostolic Church,[105] being appointed one of its 'apostles' on 25 September 1833. Prayer for the restoration of the Jews was incorporated into the liturgy of this church, although the dominant focus was 'the speedy coming of our Lord and His Kingdom.'[106] Catholic Apostolic theology owes much to Drummond's *Dialogues*, and Francis Sitwell's *The Purpose of God in Creation and Redemption*.

Francis Sitwell (1787-1864) believed that there was 'no greater source of error' than 'the culling out' of prophecies relating to Israel's restoration. He noted how the early Church had departed from the teaching of Christ and His Apostles by 'shutting her eyes…to what God had said He would do against all that should persecute them [the Jews] in the hour of their adversity'. However, there were those of his own generation who were 'able once more to pray to God in the right way' for the Jewish people.

Sitwell believed that Israel's restoration would occur in two stages: 'by natural means, and by the devices of man' *prior* to Christ's return, and 'by the mighty hand of God' *when* Christ returns. Interpreting the Bible literally, he stated that the Jews would return to the Land in unbelief, and that many would fall 'under the hands of Antichrist' and 'into the fire of that tribulation which is to come upon them to the uttermost, as a chastisement for their sin…and for the purifying of that remnant that will be left'. Many Jews would perish with 'only a third of them brought through' (Zech. 13:8-9), after which Christ would return, destroy Antichrist, and establish His millennial reign in Jerusalem.[107]

The Catholic Apostolic Church remains something of an enigma. No

---

[103] Drummond, *Dialogues: Vol. I*, pp. 6, vi-vii.

[104] Drummond, *Dialogues: Vol. III*, pp. 458, 263.

[105] Rowland A. Davenport, *Albury Apostles* (Birdlip: United Writers, 1970), p. 109.

[106] G.L. Standring, *Albury and the Catholic Apostolic Church: A Guide to the Personalities, Beliefs and Practices of the Community of Christians commonly called the Catholic Apostolic Church* (Guildford: 1985), pp. 55-57.

[107] Francis Sitwell, *The Purpose of God in Creation and Redemption: and the Successive Steps for Manifesting the Same in and by the Church*, 3rd edn (London: Hamilton, Adams, & Co., 1868), pp. 309-310, 313-316, 320-323.

provision was ever made for replacing its twelve 'apostles', since its members lived in the constant expectation of Christ's return. Although the church began to disband when the last 'apostle', Francis Valentine Woodhouse, died in 1901, some of the descendants of the early Catholic Apostolics continue to meet and pray for the Lord's return, and for the restoration and salvation of the Jews.[108]

Hugh McNeile

Chair of the Albury Park conferences was Hugh McNeile (1795-1879), a graduate of Trinity College, Dublin, whom Henry Drummond appointed rector of Albury parish in 1822. In a series of lectures he gave in London in 1827, McNeile expounded the doctrine of Israel's restoration, which, he claimed, had been 'allowed to fall into comparative neglect'.[109] He later recalled how this truth was 'just beginning to be ventilated in consequence of the labours of Mr. Louis Way and Mr. Hawtrey; and more especially in consequence of the writings of Mr. Faber, and the zealous advocacy of Mr. Simeon.'[110] McNeile introduced his lectures by describing history as 'the providence of God' and the Bible as 'the word of God', which 'mutually attest each other, on the subject of the Jewish nation, unto this day'. He was in no doubt that God had preserved the Jews and kept them distinct, and would continue to do so until the close of this present 'dispensation'. He also believed that 'the prevailing tone of Christianity', which was characterised by 'a spurious mixture', was indicative of the end-time apostasy of the Church. Like Darby, McNeile also drew a clear distinction between the heavenly realm of the Church and the earthly realm of Israel.[111]

William Cuninghame

Another regular participant at Albury was William Cuninghame of Lainshaw (1775-1849), who has been described as 'the most prolific prophetic interpreter of the time'[112] and one of the foremost historicists of his generation.[113] Cuninghame was associated with the LSPCJ for many years, serving as president of its Glasgow auxiliary committee. In his *Letters and Essays*, first published in 1822 in the LSPCJ's journal, the *Jewish Expositor*, he asserted that

---

[108] *The Liturgy and Other Divine Offices of the Church*, ed. by John Bate Cardale (London: n.d.), p. 271.

[109] Hugh McNeile, *Popular Lectures on the Prophecies Relative to the Jewish Nation* (London: J. Hatchard and Son, 1830), p. xi.

[110] Hugh McNeile, *Lectures on the Prophecies relative to the Jewish Nation*, New edn (Liverpool: E. Howell, 1866), preface.

[111] McNeile, *Popular Lectures*, pp. 1, 63, 85, 75-76, 143.

[112] Froom, *The Prophetic Faith: Vol. III*, p. 274.

[113] 'On the Gradual Unfolding of Prophecy', *The Morning Watch*, 1 (1830), 540.

Christians who renounced their obligation to the Jewish people possessed 'a superficial knowledge of the Scriptures', having 'received their views of religion from creeds and confessions composed by fallible men'.[114] Denouncing replacement theology, he argued that if there was to be no 'future redemption of this wonderful people',[115] there was 'no certain meaning in language'.[116] In a letter to Lord Shaftesbury, Cuninghame expressed his dismay at the lack of concern for Israel's restoration in the Church of England, and appealed to Shaftesbury to exercise his influence 'to aid and promote the agricultural settlement of believing Israelites in Palestine'.[117]

Lewis Way

Lewis Way (1772-1840), son of 'the fine old Dissenter Benjamin Way',[118] has been described as a man of 'intriguing eccentricities'[119] and 'the first in modern times to convince the Jews that a Christian can really love them'.[120] In her chronicles of the Way family, Anna Stirling records how, during a visit to Exmouth in 1811, Way was riding with a friend along the Exmouth-Exeter road when his attention was drawn to a strange, circular dwelling belonging to Miss Jane Parminter and her cousin. He learned that in establishing a trust for their property, the Parminters had expressed 'a preference for candidates of the Jewish race, a predilection not due apparently to any racial affinity but solely of religious origin.' The Parminters believed that the Jews were 'God's Chosen People', and that 'their eventual reinstatement in Palestine' was dependent upon their conversion to Christ. Way's friend informed him that Jane Parminter had recently died, but had stipulated in her will that a group of oak trees in the grounds of her home was to 'remain standing', and that 'the hand of man shall not be raised against them till Israel returns and is restored to the Land of Promise.' This account put his mind 'at once on fire and at rest', and inspired Way to devote the rest of his life to 'the conversion of the Jews and – what he believed to be its outcome – their restoration to Palestine.'

After covering the debts of the LSPCJ, which subsequently became an Anglican mission in 1815, Way transformed Stansted Park in Sussex into a

---

[114] William Cuninghame, *Letters and Essays, Controversial and Critical, on Subjects Connected with the Conversion and National Restoration of Israel* (London: 1822), p. vii.

[115] William Cuninghame, *A Dissertation on the Seals and Trumpets of the Apocalypse, and the Prophetical Period of Twelve Hundred and Sixty Years* (London: 1813), p. 293.

[116] Cuninghame, *Letters and Essays*, p. 282.

[117] William Cuninghame, *A Letter to the Right Honourable Lord Ashley, President of the London Society for Promoting Christianity amongst the Jews, on the Necessity of Immediate Measures for the Jewish Colonisation of Palestine* (London: 1849), p. 10.

[118] Stirling, *The Ways of Yesterday*, p. 121.

[119] Sandeen, *The Roots of Fundamentalism*, p. 9.

[120] Gidney, *The History of the London Society*, p. 150.

training centre for missionaries, having purchased the estate with a legacy he had received from John Way (no relation).[121] He was supported in the venture by his close friends, William Wilberforce and Charles Simeon.

Way wrote a number of articles for the *Jewish Expositor* under the pseudonym 'Basilicus'. In one of his articles he emphasised the importance of the Greek word *apokatastasis* in Acts 3:19-21, insisting that the 'restitution [*apokatastasis*] of all things is connected with the second advent, or rather *mission*, of Christ to the Jews.' According to Way, the Church had failed to understand the plain meaning of this passage. With typical eloquence he portrayed the Christian, who believed that the Church had replaced Israel, as one who 'takes up his station on Gerizim, and engrossing all its blessings, consigns to its original occupants the possession and curse of Ebal'.[122]

James Haldane Stewart's widely circulated pamphlet, *Thoughts on the Importance of Special Prayer for the General Outpouring of the Holy Spirit* (1821), gave Lewis Way the opportunity to correct a common misinterpretation of 'the autumn rains' in Joel 2:21-32. Like Darby,[123] Way believed that this prophecy did not apply to the Church, but foretold Israel's end-time restoration. Stewart, on the other hand, had used his pamphlet during his tours of England and Scotland to call Christians to pray for the 'latter rain' of the Holy Spirit in order to reverse Britain's moral decline.[124] Way criticised Stewart for misapplying the Scriptures, insisting that

> *special* prayer for the obtaining of the blessing, without due consideration of the *specific means* by which it is to be produced, would be to 'ask amiss,' and to 'beat the air' uncertainly; to derange the divine machinery of the promises, and invert that exact order of time, which is observable in seasons appointed of God for every work under the sun.[125]

Lewis Way, like other Restorationists, expressed his beliefs through poetry.[126] In *The Efficacy of Prayer in the Concerns of the Church*, written en route to Hanover in 1817, he appealed to Christians to 'strive in prayer to God, For Jacob's scatter'd race, 'Till he restrain the chast'ning rod, And grant his promis'd grace'.[127] However, Way made arguably his greatest contribution just

---

[121] Stirling, *The Ways of Yesterday*, pp. 125, 199-201, 305-306.

[122] Basilicus, *Thoughts on the Scriptural Expectations of the Christian Church* (Gloucester: n.d.), pp. 47, 99-100.

[123] Darby, *The Acts of the Apostles*, M4:87-93.

[124] James Haldane Stewart, *Thoughts on the Importance of Special Prayer for the General Outpouring of the Holy Spirit* (London: 1821), p. 4.

[125] Lewis Way, *The Latter Rain; with Observations on The Importance of General Prayer, for the Special Outpouring of the Holy Spirit*, 2nd edn (London: 1821), p. 7.

[126] Lewis Way, *Poems* (Stansted: 1822).

[127] Way, *The Latter Rain*, pp. 89-91. In 1794, Sir William Ashburnham unsuccessfully submitted his poem, *The Restoration of the Jews*, for Cambridge University's

before the Congress of Aix-la-Chapelle in 1818, when he travelled to Moscow to present to Czar Alexander I his *Memorial to the United Sovereigns*[128] for the emancipation of the Jews. The Czar found Way's proposal 'very interesting', and met with him on several occasions to discuss Biblical prophecy. The *Memorial* was presented to the Congress and endorsed by the emperors of Prussia, Austria, and Russia, and by notable plenipotentiaries such as Metternich, Richelieu, and Wellington.[129] As Kobler writes, 'Way's appearance in Aix-la-Chapelle represented a milestone in the history of the Restoration Movement. He was the first spokesman of the British Movement personally to plead the cause of the Jews as a nation in an inter-governmental assembly.'[130]

Edward Irving

One Albury Park delegate, who made a 'dramatic and brief'[131] impact on the Evangelical world, was Edward Irving (1792-1834). Described as 'a bizarre figure in the London of the 1820s' and 'a scrappily educated Scot', Irving achieved 'unexpected eminence'[132] after being inducted into London's Caledonian Chapel in 1822. The future Prime Minister, George Canning, attended his church and drew Parliament's attention to the tall and elegant man whose 'mind was that of a genius, though tending towards eccentricity', whose 'spirit was almost childlike in its simplicity, yet at the same time mightily masculine, full of courage and unflinching in conviction', and who, as a preacher, 'was known as "the greatest orator of the age".'[133] William Wordsworth, Samuel Taylor Coleridge, and William Gladstone also heard Irving preach in his church, which was frequently 'crowded to suffocation with grandees of all classes, peers and peeresses, lawyers, metaphysicians, philosophers of every grade, and members of literary and scientific societies.'[134]

Sadly, Edward Irving's reputation was tarnished after he was defrocked as a Church of Scotland minister in 1833 by the Presbytery of Annan, under whose jurisdiction he ministered. His dismissal followed the publication of his controversial doctrine of the Incarnation, and the outbreak of ecstatic utterances in his Regent Square church in London in 1831. Irving found himself 'an

---

prestigious Seatonian Prize. Francis Wrangham (*The Restoration of the Jews*, 1795) and John Hudson (*Cyrus and the Restoration of the Jews*, 1902) were successful.

[128] *Memoirs*, ed. by Carus, p. 501.

[129] Stirling, *The Ways of Yesterday*, pp. 174, 178-179, 197; *cf.* Lucien Wolf, *Notes on the diplomatic history of the Jewish question: with texts of protocols, treaty stipulations and other public acts and official documents* (London: 1919).

[130] Kobler, *The Vision was There*, p. 51.

[131] Sandeen, *The Roots of Fundamentalism*, p. 29.

[132] Oliver, *Prophets and Millennialists*, p. 99.

[133] Arnold Dallimore, *The Life of Edward Irving, the Fore-Runner of the Charismatic Movement* (Edinburgh: The Banner of Truth Trust, 1983), p. ix.

[134] 'The Ark of God in the Temple of Dagon', *The Morning Watch*, 5 (1832), 443.

outcast among the millenarian party, his very name transformed into a term of reproach among evangelicals and decent citizens.' Despite being likened to 'a ship without a keel',[135] he has been described as 'a man to make those tremble who never trembled before',[136] a 'holy man',[137] a 'great northern light',[138] and a man of 'torrential abilities'[139] who took London 'by storm'[140] and 'by gallantry',[141] and who helped turn the eschatological tide towards premillennialism. Before his untimely death at the age of 42, Irving's 'millenarian voice' had been heard 'in the prophetic wilderness of Scotland',[142] his 'meteoric message'[143] making a lasting impression on men like Horatius Bonar, 'the leading millenarian of the second generation'[144] and the 'chief Scottish premillennial champion'.[145]

Regrettably, the preoccupation historians have had with the controversies surrounding Edward Irving has veiled his considerable contribution to the Restorationist cause. His belief in the imminent return of Christ and the promised restoration of Israel gained prominence following the publication of his book, *Babylon and Infidelity Foredoomed* (1826). His premillennial eschatology remained 'the single most determining influence upon his thought',[146] due in no small measure to his reading of *The Coming of Messiah in Glory and Majesty*, a book which 'fired the soul of Edward Irving'[147] and propelled him to the forefront of the Restorationist movement.

The Lacunza Legacy

Written in Spanish under the pseudonym Juan Josafat Ben-Ezra, *La Venida del*

---

[135] Sandeen, *The Roots of Fundamentalism*, pp. 14-15.

[136] Holland, *Life and Letters of Zachary Macaulay*, p. 390.

[137] Andrew A. Bonar, *The Life of Robert Murray McCheyne* (London: Banner of Truth Trust, 1960), p. 35.

[138] Margaret Jean Holland, *Life and Letters of Zachary Macaulay* (London: Edward Arnold, 1900), pp. 389-390.

[139] Rennie, 'Nineteenth-Century Roots', p. 50.

[140] Rowdon, *The Origins of the Brethren*, p. 10.

[141] Drummond, *Edward Irving and His Circle*, p. 74.

[142] Sandeen, *The Roots of Fundamentalism*, p. 25.

[143] John Macleod, *Scottish Theology in Relation to Church History since the Reformation*, 2nd edn (Edinburgh: The Banner of Truth Trust, 1946), p. 277.

[144] Sandeen, *The Roots of Fundamentalism*, p. 25.

[145] David W. Bebbington, *Evangelicalism in Modern Britain: A History from the 1730s to the 1980s* (London: Unwin Hyman, 1989), p. 88.

[146] Patterson, *Designing the Last Days*, p. 18.

[147] Froom, *The Prophetic Faith: Vol. III*, p. 268; *cf.* Edward Irving, *Babylon and Infidelity Foredoomed of God: A Discourse on the Prophecies of Daniel and the Apocalypse which relate to these latter times, and until the Second Advent*, 2nd edn (Glasgow: 1828), p. 377.

Mesias en Gloria y Majestad ('The Coming of Messiah in Glory and Majesty') marked 'the decisive re-emergence of the premillennialist tradition.'[148] The author, a Jewish Jesuit by the name of Manuel Lacunza (c.1731-1801), had fled his native Chile before finding refuge in Italy. His book, which addressed the corruption within the Roman Catholic priesthood, was first printed in Spain in 1812 before being suppressed by the Spanish Inquisition. It found its way into England in 1816 and into the hands of Edward Irving in 1826. Coincidentally, Irving had been learning Spanish with a view to helping his friend, Giuseppe Sottomayor, and after being persuaded by his church to take a sabbatical, retreated to the country to translate Lacunza's work.[149]

Lacunza's primary contention was that Jesus the Messiah would return in glory to reign upon the earth, though not necessarily for one thousand years. He spoke of how 'the very feelings of the apostle' had stirred within him when reading Rom. 9:1-3,

> and perceiving that my heart was oppressed by the reawakened and renewed force of that grief, which I do almost always bear about with me, I shut the book, and hastened into the fields to relieve my heart.[150]

Seeking to offer 'some greater light, some other remedy more prompt and efficacious' to his Jewish brethren '*whose are the Fathers, and of whom is Jesus Christ according to the flesh*',[151] Lacunza launched an attack on the Roman Catholic Church, accusing its theologians of employing 'a thousand other senses besides the literal'[152] in their interpretation of the Bible, and of showing 'contempt for the Jews'.[153] He believed that the Jewish people were not 'a tree wholly withered and incapable of flourishing again, good only for the fire', but were destined by God to make 'a great figure in the grand mystery of Messiah's coming'. After being replanted in a land given to them 'in solemn and perpetual gift', they would be 'resuscitated and reanimated with that spirit of life, of which, for so many ages, they have been deprived'. This progressive restoration, Lacunza maintained, would fulfil promises 'innumerable in almost all the prophets', and be effected 'not under the old covenant, but under another covenant, new and everlasting'.[154]

Irving added his own substantial *Preliminary Discourse* to Lacunza's work,

---

[148] Bebbington, *Evangelicalism*, p. 82.
[149] Margaret Oliphant, *The Life of Edward Irving: Vol. I* (London: Hurst and Blackett, 1862), p. 385.
[150] Ben-Ezra, *The Coming of Messiah: Vol. I*, p. 21.
[151] Ben-Ezra, 'To the Messiah Jesus Christ, the Son of God, Son of the Most Holy Virgin Mary, Son of David, and Son of Abraham', in Ben-Ezra, *The Coming of Messiah: Vol. I*, pp. 9-10.
[152] Ben-Ezra, *The Coming of Messiah: Vol. I*, p. 28.
[153] Ben-Ezra, *The Coming of Messiah: Vol. II*, p. 133.
[154] Ben-Ezra, *The Coming of Messiah: Vol. I*, pp. 298-299, 342.

which inspired the 'rapid progress'[155] of the doctrine of the Second Coming in the south of England. He believed that Jesus' 'brethren according to the flesh' were to be 'gathered in great mercy, restored in great power, and possessed with an everlasting possession of the land promised to their Fathers', and despite disagreeing with his brand of futurism, conceded that Lacunza had 'awakened' in his mind

> the suspicion of a possibility, that when the time of that last great antichristian trouble shall arrive, these numbers [1260, 1290, 1335 days] may be found to have a literal application.

Irving had long suspected 'that the three years and a half duration of the Lord's suffering ministry' may have been 'a type of the duration of the sufferings of the Jewish church when it shall be again called', adding that he found 'the suffering Messiah, and the suffering Jewish church, interwoven in the prophecies of the Old Testament, especially in the Psalms.'[156]

As we shall see, Darby was familiar with Irving's work, but made no reference to Lacunza in his writings. Undeterred, Darby's amillennial, postmillennial, *and* premillennial critics have sought to discredit him by tracing his eschatology back to this Jesuit priest. There are indeed similarities between them, particularly in relation to the restoration of Israel, the apostasy of the Church, the times of the Gentiles, and the *physical* return of the Lord Jesus to the earth, but we should not be surprised when Biblical scholars, from diverse ecclesiastical traditions, arrive at similar conclusions. Having said that, it is important to point out that there are significant disparities in the theology of Darby and Lacunza, not least Lacunza's advocacy of Roman Catholic dogma, his belief in Antichrist as 'a moral body, composed of innumerable individuals...all morally united and animated with one common spirit', and his contention that Paul's letters to the Thessalonians were written to correct their 'error...of expecting every moment the coming of the Lord.'[157]

It is important to note, at this stage, that Darby has also been accused of deriving his doctrine of the pretribulation Rapture from another Jesuit priest by the name of Francisco Ribera (1537-1591). In 1590, this Spanish Jesuit from Salamanca published a substantial commentary on the book of Revelation to counter the prevailing Protestant view which identified Antichrist with the Pope. Ribera believed that with the exception of the first few chapters, events recorded in the book of Revelation related to a *future* period of 1260 *literal* days, when a personal (though not Papal) Antichrist would be received by the Jews, enthrone himself in the Third Temple, and persecute the Church. By

---

[155] William Cuninghame, *A Summary View of the Scriptural Argument for the Second and Glorious Advent of Messiah before the Millennium* (Glasgow: 1828), p. vi.

[156] Irving, 'Preliminary Discourse', pp. clix, xxix-xxxi.

[157] Ben-Ezra, *The Coming of Messiah: Vol. I*, pp. 196, 263.

locating Antichrist in the future, Ribera helped to 'deflect Protestant criticism away from Rome'.[158] His position was readily adopted by a number of Roman Catholic scholars, including Cardinal Robert Bellarmine (1542-1621), the most notable Jesuit controversialist.

Despite the similarities, any claim that Protestant futurists in general, and Darby in particular, adopted and adapted Ribera's futurism is absolutely groundless. Ribera's amillennial and Augustinian theology of replacement, and the absence of a pretribulation Rapture position in his eschatology, completely separates him from Darby on a theological level. This, coupled with the 'ample and varied arsenal of anti-Catholic polemic'[159] which Darby employed in his liberation of Irish peasants from the Church of Rome, is evidence enough to destroy the artificial link critics have forged between Darby and the Jesuits.

Irving and the Jews

Edward Irving believed that Lacunza's work had come into his hands providentially to expose the heresy of postmillennialism, which he believed was extinguishing 'the brightest candle of the apostolic and primitive church', namely the doctrine of the Second Coming. Endeavouring to help Christians 'disabuse' themselves of this 'almost universally entertained' error, Irving addressed the postmillennialist in dramatic style:

> While you are dreaming of smooth seas and a harmonious crew, and a haven hard at hand, we see the gathering of the clouds, and the curling of the waves, and a rebellious mutinous crew, and a fearful shipwreck, from which a few, a very few, of the wise and prudent will escape.[160]

He perceived the Church of Scotland to be riddled with 'pharisaical ostentation', with its 'vain parade of patriotism',[161] and accused Evangelicals in general of singing 'sweet strains of peace and prosperity, when Europe, and all the world, is rocking to and fro with the convulsions of an earthquake'.[162]

Irving was convinced that God was about to 'turn his Holy Spirit unto his ancient people the Jews, and bring unto them those days of refreshing spoken of by all the holy prophets since the world began'. This, he believed, would demonstrate 'the unchangeableness of God's grace'.[163] In *The Last Days: A*

---

[158] Thomas D. Ice, 'Francisco Ribera', in *Dictionary of Premillennial Theology*, ed. by Mal Couch (Grand Rapids, MI: Kregel Publications, 1996), p. 378.

[159] Rennie, 'Nineteenth-Century Roots', p. 51.

[160] Irving, 'Preliminary Discourse', pp. lvii, i, liii-liv.

[161] Edward Irving, 'Signs of the Times, and the Characteristics of the Church (Part II)', *The Morning Watch*, 2 (1831), 147.

[162] Edward Irving, 'Interpretation of all the Old-Testament Prophecies quoted in the New. Interpretation VII.', *The Morning Watch*, 2 (1831), 550.

[163] Irving, 'Preliminary Discourse', pp. v, xi.

Discourse on the Evil Character of these our Times (1828), he spoke of how 'Zion's recompense' would conclude 'the troublous morning of that long day, during which they [the Jews] should begin to realise all the blessings of the New Covenant, and to be irradiated with all the glory of Messiah the King'.[164] Irving and his fellow Albury delegates understood how important it was for the Church to understand the centrality of the Jews in the heart and purposes of God. As he wrote to his wife from the final Albury conference in 1830,

> The subject today has been the Jews, which always yields much matter...I feel as if far more light had been afforded me upon this subject than at any time heretofore.[165]

Irving understood that 'as the spirit cannot act of itself without the body, neither can the Christian have life perfect without knowing the purpose of God by the Jew.' Believing that 'every promise made to Abraham, and to Abraham's seed, hath received from him [Christ] the great *Amen*',[166] he found the position of those who spiritualised Scripture 'utterly incomprehensible',[167] and denounced those who had 'shut-up four-fifths, yea, nine-tenths of the sacred volume' by robbing Israel of her inheritance, as a 'whited sepulchre'.[168] Anyone who questioned that which God had promised the Jews was, in his opinion, 'a sceptic or an infidel' who 'cannot be permitted to have the name of a believer', since a believer in Christ 'is one who takes God's word as true and certain; not *so much* of it, but all of it'. Irving ardently avowed that he would 'rather have had twelve religious magazines expend their monthly venom upon [his] poor head, than have written twelve letters against the restoration of the Jews to their own land',[169] as one anonymous writer had done. In one of his most impassioned articles for *The Morning Watch*, he exclaimed:

> Ah me! why waiteth, why longeth, why groaneth not the world for the restoration of Israel, which shall be as life from the dead? Well may it be called the days of refreshing; for never till then will the barren earth be refreshed.

No matter how much zeal went into philanthropic work, missionary endeavour, and the publication of Christian literature, Irving was convinced that Christ's millennial kingdom would not be ushered in 'until the walls of Jerusalem be built up again, and Zion be made a praise in the whole earth'. He called upon

---

[164] Edward Irving, *The Last Days: A Discourse on the Evil Character of these our Times, Proving them to be the 'Perilous Times' of the 'Last Days'* (London: R.B. Seeley and W. Burnside, 1828), pp. 34-35.

[165] Oliphant, *The Life of Edward Irving: Vol. II*, p. 144.

[166] Irving, 'Interpretation III.', *The Morning Watch*, 1 (1830), 346-347.

[167] Irving, 'Interpretation V.', *The Morning Watch*, 2 (1831), 68.

[168] Irving, 'Signs of the Times...(Part II)', 142-144.

[169] Irving, 'Interpretation V.', 68-69.

true believers to pray for God to 'hasten the day of the restoration of his people, which shall be unto the world as life from the dead.'[170]

Despite Darby's negative appraisal of Irving (see below) and their radically different ecclesiologies, the similarities in their understanding of Biblical prophecy are striking. Irving, for example, used the term 'prophetic earth'[171] in confining prophecy to the Jews, understood the importance of typology,[172] referred to the present age as 'an interjected and intercalated period',[173] connected Christ's sufferings in the Psalms to the end-time sufferings of a Jewish remnant,[174] made a clear distinction between Israel and the Church, believed that the apostate Church was awaiting 'awful judgment', and assured true believers that 'there is close at hand a deliverance of God's faithful ones by translation'.[175] Although his eschatology is not as clearly defined as Darby's, it would appear from the articles he wrote for *The Morning Watch* journal, and the testimony of Robert Baxter, a once 'tender friend',[176] that Irving believed in a pretribulation Rapture. He also believed that he had a duty to the Church to 'electrify her paralysed faith, by bringing it into contact with that battery of truth concerning Israel's restoration and Immanuel's coming which is contained in the Prophets'.[177] In an article on Old Testament prophecies quoted in the New, Irving brought the following indictment against the Church:

> woe be to the man that would bereave Abraham's seed, Christ's brethren according to the flesh, of this precedency, which are written for them by the hand of Jehovah!...I cannot, I dare not, take part with those who would explain away these literal prophecies, hide them from the hope of Israel and from the desire of all the nations of the earth, in order to have them all to themselves, and leave this world the eternal habitation of devils. I openly denounce such men, as not only unbelievers in God's word, but confederate to destroy it.[178]

As we have seen, there is a clear correlation between aspects of Darby's theology and those of his contemporaries, including Edward Irving. This is to be expected, if we believe that God was raising up men during the nineteenth century to proclaim the truth of Israel's restoration and Christ's return. However, detractors who have sought to discredit the Biblical doctrine of the

---

[170] Irving, 'Interpretation VI.', *The Morning Watch*, 2 (1831), 293-294.

[171] Irving, 'Signs of the Times, and the Characteristics of the Church', *The Morning Watch*, 1 (1830), 643.

[172] Edward Irving, 'The Times and Seasons', *The Morning Watch*, 1 (1830), 44.

[173] Irving, 'Interpretation VII.II.', *The Morning Watch*, 2 (1831), 788.

[174] Irving, 'Preliminary Discourse', pp. xxx-xxxi.

[175] Irving, 'Signs of the Times...(Part II)', 156, 160.

[176] Edward Irving, 'What Caused Mr. Baxter's Fall?', *The Morning Watch*, 7 (1833), 132.

[177] Irving, 'Interpretation V.', 83.

[178] Irving, 'Interpretation VI.', 318-319.

pretribulation Rapture have made more of these similarities than is warranted. Having already broken the link between Darby and the Jesuits, we now turn our attention to Margaret MacDonald and Edward Irving, whom critics claim provided the basis for Darby's understanding of the Rapture.

The Rapture Controversy

Darby's opponents have consistently cited Samuel Tregelles when linking him to Edward Irving. In *The Hope of Christ's Second Coming* (1864), Tregelles traced Darby's doctrine back to an alleged utterance in Irving's church:

> when the theory of a secret coming of Christ was first brought forward (about the year 1832), it was adopted with eagerness: it suited certain preconceived opinions, and it was accepted by some as that which harmonised contradictory thoughts…(I am not aware that there was any definite teaching that there would be a secret Rapture of the Church at a secret coming, until this was given forth as an 'utterance' in Mr Irving's Church…But whether any one ever asserted such a thing or not, it was from that supposed revelation that the modern doctrine and the modern phraseology respecting it arose. It came not from Holy Scripture, but from that which falsely pretended to be the Spirit of God…After the opinion of a secret advent had been adopted, many expressions in older writers were regarded as supporting it).[179]

Tregelles has been dismissed as 'a prejudiced witness'[180] on the basis of the support he gave to his cousin, Benjamin Wills Newton, after Darby had charged Newton with heresy. William Kelly accused Tregelles of implicating himself in Newton's error, and of conducting a vendetta against Darby by imputing to an Irvingite spirit his doctrine of the Rapture.[181] As Huebner maintains, Tregelles' statement 'proceeded from animus'.[182]

Critics like Iain Murray are convinced that all 'the salient features of Darby's scheme are to be found in Irving'.[183] Stephen Sizer claims that there is 'compelling evidence' of 'Irving's influence' on Darby's doctrine of 'a failing church and future Jewish dispensation'.[184] Victoria Clark follows suit, stating that Darby 'honed his pre-millennialism with Irving's help',[185] while Dan Cohn-Sherbok argues that Darby's use of 'dispensation' connects him to Irving

---

[179] Samuel P. Tregelles, *The Hope of Christ's Second Coming*, 7th edn (Chelmsford: Sovereign Grace Advent Testimony, n.d.), p. 23.

[180] John F. Walvoord, *The Blessed Hope and the Tribulation: A Historical and Biblical Study of Posttribulationism* (Grand Rapids, MI: Zondervan Publishing House, 1977), p. 43.

[181] Kelly, *The Rapture of the Saints*, p. 11.

[182] Huebner, *The Truth of the Pre-Tribulation Rapture Recovered*, p. 16.

[183] Murray, *The Puritan Hope*, p. 200.

[184] Sizer, *Christian Zionism*, p. 51.

[185] Clark, *Allies for Armageddon*, p. 61.

because of Irving's prior use of the term.[186] (Cohn-Sherbok fails to realise that this terminology was common currency in the language of the day.) Sizer bases his claim that Darby simply 'developed Irving's ideas'[187] mainly on Darby's statement that the 'largest expression of piety and holiness...were found in Mr Irving's writings, and much most blessed and precious truth too'.[188] Sizer, however, misses the importance of the point he makes when asserting that this statement was made in the context of 'Darby *disassociating himself* from the fanciful prophecies of the Irvingites and the Catholic Apostolic Church'[189] (*italics* mine). He also mistakenly claims that this is the only reference to Irving 'in Darby's entire thirty-four volumes'.[190] On the contrary, Darby knew and wrote 'a great deal'[191] about the Scottish clergyman.

Darby and Irving

Despite his appreciation of Irving's 'deeply interesting and...profitable and timely sermon'[192] on intercession, Darby believed that 'the positive work of the enemy' was 'most manifest'[193] in Irving's church. In 1844, he recalled how, 'at least fourteen years ago',[194] he had disputed with Irving on the matter of spiritual gifts, and later recollected being drawn into conflict with him 'some four-and-thirty years ago', because of his 'meddling metaphysically with the Lord's Person'.[195] Darby described Irving's doctrine of the Incarnation as 'plainly wicked and evil, and contrary to God's word and Spirit'.[196] He claimed that the Irvingite gifts had been 'founded on this doctrine',[197] and lamented 'all

---

[186] Cohn-Sherbok, *The Politics of Apocalypse*, pp. 13-14.

[187] Stephen R. Sizer, *The Promised Land: A Critical Investigation of Evangelical Christian Zionism in Britain and the United States of America since 1800* (PhD: Middlesex University, 2002), p. 157.

[188] Darby, *Observations on a Tract entitled 'Remarks on the Sufferings of the Lord Jesus'*, CW15:34.

[189] Sizer, *The Promised Land*, p. 47.

[190] Sizer, *Christian Zionism*, p. 51.

[191] Darby, *Union in Incarnation*, CW29:187.

[192] Darby, *Reflections upon the Prophetic Inquiry*, CW2:19.

[193] Darby, *Letter to J.L. Harris* (Limerick, received 19 August 1833), L1:23.

[194] Darby, *On the Presence and Action of the Holy Ghost in the Church in Answer to the Work of Mr P. Wolff, entitled, 'Ministry as Opposed to Hierarchism and Chiefly to Religious Radicalism'*, CW3:264; cf. *Notes of Readings - The Acts of the Apostles*, M4:93; *The Irrationalism of Infidelity*, CW6:283.

[195] Darby, *Letter to R.T. Grant* (New York, 1866), L1:469-470.

[196] Darby, *Remarks on a Tract circulated by the Irvingites entitled, 'A Word of Instruction'*, CW15:2; *Union in Incarnation, the Root Error of Modern Theology*, CW29:186; *Christological Pantheism*, CW29:204-210.

[197] Darby, *The Irrationalism of Infidelity*, CW6:285.

poor Irving's heresies and wanderings'.[198] Darby also described elements of Irving's *Preliminary Discourse* as 'evidence, and accumulated evidence, of great carelessness', and drew attention to passages 'highly injurious to the work and honour of Christ, and in it, the just, holy, and influencing comfort of believing saints'. He also criticised Irving's sermons on Daniel's vision of the four beasts, and his interpretation of Isaiah, which he believed demonstrated 'the extreme neglect of Scripture and *even* prophecy itself, the hurried pursuit of an object in the mind'.[199] These are hardly the comments one would expect from a man allegedly impressed by, and indebted to, Edward Irving.

In a collection of Benjamin Newton's writings and conversations[200] we have an invaluable record of Darby's relationship with, and appraisal of, Edward Irving. Newton recalls how, during the formative years of the Plymouth Brethren, there were some, like Captain Percy Hall, who believed that the Bible spoke of a *secret* Rapture. Newton, who opposed the doctrine, recalls how Darby 'would take neither side', having expressed in a private letter to him 'no conviction' with regards to 'any secret coming'.[201] He also recalled a letter Darby had written to him about Thomas Tweedy, who had helped Darby clarify his thinking about the timing of the Rapture. According to William Kelly,

> no one was farther from lending an ear to the impious and profane voices of the quasi-inspired Irvingites than Mr. T. [Tweedy], unless indeed it were J.N.D. himself who had closely investigated their pretensions and judged their peculiar heterodoxy on Christ's humanity as anti-christian and blasphemous.

Kelly also noted how the Brethren had admired Irving as a preacher, but that 'no serious brother in fellowship' regarded the utterances in his church 'with less than horror, as emanating not from human excitement merely but from a demon accredited with the power of the Holy Spirit.'[202]

Darby and MacDonald

In 1830, Francis Newman received a letter from the Gare Loch region of Scotland, which was 'alive with religious fervour'.[203] The letter was passed to Newton, and Darby was duly commissioned by the Brethren to investigate the matter on their behalf. The excitement centred around the home of Isabella and Mary Campbell in Fernicarry, which had become something of a local shrine following reports that the sisters had received an ecstatic experience. God, it was claimed, was pouring out His Spirit in Scotland. According to Oliphant,

[198] Darby, *The Dispensation of the Fulness of Times*, CW13:152.
[199] Darby, *Reflections upon the Prophetic Inquiry*, CW2:6-9.
[200] Recorded by Newton's friend, Frederick Wyatt, and later copied by Alfred Fry.
[201] Fry, *The Fry MS*, pp. 237-238, 322.
[202] Kelly, *The Rapture of the Saints*, pp. 6-7.
[203] Dallimore, *The Life of Edward Irving*, p. 103.

'Almost every notable Christian man of the time took the matter into devout and anxious consideration',[204] including Edward Irving. The supernatural gifts which Mary Campbell claimed she had received commanded Irving's attention and governed his activity 'throughout the rest of his days on earth';[205] he and his associates were convinced that the 'extraordinary manifestations'[206] were 'of God'.[207] Darby did not share Irving's convictions, and the reasons he gave for dismissing these manifestations are significant. As Newton recalled,

> Darby had been most cautious, not giving us an opinion. But what decided him when on the spot was that when those who were inspired were expounding prophetic Scriptures, such as those in Isaiah, respecting Israel [and] Jerusalem they explained them as being prophetic of Christian Churches of this dispensation.- That determined me too.- I had just then been writing a 'Report' for the meeting of the Jews' Society.

Darby informed Newton 'that there wasn't a meeting or an interview in which the spirits did not dwell on the notion that the Israelitish blessings are all ours now.' As Newton recalled, 'That decided me at once, Darby too.'[208] Francis Newman, who initially believed that the alleged prophetic utterances were of God, records how his opinion changed after Darby sent him

> a full account of what he heard with his own ears; which was to the effect – that none of the sounds, vowels or consonants, were foreign;- that the strange words were moulded after the Latin grammar...so as to denote poverty of invention rather than spiritual agency;- and *that there was no interpretation*. The last point decided me, that any belief which I had in it must be for the present unpractical.[209]

In *The Irrationalism of Infidelity* (1853), Darby included an account of the MacDonald family of Port Glasgow, who were personal friends of the Campbells. Darby's personal record of his visit to the region appears to have been overlooked by most of his critics, but it is conclusive to the debate and completely exonerates him from *any* charge that he derived his doctrine of the pretribulation Rapture from the utterance of Margaret MacDonald:

> Two brothers (respectable shipbuilders at Port Glasgow, of the name M'D-), and their sister, were the chief persons who spoke, with a Gaelic maid-servant, in the tongues, and a Mrs. J-, in English. J. M'D- spoke, on the occasion alluded to, for

---

[204] Oliphant, *The Life of Edward Irving: Vol. II*, p. 134.

[205] Dallimore, *The Life of Edward Irving*, p. 106; cf. Robert Norton, *Memoirs of James & George MacDonald of Port-Glasgow* (London: John F. Shaw, 1840), pp. 74-75.

[206] 'On the Extraordinary Manifestations in Port-Glasgow', *The Morning Watch*, 2 (1831), 869-873.

[207] 'The Out-Pouring of the Holy Spirit', *The Morning Watch*, 2 (1831), 617.

[208] Fry, *The Fry MS*, pp. 236-237, 208.

[209] Newman, *Phases of Faith*, p. 119.

about a quarter of an hour, with great energy and fluency, in a semi-latin sounding speech – then sung a hymn in the same. Having finished, he knelt down and prayed there might be an interpretation...His sister got up at the opposite side of the room, and professed to give the interpretation; but it was a string of texts on overcoming, and no hymn, and one, if not more, of the texts was quoted wrongly...Once the Gaelic servant spoke briefly in 'a tongue,' not, if the 'Irish Clergyman' [Darby] remembers right, the same evening. The sense he had of the want of the power of the Holy Ghost in the Church made him willing to hear and see. Yet he went rather as deputed for others than for himself. The excitement was great, so that, though not particularly an excitable person, he felt its effects very strongly. It did not certainly approve itself to his judgment; other things contributed to form it. It was too much of a scene. Previous to the time of exercising the gifts, they read, sung psalms, and prayed, under certain persons' presidence...This being finished, the 'Irish Clergyman' was going away, when another said to him, 'Don't go: the best part is probably to come yet.' So he stayed, and heard what has just been related. He was courteously admitted, as one not believing, who came to see what was the real truth of the case. The parties are mostly dead, or dispersed, and many freed from the delusion, and the thing itself public; so that he does not feel he is guilty of any indiscretion in giving a correct account of what passed. It may be added, without of course saying anything that could point out the persons, that female vanity, and very distinct worldliness, did not confirm, to his mind, the thought that it could be the Spirit's power.[210]

William Kelly asked, 'can any fair mind in God's presence, if he knew no other facts, conceive a greater improbability than J.N.D. adopting the utterance of what he believed a demon as a truth of God?'[211] Dave MacPherson apparently can, on the basis that Darby omitted in his report any direct reference to Margaret MacDonald's *alleged* 'pre-trib' utterance. To a 'theological detective' like MacPherson, the explanation for this omission is simple: there was a 'cover-up', Darby having stolen the doctrine of the pretribulation Rapture from MacDonald. MacPherson recklessly suggests that by the time Darby wrote his account in 1853,

> he had preserved an understandably special interest in the young and unassuming Scottish lassie from whom he had borrowed a key ingredient for his dispensational system of prophetic interpretation!

Despite conceding that the 'lassie' in question 'saw a series of raptures', only the first of which he claims was a 'pre-trib translation', and despite labelling her as 'a partial rapturist', he insists that 'Darby borrowed from her, modified her views, and then popularised them under his own name without giving her

---

[210] Darby, *The Irrationalism of Infidelity*, CW6:284-285; *cf. Letter to a Sister* (5 March 1845), L1:76-77; *Letter to C. McAdam* (Chicago, May 1875), L2:346.

[211] Kelly, *The Rapture of the Saints*, p. 12.

credit'.[212] Such unrestrained allegations not only fail to inflict 'a devastating wound on the pre-trib camp',[213] as is claimed, but do not match the portrait we have of Darby from his writings, and from the testimonies of those closest to him. MacPherson's 'breezy journalistic style'[214] may be conducive to book selling, but it contributes little to critical research and damages the integrity and reputation of a man whose 'one aim' was 'the glory of God'.[215] John Nelson Darby was a careful student of the Bible who found an exegetical basis for his doctrine of the pretribulation Rapture in the Scriptures, which he consistently maintained had been his sole guide.

Margaret MacDonald's personal account of her 1830 utterance (see Appendix) is quoted in Robert Norton's *Memoirs of James & George MacDonald of Port-Glasgow* (1840), and warrants closer scrutiny. Rennie concedes that her utterance was not as clear as MacPherson suggests.[216] There is certainly no 'series of raptures' as MacPherson claims. From a careful reading of MacDonald's account, we may reasonably conclude that she was, in fact, advocating a *post*tribulation Rapture, the Great Tribulation being 'the fiery trial which is to try *us*' and which will be 'for the purging and purifying of *the real members* of the body of Jesus'. She also described this period as being 'from Antichrist', when Satan 'will try to shake in every thing *we* have believed', when 'the awful sight of a false Christ [will] be seen on this earth', and when 'nothing but the living Christ *in us* can detect this awful attempt of the enemy to deceive'[217] (*italics* mine). MacDonald included herself among the faithful to be tried *after* Antichrist has been revealed and *during* the Tribulation period. These 'revelations' are completely inconsistent with Darby's teaching.

Exploding the Myth

Despite doubting MacPherson and affirming that Darby did indeed reject the Port Glasgow manifestations as a delusion, Ian Rennie stubbornly refuses to let go in this 'tug-of-war with the truth'.[218] Reluctant to absolve Darby completely, he suggests that MacDonald's utterance was 'grist for Darby's mill', and that as he left Scotland he 'carried with him impressions which, after some years of reflection, would play their part in the formation of the teaching of the secret pretribulation rapture.'[219]

---

[212] Dave MacPherson, *The Incredible Cover-Up: Exposing the Origins of Rapture Theories* (Medford, OR: Omega Publications, 2001), pp. 94, v, 85.

[213] North, *Rapture Fever*, p. 137.

[214] Rennie, 'Nineteenth-Century Roots', p. 51.

[215] Carron, *The Christian Testimony*, pp. 346-347.

[216] Rennie, 'Nineteenth-Century Roots', p. 52.

[217] MacPherson, *The Incredible Cover-Up*, p. 153.

[218] Strandberg and James, *Are You Rapture Ready?*, p. 56.

[219] Rennie, 'Nineteenth-Century Roots', p. 52.

Flegg and Weber are among those who have expressed dissatisfaction with Tregelles and the 'hardly convincing'[220] claims of MacPherson, concluding that 'their arguments do not stand up to serious criticism'.[221] Sandeen accuses those who have cited Tregelles against Darby of bringing 'a groundless and pernicious charge',[222] while MacPherson's book has been dismissed as an 'anti pre-Trib vendetta'[223] that is 'patently ridiculous'[224] and full of 'tiresome polemics'.[225] Benware and Nebeker assert that 'no clear evidence exists that Darby got his views from Margaret MacDonald or Edward Irving,'[226] and that any suggestion of a 'directly derivative link' between Darby and Irving is 'unduly reductionist'.[227] Brethren scholar F.F. Bruce also distanced Darby from Irving and MacDonald, and acknowledged that the doctrine of the pretribulation Rapture was 'in the air in the 1820s and 1830s among eager students of unfulfilled prophecy'.[228] As Weber concedes, those who have criticised Darby 'may have to settle for Darby's own explanation.'[229]

The Morning Watch

The public voice of nineteenth-century Evangelicalism in the Church of England was the *Christian Observer*, a magazine launched by the Clapham Sect. Its editors noted the premillennial awakening in the July 1825 edition, and reviewed a number of representative writings, but by 1830 their focus had shifted away from premillennialism. Premillennialists thereafter began to propagate their doctrines 'in their own periodicals',[230] which included the *Christian Herald* (Dublin, 1830-1835) and the *Investigator* (London, 1831-1836). During the Albury Conference of 1828, the decision was taken by delegates to sound a public wake-up call to the wider Church. Financed by Henry Drummond and edited by John Tudor, the *Quarterly Journal of Prophecy and Theological Review*, or *Morning Watch*, was launched. Four years later, in the final issue, Tudor stated what its founding purpose had been:

---

[220] Columba Graham Flegg, *Gathered under Apostles: A Study of the Catholic Apostolic Church* (Oxford: Clarendon Press, 1992), p. 5; cf. Timothy P. Weber, *Living in the Shadow of the Second Coming: American Premillennialism, 1875-1982* (Chicago, IL: The University of Chicago Press, 1987), pp. 21-22.

[221] Flegg, *Gathered under Apostles*, p. 436.

[222] Sandeen, *The Roots of Fundamentalism*, p. 64.

[223] LaHaye, *Rapture under Attack*, pp. 116-136.

[224] Lindsey, *The Rapture*, p. 201.

[225] Stunt, 'Influences', p. 57.

[226] Benware, *Understanding End Times Prophecy*, p. 196.

[227] Nebeker, 'John Nelson Darby', 89.

[228] F.F. Bruce, 'Book Review of *The Unbelievable Pre-Trib Origin*', *Evangelical Quarterly*, 47 (1975), 58.

[229] Weber, *Living in the Shadow of the Second Coming*, p. 22.

[230] Sandeen, *The Roots of Fundamentalism*, p. 23.

> And now, when the Protestant church is become nearly as dead and formal as the Papal; when the ample volume of the word of God, designed to fill every chamber of the soul of man, to satiate all its longings and transcend its highest imaginings; when this gift of God to all men, designed to be free as the air of heaven…has been squeezed into Articles, fettered by commentators, and the larger portion…the Prophetic portion – prohibited and proscribed by all the rulers in all the churches of the land; – at such a time, and in such circumstances, did the Morning Watch come forth, to claim the whole word of God for the whole church; to assert the right of every individual to interpret the whole of that word which reveals the Lord God, whose image and likeness we bear.[231]

Tudor believed that the world was on the brink of catastrophe, and that certain tumultuous events had been foretold in the Bible, including one 'especially singled out by God as that which shall most peculiarly redound to his glory among men…namely, the restoration of the Jews'.[232] Endeavouring to rouse the Church from its slumber, Tudor included a discourse, written in 1785 by the bishop of Lescar, in an 1833 edition of the journal. In his discourse, Lescar insisted that the 'best hopes' of the Church were 'interwoven' with Israel's restoration, and bemoaned the contempt of the Church towards the Jew:

> O ye wretched remains of that people, dragged in the dust and trampled under the feet of the nations, I am not an accomplice in the unjust contempt with which ye are laden. I adore the hand of the Almighty, which has weighed heavy on you for seventeen centuries; but I always hope in his mercy. I consider the rank of which you are stripped, and that to which you are destined; I see in you the remains of Abraham's children according to the flesh – the fathers of Abraham's children according to the Spirit…and, astonished at such transcendent privileges, I join with the church in daily prayer to God, that he would deign to perform his mercies – call you to Him, and, by your return, fulfil his promises, silence our enemies, ensure the repose, the glory, and the stability of the church.[233]

The *Morning Watch* appears to have advocated a pretribulation, and possibly 'partial', Rapture position, believing that the catching away, or translation, of the Church would be confined to those who were faithful to Christ and longing for His return. Successive editions referred to how 'God hath promised that by watchfulness and prayer *we shall escape* all those things that shall come to pass',[234] how 'the members of Christ's body are gathered to him, before the

---

[231] John Tudor, 'Conclusion of the Morning Watch', *The Morning Watch*, 7 (1833), 401.

[232] John Tudor, 'The Study of Prophecy a Question of Degree', *The Morning Watch*, 1 (1830), 186.

[233] 'Discourse of M. de Noé, Bishop of Lescar (Troyes), written in 1785', *The Morning Watch*, 6 (1833), 56-59.

[234] Fidus, 'Commentary on the Seven Apocalyptic Epistles', *The Morning Watch*, 4 (1832), 280.

limbs of Antichrist…gather against the Lamb and his armies',[235] how during the *'long period'* of His return only those 'who are watching and praying, and expecting their Lord, and to them only, will Christ be manifested at the *beginning* of the DAY of his coming',[236] and how 'we may daily expect the accomplishment' of this 'translation'[237] of the Church. Although Darby accused the journal of being 'prepossessed with its own views',[238] and rejected its underlying historicism,[239] the contribution of the *Morning Watch* to premillennialism in general and Christian Restorationism in particular was significant. Publication of the journal ended when John Tudor assumed greater responsibility in the Catholic Apostolic Church.

In Conclusion

Before we consider how Restorationism became intertwined with politics during the nineteenth century, it is important to identify those who, with Darby, were instrumental in ending the monopoly of the historicist school, which fell into disrepute in the wake of failed predictions. As Robert Anderson remarked, 'In our day prophetic students have turned prophets, and with mingled folly and daring have sought to fix the very year of Christ's return to earth.'[240]

In *The Apostles' School of Prophetic Interpretation* (1849), Charles Maitland[241] denounced the historicist school in favour of the futurism being espoused by its 'rather quiet pioneers',[242] William and Thomas Witherby, and by Samuel Roffey Maitland, William Burgh, and Joseph Tyso. In attempting to lift the veil which had shrouded Biblical prophecy for centuries, Tyso, who

---

[235] 'The Hour of Christ's Appearance', *The Morning Watch*, 4 (1832), 253.

[236] 'Present State of Prophetic Knowledge, and Progress in the Interpretation of the Apocalypse', *The Morning Watch*, 5 (1832), 374.

[237] 'Christ the Morning Star; and Lucifer Son of the Morning', *The Morning Watch*, 5 (1832), 12.

[238] Darby, *Reflections upon the Prophetic Inquiry*, CW2:20-21.

[239] See, for example, 'Germinant Fulfilment of Prophecies', *The Morning Watch*, 6 (1833), 45-49; 'The Alphabet of Prophecy', *The Morning Watch*, 7 (1833), 140-160.

[240] Sir Robert Anderson, *The Coming Prince: The Marvellous Prophecy of Daniel's Seventy Weeks concerning the Antichrist*, 14th edn (Grand Rapids, MI: Kregel Publications, 1954), p. 131.

[241] Maitland's father, Captain Charles Maitland, believed that the restoration of the Jews was 'at the door'. (Charles Maitland, *A Brief and Connected View of Prophecy: being An Exposition of the Second, Seventh, and Eighth Chapters of the Prophecy of Daniel; together with the Sixteenth Chapter of Revelation. To which are added Some Observations respecting the period and manner of the Restoration of the Jews* [London: 1814], p. 78.)

[242] Oddy, *Eschatological Prophecy*, p. 95.

described the year-day system as 'a baseless fabric',[243] distinguished between the *'literal key'* which opens 'the treasures of prophetic truth', and the *'mystic key'* which had been 'made to fit everything, but really fits nothing well'. He maintained that only by using the right key would the Church understand that the Jews were to be resettled 'in their own land', the Temple rebuilt, and the sacrificial system restored *before* Christ's return.[244]

In his *Review of Scripture* (1818), William Witherby described the restoration of the Jews as 'the prophetic burden' of the Old Testament, and asserted that Christ's resurrection confirmed 'all those promises to Israel which are the brethren of Moses and the Prophets'. He asserted that 'no part of the Revelation, as a prophecy' had been fulfilled other than 'what is declared respecting the Seven Asiatic Churches', and cited Revelation 11 as 'indisputable evidence that the Temple of God shall be restored'. He also limited Antichrist's reign to a future period of 42 months.[245]

In a series of dialogues, Thomas Witherby claimed that it was 'both the duty and the interest of Christians to examine their opinions concerning the Jews'. History, he believed, showed 'that it is an awful thing for any nation to act with hostility against the Jews without a commission from the Lord God of Israel', and even then, as with Assyria and Babylon (*cf.* Isa. 10:5; Jer. 51:20), 'the least excess committed in the execution' of that commission 'is sure to bring down heavy judgments.' Although God had prescribed judgment for the Jewish people, His Son would soon return 'to gather them together as the elect people of God, and to restore again the kingdom unto Israel, with more than tenfold splendour'. Witherby lamented the fact that in the Church of England the confession of faith 'is entirely silent upon this subject of the restoration of the Jews',[246] and conspicuously absent from the ancient creeds of the Church.

Although Darby makes no mention of Tyso or the Witherbys in his *Collected Writings*, he does refer to Maitland and Burgh. Samuel Maitland, an associate of the LSPCJ and an acquaintance of Charles Simeon, refuted as 'error' the year-day theory, arguing that the 1260 days were *'natural days'*.[247]

---

[243] Joseph Tyso, *The Year-Day System of Interpreting the Prophecies Examined* (Wallingford: 1845), p. 10.

[244] Joseph Tyso, *An Inquiry after Prophetic Truth relative to the Restoration of the Jews and the Millennium* (London: Holdsworth and Ball, 1831), pp. 111, 117, 64-87, 176-210.

[245] William Witherby, *A Review of Scripture, in Testimony of the Truth of the Second Advent, the First Resurrection, and the Millennium: with an Appendix, containing extracts from Mr. Joseph Eyre's Observations on the Prophecies Relating to the Restoration of the Jews* (London: 1818), pp. xxii, 50, xxiii, 11, 23-24.

[246] Thomas Witherby, *An Attempt to Remove Prejudices concerning the Jewish Nation by way of Dialogue* (London: 1804), pp. v-vi, 114, 262, 311.

[247] Samuel Roffey Maitland, *An Enquiry into the Grounds on which the Prophetic Period of Daniel and St. John has been supposed to consist of 1260 Years* (London: Hatchard and Son, 1826), p. 2.

This drew an exhaustive response from Edward Bishop Elliott (1793-1875), whose four-volume defence of historicism, entitled, *Horae Apocalypticae* ('Hours with the Apocalypse'), has been described as 'the standard textbook'[248] of the historicist school. Darby acquired a copy for his private collection. In the original 1844 edition, Elliott explained how Maitland's futurism

> had begun to make an evident impression on prophetic investigators, as well as on other students of biblical and ecclesiastical literature: and had caused considerable doubt in the minds of many as to the correctness of...the prophetic year-day theory, generally received in England since the Reformation.[249]

Darby was well acquainted with Maitland's work, and had 'every respect'[250] for his scholarship. He was also acquainted with the work of William Burgh, a fellow graduate of Trinity College, Dublin.

In a series of twelve lectures published in 1832, Burgh described the Jews as '*the key to prophecy*,' asserting that God 'neither has done nor will do any thing irrespective of that people.'[251] He believed that the Jewish people would return to the Land *before* acknowledging Jesus as the Messiah, and that the Antichrist would make a covenant with them before setting himself up in the Third Temple. Writing to the *Christian Herald* in 1832, Darby spoke of the 'progress of conviction as to the truth and nearness of our Lord's coming', and suggested that Burgh's writings contained 'the most popular and common exposition...current amongst the expectants of our Lord's coming.'[252]

This brief introduction to futurism not only connects Darby to a number of Evangelicals who grew increasingly disillusioned with the historicist school, but silences those critics who have portrayed him as a blot on the premillennial landscape. Certain aspects of Darby's eschatology were clearly not unique, but as Evangelical historian David Bebbington, and Eliayahu Tal of the International Forum for a United Jerusalem, have both acknowledged, John Nelson Darby was 'the most significant figure' of the nineteenth century 'to adopt a form of futurist premillennialism'.[253]

---

[248] Anderson, *Unfulfilled Prophecy*, p. 54.

[249] Elliott, *Horae Apocalypticae: Vol. I*, p. iii.

[250] Darby, *On 'Days' Signifying 'Years'*, CW2:42.

[251] William Burgh, *Lectures on the Second Advent of our Lord Jesus Christ, and Connected Events: with an Introduction on the Use of Unfulfilled Prophecy* (Dublin: 1832), p. 125.

[252] Darby, *Review of 'Lectures on the Second Advent'*, CW33:1.

[253] Bebbington, *Evangelicalism*, p. 86; cf. Eliyahu Tal, *You Don't Have to be Jewish to be a Zionist: A Review of 400 Years of Christian Zionism* (Jerusalem: International Forum for a United Jerusalem, 2000), p. 58.

Chapter 7

Rediscovering the Land of the Bible

Many of those who attended the Albury Park conferences, including Revd William 'Millennial' Marsh (1775-1864), highlighted the 'perpetually occurring'[1] references in Scripture to the inextricable link between the Jewish people and the Land of Israel. Marsh suggested that if their promised reunion was not occupying the attention of the Church as it had occupied that of the apostles and prophets of old, then 'we are not of the same spirit with them.'[2] As the nineteenth century progressed, men and women from all walks of life became captivated with a land and people long forsaken and neglected.

The Desolate Land

In the fifth of his *Popular Lectures on the Prophecies Relative to the Jewish Nation*, Hugh McNeile confidently predicted that *Eretz Yisrael* would experience 'a literal renovation to beauty and fertility, accompanied by a multiplication of beasts upon it, as well as men'.[3] The consistent testimony of nineteenth-century travellers and explorers was that the land of the proverbial milk and honey was 'still in the Middle Ages',[4] abandoned and in ruins.[5] The most celebrated account was written by Samuel L. Clemens, alias Mark Twain, who published a chronicle of his travels to the Middle East. In *The Innocents Abroad* (1869), he wrote the following:

> Palestine sits in sackcloth and ashes. Over it broods the spell of a curse that has withered its fields and fettered its energies...Nazareth is forlorn; about that ford of

---

[1] William Marsh, *A Few Plain Thoughts on Prophecy* (Colchester: n.d.), p. 36.

[2] William Marsh, 'Preface', in *Israel's Sins, and Israel's Hopes. Being Lectures delivered during Lent, 1846, at St. George's, Bloomsbury. By twelve Clergymen of the Church of England. With a Preface by the Rev. William Marsh* (London: James Nisbet and Co., 1846), p. vi.

[3] McNeile, *Popular Lectures*, p. 139.

[4] Herbert Sidebotham, *Great Britain and Palestine* (London: MacMillan and Co. Limited, 1937), p. 83.

[5] Maundrell and Joliffe's accounts of the ruin of the Land are cited in Henry Smith, *The Protestant Bishopric in Jerusalem: Its Origin and Progress from the Official Documents published by Command of His Majesty the King of Prussia and from other Authentic Sources* (London: B. Wertheim, Aldine Chambers, 1847), p. 2.

Jordan where the hosts of Israel entered the Promised Land with songs of rejoicing, one finds only a squalid camp of fantastic Bedouins of the desert...Bethlehem and Bethany, in their poverty and their humiliation, have nothing about them now to remind one that they once knew the high honour of the Saviour's presence...Jerusalem itself, the stateliest name in history, has lost all its ancient grandeur, and is become a pauper village...Capernaum is a shapeless ruin...Palestine is desolate and unlovely. And why should it be otherwise? Can the *curse* of the Deity beautify a land?[6]

There was no need to 'multiply quotations to prove the desolation of a country which the Turks have possessed, and which the Arabs have plundered for centuries,'[7] for the Land had been rendered 'more a museum of church history than of the Bible',[8] a mere relic of a bygone era. Ben-Arieh describes Israel at that time as 'a derelict province' and 'a sad backwater of a crumbling empire'.[9] In his book, *With Our Army in Palestine* (1919), Antony Bluett, who served with the Egyptian Camel Transport Corps of the British Army, described how he saw 'the imprint of the oppressor in the very land itself'. Although there were still 'patches of cultivation' to be seen, the Land had been abandoned by the Ottomans 'to a stony barrenness.'[10] In 1939, soil conservationist Walter Clay Lowdermilk witnessed for himself the 'doleful ruins' as he contemplated 'the tragedy of this land'.[11] However, for the Jews who began to resettle there during the nineteenth century, the desolation they encountered was overcome by an imagination 'fired by the brilliant image of Zion rebuilt in glory'.[12]

The Church of Scotland Mission

In 1839, Evangelical hearts were fired by the report of a Church of Scotland deputation which had been sent to 'Palestine' to report on the condition of the Jewish population. One member of the four-man team was Robert Murray McCheyne (1813-1843). Writing to his parents on 26 June 1839, he spoke of how Judah had 'gone into captivity' with only a 'few men left in the land', and

---

[6] Mark Twain, *The Innocents Abroad* (London: Readers Library Publishing Co. Ltd., n.d.), pp. 234-235.

[7] Smith, *The Protestant Bishopric*, p. 2.

[8] George Adam Smith, *The Historical Geography of the Holy Land* (London: Collins, 1966), p. 50. David Lloyd George instructed General Allenby to read Smith's book before embarking on his 'Palestine' campaign. (David Lloyd George, *War Memoirs of David Lloyd George: Vol. II* [London: Odhams Press Limited, n.d.], p. 1090.)

[9] Yehoshua Ben-Arieh, *The Rediscovery of the Holy Land in the Nineteenth Century* (Jerusalem: Magnes Press, Hebrew University, 1979), p. 11.

[10] Antony Bluett, *With Our Army in Palestine* (London: Andrew Melrose Ltd., 1919), pp. 214-215.

[11] Lowdermilk, *Palestine*, p. 24.

[12] Amos Elon, *The Israelis: Founders and Sons* (Harmondsworth: Penguin Books Ltd., 1981), p. 87.

how Jerusalem lay 'very desolate' with most of Judah's cities 'all waste'. McCheyne prayed that God would use the deputation to 'stir up Christians to love Zion', for theirs had been a 'mission of love to Israel'. The excitement generated by the report in Scotland was 'very great', awakening 'deeper feelings...of a Scriptural persuasion that Israel was still "beloved for the fathers' sake"'. McCheyne believed that the proper Christian response was to become 'like God in his peculiar affections', since the Bible showed that 'God has ever had, and still has, a peculiar love to the Jews.'[13] Andrew Bonar, another member of the deputation, believed that the very future of the Church of Scotland depended on its response. He wrote:

> If the Church of Scotland in these perilous times 'take hold of the skirt of the Jew' [Zech. 8:23], God may remember her for Zion's sake...May the God of Israel, for his ancient people's sake, make this work useful in kindling a brighter flame of love to the Jews in the bosom of all who are 'the Lord's remembrancers' in Scotland.[14]

From the statement it issued in May 2007 denouncing Christian Zionism, it is clear that the Church of Scotland has ignored Bonar's warning. On 24 May 1889, on the occasion of the jubilee of the Scottish mission, Adolph Saphir, a Jewish Christian, implored the General Assembly of the Free Church of Scotland 'not to forget *the love to Israel* which at that time so eminently characterised you.' He believed that if Christians truly loved Christ, they would not only 'love the Jews' but understand 'something of those tears which Jesus shed when He wept over Jerusalem.'[15]

The third member of the deputation was Alexander Keith (1791-1880), whose *Evidence of the Truth of the Christian Religion derived from the Literal Fulfilment of Prophecy* (1828) underwent six editions in four years. Thomas Chalmers described it as a work 'recognised in our halls of theology as holding a high place in sacred literature', and one which could be found 'in almost every home and known as a household word throughout the land'.[16] Keith famously declared that 'the land [of Israel] is a witness as well as the people', the period of its desolation being 'commensurate with the dispersion' of the Jews. He believed that only when the Jews had been regathered from the *Diaspora* would the Land no longer be desolate, 'nor the people termed forsaken any more.'[17]

---

[13] Bonar, *The Life of Robert Murray McCheyne*, pp. 121-122, 102-104.

[14] Andrew A. Bonar and Robert Murray McCheyne, *Narrative of a Mission of Inquiry to the Jews from the Church of Scotland in 1839* (Edinburgh: William Whyte and Co., 1850), p. vi.

[15] Saphir, *Christ and Israel*, pp. 14, 134.

[16] Quoted in Elmore, *A Critical Examination*, p. 67.

[17] Alexander Keith, *Evidence of the Truth of the Christian Religion derived from the Literal Fulfilment of Prophecy; Particularly as Illustrated by the History of the Jews,*

This same conviction was expressed by John Duncan (1796-1870), the first missionary to the Jews appointed by the Church of Scotland after the 1839 mission. Affectionately known as 'Rabbi Duncan' on account of his 'deep interest in Israel', he described the Jewish nation as *'primus inter pares* (first among equals)' and the Church as 'the younger son and pardoned prodigal'. On 24 May 1867, he made the following entry in his journal:

> Sailing from Dover to Ostend, on my way first to Pesth, we found a Jewish family on board, of which fact I became aware by seeing on their carriage the motto, 'Fuimus erimus.' (We have been; we shall be.) There was no 'Iumus.' (We are.) Israel hath indeed a present, though a most lamentable one; but what a glorious past! What a still more glorious future!...Oh, the bitter weeping – the burning blush of shame – the tender kiss of reconciliation – the jubilant anthems of the long-estranged, now in everlasting loving-kindness reclaimed, never more to part! And this *redintegratio amoris* (restoration of love) will tell most blessedly upon us; it will be as life from the dead.[18]

The Stones Cry Out

During the first half of the nineteenth century the Ottoman Empire was shaken by internal revolt following its protracted conflict with Mehemet Ali, the Pasha of Egypt. European powers began to flex their muscles in anticipation of a great spoil on 'the field of glory where the epic, the imperishable reputations had been made.'[19] The Holy Land stood at the geographical, commercial, and political crossroads of the world, a narrow land bridge connecting three continents and serving as 'a highway of empires'.[20]

In 1838, Lord Shaftesbury expressed his hope that the Land, 'when dug and harrowed', would provide 'the testimony of the authenticity of the Bible'.[21] As reports came in that precious minerals and metals had been discovered in the Land, many in Britain believed that God's promised restoration of Israel was imminent. In his letters to Shaftesbury, William Gosling likened this news to 'cold water to a thirsty soul'. He believed that the Land was 'being healed'[22]

---

and by the Discoveries of Recent Travellers, 37th edn (London: T. Nelson and Sons, 1859), pp. 98, 105.

[18] *Rich Gleanings after the Vintage from 'Rabbi' Duncan*, ed. by James S. Sinclair (Glasgow: Free Presbyterian Publications, 1984), pp. 13, 372-373, 385.

[19] Barbara W. Tuchman, *Bible and Sword: How the British came to Palestine* (London: Papermac, 1982), p. 165.

[20] Silberman, *Digging for God and Country*, p. 14.

[21] Quoted in A.L. Tibawi, *British Interests in Palestine 1800-1901: A Study of Religious and Educational Enterprise* (Oxford: Oxford University Press, 1961), p. 183.

[22] William Gosling, *Two Letters to the Right Honourable the Earl of Shaftesbury, on the Speedy Restoration of the Jews to Palestine, through the Discovery of Gold and Silver in that Land. To which is added Two Letters on the Preparation of the Land for their*

before their eyes, and that such discoveries would provide a strong incentive for the Jews to return to their homeland.

Britain's link with the Holy Land had been severed during the time of the Protestant Reformation, when 'fear of war, Popery, and the Turk deterred any would-be travellers'.[23] Although periodically visited by European explorers before the nineteenth century, the Land remained a virtual *'terra incognita'*[24] as far as scientific research was concerned. Early nineteenth-century explorers who began to open up this unknown country to a wider, and predominantly Christian public included Ulrich Seetzen, Johann Burckhardt, James Silk Buckingham, and Lady Hester Stanhope. One member of the Christian public who journeyed to 'Palestine' was the 25th Earl of Crawford, Alexander Lindsay, who in a letter to his mother in 1838 described the Bible as 'the only safe guide-book in this land of ignorance and superstition'. Addressing the indigenous belief that a curse rested on the soil itself, Lindsay wrote:

> No other curse...rests upon it, than that induced by the removal of the ancient inhabitants, and the will of the Almighty that the modern occupants should never be so numerous as to invalidate the prophecy that the land should enjoy her Sabbaths so long as the rightful heirs remain in the land of their enemies.

Lindsay reported that there were still pockets of land which 'smile like the Land of Promise', and 'oases of fertility' which proved that it 'only waits the return of her banished children...to burst once more into universal luxuriance, and be all that she ever was in the days of Solomon.' When Lindsay reached Jerusalem and sat on the Mount of Olives, he viewed the promised reunion of land and people against the more magnificent backdrop of Christ's return, urging Christians to 'watch and be ready for his coming!'[25] Lindsay's *Letters on Egypt, Edom, and the Holy Land* was 'the first in that flood of Holy Land travel books that over the next forty years was to saturate the British public'.[26]

In the winter of 1839, the 'photographic heritage'[27] of 'Palestine' began to develop when the French photographer, Frédéric Goupil-Fesquet, took the first daguerreotype of Jerusalem. Soon, images were circulating around the world. In 1844, George Skene Keith, son of Alexander Keith, connected the geography of the Land with its Biblical history, his photographs being included

---

Return, the Building of the Temple, and Second Coming of Messiah (London: Houlston & Stoneman, 1853), pp. 20-21.

[23] John James Moscrop, *Measuring Jerusalem: The Palestine Exploration Fund and British Interests in the Holy Land* (London: Leicester University Press, 2000), p. 215.

[24] Ben-Arieh, *The Rediscovery of the Holy Land*, p. 5.

[25] Lord Lindsay, *Letters on Egypt, Edom, and the Holy Land*, 4th edn (London: Henry Colburn, 1847), pp. 243-244, 251.

[26] Tuchman, *Bible and Sword*, p. 191.

[27] *Photographic Heritage of the Holy Land 1839-1914*, ed. by Eyal Onne (Manchester: Institute of Advanced Studies, Manchester Polytechnic, 1980), pp. 7-8.

as engravings in his father's book. Illustrated Bibles, paintings by David Roberts and William Holman Hunt, and photographic albums soon awakened interest in the Holy Land, and between 1840 and 1880 over 1,600 travel books were published in England alone. Whereas Jewish travelogues 'fixed a sad eye' upon the ruin and desolation of the Land, their Christian counterparts were often written 'in a tone of breathless excitement'.[28]

Ruth Goldschmidt-Lehmann notes 'the quite remarkable interest Britons had in the Holy Land' during the nineteenth century. There was simply 'no limit to the literature'[29] which resulted from pilgrimage tours, archaeological research, and scientific expeditions. This was the 'Age of Rediscovery',[30] the age of the topographer, painter, cartographer, archaeologist, traveller, and missionary. In 1862, A.P. Stanley, author of *Sinai and Palestine in Connection with their History* (1856), served as a guide to the Prince of Wales (later Edward VII) on his tour of 'Palestine', a visit which further heightened public awareness of, and interest in, the land of the Bible.

Edward Robinson

William McClure Thomson (1806-1894), an American missionary who was resident in 'Palestine' for many years, described his adopted home as

> one vast tablet whereupon God's messages to men have been drawn, and graven deep in living characters by the Great Publisher of glad tidings, to be seen and read of all to the end of time.[31]

Edward Robinson (1794-1863) was the man most responsible for unearthing this 'ancient tablet' during an expedition he undertook in 1838 with American missionary, Eli Smith. According to Silberman, Robinson and Smith set about rescuing 'the historical soul of Palestine' through their 'stubborn search for the past'.[32] Robinson's account of how 'the Promised Land unfolded itself'[33] to their eyes was published in 1841 under the title, *Biblical Researches in Palestine, Mount Sinai and Arabia Petraea*, a copy of which Darby owned.

Edward Robinson, the doyen of Biblical archaeology, led a long line of

---

[28] Elon, *The Israelis*, pp. 84-85.

[29] Ruth P. Goldschmidt-Lehmann, *Britain and the Holy Land 1800-1914: A Select Bibliography* (London: The Jewish Historical Society of England, 1995), p. vii.

[30] Ben-Arieh, *The Rediscovery of the Holy Land*, p. 230.

[31] William McClure Thomson, *The Land and the Book; or, Biblical Illustrations drawn from the Manners and Customs, the Scenes and Scenery of the Holy Land* (London: T. Nelson and Sons, 1901), p. xvi.

[32] Silberman, *Digging for God and Country*, p. 47.

[33] Edward Robinson and Eli Smith, *Biblical Researches in Palestine, Mount Sinai and Arabia Petraea. A Journal of Travels in the Year 1838: Vol. I* (London: John Murray, 1841), p. v.

Evangelicals who were deeply moved during their travels to the Holy Land.[34] So great was the impact of the research of this 'scriptural geographer' that he was followed by 'a long cavalcade of geographers, missionaries and Protestant clergymen, all of whom were concerned primarily with underwriting the truth of the Bible'. Robinson's *Biblical Researches* triggered an 'avalanche of books',[35] and became a standard textbook in theological colleges and universities around the world.[36] Ben-Arieh describes it as 'a cornerstone of 19th century Palestine exploration',[37] while Isaac Da Costa, an eminent Dutch poet and theologian who helped to instil a 'deep respect and love'[38] for the Jewish people into Corrie ten Boom's family, noted how, through the work of men like Edward Robinson, 'the ruins of Jerusalem, as well as the dry bones of scattered Israel, present an appeal to the heart and mind of the Christian'.[39]

The Palestine Exploration Fund

Colonel George Gawler (1796-1869), a veteran of Waterloo and founder of the Association for Promoting Jewish Settlement in Palestine (1852), was one of many who sought to remedy the desolate state of the Land. In his book, *Tranquillisation of Syria and the East* (1845), he suggested that it was time to 'replenish the deserted towns and fields of Palestine with the energetic people whose warmest affections are rooted in the soil.'[40] Championing the cause of Jewish emancipation in Britain, Gawler connected the restoration of the Jews with British imperial interests,[41] and in 1849 accompanied Sir Moses Montefiore, president of the Board of Deputies of British Jews, on one of his seven visits to the Land. Ever the pragmatist, Gawler was instrumental in persuading Montefiore to establish agricultural settlements in *Eretz Yisrael*.

Following a meeting of clergymen and archaeologists at Westminster Abbey,[42] the Palestine Exploration Fund (P.E.F.) was founded on 22 June 1865

---

[34] Robinson and Smith, *Biblical Researches: Vol. III*, p. 75.

[35] Naomi Shepherd, *The Zealous Intruders* (London: Collins, 1987), pp. 14, 78.

[36] Moscrop, *Measuring Jerusalem*, p. 20.

[37] Ben-Arieh, *The Rediscovery of the Holy Land*, p. 90.

[38] Corrie ten Boom, *Father ten Boom: God's Man* (Eastbourne: Kingsway Publications, 1980), p. 33.

[39] Da Costa, *Israel and the Gentiles*, p. 15.

[40] George Gawler, *Tranquillisation of Syria and the East: Observations and practical suggestions, in furtherance of the establishment of Jewish colonies in Palestine, the most sober and sensible remedy for the miseries of Asiatic Turkey* (London: T.&W. Boone, 1845), p. 6.

[41] John M. Shaftesley and Norman Bentwich, 'Forerunners of Zionism in the Victorian Era', in *Remember the Days: Essays on Anglo-Jewish History presented to Cecil Roth by Members of the Council of the Jewish Historical Society of England*, ed. by John M. Shaftesley (London: The Jewish Historical Society of England, 1966), p. 214.

[42] Moscrop, *Measuring Jerusalem*, pp. 70-71.

to investigate 'the archaeology, geography, geology and natural history of the Holy Land'.[43] Sir George Grove and Arthur P. Stanley established the Fund on a non-sectarian basis to secure the support of Christian Restorationists like Lord Shaftesbury and James Finn, and Jewish leaders such as Montefiore and Baron Lionel de Rothschild. Queen Victoria served as patron.[44] When Shaftesbury was appointed president in 1875, he declared in his opening address:

> Let us not delay to send out the best agents...to search the length and breadth of Palestine, to survey the land, and if possible to go over every corner of it, drain it, measure it, and...prepare it for the return of its ancient possessors, for I must believe that the time cannot be far off before that great event will come to pass.[45]

Work on the *Ordnance Survey of Jerusalem* began in 1864 under the command of British army officer and later chairman of the P.E.F., Sir Charles Wilson (1836-1905). The Jerusalem excavations of General Sir Charles Warren (1840-1927) soon followed. In his *Survey*, Wilson described the holy city as 'one of the most unhealthy places in the world' due to 'the inferior quality of the water and the presence of an enormous mass of rubbish which had been accumulating for centuries.' It is apparent, when reading their findings, that Wilson and Warren were well versed in Scripture, a common feature among explorers, surveyors, and archaeologists in the Victorian era. Their work was later edited and republished to 'serve as a further aid to real students of the Book'.[46]

In the same year that the P.E.F. was established, Charles F. Zimpel, a civil engineer and German Lutheran, published an appeal to the Jewish people to use their wealth and intellect 'to bring about such events which finally will and must lead to the restoration of your nation to that land which by divine promise, actually and principally, belongs to you by right.'[47] Over 100,000 copies of his appeal, which was translated into various languages, were sold. To assist the Jews, Zimpel proposed the construction of a railway in the Holy Land, and addressed his appeal for £1,000,000 to

> all true Christians who, according to Isa. lxvi.10-14, love Jerusalem, and believe the whole Bible, and therefore the personal return of our *Lord and Saviour Jesus Christ* to establish His *Millennium* on earth.

---

[43] Quoted in Tibawi, *British Interests in Palestine*, p. 184.

[44] Palestine Exploration Fund, 'Brief Narrative of the Proceedings of the Palestine Exploration Fund', *Palestine Exploration Fund*, 1 (1870), 10-12.

[45] Quoted in Tuchman, *Bible and Sword*, pp. 249-250.

[46] *The Recovery of Jerusalem: A Narrative of Exploration and Discovery in the City and the Holy Land, by Capt. Wilson, R.E., Capt. Warren, R.E., with an introduction by Arthur Penrhyn Stanley: Vol. I*, ed. by Walter Morrison (London: Richard Bentley, 1871), pp. 3, v.

[47] Charles F. Zimpel, *An Appeal to all Christians and the Jewish Nation to Liberate Jerusalem* (London: G.J. Stevenson, 1865), p. 12.

Zimpel was convinced that the signs of the times pointed to Christ's imminent return, the most notable being the rise of anti-Semitism in Europe, especially in Poland. He foresaw the day when the nations would seize the first opportunity 'to get rid of their [Jewish] creditors, and drive them from their homes', and believed that the only option for the Jews would be to emigrate to 'their proper home' and so 'verify all the prophets'.[48]

In 1872, cartographer Claude Regnier Conder (1848-1910), whose maps of the Holy Land were used by General Allenby during his 'Palestine' campaign and who achieved international acclaim for his translation of the Tel-Amarna tablets, began the *Survey of Western Palestine*. In *The City of Jerusalem* (1888), Conder declared: 'We no longer depend on the writings of Josephus and Tacitus, or on the confused accounts of mediaeval pilgrims. Our ideas are founded on existing remains.'[49] In 1892, he addressed the London branch of the *Chibbath Zion* movement, insisting that the agricultural settlement of the Land could only be achieved by the Jews themselves. As Tuchman concluded,

> It was the great work of the P.E.F...to show that Palestine had once been habitable by a much larger population and a more advanced civilisation than was commonly supposed and therefore could be again.[50]

Thomas Cook's Tours

Shortly before the opening in 1869 of the Suez Canal, which David Lloyd George later described as the 'jugular vein'[51] of the British Empire, English Baptist preacher Thomas Cook (1808-1892) capitalised on public interest in the Middle East by launching his 'Eastern Tours'. Cook soon 'cornered the market' in Holy Land travel with his 'Biblical Educational and General Tours' for ministers, Sunday school teachers, and Bible educators. These proved extremely popular,[52] and by 1882, over four thousand people had travelled on a Cook's tour. His *Handbook for Palestine and Syria* not only described 'all the principal places of interest and the best way of visiting them', but also gave 'concise information bearing on the historical associations of Palestine' and corroborated the Biblical record. Cook referred to Jerusalem in poignant terms:

---

[48] Charles F. Zimpel, *Railway between the Mediterranean, the Dead Sea, and Damascus, by way of Jerusalem, with branches to Bethlehem, Hebron, Nablous, Nazareth, and Tiberias* (London: G.J. Stevenson, 1865), pp. 23, 15.

[49] Claude Reignier Conder, *The City of Jerusalem* (London: John Murray, 1909), p. 2.

[50] Tuchman, *Bible and Sword*, p. 249.

[51] Lloyd George, *War Memoirs: Vol. II*, p. 1070.

[52] Shepherd, *The Zealous Intruders*, pp. 176, 180.

No one reading the brief summary of the history of Jerusalem, or the pathetic details of its fall, can help recalling some of those touching voices of prophecy which, like a long wail through the ages, have mourned for Zion.[53]

Lord Shaftesbury

As previously noted, one man who was inspired by archaeological reports from the Holy Land was Christian philanthropist and seventh Earl of Shaftesbury, Anthony Ashley Cooper (1801-1885). Shaftesbury's 'passionate faith in the Jewish Scriptures'[54] owed much to his nanny, Maria Millis, while his premillennial beliefs took shape following a meeting with Edward Bickersteth in 1835.[55] These beliefs formed the basis of Shaftesbury's article, *The State and Prospects of the Jews*, which appeared in the December 1838 edition of the prestigious Church of England magazine, the *Quarterly Review*. The article included a review of Lord Lindsay's *Letters on Egypt, Edom, and the Holy Land*. In extracts printed in *The Times* newspaper, Shaftesbury alluded to 'the approximation of spirit between Christian and Hebrews, to entertain the same belief of the future glories of Israel, to offer up the same prayer, and look forward to the same consummation.' As *The Times* recorded, Shaftesbury had 'turned the public attention to the claims which the Jewish people still have upon the land of Israel as their rightful inheritance'.[56]

Convinced that Britain was God's appointed instrument for the restoration of the Jews, Shaftesbury urged his stepfather-in-law, Henry John Temple Palmerston, then British foreign secretary and later Prime Minister, to establish a British consulate in Jerusalem. Palmerston was 'one of the most colourful of Queen Victoria's cabinet ministers'[57] whose interest in the Jews stemmed purely from imperial, rather than Evangelical, interests. If Shaftesbury 'represented the Bible', Palmerston represented 'the sword.'[58] When Palmerston approved the establishment of a consulate, Shaftesbury believed that Britain had 'attained the praise of being the first of the Gentile nations that has ceased *"to tread down Jerusalem!"*'[59] Crombie describes its official opening in March 1839, and the appointment of William Tanner Young as vice-consul, as 'a sound geo-political move'[60] which enabled Britain to keep a

---

[53] Thomas Cook, *Cook's Tourist's Handbook for Palestine and Syria*, Revised edn (London: Thomas Cook & Son, 1911), pp. vi, 66.

[54] Hamilton, *God, Guns and Israel*, p. 67.

[55] Geoffrey B.A.M. Finlayson, *The Seventh Earl of Shaftesbury 1801-1885* (London: Eyre Methuen Ltd., 1981), p. 104.

[56] *The Times*, 24 January (1839), 3.

[57] Hamilton, *God, Guns and Israel*, p. 64.

[58] Tuchman, *Bible and Sword*, p. 176.

[59] *The Times*, 24 January (1839), 3.

[60] Crombie, *A Jewish Bishop in Jerusalem*, p. 57.

watchful eye on Russia and France in the region. This was the first consulate to be opened in Jerusalem by a European power,[61] and the first time a European nation had expressed concern for the protection of the Jewish population.[62] As Young stated in a letter to Palmerston dated 25 May 1839, 'the Jew in Jerusalem is not estimated in value, much above a dog'.[63]

Correspondence between the Foreign Office and the Consulate illustrates not only how important the protection of the Jews was to British imperial interests, but also how alert the Foreign Office was to those who were observing developments through the lens of Biblical prophecy. In a letter to Sir Stratford Canning dated 8 January 1844, Young mentions an anonymous party 'which is looking to Jerusalem and Palestine as the great Theatre on which the fulfilment of Prophecy is speedily to be accomplished respecting the restoration of the Jews'. Although Young dismissed what he termed 'Speculative Theories regarding a superhuman view of the future',[64] he did consider the Jews to be the people 'unto whom God originally gave this land for a possession'.[65]

English newspapers not only devoted considerable space to the proposed restoration of the Jewish homeland, but also to the 'horrible persecution' which the Jews suffered in the wake of the Damascus 'blood libel' in 1840. This generated 'extraordinary interest…all over Europe',[66] and on 6 July 1840, *The Times* devoted 'a very large portion'[67] of space to what Epstein describes as 'an overture to the opera of modern prejudice'.[68] Several articles condemning the 'blood libel' as completely unfounded appeared in subsequent editions,[69] as did Menasseh ben Israel's letter to Oliver Cromwell in 1656, which had called for the refutation of similar charges against the Jews.[70] In its lead article for 17 August 1840, the newspaper noted how 'the minds of the Jews' had been directed towards the land of their forefathers 'in anticipation of a reconstruction of the Jewish state', and how Christians were endeavouring 'to create facilities and to remove obstructions' while 'intently watching those coming events whose shadows are believed to be now passing over the political horizon.'[71]

---

[61] Albert M. Hyamson, 'Preface', in Hyamson, *The British Consulate*, p. ix.

[62] Albert M. Hyamson, 'Introduction', in Hyamson, *The British Consulate*, p. xxxiii.

[63] 'WM.T. Young to Viscount Palmerston, F.O.78/368 (No.13), 25 May 1839', in Hyamson, *The British Consulate*, p. 6.

[64] 'WM.T. Young to Sir Stratford Canning, F.O.78/581 (No.1), 8 January 1844', in Hyamson, *The British Consulate*, pp. 64-65.

[65] 'WM.T. Young to Viscount Palmerston, F.O.78/368 (No.8), 14 March 1839', in Hyamson, *The British Consulate*, pp. 3-4.

[66] *The Times*, 25 June (1840), 12.

[67] *The Times*, 6 July (1840), 12.

[68] Lawrence J. Epstein, *Zion's Call: Christian Contributions to the Origins and Development of Israel* (London: University Press of America, 1984), p. 31.

[69] Crombie, *A Jewish Bishop in Jerusalem*, pp. 59-60.

[70] *The Times*, 6 July (1840), 8.

[71] *The Times*, 17 August (1840), 4.

On 26 August 1840, *The Times* printed the *Memorandum, to the Protestant Powers of the North of Europe and America*, which had been signed and sealed in London on 8 January 1839 'on behalf of many who wait for the redemption of Israel'. Citing Scripture, the *Memorandum* highlighted the persecution of the Jews by the nations, emphasised the 'unrepealed' nature of the Abrahamic Covenant, announced that 'the fig-tree putteth forth her leaves again (Matt.xxiv.32)', and reminded Christians that God had 'given his waiting people [the Church] to hear the sound of His approaching footsteps, and to mark the signs of His drawing near (1 Thess.v.4)'. The *Memorandum* concluded with an appeal to the Western powers[72] to take up the mantle of Cyrus and facilitate the return of the Jews to their ancient homeland. The newspaper editorial suggested that, however improbable, 'the restoration and nationalisation of the Jewish people...may ultimately become the means...of establishing a new focus of civilisation in that interesting region.'[73]

On 24 July 1840, Shaftesbury made the following entry in his diary: 'Anxious about the hopes and prospects of the Jewish people. Everything seems ripe for their return to Palestine; "the way of the kings of the East is prepared".' On 1 August 1840, after expounding his scheme for Jewish resettlement to Palmerston over dinner, he wrote:

> Palmerston has already been chosen by God to be an instrument of good to His ancient people; to do homage, as it were, to their inheritance, and to recognise their rights without believing their destiny...But though the motive be kind, it is not sound. I am forced to argue politically, financially, commercially; these considerations strike him home; he weeps not like his Master over Jerusalem, nor prays that now, at last, she may put on her beautiful garments.[74]

On 11 August 1840, Palmerston wrote to Viscount Ponsonby, the British ambassador in Constantinople, to inform him of the 'strong notion' among European Jews 'that the Time is approaching when their Nation is to return to Palestine; and consequently their wish to go thither has become more keen'.[75] In his opinion it was in the best interests of the Sultan of Turkey to encourage

---

[72] *The Times*, 26 August (1840), 5; 17 August (1840), 4. It was addressed to 'Victoria, by the Grace of God, Queen of Great Britain and Ireland; Frederick (William) III, King of Prussia; William (Frederick) King of the Netherlands; Charles (John) XIV, King of Sweden and Norway; Frederick VI, King of Denmark; Ernest Augustus, King of Hanover; William, King of Wurtenberg; The Sovereign Princes and Electors of Germany; The Cantons of the Swiss Confederation Professing the Reformed Religion; and The States of North America, Zealous for the Glory of God'.

[73] *The Times*, 26 August (1840), 4.

[74] Edwin Hodder, *The Life and Work of the Seventh Earl of Shaftesbury, K.G.: Vol. I* (London: Cassell & Company Ltd., 1886), pp. 310-311.

[75] 'Viscount Palmerston to Viscount Ponsonby, F.O.78/390 (No.134), 11 August 1840', in Hyamson, *The British Consulate*, pp. 33-34.

the Jews to settle in the Land over which he had jurisdiction. On 17 August 1840, *The Times* described 'the proposed restoration' as 'a new element of the Eastern question', and despite conceding that it had no remit to discuss the Biblical basis for their return, noted how the Jews, 'although bereft of their temple, their city, and their country, have never ceased to be a people.'[76] Shaftesbury could not contain his excitement, as he recorded in his diary:

> Now who could have believed, a few years ago, that this subject could have been treated in a newspaper of wide circulation, gravely, sincerely, and zealously, yet so it is; and who sees not the handwriting of God upon the wall?...What a chaos of schemes and disputes is on the horizon, for the time when the affairs of the Jews shall be really and fully before the world!...What a stir of every passion and every feeling in men's hearts![77]

On 25 September 1840, Shaftesbury presented his proposals to Palmerston 'for the recall of the Jews to their ancient land'.[78] On 23 October, in the wake of the Church of Scotland deputation to the Holy Land, *The Memorial of the Acting Committee of the General Assembly of the Church of Scotland for promoting Christianity among the Jews* was also presented to Palmerston, appealing for the protection of Jews in 'Palestine' against their Arab neighbours. A copy was forwarded to Ambassador Ponsonby in Constantinople.[79] On 2 March 1841, the *Humble Memorial of the Undersigned Inhabitants of Carlow and its Vicinity*, signed by 320 Irish signatories, called upon the British government to emulate Cyrus and remember the 'irreversible decree of Heaven that "the Nation or Kingdom that will not serve Israel shall perish" [Isa. 60:12].'[80] Three years later, a clergyman by the name of Samuel Alexander Bradshaw presented to Parliament his own *Plea for the Jews*, in which he called for £5 million to be set aside by the government for the rebuilding of Jerusalem.[81] These were remarkable times for Britain, and for the Restorationist movement in particular.

The Jerusalem Bishopric

While on holiday in Italy in 1834, Shaftesbury made the acquaintance of the Prussian envoy to Switzerland, Chevalier (Baron Christian Karl Josias) Bunsen.[82] This led to a warm exchange of correspondence with King Frederick

---

[76] *The Times*, 17 August (1840), 4.
[77] Hodder, *Shaftesbury: Vol. I*, p. 311.
[78] Tuchman, *Bible and Sword*, p. 198.
[79] 'Viscount Palmerston to Viscount Ponsonby, F.O.78/391 (No.248), 24 November 1840', in Hyamson, *The British Consulate*, pp. 34-35.
[80] Kobler, *The Vision was There*, p. 63.
[81] Samuel Alexander Bradshaw, *A Tract for the Times, being A Plea for the Jews* (London: Edwards & Hughes, 1844).
[82] Crombie, *A Jewish Bishop in Jerusalem*, pp. 52-53.

William IV of Prussia, which in turn paved the way for the establishment, by Britain and Prussia, of the Jerusalem bishopric.[83] The move was designed not only to aid the proclamation of the Gospel in the Holy Land, but to protect Protestant interests, facilitate unity between the Protestant churches, and resist 'the encroachments of the See of Rome'.[84] Royal assent for the bishopric was granted on 5 October 1841, which led to the resignation from the Church of England of John Henry Newman, who joined the Church of Rome. Alexander McCaul of the LSPCJ was invited to become the first Anglican bishop of Jerusalem,[85] but after he declined the position, Shaftesbury proposed Michael Solomon Alexander, a converted Prussian rabbi who had previously served with the Society.[86] Alexander had been ordained as a deacon in the Church of Ireland on 10 June 1827 by Archbishop William Magee,[87] who, a year earlier, had ordained Darby as a priest. Alexander was consecrated as 'Bishop of the united Church of England and Ireland in Jerusalem'[88] at Lambeth Palace on 7 November 1841. Shaftesbury recorded the occasion:

> The whole thing was wonderful, and to those who have long laboured and prayed in the Jewish cause, nearly overwhelming to see a native Hebrew appointed, under God, by the English Church to revive the Episcopate of St. James, and carry back to the Holy City the truths and blessings we Gentiles had received from it…The order of Providence now seems to demand that in proportion as we have abased the Jew, so shall we be compelled to abase ourselves. His future dignity shall be commensurate with his past degradation. Be it so; I can rejoice in Zion for a capital, in Jerusalem for a church, and in a Hebrew for a king.[89]

In 1849, the first Protestant church in Jerusalem was consecrated. Its name, Christ Church, was given

> in memorial of the earnest desire of the promoters of the undertaking, that this Church should stand on Mount Zion, dedicated to the Messiah, in testimony not only of their own love for the nation and city of the Jews, but also of the

---

[83] Finlayson, *The Seventh Earl of Shaftesbury*, p. 115.

[84] *The Church of England 1815-1948: A Documentary History*, ed. by R.P. Flindall (London: SPCK, 1972), p. 102.

[85] Crombie, *A Jewish Bishop in Jerusalem*, pp. 79-80; A. Bernstein, *Jewish Witnesses for Christ* (Jerusalem: Keren Ahvah Meshihit, 1999), p. 81.

[86] See John Hatchard, *The Predictions and Promises of God respecting Israel. A Sermon preached on Wednesday, June 22nd, 1825, in the Parish Church of St. Andrew's, Plymouth, on the Baptism of Mr. Michael Solomon Alexander, late reader in the Jewish Synagogue* (Plymouth: 1825), pp. 37-40.

[87] Crombie, *A Jewish Bishop in Jerusalem*, pp. 30-32.

[88] Owen Chadwick, *The Victorian Church, Part I* (London: Adam & Charles Black, 1966), p. 191.

[89] Hodder, *Shaftesbury: Vol. I*, pp. 379-380.

adherence of the Church of England to the simple doctrines of the Gospel, in opposition to all superstitious and idolatrous worship.[90]

With the mighty Ottoman Empire beginning to crumble, the question of who would govern its territories was raised. As far as Shaftesbury was concerned, 'There is a country *without a nation*; and God now, in His wisdom and mercy, directs us to *a nation without a country*. His own once loved, nay, still loved people, the sons of Abraham, of Isaac, and of Jacob.'[91] In his tribute to Shaftesbury, 'Palestine's venerable champion',[92] Hodder writes:

> It was his daily prayer, his daily hope. 'Oh, pray for the peace of Jerusalem!' were the words engraven on the ring he always wore on his right hand – the words, too, that were engraven on his heart. His study of the prophetic Scriptures led him to associate the return of the Jews with the Second Advent of our Lord, and this was the hope that animated every other.[93]

Although plans for the restoration of the Jews were suspended during the Crimean War (1854-1856), Shaftesbury never lost hope. The quest for Biblical antiquities, described as 'a quiet extension of the "Eastern Question" waged on the battlefield of the past',[94] ensured that 'Palestine' remained in view. Other personalities now emerged who indirectly championed the Restorationist cause, including George Eliot, whose novel, *Daniel Deronda* (1876), has been described as 'the proudest testimony to English recognition of the Zionist idea'.[95] Another notable advocate was Benjamin Disraeli, whose support was expressed in his novels *Alroy* (1833), *Tancred* (1844), and *Coningsby* (1847). When the parliamentary oaths bill received its second reading in the House of Commons on 25 May 1854, Disraeli made 'a guarded and weighty speech' in favour of allowing Jews to sit in Parliament. He reminded the House that, as a 'Christian' assembly, it owed an immeasurable debt to the Jews, for without the Bible there would have been no House of Commons. He also pointed out that the Jews were 'an ancient people, a famous people, an enduring people' who had 'outlived Assyrian kings, Egyptian Pharaohs, Roman Caesars, and Arabian caliphs'. It was wise, he believed, for England to grant them full emancipation, since 'no country which had persecuted the Hebrew race had prospered.'[96]

---

[90] William Ayerst, *The Jews of the Nineteenth Century: A Collection of Essays, Reviews, and Historical Notices, originally published in the 'Jewish Intelligence'* (London: 1848), p. 394.
[91] Hodder, *Shaftesbury: Vol. II*, p. 478.
[92] Tuchman, *Bible and Sword*, pp. 176, 249.
[93] Hodder, *Shaftesbury: Vol. II*, p. 477.
[94] Silberman, *Digging for God and Country*, p. 4.
[95] Sokolow, *History of Zionism: Vol. I*, p. 212.
[96] Alexander Charles Ewald, *The Right Hon. Benjamin Disraeli, Earl of Beaconsfield, K.G., and his Times: Vol. I* (London: William Mackenzie, 1882), pp. 290-291.

William Henry Hechler

We now turn our attention to the man whom Jewish Zionists appear unwilling to credit, but who opened the door for Theodor Herzl and his Zionist manifesto. Appointed chaplain to the British Embassy in Vienna in 1885, William Hechler (1845-1931) was invited to the First Zionist Congress in Basle, where he received a public expression of thanks from Herzl.[97] Hechler first met the Zionist leader in his study on 10 March 1896, at a time when Herzl had grown despondent after failing to secure financial backing for his manifesto from the Rothschilds.[98] Although the publication of *Der Judenstaat* in February 1896 had raised his hopes, Herzl had been unable to secure an audience with those whose political support he desperately needed. Tormented and miserable,[99] he 'looked around for a grand diplomatic opening which might resolve his problem in one stroke. Quite unexpectedly, it walked through his door one day in the person of a long-bearded, eccentric English parson'[100] by the name of William Hechler, a man who has been described as 'the secret agent of a very concise politics: that of God, Who was guiding His people's history in its zionist premessianic period'.[101]

In his diaries, Herzl speaks warmly of Hechler, describing this 'naïve visionary' as a 'likeable, sensitive man with the long grey beard of a prophet', who was 'peculiar and complex'[102] but 'thoroughly honest'.[103] Although Hechler claimed that he had foreseen Herzl's day, he insisted that he was 'not a prophet, nor the son of a prophet, but only a humble student of prophecy, watching the signs of the times',[104] and that his involvement in the Restorationist movement was simply 'as a Christian and a believer in the Truth of the Bible'.[105] After visiting Hechler on 15 March 1896, Herzl noted in his

---

[97] *Encyclopaedia of Zionism and Israel: Vol. II*, ed. by Patai, p. 950.

[98] In a letter to Baron Maurice de Hirsch on 18 June 1895, Herzl wrote: 'For the present there is no helping the Jews. If someone were to show them the promised land, they would mock him. For they are demoralised…I cannot break that wall. Not with my head alone. Therefore I am giving it up. As a practical proposition I am done with the matter'. (Amos Elon, *Herzl* [New York: Holt, Rinehart and Winston, 1975], pp. 151-152.)

[99] *The Complete Diaries: Vol. I*, ed. by Patai, p. 4.

[100] Elon, *Herzl*, p. 186.

[101] Claude Duvernoy, *The Prince and the Prophet* (Christian Action for Israel, 1979), p. 70.

[102] *The Complete Diaries: Vol. I*, ed. by Patai, pp. 310-312, 342.

[103] *The Complete Diaries: Vol. III*, ed. by Patai, p. 1020.

[104] 'Rev. W.H. Hechler to the Grand Duke Frederick of Baden. March 26, 1896', in Hermann and Bessi Ellern, *Herzl, Hechler, the Grand Duke of Baden and the German Emperor 1896-1904 / documents found by Hermann and Bessi Ellern, reproduced in facsimile* (Tel Aviv: Ellern's Bank Ltd., 1961), pp. 4-5.

[105] 'Rev. W.H. Hechler to the Grand Duke Frederick of Baden. September 3, 1896', in Ellern and Ellern, *Herzl*, p. 25.

diary that he had seen 'nothing but Bibles'[106] in Hechler's study.

Herzl's first diplomatic breakthrough came when Hechler introduced him to Grand Duke Frederick Wilhelm of Baden, whose son Hechler had tutored some years earlier. The Grand Duke was favourably disposed towards the Jewish people, having conversed with Hechler many times on prophecy, and arranged for Herzl to meet his nephew, Kaiser Wilhelm II. The Kaiser, in turn, arranged a meeting with Sultan Abdul Hamid. Writing to the Grand Duke on 26 March 1896, Hechler drew his attention to *Der Judenstaat*, and stated that it was 'a most remarkable fact' that it had appeared at a time when 100,000 Jews were living in 'Palestine', 'the only country in the whole world of which God has Himself said to whom it is to belong.'[107] Believing that the promised restoration had begun, Hechler urged the Grand Duke to promote Herzl's Zionist manifesto, and in a subsequent letter referred to over forty English newspaper cuttings which demonstrated how 'earnestly and enthusiastically'[108] the question of the return of the Jews had been taken up in Britain.

Hechler's interest in the Jews had been longstanding, his father Dietrich having joined the LSPCJ in 1854. When the Russian pogroms broke out in 1881, William Hechler joined Shaftesbury in helping to establish a committee to raise funds for the resettlement of Jewish refugees.[109] Shaftesbury addressed the House of Lords on the matter,[110] while Hechler was dispatched to Russia to urge the Jews to flee to their ancient homeland. During his visit he met Leo Pinsker in Odessa,[111] and may have helped convince Pinsker that *Eretz Yisrael* was integral to the survival of the Jewish people. Later that year, Hechler published a pamphlet outlining his belief that the return of the Jews was 'in immediate connection' with the Second Coming, and that it was the duty of every Christian 'to *pray earnestly* and to long for the restoration of *God's chosen race*, and to love the Jews'. He also issued the following warning:

> Blessed shall that nation be, which *loves the Jews*...And let us not forget the *terrible punishments* which await those who *'hate'* and *'persecute'* the Jews.[112]

In a letter to a Christian missionary in Jerusalem in 1898, Hechler wrote:

> Of course...you look for the conversion of the Jews, but the times are changing rapidly, and it is important for us to look further and higher. We are now entering,

---

[106] *The Complete Diaries: Vol. I*, ed. by Patai, p. 311.

[107] 'Hechler to Frederick. March 26, 1896', in Ellern and Ellern, *Herzl*, pp. 2-3.

[108] 'Hechler to Frederick. September 3, 1896', in Ellern and Ellern, *Herzl*, p. 23.

[109] William D. Rubinstein and Hilary L. Rubinstein, *Philosemitism: Admiration and Support in the English-Speaking World for Jews, 1840-1939* (Basingstoke: Macmillan Press, 1999), p. 43.

[110] Finlayson, *The Seventh Earl of Shaftesbury*, p. 582.

[111] *Encyclopaedia Judaica: Vol. VIII*, p. 237.

[112] William Henry Hechler, *The Restoration of the Jews to Palestine* (London: 1884).

thanks to the Zionist movement, into Israel's Messianic age. Thus, it is not a matter these days of opening the gates of their homeland, and of sustaining them in their work of clearing the land, and irrigating it and bringing water to it. All of this, dear colleague, is messianic work; all of this the breath of the Holy Spirit announces. But first the dry bones must come to life, and draw together.[113]

According to Paul Merkley, 'Everything about Hechler powerfully affected Herzl', for he represented 'the living embodiment of the path Herzl had not taken – the path of pious faith.'[114] In Herzl's mind the mission of his 'devoted friend'[115] was 'a "Biblical" one', and deserved recognition. As he wrote in his diary, 'His counsel and his precepts have been excellent to date, and unless it turns out later, somehow or other, that he is a double-dealer, I would want the Jews to show him a full measure of gratitude.'[116] (Hechler was duly awarded a monthly pension by the Zionist Organisation when he returned to England.) Herzl's admiration of his Christian friend was further evident when he asked him to write for the first edition of his Zionist journal, *Die Welt* ('The World'). In his article, Hechler made an impassioned appeal to the Jewish people:

Children of Abraham, awake! God himself, the Heavenly Father, calls you back to your ancient fatherland and wants to be your God, as He promised of old through his prophets…As a Christian, I believe as well as you in what is called the Zionist Movement, for according to the Bible and its ancient prophets a Jewish state must be raised in Palestine. I am convinced by the signs of our own time that the Jews will soon recover their beloved homeland…I am certain that the establishment of a Jewish state, with the support of the Princes of Europe, will inaugurate the salvation forecast by Isaiah, Micah, and Zechariah.[117]

One wonders how the Zionist movement would have fared had Hechler not called upon Herzl when he did. Herzl himself made a telling statement when recalling his meeting in London in 1901 with Hechler and William Bramley-Moore, a member of the Catholic Apostolic Church. In his diary, Herzl recorded how Hechler, through tears, told him that after they had left Herzl that day, they had visited the local Catholic Apostolic church to pray for the restoration of the Jews. Herzl was deeply moved and wrote: 'These simple Christian hearts are much better than our Jewish clerics who think [only] of their wedding fees from the rich Jews.'[118]

Hechler was one of the last to see Herzl at the sanatorium in Edlach, Austria,

---

[113] Quoted in Cohn-Sherbok, *The Politics of Apocalypse*, p. 67.

[114] Paul C. Merkley, *The Politics of Christian Zionism 1891-1948* (London: Frank Cass, 1998), p. 23.

[115] *Encyclopaedia of Zionism and Israel: Vol. I*, ed. by Patai, p. 482.

[116] *The Complete Diaries: Vol. I*, ed. by Patai, pp. 310, 342.

[117] Quoted in Merkley, *The Politics of Christian Zionism*, p. 31.

[118] *The Complete Diaries: Vol. III*, ed. by Patai, p. 1161.

the day before he died.[119] According to Claude Duvernoy, the friendship between Hechler and Herzl

> symbolised a reality only too rare: the friendly confluence of two Zionist streams, one Jewish and the other Christian, marching side by side toward the same kingdom and the same Jerusalem.[120]

It is important to note that in March 1914, with war imminent, Hechler visited Martin Buber in Berlin. Having failed to secure an audience with the Kaiser, Hechler brought this prophetic warning to the Jewish philosopher: 'Dr. Buber, your fatherland will soon be given back to you. For a severe crisis will break out, the deep meaning of which is the liberation of your messianic Jerusalem from the yoke of the pagan nations...We are moving toward a "Weltkrieg" [world war]'.[121] Hechler, who was in Parliament when the British officially accepted the Mandate for 'Palestine' on 22 July 1922, grew increasingly dejected as his warnings went unheeded. As David Pileggi records,

> He repeatedly warned his Jewish friends that there would be an extensive massacre of Jews in Europe...His forewarnings grew into an obsession and he made them with increasing frequency until his death in 1931. Tragically, Hechler's predictions were politely dismissed by everyone.[122]

In Conclusion

On 31 October 1917, just over a decade after Herzl's death, the British Cabinet agreed to support Zionist plans for a Jewish national home, a decision which was communicated in a letter from British Foreign Secretary Arthur James Balfour to Lord Rothschild on 2 November 1917. On 11 December 1917, British General Edmund Allenby, a direct descendant of Oliver Cromwell[123] and a man who 'consulted the Bible daily',[124] stood on the steps of the Citadel of David opposite Christ Church during the Jewish feast of Hanukkah[125] to proclaim liberation for the Jews. Sir Robert Anderson described this event as one which 'gives hope that we are nearing the age in which they [the Jews] will be restored to favour, and therefore that the Lord's coming for us, which must precede that restoration, may be close at hand.'[126] The LSPCJ gave *its* response

---

[119] Ellern and Ellern, *Herzl*, p. v.

[120] Duvernoy, *The Prince and the Prophet*, p. 100.

[121] Quoted in Duvernoy, *The Prince and the Prophet*, p. 106.

[122] Quoted in Merkley, *The Politics of Christian Zionism*, p. 34.

[123] Brian Gardner, *Allenby* (London: Cassell, 1965), p. 2.

[124] Hamilton, *God, Guns and Israel*, p. 163.

[125] Crombie, *A Jewish Bishop in Jerusalem*, p. 243.

[126] Anderson, *Unfulfilled Prophecy*, p. vii.

to events as they unfolded in this momentous year:

> With one step the Jewish cause has made a great bound forward. For centuries the Jew has been downtrodden, depressed, hated and unloved by all the nations…but now there is at least a prospect of his settling down once again in his own country, and of becoming in the eyes of men a Nation amongst the Nations…He is now to have a home for himself in his God-given land. The day of his exile is to be ended. What does all this mean for us Christians? In the light of prophetic Scripture we recognise that such an action on the part of our Government and on the part of the Allied Powers…is full of significance…Ever since AD70 Jerusalem and Palestine have been under Gentile domination, and now we seem to be on the very verge of a literal fulfilment of the last prediction, and it is certainly a distinct warning to us that the Lord 'is near, even at the very doors'.[127]

The nineteenth century witnessed an unparalleled interest in the Holy Land. In 1985, Benjamin Netanyahu, then Israel's ambassador to the United Nations, paid the following tribute at a prayer breakfast in Washington to those Christians who had supported his people during that period:

> I suggest that for those who know the history of Christian involvement in Zionism, there is nothing either surprising nor new about the steadfast support given to Israel by believing Christians all over the world. For what, after all, is Zionism but the fulfilment of ancient prophecies?…There was an ancient yearning in our common tradition for the return of the Jews to the Land of Israel. And this dream, smouldering through two millennia, first burst forth in the Christian Zionism of the 19th Century – a movement that paralleled and reinforced modern Jewish Zionism…What I am trying to sketch, however briefly, is the long, intimate, and ultimately successful support given modern Zionism by powerful forces working within the Christian community from the 19th Century on…Thus it was the impact of Christian Zionism on Western Statesmen that helped modern Jewish Zionism achieve the rebirth of Israel.[128]

---

[127] Quoted in Crombie, *ANZACS*, p. 203.
[128] Benjamin Netanyahu, 'Christian Zionism and the Jewish Restoration, 1985', <http//:www.internationalwallofprayer.org/A-091-Christian-Zionism-and-the-Jewish-Restoration.html, 15 June 2006>; cf. Benjamin Netanyahu, *A Place among the Nations: Israel and the World* (London: Bantam Press, 1993), p. 16.

Chapter 8

Darby and the United States

The Balfour Declaration

On 2 November 1917, the British government declared its 'sympathy with Jewish Zionist aspirations' in a letter written by Foreign Secretary Arthur James Balfour to Lord Rothschild, a leader of the Jewish community in Britain. The contents of the letter, which became known as the Balfour Declaration, were conveyed to the Zionist Federation and read as follows:

> Foreign Office,
> November 2nd, 1917
>
> Dear Lord Rothschild,
>
> I have much pleasure in conveying to you, on behalf of His Majesty's Government, the following declaration of sympathy with Jewish Zionist aspirations which has been submitted to, and approved by, the Cabinet.
>
> 'His Majesty's Government view with favour the establishment in Palestine of a national home for the Jewish people, and will use their best endeavours to facilitate the achievement of this object, it being clearly understood that nothing shall be done which may prejudice the civil and religious rights of existing non-Jewish communities in Palestine, or the rights and political status enjoyed by Jews in any other country.'
>
> I should be grateful if you would bring this declaration to the knowledge of the Zionist Federation.
>
> Yours sincerely,
> Arthur James Balfour

Many Jews believed that their 'spiritual homelessness'[1] was about to end.

---

[1] Solomon Grayzel, *A History of the Jews: From the Babylonian Exile to the Establishment of Israel* (Philadelphia, PA: The Jewish Publication Society of America, 1953), p. 719.

The year 1917 also witnessed the deliverance of Jerusalem from the Turks, which, in the process, prepared the way for the conferment of the 'Palestine Mandate' on the British government. According to Herbert Sidebotham,

> The whole world looked on, and the ghosts of three thousand years' history walked again to see how this great England would acquit herself on this magnificent stage. Never had the glory of England stood higher.[2]

By 1939, with the issuing of the British White Paper, her glory lay in tatters. The premature end of Britain's support for the Zionist movement heralded the transfer of patronage across the Atlantic, as America emerged as the political *and* theological friend of Israel. As we shall see, John Nelson Darby's preaching tours to the United States had already prepared many within the American Evangelical Church for such a transfer.

A Window of Opportunity

As the last rites were being administered to the 'sick man of Europe', nations seeking to protect their interests and consolidate their position in the Middle East strategically positioned themselves for the 'carving up' of the Ottoman Empire. As Hamilton writes, 'the long-held Jewish dream of a homeland in Palestine became a reality as a result of a remarkable military, political and theological confluence.'[3]

Eighteen months prior to the issuing of the Balfour Declaration, Sidebotham had submitted a memorandum to the British Foreign Office on behalf of an influential group of Zionists based in Manchester; this group included Chaim Weizmann, Simon Marks, Israel Sief, and Harry Sacher. The memorandum called for the establishment of a Jewish buffer state to protect Britain's interests in the Middle East. An Englishman of Zionist 'sentiment', Sidebotham had previously advocated 'a close alliance'[4] with the Zionist movement in a series of articles he had written for the *Manchester Guardian*.

During the First World War, Britain found herself in a 'chemical dilemma' owing to a shortage of acetone, which was used in the production of munitions. David Lloyd George, then chairman of the Munitions of War Committee, sought advice from his 'close friend and confidant',[5] C.P. Scott, who was the editor of the *Manchester Guardian*. Scott referred him to 'a very remarkable professor of chemistry' at Manchester University by the name of Chaim Weizmann (1874-1952), and the two met in London in December 1914. Lloyd George took to Weizmann 'at once', describing him as a man of 'very

---

[2] Sidebotham, *Great Britain and Palestine*, p. 146.

[3] Hamilton, *God, Guns and Israel*, pp. 186, ix.

[4] Sidebotham, *Great Britain and Palestine*, p. v.

[5] Daphna Baram, *Disenchantment: the Guardian and Israel* (London: Guardian Books, 2004), p. 22.

remarkable personality'.[6] Weizmann was subsequently appointed director of the British Admiralty laboratories, and effectively rescued Britain's war effort by producing synthetic acetone from maize. In the process, he 'pulled the Zionists through a brief window of opportunity, fated never to open again.'[7]

Lloyd George later told the Jewish Historical Society how acetone had 'converted' him to Zionism, and how he had acquired a 'natural sympathy' and 'admiration' for the Jewish people from an early age by being taught 'far more' about *their* history than about the history of his own country. He also spoke of how his government had sought to harness that which had enabled the Jews to survive, and told the Society:

> You have been hammered into very fine steel, and that is why you can never be broken. Hammered for centuries into the finest steel of any race in the world! And therefore we wanted your help.

Lloyd George wanted to honour Weizmann for saving Britain from almost certain defeat by Germany, but the 'self-forgetful' Russian chemist asked instead for the repatriation of his people 'to the sacred land they had made famous'.[8] Lloyd George later described this episode as 'the fount and origin'[9] of the Balfour Declaration. According to Abba Eban, Weizmann's achievement represented 'the last victory of persuasion without power in modern international history.'[10]

British Field-Marshal Jan Christiaan Smuts was a member of Lloyd George's War Cabinet which formulated the Balfour Declaration. An 'ardent Zionist sympathizer'[11] and lifelong friend of Weizmann, Smuts believed that Christians who had received 'the leadership of the Prince of Peace' from the Jewish people were now able 'to make some small return for those priceless blessings, and to restore Israel to the Ancient glorious Home Land.'[12] He described the Declaration as 'a debt of honour which must be discharged in full, at all costs, and in all circumstances'.[13] However, 'without a nod' from the 'Bible-loving'[14] American President, Woodrow Wilson, 'powerful forces in London'[15] opposing it may have prevailed. One of the 'most formidable foes'[16]

[6] Lloyd George, *War Memoirs: Vol. I*, p. 348.

[7] Paul Johnson, *A History of the Jews* (London: Phoenix, 1993), p. 430.

[8] Guedalla, *Napoleon and Palestine*, pp. 47-50, 12.

[9] Lloyd George, *War Memoirs: Vol. I*, p. 349.

[10] Eban, 'Introduction', p. 10.

[11] Hamilton, *God, Guns and Israel*, p. 135.

[12] Quoted in Rubinstein and Rubinstein, *Philosemitism*, p. 169.

[13] Quoted in Tal, *You Don't Have to be Jewish to be a Zionist*, pp. 69-70.

[14] Hamilton, *God, Guns and Israel*, pp. xvii, 192.

[15] Learsi, *The Jews in America*, p. 257.

[16] Blanche E.C. Dugdale, *Arthur James Balfour, First Earl of Balfour: Vol. II* (London: Hutchinson & Co., Ltd., 1936), p. 214.

of the Balfour Declaration was the Secretary of State for India, Edwin Samuel Montagu. Feeling compromised as an Englishman and a Jew, Montagu described Zionism as 'a mischievous political creed'.[17] He was somewhat isolated, however, since Lloyd George had 'created a window of opportunity which coincided with Christian Zionist sympathizers in the War Cabinet'. One such sympathiser was Andrew Bonar Law. Named after Andrew Bonar, a member of the Church of Scotland deputation to 'Palestine' in 1839, Bonar Law helped to 'fulfil the aim of those passionate missionaries'[18] by enabling the Jews to return home.

Described as the 'charter of the Zionist movement',[19] the Balfour Declaration represented 'the decisive diplomatic victory of the Jewish people in modern history'.[20] According to 'military correspondent' and 'zealous imperialist',[21] Herbert Sidebotham, the Declaration had an ancestry 'older and more dignified than any political document',[22] an ancestry Christian Zionists have traced back to the 'signing' of the Abrahamic Covenant in Genesis 15. In a 1941 radio broadcast, Smuts declared how 'the promise to Abraham had at last become a part of international law.'[23] Upon hearing news of the Declaration in 1917, Golda Meir exclaimed: 'Now, the ingathering would really begin'.[24]

The British Mandate

On 24 July 1922, the 'Palestine' Mandate, which incorporated the Balfour Declaration and recognised 'the historical connexion of the Jewish people with Palestine',[25] was conferred upon Britain by the League of Nations. With the appointment as chief secretary of the British administration in 'Palestine' of Brigadier General Sir Wyndham Deedes, a Christian who 'wanted to do everything he could to hasten the Second Coming',[26] the Jewish homeland seemed secure. Lloyd George believed that the reason why the Jews had entrusted their cause to Britain in the twentieth century, and not to France in the eighteenth, was because they knew that 'the signature of Napoleon was not of much use', and that 'the British signature is invariably honoured.'[27]

---

[17] Sachar, *A History of Israel*, p. 107.

[18] Hamilton, *God, Guns and Israel*, pp. vi, 64.

[19] Lloyd George, *War Memoirs: Vol. I*, p. 349.

[20] Abba Eban, *My People: The Story of the Jews* (New York: Behrman House, Inc., 1968), pp. 366, 359.

[21] Baram, *Disenchantment*, p. 31.

[22] Sidebotham, *Great Britain and Palestine*, p. 4.

[23] Quoted in Tal, *You Don't Have to be Jewish to be a Zionist*, pp. 69-70.

[24] Meir, *My Life*, p. 47.

[25] Ingrams, *Palestine Papers*, p. 177.

[26] Hamilton, *God, Guns and Israel*, p. 155.

[27] Guedalla, *Napoleon and Palestine*, p. 54.

Arthur James Balfour, whose Declaration 'electrified the Jewish world',[28] spoke of the 'absolutely exceptional' case of the Jew in a speech celebrating the Mandate at the Royal Albert Hall. This 'convinced Zionist' told the predominantly Jewish audience, 'If we fail you, you cannot succeed.'[29] Having been 'steeped from early childhood in the Old Testament',[30] Balfour believed that the world owed the Jewish people 'an immeasurable debt' which had been 'shamefully ill repaid.' Upon meeting Chaim Weizmann for the first time in 1905, he had been 'impressed' by his 'absolute refusal'[31] of the British Uganda proposal. As Weizmann later explained, 'if Moses had come into the sixth Zionist Congress when it was adopting the resolution in favour of the Commission for Uganda, he would surely have broken the tablets once again.'[32]

At the opening of the Hebrew University in Jerusalem in 1925, Balfour addressed thousands who had gathered to welcome him as 'an honoured guest in their own National Home.'[33] After acknowledging the debt owed to the Jews by those 'brought up on a translation into English of the Hebrew Scripture', he concluded with the Hebrew prayer: 'Blessed art Thou, O Lord our God, King of the Universe, who hast kept us in life, and hast preserved us, and enabled us to reach this moment.'[34] He later told his niece and biographer, Blanche Dugdale, that what he had done for the Jewish people was 'the thing he looked back upon as the most worth his doing.' Just before he died, Balfour called Weizmann to his sick bed. Dugdale recalls what passed between them:

> No one but myself saw the brief and silent farewell between these two, so diverse from one another, whose mutual sympathy had been so powerful an instrument in the history of a nation...No words passed between them, or could pass, for Balfour was very weak, and Dr Weizmann much overcome. But I, who saw the look with which Balfour moved his hand and touched the bowed head of the other, have no doubt at all that he realised the nature of the emotion which, for the first, and only, time showed itself in his sick-room.

From the ghettos of Eastern Europe to the slums of New York, ceremonial candles were lit for Balfour, and the Jewish 'Memorial Prayer', known as the *Azkarah*, chanted. According to Dugdale, 'Never in living memory had this been done for any Gentile.'[35]

---

[28] Moshe Raviv, *Israel at Fifty: Five Decades of Struggle for Peace* (London: Weidenfeld and Nicolson, 1998), p. 2.

[29] *Speeches on Zionism*, ed. by Israel Cohen (New York: Kraus Reprint Co., 1971), pp. 26, 21, 31.

[30] Hamilton, *God, Guns and Israel*, p. 11.

[31] Dugdale, *Arthur James Balfour: Vol. I*, pp. 433-436.

[32] Weizmann, *Trial and Error*, p. 143.

[33] Dugdale, *Arthur James Balfour: Vol. II*, p. 367.

[34] Hamilton, *God, Guns and Israel*, pp. 216-217.

[35] Dugdale, *Arthur James Balfour: Vol. II*, pp. 235, 409-410.

Arab Appeasement and the White Paper

According to Israel Sief, Weizmann had 'a vivid prophetic revelation about the role Britain would play in the return of the Jews to the Promised Land'. Writing to his wife Vera from London in 1904, Weizmann declared: 'If help ever comes to us, it will come from England'. As an 11-year-old boy living in his home shtetl of Motol, Belarus, he had expressed the same supreme confidence in England's future role in a letter to his Hebrew teacher:

> Let us carry our banner to Zion and return to the original matter upon whose knees we were reared. For why should we expect mercy from the Kings of Europe, except that they should, in pity, give us a resting place? In vain! All have decided that the Jew is doomed to death; but England...will have mercy on us.[36]

In his address to the Fourth Zionist Congress in London in 1900, Theodor Herzl had also confidently declared: 'England, mighty England, free England, with its world-embracing outlook will understand us and our aspirations.'[37] However, as the British Administration in 'Palestine' shifted its policy in favour of the indigenous Arab population, hostility against the Jews escalated. In a letter to *The Times*, dated 19 December 1929, Balfour, Lloyd George, and Smuts expressed their 'deep anxiety' following the outbreak of Arab riots in 'Palestine', and called on the government to appoint a commission of inquiry which would show the world that Britain had not 'weakened in a task to which her honour is pledged'.[38] The commission failed, leaving Britain's reputation, integrity, and honour lying in the dust. Addressing the Jewish Historical Society on 20 October 1936, Cecil Roth spoke of Britain's 'policy of Arab appeasement',[39] and insisted that 'if by the renunciation of Zion we Jews would lose much of our inheritance, England, too, would lose no small part of hers.'[40]

At the height of the Arab crisis in 1936, Major General Orde Charles Wingate was dispatched to 'Palestine'. There he established 'Special Night Squads' of British soldiers and Jewish volunteers to quash the Arab sabotage of the British oil pipeline from Mosul to Haifa; he was awarded the Distinguished Service Order in 1938. Described as a 'passionate pro-Zionist',[41] Wingate's name became 'a by-word for daring and courage'[42] among young Jewish soldiers like Moshe Dayan, who affectionately referred to him as 'the Lawrence of Judaea'. Chaim Weizmann 'loved and revered' Wingate as a friend, and

---

[36] Quoted in Israel Sief, *The Memoirs of Israel Sief* (London: Weidenfeld and Nicolson, 1970), pp. 73-74.
[37] Culver, *Albion and Ariel*, p. 6.
[38] Quoted in Hamilton, *God, Guns and Israel*, p. 221.
[39] Teplinsky, *Why Care About Israel?*, p. 191.
[40] Quoted in Culver, *Albion and Ariel*, p. 23.
[41] Bernard Wasserstein, *Britain and the Jews of Europe 1939-1945* (London: Institute of Jewish Affairs, 1979), p. 30.
[42] Hamilton, *God, Guns and Israel*, p. 229.

pointed to his 'deep and lifelong study of the Bible'[43] as the inspiration behind his 'passionate sympathy' for the Zionist cause. It is commonly known that the Bible accompanied Wingate wherever he went. What is less well known, however, is that he was the son of 'devout members of the Plymouth Brethren',[44] and believed that in helping to establish the Jewish homeland he was fulfilling the will of God. In 1953, the Israeli village of Yemin Orde ('in the memory of Orde') was founded in Wingate's honour as a home for Holocaust orphans.

On 17 March 1939, the British government issued the White Paper, which restricted Jewish immigration into 'Palestine' to 75,000 over a period of five years. Presided over by British Colonial Secretary Malcolm MacDonald, it was issued in the wake of the Peel Commission of August 1936, which had been appointed to investigate Arab unrest in 'Palestine'. This 'reprehensible',[45] 'unconscionable',[46] and 'vicious'[47] document, which has been described by Bennett as 'political treachery',[48] was issued at a time when 'Palestine' could have offered 'some palliative'[49] to the Jews of Europe. It became known as 'the Black Paper',[50] and proved to be 'a death warrant for many thousands'[51] of Jews. As Brog poignantly writes, 'The British had closed the doors of Palestine to Jewish immigration just as Hitler was opening the door of Auschwitz.'[52] Golda Meir and Benjamin Netanyahu described the White Paper as Britain's 'betrayal'[53] of the Jewish people, and the 'betrayal of Zionism'[54] by the West. Christian Zionists are convinced that an 'historic opportunity' for Britain 'to help the Jewish people'[55] had been squandered.

In what was to be his final Zionist Congress address in Basle in 1946, an emotional Chaim Weizmann declared: 'Few documents in history have worse consequences for which to answer.'[56] Colonel Richard Meinertzhagen, General Allenby's Chief Political Officer and a key figure in the creation of the 'Uneasy Mandate',[57] described the policy shift as a 'complete abdication of Britain's

---

[43] Weizmann, *Trial and Error*, pp. 489-490.
[44] Hamilton, *God, Guns and Israel*, p. 223.
[45] Culver, *Albion and Ariel*, p. 24.
[46] Hunt, *Judgment Day*, p. 94.
[47] Duvernoy, *Controversy of Zion*, p. 107.
[48] Bennett, *Saga*, p. 152.
[49] Edelman, *Ben Gurion*, p. 111.
[50] Hamilton, *God, Guns and Israel*, p. 230.
[51] Learsi, *The Jews in America*, p. 308.
[52] Brog, *Standing with Israel*, p. 120.
[53] Meir, *My Life*, p. 160.
[54] Netanyahu, *A Place among the Nations*, pp. 69, 89.
[55] Myss, *A Call to the Nations*, p. 66.
[56] Quoted in Eban, *My People*, p. 433.
[57] Edelman, *Ben Gurion*, p. 71.

moral influence in the world'.[58] Failure in 'Palestine', he suggested, 'will be a greater disaster than is apparent to most persons', and one which 'will cost us dear'. Through his own intelligence operation, Meinertzhagen discovered that British officers had colluded with Palestinian Arabs to thwart the implementation of the Balfour Declaration. In his diary, dated 26 April 1920, he claimed that Colonel Waters-Taylor had told the Grand Mufti of Jerusalem, Haj Amin el-Husseini, that 'if disturbances of sufficient violence occurred in Jerusalem at Easter, both General Bols and General Allenby would advocate the abandonment of the Jewish Home.' Britain had become 'the champion of the Arab League',[59] and not 'the midwife of a newborn Israel as the Victorians had so much hoped'.[60] When the British administration finally sailed out of Haifa on 15 May 1948, all they left the Jewish people with was the 'sour conviction of betrayal by His Majesty's Government'.[61]

Many Christian Zionists have linked Britain's betrayal of the Jews to the collapse of the British Empire. As Mitchell writes, 'One of the foremost reasons for the decline of this once great nation is, I believe without doubt, our treatment of God's ancient people the Jews.'[62] When news broke of the White Paper, many Americans marched through the streets in protest, and a statement was drawn up by twenty-eight U.S. senators condemning Britain's policy shift as 'a tragic abandonment of a brave people in its hour of gravest need'.[63]

It is perhaps the most 'coincidental symmetry of history' that the Zionist movement was advancing under the leadership of Chaim Weizmann at the same time as 'Christian' sympathisers of Zionism were assuming positions of prominence within the British government. However, the task of ensuring the safe delivery of the Jewish State was left not to British Prime Minister Clement Atlee and his virulently anti-Semitic foreign secretary, Ernest Bevin, but to Bible-believing American President Harry S. Truman, who signalled America's recognition of the State of Israel eleven minutes after David Ben Gurion declared independence. In the words of Jill Hamilton, 'Two thousand years of prayer and longing was over. The Bible had triumphed.'[64]

---

[58] John Lord, *Duty, Honour, Empire: The Life and Times of Colonel Richard Meinertzhagen* (London: Hutchinson & Co. Ltd., 1971), p. 391.

[59] Richard Meinertzhagen, *Middle East Diary 1917-1956* (London: The Cresset Press, 1959), pp. 143, 225, 82, 226.

[60] Polowetzky, *Jerusalem Recovered*, p. 148.

[61] A.J. Sherman, *Mandate Days: British Lives in Palestine 1918-1948* (London: Thames and Hudson, 1997), p. 12.

[62] Mitchell, *Rome*, p. 151.

[63] Quoted in *America and Palestine: The Attitude of Official America and of the American People toward the Rebuilding of Palestine as a Free and Democratic Jewish Commonwealth*, Revised edn, ed. by Reuben Fink (New York: Herald Square Press, Inc., 1945), p. 62.

[64] Hamilton, *God, Guns and Israel*, pp. 261, 253.

America and the Jews

The Statue of Liberty stands as America's greatest symbol of freedom, hope, and opportunity. Engraved on a plaque over the main entrance are the words of *The New Colossus* (1883), the title of a sonnet by the Jewish poet, Emma Lazarus,[65] which calls upon the nations to give America 'your tired, your poor, your huddled masses yearning to breathe free, the wretched refuse of your teeming shore.'[66] According to Paul Johnson, Lazarus 'understood the meaning of America for world Jewry'.[67] The story of the American Jew begins in colonial times when two significant streams converged - the integration of Jewish immigrants into American society, and the identification of America with ancient Israel.

The great advantage Jewish settlers had in America was that they were 'living within a nation without a past'.[68] Few restraints were placed on the first twenty-three Sephardic immigrants who, in September 1654, sailed into New Amsterdam from Brazil on the French vessel, the *Sainte Catherine*. Although opposition arose from Dutch colonial governor and 'dyed-in-the-wool Jew-hater',[69] Peter Stuyvesant, his petition to oust those he described as 'hateful enemies and blasphemers of the name of Christ'[70] failed. The year 1654 was already proving pivotal on the other side of the Atlantic, with Menasseh ben Israel's petitioning of Oliver Cromwell for the readmission of the Jews. It is remarkable that these two nations were destined at the same time to play such a decisive role in securing the future of the Jewish people.

Colonial Zionists

The Pilgrim Fathers identified themselves with the Jews as fellow refugees fleeing oppression in search of a new homeland. The Biblical account of the 'Exodus' became a powerful motif in America at this time, and was adopted not only by English Puritans fleeing Britain during the seventeenth century, but also later by African-Americans seeking freedom from slavery during the nineteenth century. Armstrong suggests that the bond between Americans and Israelis is strong because 'each recognises the other at a deep level', America

---

[65] Emma Lazarus, *The Poems of Emma Lazarus* (New York: Houghton Mifflin Company, 1888), p. 202.

[66] Robert Ernst, 'Concepts of Americanism as Reflected in Minority Groups', in *The Writing of American Jewish History*, ed. by Moshe Davis and Isidore Meyer (New York: American Jewish Historical Society, 1957), p. 141.

[67] Johnson, *A History of the Jews*, p. 371.

[68] Leon Poliakov, *The History of Anti-Semitism: Vol. III* (London: Routledge & Kegan Paul, 1975), p. 45.

[69] Jacob R. Marcus, *The Colonial American Jew 1492-1776: Vol. III* (Detroit, MI: Wayne State University Press, 1970), p. 1135.

[70] Peter Grose, *Israel in the Mind of America* (New York: Alfred A. Knopf, 1984), p. 3.

perceiving Israel to be 'her alter ego in the Middle East'.[71] Peter Grose suggests that these two nations 'are bonded together like no two other sovereign peoples', having 'grafted the heritage of the other onto itself.'[72] This common heritage and identity was powerfully expressed by Israeli Prime Minister Ehud Olmert on 24 May 2006, in his address to the United States Congress:

> The unbreakable ties between our two nations extend far beyond mutual interests. They are based on our shared goals and values stemming from the very essence of our mutual foundations...Our two great nations share a profound belief in the importance of freedom and a common pioneering spirit deeply rooted in optimism. It was the energetic spirit of our pioneers that enabled our two countries to implement the impossible: to build cities where swamps once existed and to make the desert bloom.[73]

Early Jewish settlers made a significant contribution to the economic growth and stabilisation of seventeenth-century America by helping to 'create a little world of commerce and industry which tied the colonies together' through 'a common culture, a common country, a common spirit.'[74] The Bible occupied a central place in colonial society, many villages bearing Biblical names such as Hebron, Bethlehem, Nazareth, Salem, Shiloh, and Zion. Likewise, children were named after Old Testament characters. At this time a certain 'romance with the Hebrew language' began to run through 'the fabric of American religious and cultural life', with many early Puritans distinguishing themselves as Hebrew scholars. Cotton Mather, the 'most prolific, if not...precise, practitioner',[75] was one of the foremost Hebraists of his generation. America's education system was greatly impacted by Old Testament and Hebraic studies, with Hebrew inscriptions being incorporated into the insignias or seals of several Ivy League colleges, including Dartmouth, which 'gave Hebrew a special place of prominence.'[76] From 1638 until 1785, Hebrew was compulsory at Harvard, the oldest American institute for higher education, where 'no scholar could be admitted for a degree unless he was able to translate the Hebrew original of the Bible into Latin.'[77]

In 1630, John Winthrop, the first governor of the Massachusetts Bay Colony, wrote *A Model of Christian Charity* whilst aboard the flagship *Arbella*.

---

[71] Karen Armstrong, *Holy War: The Crusades and their Impact on Today's World* (London: Papermac, 1992), p. 529.

[72] Grose, *Israel in the Mind of America*, p. 316.

[73] Haaretz.com, 'Prime Minister Ehud Olmert's Address Before Congress', <http://www.haaretz.com/hasen/spages/719462.html, 31 May 2006>.

[74] Marcus, *The Colonial American Jew: Vol. II*, p. 845.

[75] Goldman, 'Introduction', pp. xi, xvii.

[76] Shalom Goldman, 'Biblical Hebrew in Colonial America: The Case of Dartmouth', in Goldman, *Hebrew and the Bible in America*, pp. 201-208.

[77] *America and Palestine*, ed. by Fink, p. 13.

In his treatise, Winthrop expounded his belief that God had covenanted with the Pilgrim Fathers to establish America as the new Zion. The 'Zion' motif was later employed by a number of religious movements in America wanting to assert their own sense of divine commission, including the Zionitic Brotherhood, the Shakers, the Mormons, and the Jehovah's Witnesses (formerly the Zion Watch Tower Society).[78] However, subsequent generations of Puritan scholars found 'prophetic meaning'[79] in the developing history of their nation. Men like John Cotton, Increase Mather, Samuel Sewall, and Jonathan Edwards were undoubtedly 'the most articulate' spokesmen 'for the theme of American destiny'.[80] The Great Awakening of the 1740s raised 'intense millennial expectations',[81] with many American Evangelicals believing that a new age of peace and prosperity was not only imminent, but 'attainable'.[82] In a sermon preached in Northampton in 1739, Jonathan Edwards spoke of 'multitudes flocking to Christ in one nation and another',[83] and of America being 'the first fruits of that glorious day'.[84] Isaac Backus was another who preached that the Church was not a safe haven from impending disaster, as premillennialists had taught, but 'a place to mobilise the saints and encourage their efforts to bring the Kingdom into being.'[85]

For Whom the Liberty Bell Tolls

The War of Independence (1775-1783) was the most decisive turning point in the history not only of America, but of American Jewry. With the Jewish population 'overwhelmingly on the side of the rising Revolution',[86] the War 'marked the beginning of the political existence of Jews'[87] in America, with their right to vote and serve in public office following soon after. As Poliakov writes, 'The political philosophy of the United States put the final touch to this

---

[78] Robert T. Handy, 'Zion in American Christian Movements', in *Israel: Its Role in Civilisation*, ed. by Moshe Davis (New York: The Jewish Theological Seminary of America, 1956), p. 292.

[79] Boyer, *When Time Shall Be No More*, p. 68.

[80] *God's New Israel: Religious Interpretations of American Destiny*, Revised edn, ed. by Conrad Cherry (London: The University of North Carolina Press, 1998), p. 26.

[81] Ruth H. Bloch, *Visionary Republic: Millennial Themes in American Thought, 1756-1800* (Cambridge: Cambridge University Press, 1985), p. 16.

[82] Alan Heimert, *Religion and the American Mind* (Cambridge, MA: Harvard University Press, 1966), p. 56.

[83] *A History of the Work of Redemption*, ed. by John F. Wilson (New Haven, CT: Yale University Press, 1989), p. 462.

[84] *God's New Israel*, ed. by Cherry, pp. 54-55.

[85] Heimert, *Religion and the American Mind*, p. 128.

[86] President Calvin Coolidge, quoted in *America and Palestine*, ed. by Fink, p. 18.

[87] Eli Faber, *The Jewish People in America: Vol. I* (Baltimore, MD: The Johns Hopkins University Press, 1992), p. 106.

integration, and when they drew up the birth certificate of the American nation, its founding fathers were opening up the "age of the rights of man," solemnly proclaimed by the Declaration of Independence.'[88]

Successive legislation, beginning in New York in 1777, guaranteed freedom of worship across the nation. For the Jewish communities 'the most striking feature of this new era was its emphasis on liberty – liberty from England, liberty from religious establishments, liberty of conscience, liberty for the pursuit of happiness.'[89] Tradition holds that the famous Liberty Bell, inscribed in 1752 with the words, 'Proclaim Liberty throughout all the land unto all inhabitants thereof' (Lev. 25:10), rang out in Philadelphia on 8 July 1776 at the first public reading of the Declaration of Independence.

Many churchmen now capitalised on the 'Exodus' motif. In a sermon preached in East Haven, Connecticut, in 1777, Nicholas Street portrayed King George III as 'the British tyrant' who was acting out 'the same wicked and cruel part that Pharaoh king of Egypt acted towards the children of Israel above 3000 years ago.' In 1783, Ezra Stiles declared to the General Assembly of the State of Connecticut that God had exalted His 'American Israel'.[90] Britain's defeat in the American War of Independence convinced many Americans that *their* nation had been 'graced with a millennial role in world history', a conviction Whalen notes had been 'cut from whole cloth woven in England'.[91]

A Land of Milk and Honey

A key factor which enabled the Jewish people to integrate into American society was the presence of other immigrant groups. The Jews were seen as 'just another congregation', and not as some 'special and exotic community'[92] as they had been in Europe. Humanity, it seemed, had the opportunity to make a fresh start in America, 'unshackled by the hates and prejudices that bedevilled the nations of Europe.'[93] As Poliakov writes, 'All the human groups who successively populated the United States had to suffer the same transplantation and the same ordeal'.[94]

From 1776 onwards the rights of the individual were written into state constitutions. In 1785, Virginia approved an act, originally drawn up by Thomas Jefferson, which established religious liberty in the state. However, it was the Constitutional Convention, held in Philadelphia on 25 May 1787 and

---

[88] Poliakov, *The History of Anti-Semitism: Vol. III*, p. 43.

[89] Jonathan D. Sarna and David G. Dalin, *Religion and State in the American Jewish Experience* (Notre Dame, IN: The University of Notre Dame Press, 1997), p. 61.

[90] Quoted in *God's New Israel*, ed. by Cherry, pp. 70, 84.

[91] Whalen, 'Christians Love the Jews!', 239, 226.

[92] Armstrong, *Holy War*, p. 479.

[93] Learsi, *The Jews in America*, p. 52.

[94] Poliakov, *The History of Anti-Semitism: Vol. III*, p. 44.

presided over by George Washington, which heralded a new dawn. Article VI and Amendment I of the Constitution removed the requirement of a religious test for those wishing to hold public office, and ensured that Congress could not enact laws pertaining to the establishment, or prohibition, of any religious organisation. The Jewish community in Newport, Rhode Island, which was the first of the original thirteen colonies to afford Jews equal rights, expressed its gratitude to George Washington and a government 'which to bigotry gives no sanction, to persecution no assistance, but generously affording to all liberty of conscience and immunities of citizenship'. In reply, Washington wrote:

> May the children of the stock of Abraham who dwell in this land continue to merit and enjoy the good will of the other inhabitants; while every one shall sit in safety under his own vine and fig tree and there shall be none to make him afraid.[95]

The acknowledgement of the Jews as fully-fledged citizens of a sovereign nation was unprecedented. Addressing the Hebrew Orphan Society in South Carolina in October 1806, Myer Moses praised America for the freedom, dignity, and equality the Jews had been granted, and prayed that God would gather His scattered people to this new land of milk and honey. He declared:

> I am so proud of being a sojourner in this promised land, that, had I to subsist on the spontaneous production of the earth, and each day to search a running stream to quench my thirst at, I should prefer it to all the luxuries and superfluities which ill fated Europe can boast of.[96]

Although political restrictions remained in place for a time, by 1840 equality had been granted to the Jews in twenty-one of the twenty-six states.

Campaigns to secularise America, led by Isaac Leeser and Nathaniel Levin, ensured that the Jewish people remained on an 'equal footing'[97] with their fellow Americans. Max Lilienthal, Bernhard Felsenthal, and Isaac Mayer Wise, the 'foremost apostle and architect'[98] of Reform Judaism, helped keep religion and state separate. This resulted in 'an unprecedentedly speedy Jewish acculturation, and the growth of a genuine feeling of being "at home".'[99] As immigration increased dramatically during the nineteenth century, the Jews were treated as a people who 'lived next door'.[100] In his survey of 'the inweaving of the Jews in America', Learsi suggests that 'a work of

---

[95] Sarna and Dalin, *Religion and State*, pp. 79-80.
[96] Faber, *The Jewish People in America: Vol. I*, p. 127.
[97] Sarna and Dalin, *Religion and State*, p. 121.
[98] Learsi, *The Jews in America*, p. 116.
[99] Salo W. Baron, 'Conference Theme', in Davis and Meyer, *The Writing of American Jewish History*, p. 6.
[100] Sarna and Dalin, *Religion and State*, p. 125.

encyclopaedic magnitude'[101] would be needed to tell the story of how Jewish immigrants successfully integrated into all areas of American society.

Noah and the American Eagle

Mordecai Manuel Noah (1785-1851), journalist, playwright, diplomat, politician, and editor of several New York newspapers, has been described as the 'first American Zionist'[102] and 'the first Jew in American history to gain a national hearing'.[103] Preoccupied with the welfare of his Jewish brethren from the moment he entered politics, he rose to the position of United States Consul to the Barbary States of North Africa,[104] became sheriff of New York, and even 'satirically suggested himself for President'. As Jonathan Sarna comments,

> Only in America, they proudly proclaimed, did a Jew have the right even to suggest himself for the nation's highest office. By raising the possibility, albeit in a jocular vein, that a Jew might exercise this right, Noah pointed up the gap separating myth and reality in Americans' view of the Jew.[105]

In summing up his political career, Isaac Goldberg vividly portrays Noah as the Jew who 'set the American eagle screeching all around the six points of David's Shield.'[106]

Having witnessed first hand the plight of his people in Europe, Noah purchased 2,555 acres of land on Grand Island near Buffalo, New York, in an audacious attempt to establish a safe haven for Eastern European Jews. The vision of this self-styled 'high sheriff of the Jews'[107] was to make this 'asylum' a place where they could undergo 'regeneration'[108] before returning to 'Palestine'. It was to be named 'Ararat' (Gen. 8:4). As Kleinfeld writes, 'Noah was always a proto-Zionist, although he shifted in belief from endorsing a separate Jewish colony in the New World to advocating immediate return of the

---

[101] Learsi, *The Jews in America*, pp. 343, 327.

[102] Isaac Goldberg, *Major Noah: American-Jewish Pioneer* (Philadelphia, PA: The Jewish Publication Society of America, 1936), p. 212.

[103] Jonathan D. Sarna, *Jacksonian Jew: The Two Worlds of Mordecai Noah* (New York: Holmes & Meier Publishers, 1981), p. 160.

[104] Another diplomatic envoy who believed that 'Palestine' was the most suitable home for the Jews was General Lewis Wallace, author of *Ben-Hur: A Tale of the Christ* (1880). (*America and Palestine*, ed. by Fink, pp. 25-26.)

[105] Sarna, *Jacksonian Jew*, pp. 43-44.

[106] Goldberg, *Major Noah*, p. 138.

[107] Arthur Hertzberg, *The Jews in America* (New York: Simon & Schuster Inc., 1989), p. 95.

[108] Mordecai Noah, 'The Ararat Proclamation and Speech', in *The Selected Writings of Mordecai Noah*, ed. by Michael Schuldiner and Daniel J. Kleinfeld (Westport, CT: Greenwood Press, 1999), pp. 107, 114.

238 Jews to Jerusalem.

Jews to Jerusalem.'[109] In typically theatrical style, Noah dedicated the colony in a Richard III costume,[110] and made the following proclamation on 15 September 1825, which was printed in the *Buffalo Patriot* newspaper:

> In calling the Jews together under the protection of the American Constitution and laws and governed by our happy and salutary institutions, it is proper for me to state that this asylum is temporary and provisional. The Jews never should and never will relinquish the just hope of regaining possession of their ancient heritage, and events in the neighbourhood of Palestine indicate an extraordinary change of affairs.[111]

After Noah's project ran aground on Ararat, he devoted his time to the general welfare of his people. The Plymouth Brethren were aware of his activities, with Benjamin Newton including extracts from one of his public addresses in his book, *Babylon: Its Future History and Doom*.[112] In 1844, Noah delivered his *Discourse on the Restoration of the Jews* to an audience of Jewish and Protestant leaders, claiming that political events in the Middle East were conducive to the return of his people to their ancient homeland. Noting how, on 'almost every page of the Bible we have, directly and indirectly, in positive language and in parables the literal assurance and guarantee for the restoration of the Jews to Judea,' Noah believed that the Land had been given 'as a perpetual inheritance...which we dare not surrender without at once surrendering our faith.' Trusting in the 'overruling hand of Providence', he claimed that much prophecy had already been fulfilled, and that 'what remains...will assuredly as literally be fulfilled', including the rebuilding of the Temple, the coming of the Messiah, and 'the thousand years of happiness and peace which are to ensue'. He also reminded Protestant ministers that if the Jews were ever to believe in Jesus as the Messiah, they would 'still be Jews'.[113]

Mission to the Jews

In 1814, John McDonald, a Presbyterian minister in Albany, New York, called upon his fellow believers to 'carry the tidings of joy and salvation' to their 'Saviour's kinsmen in disgrace!'[114] In 1816, Hannah Adams, a distant cousin of American Presidents John Adams and John Quincy Adams, founded the Female Society of Boston and Vicinity for Promoting Christianity amongst the

[109] Daniel J. Kleinfeld, 'Staging a Nation: Mordecai Noah and the Early Republic', in Schuldiner and Kleinfeld, *The Selected Writings*, p. 69.
[110] Sarna, *Jacksonian Jew*, p. 66.
[111] Noah, 'The Ararat Proclamation', pp. 112-114.
[112] Newton, *Babylon*, pp. 164-176.
[113] Mordecai Noah, 'Discourse on the Restoration of the Jews', in Schuldiner and Kleinfeld, *The Selected Writings*, pp. 136, 145-146.
[114] Grose, *Israel in the Mind of America*, p. 9.

Jews,[115] and later that year the American Society for Evangelising the Jews was established. In 1819, the American Board of Commissioners for Foreign Missions sent missionaries out to 'Palestine'[116] to work closely with the LSPCJ, and within a quarter of a century approximately sixty Protestant missionaries had been sent from America to Jewish communities in Israel and across the Middle East.[117] Missionary endeavour among *American* Jews, on the other hand, remained fairly sporadic until the 1880s, when the mass immigration of Jewish refugees from Russia coincided with a 'new school of premillennial hope' called dispensationalism. This 'school' inspired 'the most decisive motivation for those who have evangelised Jews in the United States'.[118]

The Revival of Premillennialism

In 1854, Methodist minister Samuel Baldwin identified the 'Israel' of Biblical prophecy with America, and dismissed belief in the restoration of the Jews as 'absurd, fanatical, and repugnant to Scripture, as well as to common sense'.[119] The American Civil War (1861-1865) soon exposed the fallacy of Baldwin's postmillennial replacementism, and paved the way for a revival in premillennial eschatology. As America was coming to terms with the carnage of Gettysburg, many Christians dismissed postmillennialism as 'a pipe dream'.[120]

Immediately prior to John Nelson Darby's first tour of North America in 1862, premillennialism was boosted by a series of publications. These included a reprint of Elhanan Winchester's premillennial lectures of 1795, Edward Winthrop's *Lectures on the Second Advent* (1843) and *Letters on the Prophetic Scriptures* (1850), Jacob Janeway's *Hope for the Jews: or, The Jews will be Converted to the Christian Faith; and Settled and Reorganised as a Nation in the Land of Palestine* (1853), two books by 'the nineteenth-century Hal Lindsey',[121] John Cumming, entitled, *Signs of the Times* (1854) and *The End* (1855), and Joseph Seiss's *The Last Times and the Great Consummation*

---

[115] A.L. Tibawi, *American Interests in Syria 1800-1901: A Study of Educational, Literary and Religious Work* (Oxford: Clarendon Press, 1966), p. 9.

[116] Vivian D. Lipman, 'America-Holy Land Material in British Archives, 1820-1930', in *With Eyes Toward Zion – Volume II: Themes and Sources in the Archives of the United States, Great Britain, Turkey and Israel*, ed. by Moshe Davis (London: Praeger, 1986), p. 26.

[117] Hertzel Fishman, *American Protestantism and a Jewish State* (Detroit, MI: Wayne State University Press, 1973).

[118] Yaakov Ariel, *Evangelizing the Chosen People: Missions to the Jews in America, 1880-2000* (Chapel Hill, NC: University of North Carolina Press, 2000), p. 2.

[119] Quoted in Boyer, *When Time Shall Be No More*, p. 84.

[120] Jeanne Halgren Kilde, 'How did Left Behind's Particular Vision of the End Times Develop? A Historical Look at Millenarian Thought', in Forbes and Kilde, *Rapture*, p. 56.

[121] Boyer, *When Time Shall Be No More*, p. 155.

(1856). The works of Cumming and Seiss exemplify the growing interest in Israel's restoration and Christ's premillennial return at that time.

Preparing the Ground

John Cumming (1807-1881) was the minister of the Scottish National Church in Covent Garden, London. A popular preacher and vociferous opponent of Roman Catholicism, he was also noted for his historicist interpretation of Biblical prophecy. In his book, *Signs of the Times* (1854), Cumming drew attention to specific signs he believed would precede the Second Coming of Christ, the most notable of which was to be the bursting forth 'into blossom, and verdure, and beauty' of the fig tree of Israel. Referring to the 'awful desolation' of the land where 'the Arab plunderer roams in every valley', he drew attention to its one redeeming feature: it was

> covered with prophetic indications of an approaching glory, when Jerusalem shall again be the world's metropolis, and Palestine once more a land overflowing with milk and honey.

Denouncing those in the Church who had eaten 'the sweet kernel' of prophecy and thrown 'the shells and husks' to the Jews, Cumming observed how the Land was fast becoming 'the source of disquiet and conflict in the most powerful cabinets of the east and west of Europe'. It was his ardent hope that Britain would 'play the most illustrious part in the restoration of the Jews'. Once restored to their land, Cumming believed that the Jews would 'build their temple, revive the sacrifices of Levi', be 'converted to the Lord,' and 'occupy a very prominent place in the age to come.' In his estimation, one could not fail to see 'the overruling hand of God in what is now taking place.'[122]

Joseph A. Seiss (1823-1904) was a popular and influential Lutheran minister from Frederick County, Maryland, in the United States. In his book, *The Last Times and the Great Consummation* (1856), Seiss, like Cumming, portrayed the Jewish people as the 'fig tree which is to have a long winter of leafless barrenness, but which is to bud again when the summer-time of the kingdom approaches'. He believed that the 'scattered family of Jacob' would one day be 'nationally restored to the land of their fathers', warning detractors not to 'bend and modify the word of God to make it harmonize' with their 'whims and jealousies'. Seiss maintained that the demise of the Ottoman Empire and the political manoeuvring of the nations were 'the preliminaries of the second Jewish exodus.' As he rhetorically asked,

> Why are the Jewish people still distinct, and Jerusalem's walls still dear, as ever? Why have Jacob's seed always refused to hold hands anywhere but in Palestine,

---

[122] John Cumming, *Signs of the Times; or, Present, Past, and Future*, New edn (London: Arthur Hall, Virtue & Co., 1854), pp. 4, 150, 155, 158, 161, 164, 242, 268, 308.

and Jerusalem always refused to give permanent habitation to any but them?...And of all that have ever tried to fix themselves in the Holy Land...none have ever been able to gain a permanent foothold in it. WHY IS ALL THIS?...God has his own settled purpose with this people and this place, holding the one in reserve for the other until each shall be forever satisfied with its own. Here, history is prophecy. And if all the holy seers were silent, the very stones themselves cry out for Israel's restoration. The rocks of Palestine will have no lord but Jacob.

Seiss, like many of his British contemporaries, predicted that the 'great maritime power' referred to in Isaiah 18 'must either be the United States, Great Britain, or perhaps both', a power which was to 'become interested in behalf of the Jews'. He believed that it would be 'from the study of prophecy, and from the will of God as thus presented, that men shall be roused up to this work', observing how America and Britain had already sent exploration teams to the Land 'as if these countries, so closely allied in so many particulars, were already laying the foundations for their work and mission in bringing back the dispersed children of Abraham.' Speaking of the 'blessed hope' of the Church, Seiss maintained that the Second Coming would consist of 'two distinct stages', and that 'the translation' of faithful believers, who were 'devoutly looking and waiting' for Christ to return, 'must *precede* the great tribulation'. It is noteworthy that Seiss included Darby's *The Hopes of the Church of God* (1840) in a section of his book on 'recent writers'.[123]

Premillennial treatises were supplemented during this period by a number of periodicals. These included *The Literalist* (1840-1842) and the *American Millenarian and Prophetic Review* (1842-1844), which reprinted works by British premillennialists Lewis Way, William Cuninghame, Hugh McNeile, and Edward Bickersteth. In 1863, *Prophetic Times* was also launched. Edited by Joseph Seiss, it was 'devoted to the exposition and inculcation of the doctrine of the speedy coming and reign of the Lord Jesus Christ, and related subjects'.[124] The way was now prepared for the propagation of a distinct form of premillennial eschatology which revived belief in the Rapture of the Church, the restoration of Israel, and the return of Jesus Christ to Jerusalem.

Dispensationalism

John Nelson Darby has been described as 'the father of modern dispensationalism',[125] its 'pioneer, systematiser, and populariser',[126] the 'first

---

[123] Joseph A. Seiss, *The Last Times and the Great Consummation: An Earnest Discussion of Momentous Themes*, Revised edn (Philadelphia, PA: Smith, English & Co., 1863), pp. 29, 185, 192, 196, 198-200, 349-350, 353, 412.

[124] Sandeen, *The Roots of Fundamentalism*, p. 94.

[125] Weremchuk, *John Nelson Darby*, p. 79.

proponent' of its 'most salient distinctives',[127] the man who 'systematised premillennial dispensationalism',[128] and 'the first to espouse dispensationalism as a discrete theological system'.[129] It is somewhat surprising, then, to find so little credit given to Darby in dispensationalist writings. Daniel Fuller found it 'refreshing…to hear one dispensationalist [Harry Ironside] fully endorse Darby as the man who rediscovered the apostolic teachings which had been lost to the Church during the sixteen-hundred-year interval.'[130]

Theologians throughout the centuries have developed their own systems of ages, economies, or dispensations,[131] but as MacLeod points out, their use of the term 'dispensation' does not make them dispensationalists.[132] This mistake is made by Arnold Ehlert in his *Bibliography of Dispensationalism*,[133] which includes those who 'were not millenarians at all'.[134] Kromminga has added to the confusion by hailing amillennialist Johannes Cocceius (1603-1669) as the 'father of dispensationalism',[135] simply on the basis that he incorporated multiple dispensations into his Reformed, covenant theology.

As we have seen, the essence of Darby's eschatology was not his 'system of dispensations',[136] but the distinction he made between Israel and the Church. Despite recent revisions by *progressive* dispensationalists, this distinction remains one of the 'indispensable factors'[137] of *true* dispensationalism.

---

[126] Larry V. Crutchfield, *The Origins of Dispensationalism: The Darby Factor* (New York: University Press of America, 1992), p. 206.

[127] Vern S. Poythress, *Understanding Dispensationalists*, 2nd edn (Phillipsburg, NJ: Presbyterian and Reformed Publishing Company, 1994), p. 14.

[128] Whalen, 'Dispensationalism', p. 134.

[129] Stephen R. Sizer, 'Dispensational Approaches to the Land', in Johnston and Walker, *The Land of Promise*, p. 147.

[130] Daniel P. Fuller, *Gospel and Law: Contrast or Continuum? The Hermeneutics of Dispensationalism and Covenant Theology* (Grand Rapids, MI: William B. Eerdmans Publishing Company, 1980), p. 12.

[131] For example, John Edwards, *A compleat history, or survey of all the dispensations* (1699); Pierre Poiret, *The divine oeconomy: or, an universal system of the works and purposes of God towards men, demonstrated* (1713); Isaac Watts, *The harmony of all the religions which God ever prescribed: containing a brief survey of the several publick dispensations of God toward man* (1742).

[132] David J. MacLeod, 'Walter Scott, A Link in Dispensationalism between Darby and Scofield?', *Bibliotheca Sacra*, 153 (Apr-Jun, 1996), 158.

[133] Arnold D. Ehlert, 'A Bibliography of Dispensationalism', *Bibliotheca Sacra*, 101-103 (1944-1946).

[134] Sandeen, *The Roots of Fundamentalism*, p. 68.

[135] Kromminga, *The Millennium in the Church*, p. 205.

[136] Sandeen, *The Roots of Fundamentalism*, p. 69.

[137] Renald E. Showers, *There Really is a Difference! A Comparison of Covenant and Dispensational Theology* (Bellmawr, NJ: The Friends of Israel Gospel Ministry, Inc., 1990), p. 52.

Darby's Letter from America

According to Joseph Canfield, Darby's seven tours to America and Canada (1862-1877) 'went largely unnoticed in Dispensational circles for many years.'[138] Writing to G.V. Wigram from Hamilton, Canada, in 1862, Darby explained the reason for his visits:

> Here and in the U.S. the church and the world are more mixed than even in England, so that the testimony of brethren is more definite and important as far as the sphere goes, and things seem to point to an awakening as to this in the States.[139]

Canada was a country for which Darby expressed 'unfeigned'[140] affection. He felt 'knit up with' and 'more attached'[141] to believers there than anywhere else. As he expressed in a letter to A. Wells, 'Canada is ever dear to me. I do not know how to account for my attachment to it, if it be not all the love I met with in it: that I ever feel.'[142] He found 'many hungry souls'[143] in Acton in 1863, enjoyed a 'delicious'[144] meeting in Toronto in 1865, and attended 'a very blessed conference'[145] in Brantford in 1876. The place he visited most frequently was Guelph, where 'a great many fresh brethren from all parts of the United States' and 'a good many Indians' met to discuss matters of 'general truth'.[146] It was there that the doctrine of the Second Coming gained 'a more actual and practical place'[147] among believers.

The purpose of Darby's first tour of the United States was to encourage French and Swiss Brethren who were struggling 'out in the prairies'. During the next couple of decades Darby travelled extensively across the country, even passing, in 1863, 'on the skirts of the [American Civil] war – though not feeling it'. In a letter to Mr Pollock from Toronto that year he recalled travelling 'about 2,000 miles in the last four weeks, besides preaching and walking.'[148] Darby found the spiritual condition of America 'frightful',[149] and though his heart soon became 'greatly knit to the States and God's people there',[150] he found the

---

[138] Canfield, *The Incredible Scofield and His Book*, p. 74.

[139] Darby, *Letter to G.V. Wigram* (Hamilton, rec'd 24 December 1862), L1:336.

[140] Darby, *Letter to A. Wells* (Geneva, 25 August 1869), L2:39.

[141] Darby, *Letter to R. Evans* (Pau, 3 March 1864), L1:371-372.

[142] Darby, *Letter to A. Wells* (3 January 1870), L2:62.

[143] Darby, *Letter to C. McAdam* (Guelph, 10 February 1863), L1:345.

[144] Darby, *Letter to W. Kelly* (Toronto, 1865), L1:398.

[145] Darby, *Letter to G. Biava* (Hamilton, 18 July 1876), L2:372.

[146] Darby, *Letter to C. McAdam* (rec'd 8 August 1866), L1:451-452.

[147] Darby, *Letter to A. Wells* (Geneva, 25 August 1869), L2:39.

[148] Darby, *Letter to Mr Pollock* (Toronto, 27 May 1863), L1:351-352.

[149] Darby, *Letter to A.B. Pollock* (Toronto, October 1866), L1:460.

[150] Darby, *Letter to F.G. Brown(e)* (London, 1869), L2:34.

country as a whole 'full of worldliness'[151] and the Church 'more worldly...than anywhere you would find it'.[152] However, by 1866 many ministers were travelling considerable distances to hear Darby and his fellow Brethren itinerants speak.[153] Writing to John Pollock from New York in 1867, he reported that 'The cloud is not bigger than a man's hand, but I believe there is unequivocal blessing', the doctrine of the Second Coming having been 'planted in many souls'.[154] Wherever Darby journeyed his ministry remained the same, namely 'to present Christ and the truth, accomplished salvation, and His coming.'[155] Most of his time in America was spent in Boston, Chicago, and St. Louis, cities which became centres of dispensationalism.

Boston

Writing to F.G. Brown(e) from Demerara in 1868, Darby described how his ministry in Boston had not been accepted as it had been elsewhere.[156] As he told G.V. Wigram, the church there was in a 'sorrowful'[157] state. In a letter from Boston in 1874, he lamented the way Evangelicals were refusing to leave their denominations, despite embracing Brethren principles:

> The state of the churches is scandalous indeed: pious souls groan, but where are instruments to be found to guide them in the good way? God has raised up a few, several ministers even have left their systems, but it is a drop of water in the wide sea, and there is a great effort to keep souls in the various systems while taking advantage of the light which brethren have...One of the most active who has visited Europe told ministers that they could not keep up with the brethren unless they read their books, but he was doing everything he could to prevent souls leaving their various...churches. It is a new wile of the enemy.[158]

Darby struggled to reconcile how ministers could so enthusiastically welcome and endorse Brethren literature, and yet 'stay where they are'.[159] However, by 1875 there had been a breakthrough, 'chiefly of converted persons coming to a knowledge of salvation, and grace and the Lord's coming.'[160] Writing to C. McAdam in February that year, Darby referred to a meeting with 'two principal Wesleyan ministers and their chief members, and some others', and how they

---

[151] Darby, *Letter to Mr Haldo* (1866), L1:472.
[152] Darby, *Letter to Mr Pollock* (Toronto, 27 May 1863), L1:351.
[153] Darby, *Letter to A.B. Pollock* (Toronto, October 1866), L1:461.
[154] Darby, *Letter to John Pollock* (New York, April 1867), L1:495-496.
[155] Darby, *Letter to G. Biava* (New York, April 1873), L2:212.
[156] Darby, *Letter to F.G. Brown(e)* (Demerara, 1868), L1:537.
[157] Darby, *Letter to G.V. Wigram* (New York, 23 June 1865), L1:401.
[158] Darby, *Letter* (Boston, 27 September 1874), L2:304.
[159] Darby, *Letter to J.G. Deck* (New York, 1874), L2:308.
[160] Darby, *Letter to C. McAdam* (Boston, March 1875), L2:337.

had spent 'all the afternoon' discussing 'deliverance from sin, full acceptance, [and] the Lord's coming.' He also mentioned meeting 'the chief Baptist minister',[161] who may well have been Adoniram Judson Gordon, who served as pastor of Clarendon Street Baptist Church for twenty-six years and who became one of the foremost propagators of dispensationalism. His son, Ernest B. Gordon, records the tribute his father paid to Darby and the Brethren:

> We might mention Darby's 'Synopsis of the Bible,' the expositions of Kelly, Newton, Tregelles, Soltau, Pridham, and Jukes. These books, especially those of the first three, have constituted the chief theological treasury of many of our evangelists. We can say for ourselves that, from the first time our eyes fell upon these treasures, we have nowhere else seen the gospel so luminously presented... The springs of great reformations are often hidden and remote, but they rarely fail to be recognised in the end...It demands a fearless candour to concede it, but we believe that truth requires us to confess that we owe a great debt, both in literature and in life, to the leaders of this ultra-Protestant movement.[162]

Chicago

Writing to Mr Robbins from Chicago in 1872, Darby referred to a Presbyterian minister who, 'by preaching what he had learned of the Lord's coming and truths connected with it, has broken up his congregation, and some thirty or forty are going to meet, waiting on the Lord to be guided'.[163] Another Chicago minister Darby impacted was Dwight L. Moody, who has been described as 'the most influential "clergyman" in America'.[164] Although Moody later became 'a potent catalyst'[165] and 'patron of dispensationalism',[166] Darby's assessment of him was mixed. After receiving news about his evangelistic campaign in Edinburgh in 1874, Darby wrote to Walter Wolston: 'I rejoice, am bound to rejoice, in every soul converted...Nor do I doubt Moody's earnestness, for I know the man well.' However, he expressed concern in this, and subsequent letters, about certain aspects of Moody's doctrine, which he believed would only 'foster worldliness in saints'.[167] He was nevertheless

---

[161] Darby, *Letter to C. McAdam* (Boston, February 1875), L2:329-330.

[162] Ernest B. Gordon, *Adoniram Judson Gordon, A Biography* (New York: Revell, 1896), pp. 86-88.

[163] Darby, *Letter to Mr Robbins* (Chicago, November 1872), L2:190.

[164] Sandeen, *The Roots of Fundamentalism*, p. 172.

[165] Peter W. Williams, *America's Religions: From their Origins to the Twenty-First Century*, 2nd edn (Chicago, IL: University of Illinois Press, 2002), p. 276.

[166] Yaakov Ariel, *On Behalf of Israel: American Fundamentalist Attitudes toward Jews, Judaism, and Zionism, 1865-1945* (Brooklyn, NY: Carlson Publishing Inc., 1991), p. 31.

[167] Darby, *Letter to Walter Wolston* (1874), L2:257; *cf. Letter to C. McAdam* (Boston, 20 February 1875), L2:334; *Letter* (Boston, 23 February 1875), L2:335; *Letter to C.*

encouraged to hear of the doctrinal progress Moody was making after reading a tract by C.H. Mackintosh, which was 'in a great measure a *résumé*'[168] of Brethren teaching. Rejoicing that Moody had 'greatly got on in truth',[169] Darby suddenly found himself 'in great vogue with a certain number'[170] in Chicago.

Moody was inspired by the devotion of the Plymouth Brethren to Scripture, and by their missionary zeal and 'uncompromising belief in the imminent, bodily, and premillennial return of the Lord Jesus Christ'[171] which, by 1877, Moody was teaching.[172] He spent considerable time among the Brethren, inviting many, including Darby, to preach in his Illinois Street Church. He also invited Darby to give a series of Bible readings in Farwell Hall.[173] Although the two men disputed on one occasion over the question of free will, prompting Darby to walk out of the meeting, Moody 'never denied' the influence of the Brethren, and like many others, 'showed his knack of drawing strength from a movement without becoming its slave.'[174]

Brethren Literature

During his time in St. Louis, Darby established 'pretty full intercourse'[175] with a number of ministers, one of whom was James Hall Brookes, the pastor of Walnut Street Presbyterian Church and the man who discipled Cyrus Scofield in the Christian faith. Besides sermons, Bible readings, and home visits, Darby's eschatology was disseminated most widely through Brethren literature. In a letter to C. Wolston in October 1866, he wrote: 'Tracts and books we cannot get enough of for the States.'[176] This need was expressed in a later letter to F. Rowan in 1872, in which Darby referred to an anonymous individual in St. Louis who 'says he is alone, and has sent for brethren's books'.[177]

The demand for literature led to a complete overhaul of Brethren printing and supply procedures.[178] Books and tracts written by Darby, William Kelly, Charles Mackintosh, and William Trotter were shipped to the United States and

---

McAdam (Boston, March 1875), L2:336; *Letter to J.B. Stoney* (March 1874), L2:259; *Letter to C. McAdam* (Springfield, 21 November 1872), L2:193.

[168] Darby, *Letter to J.B. Stoney* (March 1874), L2:259.

[169] Darby, *Letter to B.F. Pinkerton* (Chicago, 23 June 1876), L2:369.

[170] Darby, *Letter to C. McAdam* (Chicago, May 1875), L2:346.

[171] Lyle W. Dorsett, *A Passion for Souls: The Life of D.L. Moody* (Chicago, IL: Moody Publishers, 1997), p. 136.

[172] Sandeen, *The Roots of Fundamentalism*, pp. 173-174.

[173] John Reid, *F.W. Grant: His Life, Ministry and Legacy* (Plainfield, NJ: John Reid Book Fund, 1995), p. 58.

[174] John Pollock, *Moody without Sankey* (London: Hodder and Stoughton, 1983), p. 74.

[175] Darby, *Letter to F. Rowan* (St Louis, 1872), L2:180.

[176] Darby, *Letter to C. Wolston* (Toronto, October 1866), L1:459.

[177] Darby, *Letter to F. Rowan* (St Louis, 22 July 1872), L2:181.

[178] Darby, *Letter to A.B. Pollock* (Toronto, October 1866), L1:461.

distributed through publications such as James Inglis' *The Witness* and *Waymarks in the Wilderness* (1864-1872), and Charles Campbell's *The Scripture Testimony* (1863). As early as 1864, Darby's doctrine of the any-moment Rapture was promoted in a *Waymarks* article by Inglis entitled, 'The Expectation of the Church', in which Inglis claimed that 'there is not a single predicted event standing between us and the fulfilment of that hope.' A helpful summary of the progress of dispensationalism in the United States at that time is found in the September 1935 edition of *The Witness*, which included an entry about D.L. Moody taken from the February edition of *Moody Monthly*:

> He and others were beginning to get light on the Second Coming, and he asked Moorehouse if he knew anyone well posted on that truth? Moorehouse said there was a brother in New York, Richard Owens, a Dublin man...who could tell him all about it...Owens recommended him to Brother Inglis...then living in Philadelphia, and publishing a monthly paper. So Mr. Moody went to Philadelphia and sat at the feet of Inglis. Later, he met Mr. Darby, who visited the United States and who became a great friend of Dr. James H. Brookes, of St. Louis.[179]

Two men who played an important role in the publication and distribution of Brethren literature were Paul and Timothy Loizeaux. In 1876, they established the Bible Truth Depot in Vinton, Iowa, which later became known as Loizeaux Brothers. In 1870, at a Bible conference in Guelph, Paul Loizeaux met John Nelson Darby for the first time, and according to the company's centenary publication in 1976, 'The influence of this man [Darby], and many evangelists who had gathered from different parts of Canada, greatly affected his future life.'[180] The first notable Brethren scholar to have his work published by Loizeaux Brothers was C.H. Mackintosh, whose *Papers on the Lord's Coming* was one of the best-selling 'popularisations of Darby's theology'[181] in America. In his book, Mackintosh assured believers that there was

> nothing whatever to wait for – no events to transpire amongst the nations – nothing to occur in the history of Israel – nothing in God's government of the world – nothing, in short, in any shape or form whatsoever, to intervene between the heart of the true believer and his heavenly hope.[182]

---

[179] Roy A. Huebner, *Elements of Dispensational Truth: Vol. I*, 2nd edn (Morganville, NJ: Present Truth Publishers, 1998), pp. 16, 21.

[180] Marie Duvernoy Loizeaux, *A Century of Christian Publishing 1876-1976* (Neptune, NJ: Loizeaux Brothers, 1976), p. 7.

[181] Weber, *Living in the Shadow of the Second Coming*, p. 19.

[182] C.H. Mackintosh, *Papers on the Lord's Coming* (Chicago, IL: The Moody Press, n.d.), p. 22.

The Millerites

Writing to C. McAdam from Boston in 1875, Darby noted how the Brethren had become 'the subject of discussion everywhere', with 'evil doctrine...less rampant'[183] due to their influence. One of the 'doctrines' Darby consistently targeted was that of Millerism,[184] which was named after William Miller (1782-1849), a 'New England farmer turned prophetic interpreter'.[185]

In 1840, Miller announced that the Second Coming would take place some time between 21 March 1843 and 21 March 1844. When nothing happened, a revised date of 22 October 1844 was set and the Millerites duly gathered to meet Jesus, only to be met with despair. As the day closed, 'the sun sank as it had on every other day since creation, and Christ had not come.'[186] What became known as 'The Great Disappointment' proved to be an 'irredeemable error'. However, Millerism was soon revived by the 'imaginative theology'[187] of those who broke away from the movement to form the Seventh-day Adventists and the Branch Davidians. Darby's denunciation of the Millerites, and his refusal to set dates for the Second Coming, helped to secure an audience for his eschatology.

Darby's Farewell to America

In his final letter from America, written to Mr Brockhaus in June 1877, Darby summed up how the Brethren had been received by the American Church:

> There is an acknowledgment here in the United States of their acquaintance with the word such as nowhere else. They are not the less opposed to us; but they buy the books, and come in numbers to the Bible readings: they feel they must reckon with us, as they say. The Presbyterians, the Methodists, the Baptists, are minded to oppose. The first are unanimous, the ministers, as everywhere, opposing our work, and some write about it...The godly ones are discontented with the sermons [in their own churches], and some, like Moody, endeavour to help by a strenuous effort of activity...The truth is spreading...For some time the coming of the Lord has wrought in souls far and wide, and the doctrine is spreading wonderfully.[188]

By the time Darby left America, eighty-eight regular Brethren Bible-reading meetings had been established.[189] His achievement is best expressed, however,

---

[183] Darby, *Letter to C. McAdam* (Boston, February 1875), L2:329-330.

[184] Darby, *Letter to G.V. Wigram* (New York, 23 June 1865), L1:402; *Letter to C. McAdam* (Chicago, May 1875), L2:347; *Letter* (Ottawa, 4 June 1877), L2:394.

[185] Newport, *Apocalypse and Millennium*, p. 154.

[186] Sandeen, *The Roots of Fundamentalism*, p. 54.

[187] Newport, *Apocalypse and Millennium*, p. 165.

[188] Darby, *Letter to Mr Brockhaus* (7 June 1877), L2:395.

[189] Sandeen, *The Roots of Fundamentalism*, p. 79.

in terms of the 'sheer momentum'[190] he generated, a momentum carried forward by the American Bible and Prophecy Conference movement, which put Darby's dispensationalist eschatology firmly on America's theological map.

The Bible and Prophecy Conference Movement

James Inglis, Charles Campbell, and George Needham were among those who gathered for the first of a series of informal meetings in New York in 1868. Following the death of Inglis, these were suspended until the summer of 1875, when six men, including Nathaniel West, James H. Brookes, and W.J. Erdman, gathered near Chicago to study the Bible. Adoniram Judson Gordon joined the following summer when they met in Swampscott, Massachusetts. On the conference agenda that week was 'Dispensational Truth',[191] which included an exposition of the pretribulation Rapture by the 'founding father and controlling spirit'[192] of the conference, James H. Brookes, who had been influenced by the dispensationalism of G.B.M. Clouser and W.C. Bayne. Brookes described Darby and the Brethren as 'a people who are on the whole the soundest in faith, and most intelligent in the knowledge of our Lord Jesus Christ'.[193] He later recalled how he had 'often heard with great pleasure and profit Mr. Darby',[194] who had 'preached in his church in St. Louis at various times.'[195]

The Niagara Conference

At the close of the Swampscott meeting in 1876, it was decided to reconvene the following year at Watkins' Glen, New York, under the name of the Believers' Meeting for Bible Study. In the conference report it was noted how 'the coming of the Lord in its bearing upon Israel, the Church, and the world at large, received much attention, and of course it was found to be a most profitable subject for study and meditation.'[196] For the next three years delegates assembled at Clifton Springs, New York,[197] the method of 'Bible readings' adopted at these conferences, and the topics under discussion,

---

[190] Gribben, 'Introduction: Antichrist in Ireland', p. 16.

[191] C. Norman Kraus, *Dispensationalism in America* (Richmond, VA: John Knox Press, 1958), p. 78.

[192] Sandeen, *The Roots of Fundamentalism*, p. 134.

[193] Quoted in Kraus, *Dispensationalism in America*, pp. 37-38, 47; James H. Brookes, *I am Coming*, 7th edn (Edinburgh: Pickering & Inglis, n.d.), p. 98.

[194] Quoted in Huebner, *Elements of Dispensational Truth: Vol. I*, p. 20.

[195] Reid, *F.W. Grant*, p. 29.

[196] Quoted in Kraus, *Dispensationalism in America*, pp. 77-79.

[197] Arno C. Gaebelein, *The History of the Scofield Reference Bible* (Spokane, WA: Living Words Foundation, 1991), pp. 31-32.

strongly suggesting Brethren influence.[198] As Kraus writes,

> When we recall that Darby himself had been in the States for an extended ministry in the years immediately preceding the rise of the Bible conference movement, and, further, that he had ministered in the pulpits of the very men who gave the initial impetus to the movement, there can be little room for doubt that Darby and other early Plymouth Brethren preachers gave direct stimulus and at least indirect guidance to the movement.[199]

The Believers' Meeting quickly gathered momentum, delegates assembling in Old Orchard, Maine, in 1881, Mackinac Island, Michigan, in 1882, and Niagara-on-the-Lake, Ontario, from 1883-1897, where the Meeting changed its name to the Niagara Conference. Under the leadership of Brookes, and attended by all the leading premillennialists of the day, the Conference was 'the catalyst for the spread of…dispensational thinking in North America'.[200] The Believers' Meeting also provided the impetus for the First American Bible and Prophetic Conference, which opened in New York on 30 October 1878. Nathaniel West, who organised the Conference, issued the following invitation:

> The precious doctrine of Christ's second personal appearing has, we are forced to believe, long lain under such neglect and misapprehension…In view of these facts, it has seemed desirable that those who hold to the personal, premillennial advent of our Lord Jesus Christ, and who are 'looking for that blessed hope,' should meet together in conference, as our honoured brethren in England have recently done, to set forth on clear terms the grounds of their hope.[201]

West highlighted the 'almost fabulous increase of prophetic and apocalyptic literature' in his day, but conceded that the professing Church had largely adopted a 'false spiritualising, allegorising, and idealising, interpretation' of the Scriptures. This, he believed, had 'contributed to rob the predictions concerning Israel of their realistic value', and had helped to fuel anti-Semitism.[202] This conference is probably the 'congress at New York' which Darby referred to in a letter to H. Talbot in 1879, its major achievement having been 'the positive good of bringing the coming of the Lord publicly forward'.[203] According to Wilbur Smith, the conference papers contained 'the most important history of Premillennialism that exists in the literature of that generation'.[204]

On 16 November 1886, a second conference was convened at Farwell Hall,

---

[198] Bruce L. Shelley, 'Niagara Conferences', in *The New International Dictionary of the Christian Church*, ed. by J.D. Douglas (Exeter: The Paternoster Press, 1974), p. 706.

[199] Kraus, *Dispensationalism in America*, p. 79.

[200] *Three Central Issues in Contemporary Dispensationalism*, ed. by Bateman, p. 43.

[201] Quoted in Gaebelein, *The History of the Scofield Reference Bible*, pp. 33-34.

[202] West, *The Thousand Year Reign of Christ*, pp. xi-xii.

[203] Darby, *Letter to H. Talbot* (Pau, 1879), L2:499.

[204] Wilbur M. Smith, 'Foreword', in West, *The Thousand Year Reign of Christ*, p. viii.

Chicago, where advocates of Darby's dispensationalism, including A.J. Frost, A.T. Pierson, H.M. Parsons, W.R. Nicholson, and W.E. Blackstone, were prominent. According to Kraus, 'what one might call the dispensationalist mood...settled over the assembly.'[205] It is interesting to note that an advertisement of Darby's *Lectures on the Book of Revelation* was included in the publication of the conference papers.[206]

In 1890, the fourteen-point Niagara Creed, which had been drawn up by James H. Brookes in 1878, was officially adopted. Article XIV of the Creed 'reflects its background in the teachings of Darby':[207]

> We believe that the world will not be converted during the present dispensation, but is fast ripening for judgment, while there will be a fearful apostasy in the professing Christian body; and hence that the Lord Jesus will come in person to introduce the millennial age, when Israel shall be restored to their own land, and the earth shall be full of the knowledge of the Lord; and that this personal and premillennial advent is the blessed hope set before us in the Gospel for which we should be constantly looking: Luke 12:35-40; 17:26-30; 18:8; Acts 15:14-17; 2 Thess. 2:3-8; 2 Tim. 3:1-5; Tit. 2:11-15.

During the 1884 Niagara Conference, Canadian Baptist, Robert Cameron, challenged Nathaniel West over the veracity of the doctrine of the any-moment Rapture, which had become increasingly prominent at these conferences. West was finally won over to Cameron's position, which sparked a crisis within the Conference movement. In 1893, he published *The Apostle Paul and the 'Any Moment' Theory*, describing the 'Darby-Doctrine' as having 'nothing new in it that is true and nothing true in it that is new.'[208] In the October 1896 edition of *The Watchword*, Cameron suggested that 'the writings of Mr. Darby and the "brethren"...have moulded the teachings of nearly all the recent writers on prophetic subjects.'[209] He was determined to break the mould.

In 1898, the conference moved to Point Chautauqua near Jamestown, New York, and then to Asbury Park, New Jersey, where several speakers who had been influenced by Cameron voiced their opposition to Darby's doctrine of the Rapture. By this time Brookes had passed away, 'his voice...hushed and his able pen...no longer active,'[210] and it fell to Arno C. Gaebelein and Cyrus I. Scofield to take up the dispensationalist mantle. A new conference, known as the Sea Cliff Bible Conference, was convened on Long Island in July 1901, and sponsored by several wealthy Plymouth Brethren. The breach in the Conference movement widened when Cameron published a personal attack on Gaebelein,

---

[205] Kraus, *Dispensationalism in America*, p. 97.

[206] Huebner, *Elements of Dispensational Truth: Vol. I*, p. 19.

[207] Shelley, 'Niagara Conferences', p. 706.

[208] Quoted in Sandeen, *The Roots of Fundamentalism*, pp. 276-277, 210-211.

[209] Kraus, *Dispensationalism in America*, p. 48.

[210] Gaebelein, *The History of the Scofield Reference Bible*, p. 41.

suggesting that belief in a pretribulation Rapture could be traced back to Edward Irving and 'the testimony of demons'.[211] Scofield wrote the following anonymous response in Gaebelein's *Our Hope* magazine:

> To the *personal* reference we shall…make no reply. We cannot, however, in the interests of truth, allow the statement to stand that 'until the days of Edward Irving…no one ever heard of this "coming for" and "coming with His saints".'[212]

Despite the unfolding crisis in the Conference movement, its members were united in their opposition to 'rationalistic modernism'[213] which, by the early 1900s, was impacting churches and theological institutions across America. This united response laid the foundation for the Fundamentalist movement.

The Fundamentalist Movement

The increasing secularisation of American society, the theological impact of higher criticism and comparative religion, the emergence of 'Christian' cults, and the general breakdown of Judeo-Christian values, not only changed the cultural milieu in America but convinced many Evangelicals that the end of the age was near. A return to Biblical fundamentals was seen as the only bulwark against the rising tide of Modernism, and it was the dispensationalists, with their high view of Scripture and literalist approach to Biblical interpretation, who led the theological fight back. As Weber sums up,

> In the religiously factious decades before and after World War I, when popular notions of the Bible were changing, nobody could out-Bible the dispensationalists…Their worldview still had room for angels, demons, lakes of fire that burned forever, and a Saviour whose personal return would put an end to evil and establish the perfect world order.[214]

George Marsden has defined the Fundamentalist movement as 'a loose, diverse, and changing federation of co-belligerents united by their fierce opposition to modernist attempts to bring Christianity into line with modern thought.'[215] Sandeen suggests that premillennialism 'gave life and shape to the Fundamentalist movement',[216] while Kraus is more specific, and accurate, in his claim that dispensationalism was 'the vanguard of the modern fundamentalist

---

[211] Sandeen, *The Roots of Fundamentalism*, p. 218.

[212] Quoted in Gaebelein, *The History of the Scofield Reference Bible*, p. 43.

[213] Gaebelein, *The Conflict of the Ages*, p. 64.

[214] Weber, *On the Road to Armageddon*, pp. 36, 42.

[215] George M. Marsden, *Fundamentalism and American Culture* (New York: Oxford University Press, 1980), p. 4.

[216] Sandeen, *The Roots of Fundamentalism*, p. xv.

movement'.[217] Twelve volumes of essays, written by sixty-four British and American Evangelicals who were determined to uphold the fundamentals of the Christian faith, were compiled under the supervision of dispensationalists A.C. Dixon, Louis Meyer, and Reuben A. Torrey. Published between 1910 and 1915, they were collectively entitled, *The Fundamentals: A Testimony to the Truth*, and were initially distributed free of charge to thousands of Bible teachers, Sunday School superintendents, and missionaries across the United States and overseas. Financially backed by Lyman Stewart, a follower of Darby and co-founder of the Bible Institute of Los Angeles (BIOLA), *The Fundamentals* represented 'the epitome of Fundamentalist belief'.[218] Among the sixty-four writers were nineteen dispensationalists, including A.T. Pierson, J.H. Gray, L.W. Munhall, A.C. Gaebelein, and C.I. Scofield.

It is noteworthy that dispensationalists like Pierson and Torrey, along with Lewis Sperry Chafer and Harry Ironside, were invited to address the Keswick 'higher life' conventions in Britain, which began in 1875. According to Peter Williams, this ensured that Darby's dispensational premillennialism became 'a major doctrinal undergirding'[219] of the Keswick movement.

It is also important to note that dispensationalism influenced many of the early Pentecostal pioneers, who saw its eschatology as 'a helpful aid to emphasizing the premillennial second coming of Christ, the Rapture of the church, the seven years of the great Tribulation, the Millennium, and the cataclysmic Judgment that will mark the end of the present order.'[220] The essential features of dispensationalism, including Israel's place in the end-times, remain foundational doctrines for the Assemblies of God (USA), the world's largest Pentecostal denomination. According to Grant Wacker,

> Whether we rely upon 'hard' poll data, or sales figures of books and periodicals, or an endless stream of anecdotal evidence, Darbyite premillennialism proves to be one of the most resilient and widely held belief systems that has ever gripped the American imagination.[221]

Wearing Darby's Mantle

Among those who were profoundly influenced by Darby's writings were William E. Blackstone, Arno C. Gaebelein, and Cyrus I. Scofield, arguably the

---

[217] Kraus, *Dispensationalism in America*, p. 7.

[218] Sandeen, *The Roots of Fundamentalism*, p. 189.

[219] Williams, *America's Religions*, p. 271.

[220] *The New International Dictionary of Pentecostal and Charismatic Movements*, Revised and expanded edn, ed. by Stanley M. Burgess and Eduard M. van der Maas (Grand Rapids, MI: Zondervan, 2002), p. 585.

[221] Grant Wacker, 'Planning Ahead: The Enduring Appeal of Prophecy Belief', *The Christian Century*, 111 (January, 1994), 48.

three most influential popularisers of his eschatology in the United States.

William Eugene Blackstone

William Blackstone (1841-1935), a Chicago businessman turned 'clergyman of national repute',[222] is described in the *Encyclopaedia Judaica* as the 'most famous of the Zionist millenarians in the United States'.[223] According to Timothy Weber, 'No American premillennialist earned more acclaim among Zionists'.[224] In 1956, Israel named a forest in his honour. In his own eyes, however, he was simply 'God's little errand boy'.[225]

Blackstone was the author of *Jesus is Coming* (1878), 'probably the most widely read premillennialist book of its time'[226] and America's first dispensationalist best seller. In 1917, Moody Bible Institute sent presentation copies to its ministers, missionaries, and theological students. The book went through three editions and was translated into forty-two languages, including Yiddish and Hebrew, and by the time of Blackstone's death in 1935, over 1.3 million copies had been printed. In his book, Blackstone likened 'dispensational truth' to 'the red thread in the British rigging', because it ran 'through the whole Bible'. His book was written to show how Israel's restoration 'is an incontrovertible fact of prophecy...intimately connected with our Lord's appearing'. Blackstone made the following appeal to detractors:

> But, perhaps, you say: 'I don't believe the Israelites are to be restored to Canaan, and Jerusalem rebuilt.' Dear reader! have you read the declarations of God's word about it? Surely nothing is more plainly stated in the Scriptures...We beg of you to read them thoroughly. Divest yourself of prejudice and preconceived notions, and let the Holy Spirit show you, from His word, the glorious future of God's chosen people, 'who are beloved' (Rom.11:28), and dear unto Him as 'the apple of His eye.' Zech.2:8.[227]

Seeking to promote the welfare of Jewish immigrants in America, while presenting Jesus to them as their Messiah, Blackstone founded the Hebrew Christian Mission in November 1887. It was renamed the Chicago Hebrew Mission in 1889, the American Messianic Fellowship in 1953, and is now known as AMF International. In November 1890, Blackstone organised a conference on 'The Past, Present and Future of Israel', during which a petition was drawn up addressing the plight of Russian Jews. It was signed by 413

---

[222] *America and Palestine*, ed. by Fink, p. 21.
[223] *Encyclopaedia Judaica: Vol. XVI*, p. 1154.
[224] Weber, *Living in the Shadow of the Second Coming*, p. 137.
[225] William E. Currie, 'God's Little Errand Boy', <http://www.amfi.org/errandboy.htm, 6 June 2005>.
[226] Weber, *Living in the Shadow of the Second Coming*, p. 137.
[227] Blackstone, *Jesus is Coming*, pp. 235, 176, 162.

politicians, clergymen, Jewish leaders, journalists, and industrialists who represented 'a veritable "Who's Who" among the leaders in the United States'.[228] On 5 March 1891, the petition, known as the *Blackstone Memorial*, was presented to President Benjamin Harrison and Secretary of State James Blaine. Blackstone urged them to persuade the crown heads of Europe to convene a conference which would 'consider the condition of the Israelites and their claims to Palestine as their ancient home', and 'promote, in all other just and proper ways, the alleviation of their suffering condition.'

Not since the days of Cyrus had 'any mortal' been given 'such a privileged opportunity to further the purposes of God concerning His ancient people'. Blackstone asked why 'Palestine' could not be given back to the Jews, since it was their 'inalienable possession' from which they had been 'expelled by force.' He argued that a precedent had been set by the Treaty of Berlin in 1878, when Bulgaria had been given to the Bulgarians, Serbia to the Serbs, and Romania and Montenegro wrested from Turkish control. He believed that it was 'an appropriate time for all nations and especially the Christian nations of Europe to show kindness to Israel' by restoring the Jews to 'the land of which they were so cruelly despoiled by our Roman ancestors.'[229] Blackstone's *Memorial* failed to win the necessary presidential support, and was equally unsuccessful when it was later re-presented to President Woodrow Wilson on 30 June 1917. Undeterred by the setback, Blackstone continued to express his love for the Jewish people and his *Biblical* support for the Zionist cause. At a Zionist gathering in Los Angeles on 27 January 1918, he declared:

> I wish all of you Gentiles were true Israelites in your religious life, and I wish all of you Jews were true Christians. I am and for over thirty years have been an ardent advocate of Zionism. This is because I believe that true Zionism is founded on the plan, purpose, and fiat of the everlasting and omnipotent God, as prophetically recorded in His Holy Word, the Bible.[230]

Blackstone had once expressed despair at Theodor Herzl's indifference towards *Eretz Yisrael*, so much so that he sent him an Old Testament in which he had marked those scriptures which spoke of the return of the Jews to the Land. By 1932, however, he was in no doubt that 'God's hand' was in the Zionist movement Herzl had founded. Blackstone saw developments in the Middle East and Europe as 'wonderful signs for every believer in the Scriptures that they will be completely fulfilled,' and encouraged all who wished to know the

---

[228] *America and Palestine*, ed. by Fink, p. 22.

[229] 'Palestine for the Jews: Copy of Memorial Presented to President Harrison, March 5th, 1891', in *Christian Protagonists for Jewish Restoration* (New York: Arno Press, 1977), pp. 1-14.

[230] Quoted in David A. Rausch, *Zionism within early American Fundamentalism 1878-1918* (New York: The Edwin Mellen Press, 1979), p. 268.

prophetic time to look at Israel, 'God's sun-dial'.[231]

Arno C. Gaebelein

Another American Evangelical who sounded the 'midnight cry' of Christ's return, and who helped to provide 'the spark for the millenarian movement during the first two decades of the twentieth century',[232] was Arno C. Gaebelein (1861-1945). In *The Gospel of Matthew*, Gaebelein described how the midnight cry had sounded 'toward the middle' of the nineteenth century, when

> the Holy Spirit through mighty instruments, though humble, gave a revival of the blessed Hope and all that which is connected with it. And this cry is still heard, 'Behold the Bridegroom! go ye forth to meet him.' The enemy would silence this blessed word, but he cannot do it…The midnight cry is given that we may go forth to meet Him and be truly separated unto Him, who is soon coming. And if we have heard that cry by the power of the Spirit of God and are gone forth to meet the Bridegroom, we have a responsibility to take it up and sound it forth.[233]

A Jewish immigrant from Thuringia, Germany, Gaebelein served for many years as a Methodist minister in the United States before establishing The Hope of Israel mission on the Lower East Side of New York, where many of his fellow Jewish immigrants lived. Gaebelein and his associate, Ernest Stroeter, revolutionised Christian outreach to the Jews by insisting that those who received Jesus as their Messiah did not have to 'Gentilise', but could retain their Jewish identity.[234] This approach was strongly affirmed by dispensationalists in Britain including Sir Robert Anderson, the celebrated Assistant Commissioner of the Metropolitan Police who served as Chief of Scotland Yard's Criminal Investigation Department during the infamous 'Jack the Ripper' case. A member of the Plymouth Brethren and a friend of John Nelson Darby, Anderson dismissed any suggestion that Jews who accepted Christ ceased to be Jews as 'absolutely grotesque in its absurdity.'[235] By adopting Jewish symbols, meeting on the Sabbath, and incorporating Jewish feasts into their Christian liturgy, Gaebelein and Stroeter 'promoted the idea that the acceptance of the Christian faith was compatible with the Jewish faith', and represented the 'fulfilment of one's Jewish destiny.'[236]

Gaebelein staunchly opposed the 'horrors of anti-Semitism', adding his

---

[231] Blackstone, *Jesus is Coming*, pp. 242, 234.

[232] Sandeen, *The Roots of Fundamentalism*, p. 221.

[233] A.C. Gaebelein, *The Gospel of Matthew* (New York: Loizeaux Brothers, 1961), pp. 531-532.

[234] Ariel, *On Behalf of Israel*, p. 104.

[235] Sir Robert Anderson, *The Silence of God* (Grand Rapids, MI: Kregel Publications, 1978), p. 85.

[236] Ariel, *Evangelizing the Chosen People*, pp. 14-15.

signature to a statement denouncing the *Protocols of the Elders of Zion* and publishing detailed accounts of Nazi atrocities against the Jews. His lament over 'the contempt expressed by certain "Christians" to the Jew' was based on his own 'deep love for'[237] and 'deep kinship'[238] with the Jewish people. As he expressed in his book, *The Jewish Question*,

> The knowledge of Israel's place and position in God's revealed plan is of incalculable importance. All the confusion in doctrine and practice we see about us, is more or less the result of a deplorable ignorance which exists throughout Christendom concerning Israel's place and future.[239]

In 1898, Gaebelein met New York printer Francis E. Fitch, a Plymouth 'brother' who introduced him to the works of Darby and the Brethren. Although Gaebelein was not enamoured with their ecclesiology, he wrote enthusiastically about the Brethren in his autobiography, *Half a Century*:

> Through these brethren beloved I had become acquainted with the works of those able and godly men who were used in the great spiritual movement of the Brethren in the early part of the nineteenth century, John Nelson Darby and others. I found in his writings, in the works of William Kelly, Mackintosh, F.W. Grant, Bellett and others the soul food I needed. I esteem these men next to the Apostles in their sound and spiritual teaching.[240]

Gaebelein described Darby as the 'most outstanding' among 'the mighty men of God'[241] of the Plymouth Brethren, and as 'one of the most eminent scholars who ever lived and possessed insight in the word of God, which made him one of the greatest gifts the Lord ever gave to His church. And yet he was a very humble man.'[242] Gaebelein's son, Frank, later wrote:

> My father was definitely a dispensationalist. I believe his dispensationalism came from his association with the Plymouth Brethren and through reading the writings of John Nelson Darby, William Kelly, C.H. Mackintosh, and F.W. Grant, and through knowing and also working with men like F.C. Jennings, W.J. Erdman, A.T. Pierson, Nathaniel West and C.I. Scofield.[243]

After retiring from missionary work to support the fundamentalist cause,

---

[237] David A. Rausch, 'Introduction', in Gaebelein, *The Conflict of the Ages*, pp. ix-xviii.

[238] Donn M. Gaebelein, 'Foreword', in Gaebelein, *The Conflict of the Ages*, p. viii.

[239] Arno C. Gaebelein, *The Jewish Question* (New York: Our Hope, 1912), p. 1.

[240] Arno C. Gaebelein, *Half a Century: The Autobiography of a Servant* (New York: Our Hope, 1930), pp. 83-85.

[241] Gaebelein, *The Conflict of the Ages*, p. 62.

[242] Quoted in Huebner, *Elements of Dispensational Truth: Vol. I*, p. 16.

[243] David A. Rausch, *Arno C. Gaebelein 1861-1945 Irenic Fundamentalist and Scholar* (New York: Edwin Mellen Press, 1983), p. 239.

Gaebelein was invited by his friend, Lewis Sperry Chafer, to help establish the Evangelical Theological College in Dallas in 1924. Known today as Dallas Theological Seminary, the 'college' quickly became the flagship, or 'centre of institutional dispensationalism',[244] staffing many theological establishments. In 1905, Gaebelein received a letter from Cyrus Scofield thanking him for his help in the compilation of his *Reference Bible*. Scofield paid Gaebelein the highest tribute when he wrote: 'I sit at your feet when it comes to prophecy'.[245]

Cyrus Ingerson Scofield

After serving in the Confederate Army, Cyrus Scofield (1843-1921) moved to St. Louis to pursue a legal career. He was appointed district attorney for Kansas by President Ulysses S. Grant, a position he held for two years before returning to St. Louis where, in 1879, he was converted to Christ. Scofield was discipled by James H. Brookes, whom he described as 'the greatest Bible student' he had ever known and who was 'an amazing blessing' to him. Scofield also met D.L. Moody during one of his evangelistic campaigns in St. Louis, describing him as 'one of the greatest men of his generation'.[246] Scofield later pastored Moody's church at East Northfield, Massachusetts. In 1890, he launched his *Bible Correspondence School Course of Study*, which was later used by Moody Bible Institute to promote dispensationalism around the world.

Like Darby, Scofield believed that the study of prophecy was not a means of indulging in 'idle and profitless speculations', but an occupation which ought to encourage 'intimacy with God'. Having at one time dismissed God's promises to Israel as irrelevant, Scofield's attitude changed when he realised that by doing so he was 'refusing the most intimate fellowship with the Lord'. From that point on he saw the Jew as 'the miracle of history' who can 'no more be understood apart from God than the universe can'.[247]

Scofield believed that all was 'contrast' when Israel and the Church were referred to in Scripture, insisting that prophecy was to be interpreted 'in the literal, natural and unforced meaning of the words', so that 'Jerusalem is always Jerusalem, Israel always Israel, Zion always Zion.'[248] He accused those who stole from Israel 'her promises of earthly glory' of having done 'more to swerve the Church from the appointed course than all other influences put together'.

Like Darby, Scofield highlighted the prophetic element in the Psalms, and interpreted the Jewish feasts typologically. He also believed in a two-stage

---

[244] Weber, *Living in the Shadow of the Second Coming*, p. 238.

[245] Quoted in Gaebelein, *The History of the Scofield Reference Bible*, pp. 32-33.

[246] Charles Gallaudet Trumbull, *The Life Story of C.I. Scofield* (New York: Oxford University Press, 1920), pp. 28, 35-36, 52.

[247] Scofield, *Prophecy made Plain*, pp. 10, 74-75, 12-13, 57.

[248] Scofield, *The Scofield Bible Correspondence School: Vol. I*, pp. 23-25, 128, 46.

Second Coming, the first being the Rapture of 'the real Church composed of true believers since the crucifixion',[249] and the second being Christ's 'subsequent coming to the earth with His saints.'[250] He further maintained that the Rapture would herald the time of 'Jacob's trouble',[251] a period which would be characterised by the revival of the Roman Empire, the rise of Antichrist, and the Second Coming of Jesus to establish His millennial reign on earth.[252]

When Scofield was beginning work on his *Reference Bible*, Timothy and Paul Loizeaux introduced him to Miss Emily Farmer, who was duly assigned to assist him. Farmer later recalled that 'the two sets of reference books on Dr. Scofield's desk to which he referred constantly, were the *Synopsis of the Books of the Bible* by J.N. Darby and the *Numerical Bible* by F.W. Grant.'[253]

Between 1904 and 1907, Scofield travelled to London and Montreux to undertake further research. Trumbull records how, on one occasion during his two-year stay in England, Scofield and his wife 'found spiritual fellowship and comfort in a little gathering of Plymouth Brethren'[254] in Oxford.

The *Scofield Reference Bible* was finally published in 1909, reprinted in 1917, and revised and republished in 1967. It remains the most systematic and popular expression of classical dispensationalism, and proved to be a potent weapon in the Fundamentalist fight against Modernism. It was completed 'with the invaluable collaboration of a wide circle of spiritual and experienced Bible students and teachers, in England and the United States,'[255] to whom Scofield acknowledged his debt.

In Conclusion

In 1654, twenty-three Sephardic immigrants arrived in New York. In the same year, Menasseh ben Israel petitioned Oliver Cromwell to readmit the Jews to England. It was unclear, however, which nation would prove to be the staunchest ally of the Jewish people. Following Britain's abdication of responsibility and her betrayal of the Jewish people during the 'Mandate' period, it fell to America to assume the role of patron of Israel. This patronage was given voice in 2001 by newly elected President George W. Bush, who declared:

---

[249] Scofield, *Prophecy made Plain*, pp. 13, 52, 120.

[250] Scofield, *The Scofield Bible Correspondence School Course of Study, Vol. II: The New Testament*, 9th edn (London: Morgan and Scott, n.d.), p. 243.

[251] Scofield, *Prophecy made Plain*, pp. 122, 130-131, 119.

[252] Scofield, *The Scofield Bible Correspondence School: Vol. II*, p. 340.

[253] Quoted in Reid, *F.W. Grant*, pp. 27-28.

[254] Trumbull, *The Life Story of C.I. Scofield*, pp. 108, 117.

[255] C.I. Scofield, 'Introduction', in *The First Scofield Reference Bible* (Sunbury, PA: Believers Bookshelf Inc., 1986), p. ii.

I am a Christian, but I believe with the psalmist that the Lord God of Israel neither slumbers nor sleeps...My administration will be steadfast in supporting Israel against terrorism and violence, and in seeking the peace for which all Israelis pray.[256]

Dispensationalism has endured in the United States because 'it was able to create a new subculture'[257] among Evangelical leaders who were happy to adopt Darby's eschatology, while remaining within their own denominational structures. Such men founded Bible colleges, institutes, and theological seminaries which 'expounded dispensational pretribulationism'[258] and laid a firm Christian Zionist foundation within the American Evangelical Church.[259] As one notable critic of dispensationalism conceded,

It is doubtful if there has been any other circle of men who have done more by their influence, in preaching, teaching and writing, to promote a love for Bible study, a hunger for the deeper Christian life, a passion for evangelism and zeal for missions, in the history of American Christianity.[260]

The very ethos of the United States enabled an unassuming 'Irish clergyman' to lay the foundations for a distinct form of Evangelicalism which has greatly impacted American Christianity. By heralding the any-moment Rapture of the Church, the national restoration of Israel, and the Second Coming of Jesus Christ, John Nelson Darby raised a banner for Biblical truth in the nineteenth century beneath which successive generations of true believers have rallied. As Thomas Ice rightly points out in the Foreword, Darby's 'importance and impact has remained hidden for too long.'

---

[256] Stephen Mansfield, *The Faith of George W. Bush* (New York: Jeremy P. Tarcher, 2003), pp. 124-125.

[257] Weber, *On the Road to Armageddon*, p. 43.

[258] Hitchcock and Ice, *The Truth behind Left Behind*, p. 201.

[259] Craig A. Blaising and Darrell L. Bock, *Progressive Dispensationalism* (Grand Rapids, MI: Bridgepoint Books, 2002), p. 12.

[260] George Eldon Ladd, *Crucial Questions about the Kingdom of God* (Grand Rapids, MI: William B. Eerdmans Publishing Company, 1977), p. 49.

Afterword

Probably no Christian thinker in the last two hundred years has so affected the way in which English-speaking Christians view the faith, and yet has received so little recognition of his contribution, as John Nelson Darby.[1]

Few academic historians are comfortable with Christian theology; fewer still are prepared to grapple with the nuances of Christian eschatology. They have been inclined instead to focus on sociological, economic, and political factors in their surveys of Church history. In so doing, they have failed to understand, and do justice to, Christian Zionism and its leading architect and patron, John Nelson Darby. Eminent historians of the calibre of Ernest Sandeen have despaired of understanding Darby's eschatology, and have rather arrogantly dismissed it as unintelligible. Although Darby expressed himself rather awkwardly at times, his commanding intellect and devout Christian faith inspired one of the most comprehensive and coherent theological systems in the history of the Church, one which enabled Evangelicals to resist the onslaught of Modernism and Liberalism, and sound the midnight cry, 'Behold, the Bridegroom!' (Matt. 25:6; RSV).

The distinctions made in this book between premillennialism and postmillennialism, historicism and futurism, and pretribulationism and posttribulationism, may seem hair-splitting to the outsider, but they are of critical importance to the Church, especially in light of its 'blessed hope' (Tit. 2:13). Another important distinction has also been made between Christian Zionism and Restorationism, the latter being far too broad a term and one which has been used to create artificial and misleading genealogies which have underplayed the crucial role of eschatology. By identifying Christian Zionism as a distinct *form* of Restorationism, rather than as its equivalent, the necessary means of correctly classifying individuals, organisations, and movements which have promoted, in one form or another, belief in the restoration of Israel, has been provided.

This book also demonstrates the need to re-evaluate Darby the man. Darby's powerful and uncompromising personality polarised people during his lifetime, and has continued to do so to the present day. It is difficult to remain impartial when reading his work and the early history of the Plymouth Brethren movement, but followers and critics alike have tended to ignore the man behind the ministry. Consequently, distorted impressions, even grotesque caricatures, have been created, which have veiled Darby's enormous contribution to the

---

[1] Melton, *The Encyclopedia of American Religions: Vol. I*, p. 411.

Evangelical Church. It is imperative, therefore, that we understand his theology against the backdrop of his personal and ministerial life. Whereas in public Darby was tenacious when it came to defending the fundamental doctrines of the Christian faith, a rather different portrait emerges from his private correspondence, and from the testimony of those who knew him best. Darby was a man of considerable personal warmth and compassion who was able to inspire loyalty and affection among those who knew him. A world-denying visionary, he forsook a comfortable life of financial security and upper class privilege, along with a career in law, to practise what he preached. Wholeheartedly devoted to his Lord and Saviour Jesus Christ, he preached the Good News to the sinner and prepared the Church to meet her Heavenly Bridegroom.

Key elements of Christian Zionist doctrine can be traced back to the early Puritan period, when God began to awaken Christians to the truth concerning Israel's restoration, which had long been suppressed by amillennial replacementism. The survey of nineteenth-century Restorationism shows how integral that truth was to Evangelicalism at that time, and how considerable its impact was not only on the British Church, but also on the nation as a whole. However, it is in Darby's writings that we first discover *all* the key elements of Christian Zionism in one coherent, theological package. Among the most important of these are a clear distinction between Israel and the Church, a consistently literal interpretation of Biblical prophecy in relation to the end-times, the inherent *Jewishness* of scriptures relating to the Great Tribulation, and the location of the Rapture *before* the time of Jacob's trouble.

Few Christians have left a legacy as enduring as that of John Nelson Darby, to whom Evangelicals owe a considerable debt of gratitude. Darby was raised up by God at a crucial time in history to recover, and proclaim, the truth of Israel's restoration and the *any-moment* Rapture of the Church. A year before his death, he expressed his deep longing for the Lord's return in a hymn entitled, 'Hope' (1881). That same longing abides in the hearts of all true believers today:

> And shall we see Thy face,
> And hear Thy heavenly voice,
> Well known to us in present grace!
> Well may our hearts rejoice.

> With Thee in garments white,
> O Jesus, we shall walk;
> And, spotless in that heavenly light,
> Of all Thy sufferings talk.

Close to Thy trusted side,
In fellowship divine,
No cloud, no distance, e'er shall hide
Glories that there shall shine.

Fruit of Thy boundless love
That gave Thyself for us –
For ever we shall with Thee prove
That Thou still lov'st us thus.

And we love Thee, blest Lord,
E'en now, though feeble here;
Thy sorrows and Thy cross record
What makes us know Thee near.

We wait to see Thee, Lord!
Yet now within our hearts
Thou dwell'st in love, that doth afford
The joy *that* love imparts.

Yet still we wait for Thee,
To see Thee as Thou art,
Be with Thee, like Thee, Lord, and free
To love with all our heart.

'I have finished the race, I have kept the faith. Henceforth the crown of righteousness is laid up for me, which the Lord, the righteous Judge, will render to me in that day; but not only to me, but also to all who love His appearing.'
(2 Tim. 4:7-8; *Darby's Translation*)

Appendix

Margaret MacDonald's Utterance

It was first the awful state of the land that was pressed upon me. I saw the blindness and infatuation of the people to be very great. I felt the cry of Liberty just to be the hiss of the serpent…I repeated the words, Now there is distress of nations, with perplexity, the seas and the waves roaring, men's hearts failing them for fear – now look out for the sign of the Son of man. Here I was made to stop and cry out, O it is not known what the sign of the Son of man is; the people of God think they are waiting, but they know not what it is. *I felt this needed to be revealed, and that there was great darkness and error about it; but suddenly what it was burst upon me with a glorious light. I saw it was just the Lord himself descending from Heaven with a shout, just the glorified man, even Jesus; but that all must, as Stephen was, be filled with the Holy Ghost, that they might look up, and see the brightness of the Father's glory…Many passages were revealed, in a light in which I had not before seen them…'*But be ye not unwise, but understanding what the will of the Lord is; and be not drunk with wine *wherein is excess, but be filled with the Spirit.' This was the oil the wise* virgins *took in their vessels – this is the light to be kept burning – the light of God – that we may discern that which cometh not with observation to the natural eye. Only those who have the light of God within them will see the sign of his appearance…'*Tis Christ in us that will lift us up – he is the light – 'tis only those that are alive in him that will be caught up to meet him in the air. *I saw that we must be in the Spirit, that we might see spiritual things…But I saw that the glory of the ministration of the Spirit had not been known. I repeated frequently, but the spiritual temple must and shall be reared, and the fullness of Christ* be *poured into his body, and then shall we be caught up to meet him. Oh none will be counted worthy of this calling but his body,* which is *the church,* and which must be *a candlestick all of gold.* I often said, *Oh the glorious inbreaking of God* which is *now about to burst on this earth*; Oh *the glorious temple* which is *now about to be reared, the bride adorned for her husband; and Oh what a holy, holy bride she must be, to be prepared for such a glorious bridegroom.* I said, Now shall the people of God have to do with realities – *now shall the glorious mystery of God in our nature be known – now shall it be known what it is for man to be glorified.* I felt that the revelation of Jesus Christ had yet to be opened up – it is not knowledge about God that it contains, but it is an entering into God – I saw that there was a glorious breaking in of God to be. *I felt as Elijah, surrounded with chariots of fire. I saw as it were, the spiritual temple reared, and the Head Stone brought forth with shoutings of* *grace, grace, unto it. It was a glorious light above the brightness of the sun, that shone round about me. I felt that those who were filled with the Spirit could see spiritual things...while those who had not the Spirit could see nothing...I saw the people of God in an awfully dangerous situation,* surrounded by nets and entanglements, about to be tried, and many about to be deceived and fall. *Now will THE WICKED be revealed, with all power and signs and lying wonders, so that if it were possible the very elect will be deceived.*– This is the fiery trial which is to try us.– It will be for the purging and purifying of the real members of the body of Jesus; but Oh *it will be a fiery trial. Every soul will be shaken to the very centre.* The enemy will try to shake in every thing we have believed...*The stony-ground hearers will be made manifest – the love of many will wax cold. I* frequently *said* that night, and often since, *now shall the awful sight of a false Christ be seen on this earth, and nothing but* the living *Christ in us can detect this awful attempt of the enemy to deceive – for it is with all deceivableness of unrighteousness he will work – he will have a counterpart for every part of God's truth, and an imitation for every work of the Spirit.* The Spirit must and will be poured out on the church, that she may be purified and filled with God – and just *in proportion as the Spirit of God works, so will he – when our Lord anoints men with power, so will he. This is* particularly the nature of *the trial, through which those are to pass who will be counted worthy to stand before the Son of man. There will be outward trial* too, *but 'tis principally temptation. It is brought on by the outpouring of the Spirit, and will* just *increase in proportion as the Spirit is poured out.* The trial of the Church is from Antichrist...*I frequently said, Oh be filled with the Spirit – have the light of God in you, that you may detect satan – be full of eyes within – be clay in the hands of the potter – submit to be filled,* filled *with God. This* will build the temple...*This will fit us to enter into the marriage supper of the Lamb. I saw it to be the will of God that all should be filled. But what hindered the* real *life of God from being received by his people, was their turning from Jesus,* who is the way to the Father...They were *passing the cross, through which every drop of the Spirit of God flows to us.* All power that comes not through the blood of Christ is not of God...*I saw that night, and often since, that there will be an outpouring of the Spirit* on the body, *such as has not been, a baptism of fire, that all the dross may be put away.* Oh there must and will be such an indwelling of the living God as has not been – *the servants of God sealed in their foreheads* – great conformity to Jesus – *his holy* holy *image* seen *in his people*...This is what we are at present made to pray much for, that speedily we may all be made ready to meet our Lord in the air – and it will be. *Jesus wants his bride. His desire is toward us. He that shall come, will come, and will not tarry.* Amen and Amen. Even so come Lord Jesus.[1]

---

[1] Quoted in MacPherson, *The Incredible Cover-Up*, pp. 151-154. MacPherson combines MacDonald's account in Norton's *Memoirs* (1840; pp. 171-176) and *The Restoration of Apostles and Prophets* (1861; pp. 15-18). The portions in italics are from the latter.

Bibliography

Abbott, Wilbur Cortez, *The Writings and Speeches of Oliver Cromwell*. *Vol. III* (Cambridge, MA: Harvard University Press, 1945).

Adler, Joseph, *Restoring the Jews to their Homeland: Nineteen Centuries in the Quest for Zion* (Northvale, NJ: Jason Aronson Inc., 1997).

Ahlstrom, Sydney E., *A Religious History of the American People* (New Haven, CT: Yale University Press, 1972).

Alexander, Philip S., 'Dispensationalism, Christian Zionism and the State of Israel', *Presidential Lecture for the Manson Society* (Manchester: Faculty of Humanities, University of Manchester, 2001).

Allen, Ronald B., 'The Land of Israel', in House, *Israel*, pp. 17-33.

Allis, Oswald T., *Prophecy and the Church* (Nutley, NJ: The Presbyterian and Reformed Publishing Company, 1972).

Anderson, Irvine H., *Biblical Interpretation and Middle East Policy: The Promised Land, America, and Israel, 1917-2002* (Gainesville, FL: University Press of Florida, 2005).

Anderson, John A., *Heralds of the Dawn* (Aberdeen: 1933).

Anderson, Sir Robert, *Unfulfilled Prophecy; and The Hope of the Church*, 2nd edn (London: James Nisbet & Co. Ltd., 1918).

— *The Coming Prince: The Marvellous Prophecy of Daniel's Seventy Weeks concerning the Antichrist*, 14th edn (Grand Rapids, MI: Kregel Publications, 1954).

— *The Silence of God* (Grand Rapids, MI: Kregel Publications, 1978).

Archer, Gleason L., et al., *The Rapture: Pre-, Mid-, or Post-Tribulational?* (Grand Rapids, MI: Academie Books, 1984).

Archer, Henry, *The Personall Raigne of Christ upon Earth* (London: 1642).

Ariel, Yaakov, *On Behalf of Israel: American Fundamentalist attitudes toward Jews, Judaism, and Zionism, 1865-1945* (Brooklyn, NY: Carlson Publishing Inc, 1991).

— *Evangelizing the Chosen People: Missions to the Jews in America, 1880-2000* (Chapel Hill, NC: University of North Carolina Press, 2000).

— 'How are Jews and Israel Portrayed in the Left Behind Series? A Historical Discussion of Jewish-Christian Relations', in Forbes and Kilde, *Rapture*, pp. 131-166.

Armerding, Carl E., and W. Ward Gasque, (eds.), *A Guide to Biblical Prophecy* (Peabody, MA: Hendrickson Publishers, 1989).

Armstrong, Karen, *Holy War: The Crusades and their Impact on Today's World* (London: Papermac, 1992).

Arnold, Jon, and Stephen R. Sizer, *A Panorama of the Holy Land* (Guildford: Eagle, 1998).

Ashburnham, William, *The Restoration of the Jews, a Poem* (London: 1794).

Ateek, Naim, *Justice, and Only Justice: A Palestinian Theology of Liberation* (Maryknoll, NY: Orbis Books, 1990).

Ateek, Naim, 'Jerusalem in Islam and for Palestinian Christians', in Walker, *Jerusalem*, pp. 125-154.

— 'A Palestinian Theology of Jerusalem', in Ateek, Duaybis, and Schrader, *Jerusalem*, pp. 94-106.

— 'Zionism and the Land: a Palestinian Christian Perspective', in Johnston and Walker, *The Land of Promise*, pp. 201-214.

— 'Christian Zionism: The Dark Side of the Bible', *Cornerstone*, 30 (Winter, 2003), 1-2.

— 'Introduction: Challenging Christian Zionism', in Ateek, Duaybis, and Tobin, *Challenging Christian Zionism*, pp. 13-19.

Ateek, Naim, Marc H. Ellis, and Rosemary Radford Ruether, (eds.), *Faith and the Intifada: Palestinian Christian Voices* (Maryknoll, NY: Orbis Books, 1992).

Ateek, Naim, Cedar Duaybis, and Marla Schrader, (eds.), *Jerusalem: What Makes for Peace! A Palestinian Christian Contribution to Peacemaking* (London: Melisende, 1997).

Ateek, Naim, and Michael Prior, (eds.), *Holy Land Hollow Jubilee: God, Justice and the Palestinians* (London: Melisende, 1999).

Ateek, Naim, Cedar Duaybis, and Maurine Tobin, *Challenging Christian Zionism: Theology, Politics and the Israel-Palestine Conflict* (London: Melisende, 2005).

Aune, David E., and Eric Stewart, 'From the Idealised Past to the Imaginary Future: Eschatological Restoration in Jewish Apocalyptic Literature', in Scott, *Restoration*, pp. 147-177.

Ausubel, Nathan, *The Book of Jewish Knowledge: An Encyclopedia of Judaism and the Jewish People, Covering all Elements of Jewish Life from Biblical Times to the Present* (New York: Crown Publishers, Inc., 1964).

Ayerst, William, *The Jews of the Nineteenth Century: A Collection of Essays, Reviews, and Historical Notices, originally published in the 'Jewish Intelligence'* (London: 1848).

Bahnsen, Greg L., and Kenneth L. Gentry, Jr, *House Divided: The Break-Up of Dispensational Theology* (Tyler, TX: Institute for Christian Economics, 1989).

Bailey, Mark, 'The Tribulation', in Swindoll et al., *The Road to Armageddon*, pp. 49-77.

Baillie, John, *Two Sermons: The First on the Divinity of Jesus Christ; the Second on Time, Manner, and Means of the Conversion and Universal Restoration of the Jews*, 2nd edn (London: 1792).

Baker, H.A., 'A "Pre-Tribulation Rapture" is a New Theory', *Watching and Waiting*, July-August (1956), 241-244.

Ball, Bryan W., *A Great Expectation: Eschatological Thought in English Protestantism to 1660* (Leiden: E.J. Brill, 1975).

Balleine, G.R., *A History of the Evangelical Party in the Church of England* (London: Church Book Room Press Ltd., 1951).

Baram, Daphna, *Disenchantment: the Guardian and Israel* (London: Guardian Books, 2004).

Barbieri, Louis A., 'The Church: Watching for our Blessed Hope', in Dyer, *Storm Clouds on the Horizon*, pp. 33-46.

Baron, David, *Israel in the Plan of God* (Grand Rapids, MI: Kregel Publications, 1983).

Baron, Salo W., 'Conference Theme', in Davis and Meyer, *The Writing of American Jewish History*, pp. 5-8.

Barr, James, *Fundamentalism* (London: SCM Press Ltd., 1981).

Bar-Yosef, Eitan, 'Christian Zionism and Victorian Culture', *Israel Studies*, 8.2 (2003).

Basilicus, *Thoughts on the Scriptural Expectations of the Christian Church* (Gloucester: n.d.).

Bass, Clarence B., *Backgrounds to Dispensationalism* (Grand Rapids, MI: Baker Book House, 1978).

Bateman IV, Herbert W., (ed.), *Three Central Issues in Contemporary Dispensationalism: A Comparison of Traditional and Progressive Views* (Grand Rapids, MI: Kregel Publications, 1999).

Bauckham, Richard, *Tudor Apocalypse* (Oxford: The Sutton Courtenay Press, 1978).

Bayliss, Robert H., *My People: The History of those Christians sometimes called Plymouth Brethren* (Wheaton, IL: Harold Shaw Publishers, 1995).

Bebbington, David W., *Evangelicalism in Modern Britain: A History from the 1730s to the 1980s* (London: Unwin Hyman, 1989).

Beere, Richard, *A Dissertation on the 13th and 14th verses of the 8th chapter of Daniel; containing strong and cogent arguments, to prove that the commencement of the final restoration of the Jews, to the Holy Land, is to take place in the ensuing year, A.D. 1791* (London: 1790).

Bellett, John Gifford, *Interesting Reminiscences of the Early History of "Brethren": with Letter from J.G. Bellett to J.N. Darby* (London: Alfred Holness, n.d.).

Bellett, L.M., *Recollections of the Late J.G. Bellett* (London: James Carter, 1895).

— *Recollections of the Late J.G. Bellett. With sequel: 'The Memory of a Dearly Loved and only Son'* (London: A.S. Rouse, 1895).

Ben-Arieh, Yehoshua, *The Rediscovery of the Holy Land in the Nineteenth Century* (Jerusalem: Magnes Press, Hebrew University, 1979).

Ben-Ezra, Juan Josafat [Manuel Lacunza], *The Coming of Messiah in Glory and Majesty, by Juan Josafat Ben-Ezra, a Converted Jew, translated from the Spanish, with a Preliminary Discourse, by the Rev. Edward Irving, A.M.* (London: L.B. Seeley and Son, 1827), 2 vols.

Ben Israel, Menasseh, *The Hope of Israel*, 2nd edn (London: 1651).

Bennett, Ramon, *Saga: Israel and the Demise of Nations* (Jerusalem: Arm of Salvation, 1993).

— *Philistine: The Great Deception* (Jerusalem: Arm of Salvation, 1995).

— *When Day and Night Cease*, Revised edn (Jerusalem: Arm of Salvation, 1996).

— *The Wall: Prophecy, Politics and Middle East 'Peace'* (Citrus Heights, CA: Shekinah Books, Ltd., 2000).

Benware, Paul N., *Understanding End Times Prophecy* (Chicago, IL: Moody Press, 1995).

Bernstein, A., *Jewish Witnesses for Christ* (Jerusalem: Keren Ahvah Meshihit, 1999).

Beveridge, Henry, (ed.), *Commentary Upon the Acts of the Apostles by John Calvin. Vol. I* (Edinburgh: 1844).

Bicheno, James, *The Restoration of the Jews the Crisis of all Nations; to which is now prefixed, A Brief History of the Jews, from their First Dispersion, to the Calling of their Grand Sanhedrin at Paris, October 6th, 1806. And An Address on the Present State of Affairs, in Europe in General, and in this Country in Particular*, 2nd edn (London: 1807).

Bickersteth, Edward, *The Restoration of the Jews to their own Land, in Connection with their Future Conversion and the Final Blessedness of our Earth*, 2nd edn (London: R.B. Seeley and W. Burnside, 1841).

Bietenhard, Hans, 'The Millennial Hope in the Early Church', *Scottish Journal of Theology*, 6 (1953), 12-30.

Blackstone, William Eugene, *Jesus is Coming* (Chicago, IL: Fleming H. Revell Company, 1932).

Blaising, Craig A., and Darrell L. Bock, *Progressive Dispensationalism* (Grand Rapids, MI: Bridgepoint Books, 2002).

Bloch, Ruth H., *Visionary Republic: Millennial Themes in American Thought, 1756-1800* (Cambridge: Cambridge University Press, 1985).

Bluett, Antony, *With Our Army in Palestine* (London: Andrew Melrose Ltd., 1919).

Boice, James Montgomery, *The Last and Future World* (Grand Rapids, MI: Zondervan, 1974).

Bokser, Ben Zion, (ed.), *Abraham Isaac Kook: The Lights of Penitence, The Moral Principles, Lights of Holiness, Essays, Letters, and Poems* (New York: Paulist Press, 1978).

Bonar, Andrew A., and Robert Murray McCheyne, *Narrative of a Mission of Inquiry to the Jews from the Church of Scotland in 1839* (Edinburgh: William Whyte and Co., 1850).

Bonar, Andrew A., *The Life of Robert Murray McCheyne* (London: Banner of Truth Trust, 1960).

— *Memoir and Remains of Robert Murray McCheyne* (Edinburgh: The Banner of Truth Trust, 1978).

Boreland, Stephen, *Some Golden Daybreak: A Defence of the Pretribulation Rapture* (Pearl Publishing Press, 2001).

Bowie, Fiona, (ed.), *The Coming Deliverer: Millennial Themes in World Religions* (Cardiff: University of Wales Press, 1997).

Boyer, Paul S., *When Time Shall Be No More: Prophecy Belief in Modern American Culture* (Cambridge, MA: Belknap Press, 1999).

Bradshaw, Samuel Alexander, *A Tract for the Times, being A Plea for the Jews* (London: Edwards & Hughes, 1844).

Brady, David, *The Christian Brethren Archive in the John Rylands University Library of Manchester* (Firenze, 1988).

Bramley-Moore, William, *The Church's Forgotten Hope, or Scriptural Studies on the Translation of the Saints*, 2nd edn (London: George J.W. Pitman, 1903).

Brasher, Brenda E., (ed.), *Encyclopedia of Fundamentalism* (London: Routledge, 2001).

Brayer, Lynda, 'The Separation of Jerusalem from the West Bank and Gaza', in Ateek, Duaybis, and Schrader, *Jerusalem*, pp. 141-153.

Brearley, Margaret, 'Jerusalem in Judaism and for Christian Zionists', in Walker, *Jerusalem*, pp. 99-124.

Breunig, Charles, *The Age of Revolution and Reaction 1789-1850* (London: Weidenfeld and Nicolson, 1970).

Brickner, David, *Future Hope: A Jewish Christian Look at the End of the World*, 2nd edn (San Francisco, CA: Purple Pomegranate Productions, 1999).

Brightman, Thomas, *A Revelation of the Apocalyps* (Amsterdam: 1611).

Brimmer, Rebecca J., and Bridges for Peace Leaders, *Israel and the Church: God's Road Map* (Jerusalem: Bridges for Peace International, 2006).

Brimmer, Rebecca J., 'Israel-Miracle Nation', in Brimmer, *Israel*, pp. 129-141.

British Council of Churches, *Israel and the Land: A Symposium* (London: British Council of Churches, 1989).

Brog, David, *Standing with Israel: Why Christians Support the Jewish State* (Lake Mary, FL: FrontLine, 2006).

Brookes, James H., *I am Coming*, 7th edn (Edinburgh: Pickering & Inglis, n.d.).

Brooks, Joshua W., (ed.), *A Dictionary of Writers on the Prophecies, with the Titles and Occasional Description of their Works* (London: Simpkin, Marshall and Co., 1835).

Broughton, Hugh, *The Works of the Great Albionean Divine* (London: 1662).

— 'To the Right Honorable, the Temporal Lords of the Queen of Englands most Excellent Privy Councell (29 July 1599)', in Broughton, *The Works*, p. 673.

— 'A Supplication to the Kings Majesty, concerning Piety towards the Jews of our Constantines Town', in Broughton, *The Works*, p. 696.

Brown, John Aquila, *The Jew, the Master-Key of the Apocalypse; in answer to Mr. Frere's 'General Structure,' and the Dissertations of the Rev. Edw. Irving, and Other Commentators* (London: 1827).

Brown, John, *The Self-Interpreting Bible* (Glasgow: Blackie & Son, 1845).

Brown, Michael L., *Our Hands are Stained with Blood: The Tragic Story of the 'Church' and the Jewish People* (Shippensburg, PA: Destiny Image Publishers, Inc., 1992).

Brown, Michael L., *Israel's Divine Healer* (Carlisle: Paternoster Press, 1995).

Bruce, F.F., 'Book Review of *The Unbelievable Pre-Trib Origin*', *Evangelical Quarterly*, 47 (1975), 58.

Buchanan, Claudius, *Christian Researches in Asia*, 3rd edn (Edinburgh: 1812).

Burge, Gary M., *Whose Land? Whose Promise?* (Cleveland, OH: The Pilgrim Press, 2003).

— 'Theological and Biblical Assumptions of Christian Zionism', in Ateek, Duaybis, and Tobin, *Challenging Christian Zionism*, pp. 45-58.

Burgess, Stanley M., and Eduard M. van der Maas, (eds.), *The New International Dictionary of Pentecostal and Charismatic Movements*, Revised and expanded edn, (Grand Rapids, MI: Zondervan, 2002).

Burgh, William, *Lectures on the Second Advent of our Lord Jesus Christ, and Connected Events: with an Introduction on the Use of Unfulfilled Prophecy* (Dublin: 1832).

Burke, Peter, and Roy Porter, (eds.), *Language, Self and Society: A Social History of Language* (Cambridge: Polity Press, 1991).

Burnham, Jonathan D., *A Story of Conflict: The Controversial Relationship between Benjamin Wills Newton and John Nelson Darby* (Milton Keynes: Paternoster, 2004).

Burtchaell, G.D., and T.V. Sadler, (eds.), *Alumni Dublinenses: A Register of the Students, Graduates, Professors, and Provosts of Trinity College, in the University of Dublin* (London: Williams and Norgate, 1924).

Canfield, Joseph M., *The Incredible Scofield and His Book* (Vallecito, CA: Ross House Books, 1988).

Capp, Bernard S., *The Fifth Monarchy Men: A Study in Seventeenth-century English Millenarianism* (London: Faber and Faber, 1972).

Cardale, John Bate, (ed.), *The Liturgy and Other Divine Offices of the Church* (London: n.d.).

Carron, T.W., *The Christian Testimony through the Ages* (London: G. Morrish, 1956).

Carter, Grayson, *Anglican Evangelicals: Protestant Secessions from the Via Media, c.1800-1850* (Oxford: Oxford University Press, 2001).

Carus, William, (ed.), *Memoirs of the Life of the Rev. Charles Simeon*, 2nd edn (London: J. Hatchard & Son, 1847).

Catalogue of the Library of the late John Nelson Darby, Esq. Comprising Important Works relating to Theology, History, Geography, Archaeology, Voyages and Travels, & c. Benedictine and Best Editions of the Fathers of the Church, Rare Editions of the Scriptures, Bibliography, Dictionaries, & c. Which will be sold by auction, by Messrs Sotheby, Wilkinson & Hodge...On Monday, 25th November, 1889, and following day (London: J. Davy & Sons, 1889; CBA/12002).

Chacour, Elias, *Blood Brothers: A Palestinian's Struggle for Reconciliation in the Middle East* (Eastbourne: Kingsway Publications, 1984).

— *We Belong to the Land* (London: Marshall Pickering, 1992).

— 'A Palestinian Christian Challenge to the West', in Ateek, Ellis, and Ruether, *Faith and the Intifada*, pp. 85-90.

— 'Empty Tomb and Risen Lord', in Ateek, Duaybis, and Schrader, *Jerusalem*, pp. 13-16.

— 'Reconciliation and Justice: Living with the Memory', in Ateek and Prior, *Holy Land Hollow Jubilee*, pp. 111-115.

Chadwick, Owen, *The Victorian Church. Part I* (London: Adam & Charles Black, 1966).

Chafer, Lewis Sperry, *He that is Spiritual: A Classic Study of the Biblical Doctrine of Spirituality*, Revised edn (Grand Rapids, MI: Zondervan, 1967).

— *Systematic Theology, Volume IV: Ecclesiology – Eschatology* (Dallas, TX: Dallas Seminary Press, 1978).

Chapman, Colin, 'Ten Questions for a Theology of the Land', in Johnston and Walker, *The Land of Promise*, pp. 172-187.

— *Whose Promised Land? The Continuing Crisis over Israel and Palestine* (Oxford: Lion, 2002).

Chaucer, Geoffrey, *The Canterbury Tales* (London: Marshall Cavendish Partworks Ltd., 1988).

Cherry, Conrad, (ed.), *God's New Israel: Religious Interpretations of American Destiny*, Revised edn (London: The University of North Carolina Press, 1998).

'Christ the Morning Star; and Lucifer Son of the Morning', *The Morning Watch*, 5 (1832), 1-16.

Christian Protagonists for Jewish Restoration (New York: Arno Press, 1977).

Clark, Henry W., *History of English Nonconformity. Vol. II* (London: Chapman and Hall Limited, 1913).

Clark, Samuel, and James S. Donnelly, Jr, (eds.), *Irish Peasants: Violence & Political Unrest 1780-1914* (Manchester: Manchester University Press, 1983).

Clark, Victoria, *Allies for Armageddon: The Rise of Christian Zionism* (New Haven, CT: Yale University Press, 2007).

Coad, F. Roy, *Prophetic Developments with Particular Reference to the early Brethren Movement* (Pinner: CBRF Publications, 1966).

— *A History of the Brethren Movement* (Exeter: The Paternoster Press Ltd., 1976).

Cogley, Richard W., 'The Fall of the Ottoman Empire and the Restoration of Israel in the "Judeo-centric" Strand of Puritan Millenarianism', *Church History*, 72.2 (June, 2003), 304-332.

Cohen, Gerson D., *Jewish History and Jewish Destiny* (New York: The Jewish Theological Seminary of America, 1997).

Cohen, Israel, *A Short History of Zionism* (London: Frederick Muller Ltd., 1951).

— *Speeches on Zionism* (New York: Kraus Reprint Co., 1971).

Cohn, Norman, *The Pursuit of the Millennium* (London: Secker & Warburg, 1957).

Cohn-Sherbok, Dan, *The Politics of Apocalypse: The History and Influence of Christian Zionism* (Oxford: Oneworld Publications Limited, 2006).

Collet, Samuel, *A Treatise of the Future Restoration of the Jews and Israelites to their own Land. With some Account of the Goodness of the Country, and their Happy Condition there, till they shall be Invaded by the Turks: With their Deliverance from all their Enemies, when the Messiah will establish his Kingdom at Jerusalem, and bring in the last Glorious Ages. Addressed to the Jews* (London: 1747).

Collingwood, William, *The Brethren: A Historical Sketch* (Glasgow: Pickering & Inglis, 1899).

Collinson, Patrick, *The Birthpangs of Protestant England: Religious and Cultural Change in the Sixteenth and Seventeenth Centuries* (Basingstoke: Macmillan Press, 1988).

Conder, Claude Reignier, *The City of Jerusalem* (London: John Murray, 1909).

Cook, Thomas, *Cook's Tourist's Handbook for Palestine and Syria*, Revised edn (London: Thomas Cook & Son, 1911).

Cooper, William, *Christ the True Messiah: A Sermon, Preached at Sion-Chapel, Whitechapel, to God's Ancient Israel, the Jews, on Sunday, August 28, 1796* (London: 1796).

— *Daniel's Seventy Weeks: A Sermon Preached at Sion-Chapel, on Sunday afternoon, September 18, 1796, to the Jews*, 3rd edn (London: 1796).

— *The Promised Seed: A Sermon, Preached to God's Ancient Israel, the Jews, at Sion-Chapel, Whitechapel, on Sunday afternoon, August 28, 1796*, 3rd edn (London: 1796).

Corbon, Jean, et al., 'What is Required of the Christian Faith concerning the Palestine Problem: A Memorandum by a Group of Middle Eastern Theologians', in The Institute for Palestine Studies, *Christians*, pp. 69-76.

Cornish, Francis Warre, *The English Church in the Nineteenth Century. Part I* (New York: AMS Press, n.d.).

Couch, Mal, *Dictionary of Premillennial Theology* (Grand Rapids, MI: Kregel Publications, 1996).

Couper, W.J., *Zionism and Christian Missions* (Edinburgh: United Free Church of Scotland, 1920).

Cragg, Kenneth, *This Year in Jerusalem* (London: Darton, Longman & Todd, 1982).

— *The Arab Christian: A History in the Middle East* (London: Mowbray, 1992).

Crombie, Kelvin, *For the Love of Zion* (London: Hodder & Stoughton, 1991).

— *ANZACS, Empires and Israel's Restoration 1798-1948* (Osborne Park: Vocational Education & Training Publications, 1998).

— *A Jewish Bishop in Jerusalem: The Life Story of Michael Solomon Alexander* (Jerusalem: Nicolayson's Ltd., 2006).

Croskery, Thomas, *A Catechism on the Doctrines of the Plymouth Brethren*, 5th edn (London: James Nisbet & Co., 1866).

Cross, E.N., (ed.), *John Nelson Darby: Compiled from Reliable Resources chiefly by W.G. Turner* (London: Chapter Two, 1990).

Crutchfield, Larry V., *The Origins of Dispensationalism: The Darby Factor* (New York: University Press of America, 1992).

Culver, Douglas J., *Albion and Ariel: British Puritanism and the Birth of Political Zionism* (New York: Peter Lang, 1995).

Cumming, John, *Signs of the Times; or, Present, Past, and Future*, New edn (London: Arthur Hall, Virtue & Co., 1854).

Cuninghame, William, *A Dissertation on the Seals and Trumpets of the Apocalypse, and the Prophetical Period of Twelve Hundred and Sixty Years* (London: 1813).

— *Letters and Essays, Controversial and Critical, on Subjects Connected with the Conversion and National Restoration of Israel* (London: 1822).

— *A Summary View of the Scriptural Argument for the Second and Glorious Advent of Messiah before the Millennium* (Glasgow: 1828).

— *A Letter to the Right Honourable Lord Ashley, President of the London Society for Promoting Christianity amongst the Jews, on the Necessity of Immediate Measures for the Jewish Colonization of Palestine* (London: 1849).

Da Costa, Isaac, *Israel and the Gentiles: Contributions to the History of the Jews from the Earliest Times to the Present Day* (London: James Nisbet and Co., 1850).

Dallimore, Arnold, *The Life of Edward Irving, the Fore-Runner of the Charismatic Movement* (Edinburgh: The Banner of Truth Trust, 1983).

Daly, Robert, (ed.), *Letters and Papers of the Late Theodosia A. Viscountess Powerscourt*, New edn (London: G. Morrish, n.d.).

Daniell, David, *The Bible in English: Its History and Influence* (New Haven, CT: Yale University Press, 2003).

Darby, John Nelson, *How the Lost Sheep was Found: An Incident in the Life of the Late J.N. Darby* (Kingston-on-Thames: Stow Hill Bible & Tract Depot, n.d.).

— *Joying in God and Waiting for Christ* (London: Gospel Tract Depot, n.d.).

— *Letters of J.N.D.* (Kingston-on-Thames: Stow Hill Bible & Tract Depot, n.d.), 3 vols.

— *Miscellaneous Writings of J.N.D., Volumes 4 and 5* (Oak Park, IL: Bible Truth Publishers, n.d.).

— *Notes and Comments on Scripture* (Kingston-on-Thames: Stow Hill Bible & Tract Depot, n.d.), 7 vols.

— *Notes and Jottings from Various Meetings with J.N. Darby* (Kingston-on-Thames: Stow Hill Bible & Tract Depot, n.d.).

— *Synopsis of the Books of the Bible* (London: G. Morrish, n.d.), 5 vols.

— *The Christian's Attitude towards the World* (London: G. Morrish, n.d.).

— *The Closing Days of Christendom* (London: C.A. Hammond, n.d.).

— *The Collected Writings of J.N. Darby*, ed. by William Kelly (Kingston-on-Thames: Stow Hill Bible & Tract Depot, n.d.), 34 vols.

— *The Non-Atoning Sufferings of Christ, 1864. Translated from the French of J.N.D.* (London: G. Morrish, n.d.).

— *Address, delivered at Manchester, June 19, 1873* (N.pl., n.d.).

— *The 'Holy Scriptures': A New Translation from the Original Languages* (Kingston-on-Thames: Stow Hill Bible & Tract Depot, 1961).

— *Spiritual Songs* (Lancing: Kingston Bible Trust, 1974).

Davenport, Rowland A., *Albury Apostles* (Birdlip: United Writers, 1970).

Davidson, Elishua, *Islam, Israel, and the Last Days* (Eugene, OR: Harvest House Publishers, 1991).

Davies, Philip R., *In Search of 'Ancient Israel'* (Sheffield: Sheffield Academic Press, 1992).

Davies, W.D., *The Gospel and the Land: Early Christianity and Jewish Territorial Doctrine* (London: University of California Press, 1974).

— *The Territorial Dimension of Judaism* (London: University of California Press, 1982).

Davis, Moshe, (ed.), *Israel: Its Role in Civilisation* (New York: The Jewish Theological Seminary of America, 1956).

Davis, Moshe, and Isidore Meyer, (eds.), *The Writing of American Jewish History* (New York: American Jewish Historical Society, 1957).

Davis, Moshe, (ed.), *With Eyes Toward Zion – Volume II: Themes and Sources in the Archives of the United States, Great Britain, Turkey and Israel* (London: Praeger, 1986).

Davis, Uri, *Israel: An Apartheid State* (London: Zed Books Ltd., 1987).

Dayan, Moshe, *Story of My Life* (London: Sphere Books Limited, 1978).

De Haan, Richard W., *Israel and the Nations in Prophecy* (Grand Rapids, MI: Zondervan Publishing House, 1968).

De Jong, J.A., *As the Waters Cover the Sea: Millennial Expectations in the Rise of Anglo-American Missions 1640-1810* (Kampen: J.H. Kok, 1970).

Dell, Robert S., 'Simeon and the Bible', in Pollard and Hennell, *Charles Simeon*, pp. 29-47.

Dennett, Edward, *The Blessed Hope: Being Papers on the Lord's Coming and Connected Events* (London: G. Morrish, 1910).

De Tocqueville, Alexis, *Journeys to England and Ireland* (New York: Arno Press, 1979).

Dimont, Max I., *Jews, God and History* (New York: The New American Library, Inc., 1962).

Diprose, Ronald E., *Israel and the Church: The Origins and Effects of Replacement Theology* (Rome: Istituto Biblico Evangelico Italiano, 2000).

'Discourse of M. de Noé, Bishop of Lescar (Troyes), written in 1785', *The Morning Watch*, 6 (1833), 49-80.

Dixon, Larry E., 'The Importance of J.N. Darby and the Brethren Movement in the History of Conservative Theology', *Christian Brethren Review*, 41 (1990), 42-55.

Dixon, Murray, *The Rebirth and Restoration of Israel* (Chichester: Sovereign World, 1988).

Dolan, David, *Israel at the Crossroads: Fifty Years and Counting* (Grand Rapids, MI: Fleming H. Revell, 1998).

— *Israel in Crisis: What Lies Ahead?* (Grand Rapids, MI: Fleming H. Revell, 2002).

Donnelly, James S., Jr, 'Pastorini and Captain Rock: Millenarianism and Sectarianism in the Rockite Movement of 1821-4', in Clark and Donnelly, Jr, *Irish Peasants*, pp. 102-139.

Dorman, William Henry, *The Close of Twenty-Eight Years of Association with J.N.D.: And of Fellowship and Ministry amongst those who adopt his Doctrines concerning the Sufferings of Christ* (London: Houlston & Wright, 1866).

Dorsett, Lyle W., *A Passion for Souls: The Life of D.L. Moody* (Chicago, IL: Moody Publishers, 1997).

Douglas, J.D., (ed.), *The New International Dictionary of the Christian Church* (Exeter: The Paternoster Press, 1974).

Doyle, Tom, *Two Nations Under God: Why Should America Care About Israel and the Middle East* (Nashville, TN: Broadman & Holman Publishers, 2004).

Drummond, Andrew Landale, *Edward Irving and His Circle: Including some Consideration of the 'Tongues' Movement in the Light of Modern Psychology* (London: James Clarke & Co. Ltd., n.d.).

Drummond, Henry, *A Defence of the Students of Prophecy, in Answer to the Attack of the Rev. Dr. Hamilton, of Strathblane* (London: James Nisbet, 1828).

— *Dialogues on Prophecy* (London: James Nisbet, 1828), 3 vols.

— *Narrative of the Circumstances which led to the setting up of the Church of Christ at Albury* (1834).

— *Tracts for the Last Days* (London: William Edward Painter, 1844).

Dugdale, Blanche E.C., *Arthur James Balfour, First Earl of Balfour* (London: Hutchinson & Co., Ltd., 1936), 2 vols.

Duvernoy, Claude, *The Prince and the Prophet* (Christian Action for Israel, 1979).

— *Controversy of Zion: A Biblical View of the History and Meaning of Zion* (Green Forest, AR: New Leaf Press, 1987).

Dyer, Charles H., *The Rise of Babylon: Sign of the End Times* (Wheaton, IL: Tyndale House Publishers, Inc., 1991).

— (ed.), *Storm Clouds on the Horizon* (Chicago, IL: Moody Press, 2001).

— 'Jerusalem: The Eye of the Storm', in Dyer, *Storm Clouds on the Horizon*, pp. 65-80.

Eaton, Kent, 'Beware the Trumpet of Judgement!: John Nelson Darby and the Nineteenth-Century Brethren', in Bowie, *The Coming Deliverer*, pp. 119-162.

Eban, Abba, 'Introduction', in Frankel, *Israel*, pp. 7-17.

— *My People: The Story of the Jews* (New York: Behrman House, Inc., 1968).

Edelman, Maurice, *Ben Gurion: A Political Biography* (London: Hodder and Stoughton, 1964).

Edelstein, Alan, *An Unacknowledged Harmony: Philo-Semitism and the Survival of European Jewry* (London: Greenwood Press, 1982).

Ehlert, Arnold D., 'A Bibliography of Dispensationalism', *Bibliotheca Sacra*, 101-103 (1944-1946).

Eisen, Paul, 'Speaking the Truth to Jews', in Prior, *Speaking the Truth*, pp. 190-206.

El-Assal, Riah Abu, *Caught in Between: The Extraordinary Story of an Arab Palestinian Christian Israeli* (London: SPCK, 1999).

Ellern, Hermann, and Bessi Ellern, *Herzl, Hechler, the Grand Duke of Baden and the German Emperor 1896-1904 / documents found by Hermann and Bessi Ellern, reproduced in facsimile* (Tel Aviv: Ellern's Bank Ltd., 1961).

Elliott, E.B., *Horae Apocalypticae, or A Commentary on the Apocalypse, Critical and Historical; Including also an Examination of the Chief Prophecies of Daniel*, 2nd edn (London: Seeley, Burnside, and Seeley, 1846), 4 vols.

Ellis, Marc H., 'The Boundaries of Our Destiny: A Jewish Reflection on the Biblical Jubilee on the Fiftieth Anniversary of Israel', in Ateek and Prior, *Holy Land Hollow Jubilee*, pp. 236-246.

— *O, Jerusalem! The Contested Future of the Jewish Covenant* (Minneapolis, MN: Fortress Press, 1999).

Ellisen, Stanley A., *The Arab-Israeli Conflict: Who Owns the Land?* (Portland, OR: Multnomah Press, 1991).

Ellison, H.L., *The Mystery of Israel* (Exeter: The Paternoster Press, 1966).

Elmore, Floyd Saunders, *A Critical Examination of the Doctrine of the Two Peoples of God in John Nelson Darby* (ThD: Dallas Theological Seminary, 1991).

Elon, Amos, *Herzl* (New York: Holt, Rinehart and Winston, 1975).

— *The Israelis: Founders and Sons* (Harmondsworth: Penguin Books Ltd., 1981).

Embley, Peter L., *The Origins and Early Development of the Plymouth Brethren* (PhD: St. Paul's College, Cheltenham, 1996).

Encyclopaedia Judaica (Jerusalem: Keter Publishing House Ltd., c.1971), 16 vols.

Endelman, Todd M., *The Jews of Georgian England, 1714-1830* (Philadelphia, PA: Jewish Publication Society of America, 1979).

English, E. Schuyler, *Re-Thinking the Rapture* (Neptune, NJ: Loizeaux Brothers, 1954).

Epstein, Lawrence J., *Zion's Call: Christian Contributions to the Origins and Development of Israel* (London: University Press of America, 1984).

Ernst, Robert, 'Concepts of Americanism as Reflected in Minority Groups', in Davis and Meyer, *The Writing of American Jewish History*, pp. 136-156.

Ewald, Alexander Charles, *The Right Hon. Benjamin Disraeli, Earl of Beaconsfield, K.G., and his Times, Vol. I* (London: William Mackenzie, 1882).

Eyre, Joseph, *Observations upon the Prophecies relating to the Restoration of the Jews* (London: 1771).

Faber, Eli, *The Jewish People in America, Vol. I* (Baltimore, MD: The Johns Hopkins University Press, 1992).

Faber, George Stanley, *A General and Connected View of the Prophecies, relative to the Conversion, Restoration, Union, and Future Glory, of the Houses of Judah and Israel; the Progress, and Final Overthrow, of the Antichristian Confederacy in the Land of Palestine; and the Ultimate General Diffusion of Christianity*, 2nd edn (London: 1809), 2 vols.

— *The Conversion of the Jews to the Faith of Christ, the true Medium of the Conversion of the Gentile World. A Sermon Preached before the London Society for Promoting Christianity amongst the Jews, 18 Ap. 1822, Covent Garden, Parish Church of St. Paul* (London: 1822).

— *The Predicted Downfall of the Turkish Power the Preparation for the Return of the Ten Tribes* (London: Thomas Bosworth, 1853).

Feinberg, Charles L., (ed.), *Prophetic Truth Unfolding Today* (Westwood, NJ: Fleming H. Revell, 1968).

— 'The Rebuilding of the Temple', in Henry, *Prophecy in the Making*, pp. 91-112.

— *Israel at the Centre of History and Revelation*, 3rd edn (Portland, OR: Multnomah Press, 1980).

Feinberg, Paul D., 'The Case for the Pretribulation Rapture Position', in Archer et al., *The Rapture*, pp. 47-86.

Ferguson, Sinclair B., and David F. Wright, (eds.), *New Dictionary of Theology* (Leicester: Inter-Varsity Press, 1994).

Fidus, 'Commentary on the Seven Apocalyptic Epistles', *The Morning Watch*, 4 (1832), 255-294.

Finch, Henry, *The Worlds Great Restauration, or The Calling of the Jewes, and with them of all the Nations and Kingdomes of the Earth, to the Faith of Christ* (London: William Gouge, 1621).

Finestein, Israel, *Jewish Society in Victorian England* (London: Vallentine Mitchell & Co., 1993).

Fink, Reuben, (ed.), *America and Palestine: The Attitude of Official America and of the American People toward the Rebuilding of Palestine as a Free and Democratic Jewish Commonwealth*, Revised edn (New York: Herald Square Press, Inc., 1945).

Finkelstein, Norman G., *The Holocaust Industry: Reflections on the Exploitation of Jewish Suffering* (London: Verso, 2000).

Finlayson, Geoffrey B.A.M., *The Seventh Earl of Shaftesbury 1801-1885* (London: Eyre Methuen Ltd., 1981).

Firth, Katherine R., *The Apocalyptic Tradition in Reformation Britain 1530-1645* (Oxford: Oxford University Press, 1979).

Fishman, Hertzel, *American Protestantism and a Jewish State* (Detroit, MI: Wayne State University Press, 1973).

Flegg, Columba Graham, *Gathered under Apostles: A Study of the Catholic Apostolic Church* (Oxford: Clarendon Press, 1992).

Flindall, R.P., (ed.), *The Church of England 1815-1948: A Documentary History* (London: SPCK, 1972).

Forbes, Bruce David, and Jeanne Halgren Kilde, (eds.), *Rapture, Revelation, and the End Times: Exploring the Left Behind Series* (New York: Palgrave Macmillan, 2004).

Frankel, Jonathan, *The Damascus Affair: 'Ritual Murder,' Politics, and the Jews in 1840* (Cambridge: Cambridge University Press, 1997).

Frankel, William, (ed.), *Israel: The First Forty Years* (London: Thames and Hudson Ltd., 1987).

Freeman-Attwood, Marigold, *Leap Castle: A Place and its People* (Norwich: Michael Russell, 2001).

Froese, Arno, *The Great Mystery of the Rapture* (West Columbia, SC: The Olive Press, 1999).

Fromow, George H., (ed.), *B.W. Newton and Dr S.P. Tregelles: Teachers of the Faith and the Future*, 2nd edn (Chelmsford: Sovereign Grace Advent Testimony, 1969).

Froom, Le Roy Edwin, *The Prophetic Faith of our Fathers* (Washington, D.C.: Review and Herald, 1950), 4 vols.

Fruchtenbaum, Arnold G., *The Footsteps of the Messiah: A Study of the Sequence of Prophetic Events* (Tustin, CA: Ariel Press, 1984).

— *Israelology: The Missing Link in Systematic Theology* (Tustin, CA: Ariel Ministries Press, 1993).

Fry, Alfred C., *The Fry Manuscript* (Manchester: Christian Brethren Archive, John Rylands University Library of Manchester).

Fry, John, *The Second Advent; or, the Glorious Epiphany of our Lord Jesus Christ. Being an attempt to elucidate, in chronological order, the Prophecies both of the Old and New Testaments, Vol. I* (London: 1822).

Fuller, Daniel P., *Gospel and Law: Contrast or Continuum? The Hermeneutics of Dispensationalism and Covenant Theology* (Grand Rapids, MI: William B. Eerdmans Publishing Company, 1980).

Gaebelein, Arno C., *The Jewish Question* (New York: Our Hope, 1912).

— *Half a Century: The Autobiography of a Servant* (New York: Our Hope, 1930).

— *The Gospel of Matthew* (New York: Loizeaux Brothers, 1961).

— *The Conflict of the Ages*, Revised edn (Neptune, NJ: Loizeaux Brothers, 1983).

— *The History of the Scofield Reference Bible* (Spokane, WA: Living Words Foundation, 1991).

Gardner, Brian, *Allenby* (London: Cassell, 1965).

Garrett, Clarke, *Respectable Folly: Millenarians and the French Revolution in France and England* (London: The John Hopkins University Press, 1975).

Gawler, George, *Tranquillisation of Syria and the East: observations and practical suggestions, in furtherance of the establishment of Jewish colonies in Palestine, the most sober and sensible remedy for the miseries of Asiatic Turkey* (London: T.&W. Boone, 1845).

George, David Lloyd, *War Memoirs of David Lloyd George* (London: Odhams Press Limited, n.d.), 2 vols.

'Germinant Fulfilment of Prophecies', *The Morning Watch*, 6 (1833), 45-49.

Gerstner, John H., *Wrongly Dividing the Word of Truth: A Critique of Dispensationalism*, 2nd edn (Morgan, PA: Soli Deo Gloria Publications, 2000).

Gidney, W.T., *The Jews and their Evangelization* (London: Student Volunteer Missionary Union, 1899).

— *The History of the London Society for Promoting Christianity amongst the Jews, from 1809-1908* (London: LSPCJ, 1908).

Gilbert, Martin, *Letters to Auntie Fori: The 5,000-Year History of the Jewish People and their Faith* (London: Weidenfeld & Nicolson, 2002).

Gilley, Sheridan, and W.J. Sheils, (eds.), *A History of Religion in Britain* (Oxford: Blackwell, 1994).

Gilley, Sheridan, 'The Church of England in the Nineteenth Century', in Gilley and Sheils, *A History of Religion in Britain*, pp. 291-305.

Glaser, Mitch, and Zhava Glaser, *The Fall Feasts of Israel* (Chicago, IL: Moody Press, 1987).

Glatstein, Jacob, Israel Knox, and Samuel Margoshes, (eds.), *Anthology of Holocaust Literature* (New York: Atheneum, 1968).

Goldberg, David J., *To the Promised Land: A History of Zionist Thought from its Origins to the Modern State of Israel* (London: Penguin Books, 1996).

Goldberg, Isaac, *Major Noah: American-Jewish Pioneer* (Philadelphia, PA: The Jewish Publication Society of America, 1936).

Goldberg, Louis, 'Historical and Political Factors in the Twentieth Century affecting the Identity of Israel', in House, *Israel*, pp. 113-141.

Goldman, Shalom, (ed.), *Hebrew and the Bible in America: The First Two Centuries* (London: University Press of New England, 1993).

— 'Biblical Hebrew in Colonial America: The Case of Dartmouth', in Goldman, *Hebrew and the Bible in America*, pp. 201-208.

Goldschmidt-Lehmann, Ruth P., *Britain and the Holy Land 1800-1914: A Select Bibliography* (London: The Jewish Historical Society of England, 1995).

Gordon, Ernest B., *Adoniram Judson Gordon, A Biography* (New York: Revell, 1896).

Gordon, Sam, *Hope and Glory: Jesus is Coming Again, The Timeless Message of 1 & 2 Thessalonians* (Greenville, SC: Ambassador International, 2005).

Gosling, William, *Two Letters to the Right Honourable the Earl of Shaftesbury, on the Speedy Restoration of the Jews to Palestine, through the Discovery of Gold and Silver in that Land. To which is added Two Letters on the Preparation of the Land for their Return, the Building of the Temple, and Second Coming of Messiah* (London: Houlston & Stoneman, 1853).

Gould, Allan, ed., *What did they think of the Jews?* (Northvale, NJ: Jason Aronson Inc., 1997).

Graves, Richard, *A Sermon Preached in St. Andrew's Church, Dublin, on Sunday, 21 April, 1811 in aid of the London Society for Promoting Christianity amongst the Jews* (Dublin: 1811).

Grayzel, Solomon, *A History of the Jews: From the Babylonian Exile to the Establishment of Israel* (Philadelphia, PA: The Jewish Publication Society of America, 1953).

Gribben, Crawford, *The Puritan Millennium: Literature and Theology 1550-1682* (Dublin: Four Courts Press Ltd., 2000).

— *The Irish Puritans: James Ussher and the Reformation of the Church* (Darlington: Evangelical Press, 2003).

— *Rapture Fiction and the Evangelical Crisis* (Darlington: Evangelical Press, 2006).

— 'Introduction: Antichrist in Ireland – Protestant Millennialism and Irish Studies', in Gribben and Holmes, *Protestant Millennialism*, pp. 1-30.

Gribben, Crawford, and Timothy C.F. Stunt, (eds.), *Prisoners of Hope? Aspects of Evangelical Millennialism in Britain and Ireland, 1800-1880* (Carlisle: Paternoster Press, 2004).

Gribben, Crawford, and Andrew R. Holmes, (eds.), *Protestant Millennialism, Evangelicalism and Irish Society, 1790-2005* (Basingstoke: Palgrave Macmillan, 2006).

Grier, W.J., *The Momentous Event: A Discussion of Scripture Teaching on the Second Advent* (London: Banner of Truth, 1970).

Grose, Peter, *Israel in the Mind of America* (New York: Alfred A. Knopf, 1984).

Groves, Harriet, *Memoir of Anthony Norris Groves, compiled chiefly from his Journals and Letters; to which is added a Supplement, containing Recollections of Miss Paget, and Accounts of Missionary Work in India, & c.*, 3rd edn (London: James Nisbet & Co., 1869).

Groves, Henry, *Darbyism: Its Rise and Development, and a Review of 'The Bethesda Question'* (London: Houlston and Wright, n.d.).

Grudem, Wayne, *Systematic Theology: An Introduction to Biblical Doctrine* (Leicester: IVP, 1994).

Guedalla, Philip, *Napoleon and Palestine* (London: George Allen & Unwin Ltd., 1925).

Guinness, H. Grattan, *Light for the Last Days: A Study in Chronological Prophecy*, Revised edn (London: Morgan & Scott Ltd., 1917).

H., J.M., *Last Words of Five Hundred Remarkable Persons*, 2nd edn (London: Gospel Publication Depot, n.d.).

Hagee, John, *Jerusalem Countdown: A Warning to the World* (Lake Mary, FL: FrontLine, 2006).

Haller, William, *Foxe's Book of Martyrs and the Elect Nation* (London: Jonathan Cape, 1963).

Hallie, Philip, *Lest Innocent Blood be Shed: The Story of the Village of Le Chambon and how Goodness happened there* (London: Harper Torchbooks, 1985).

Halpern, Ben, *The Idea of the Jewish State*, 2nd edn (Cambridge, MA: Harvard University Press, 1969).

Halsell, Grace, *Prophecy and Politics: Militant Evangelists on the Road to Nuclear War* (Bullsbrook: Veritas Publishing Company Pty. Ltd., 1987).

— *Forcing God's Hand: Why Millions Pray for a Quick Rapture...and Destruction of Planet Earth* (Beltsville, MD: Amana Publications, 2003).

Hamilton, Floyd E., *The Basis of Millennial Faith* (Grand Rapids, MI: William B. Eerdmans Publishing Company, 1955).

Hamilton, Jill, *God, Guns and Israel: Britain, the First World War and the Jews in the Holy Land* (Stroud: Sutton Publishing Limited, 2004).

Handy, Robert T., 'Zion in American Christian Movements', in Davis, *Israel: Its Role in Civilisation*, pp. 284-297.

Hanson, Calvin B., *A Gentile, With the Heart of a Jew* (Nyack, NY: Parson Publishing, 1979).

Harrison, J.F.C., *The Second Coming: Popular Millenarianism 1780-1850* (London: Routledge & Kegan Paul Ltd., 1979).

Hatchard, John, *The Predictions and Promises of God respecting Israel. A Sermon preached on Wednesday, June 22nd, 1825, in the Parish Church of St. Andrew's, Plymouth, on the Baptism of Mr. Michael Solomon Alexander, late reader in the Jewish Synagogue* (Plymouth: 1825).

Hechler, William Henry, *The Restoration of the Jews to Palestine* (London: 1884).

Hedding, Malcolm, *Christian Zionism and its Biblical Basis* (Jerusalem: International Christian Embassy Jerusalem, 1988).

Heimert, Alan, *Religion and the American Mind* (Cambridge, MA: Harvard University Press, 1966).

Hein, Virginia H., *The British Followers of Theodor Herzl: English Zionist Leaders, 1896-1904* (New York: Garland Publishing Inc., 1987).

Heller, Joseph, *The Zionist Idea* (New York: Schocken Books, 1949).

Hempton, David N., *Religion and Political Culture in Britain and Ireland* (Cambridge: Cambridge University Press, 1996).

Hender, Don, *The Nation of Israel: Its Foundation, Function, Failure, and Future* (Pearl Publishing Press, 2001).

Henry, Carl F.H., (ed.), *Prophecy in the Making: Messages Prepared for Jerusalem Conference on Biblical Prophecy* (Carol Stream, IL: Creation House, 1971).

Henzel, Ronald M., *Darby, Dualism and the Decline of Dispensationalism* (Tucson, AZ: Fenestra Books, 2003).

Hertzberg, Arthur, (ed.), *The Zionist Idea* (Westport, CT: Greenwood Press, 1959).

— *The Jews in America* (New York: Simon & Schuster Inc., 1989).

Herzl, Theodor, *The Jewish State*, 6th edn (London: H. Pordes, 1972).

Hill, Christopher, *Antichrist in Seventeenth-Century England* (London: Oxford University Press, 1971).

— *The Experience of Defeat* (London: Faber & Faber, 1984).

— 'Till the Conversion of the Jews', in Popkin, *Millenarianism*, pp. 12-36.

— *The English Bible and the Seventeenth-Century Revolution* (London: The Penguin Press, 1993).

Hilton, Boyd, *The Age of Atonement: The Influence of Evangelicalism on Social and Economic Thought, 1795-1865* (Oxford: Clarendon Press, 1988).

Hitchcock, Mark, *Is the Antichrist Alive Today?* (Sisters, OR: Multnomah Publishers, Inc., 2002).

— *Could the Rapture Happen Today?* (Sisters, OR: Multnomah Publishers, 2005).

— *Iran: The Coming Crisis* (Sisters, OR: Multnomah Publishers, 2006).

Hitchcock, Mark, and Thomas Ice, *The Truth behind Left Behind: A Biblical View of the End Times* (Sisters, OR: Multnomah Publishers, Inc., 2004).

Hodder, Edwin, *The Life and Work of the Seventh Earl of Shaftesbury, K.G.* (London: Cassell & Company Ltd., 1886), 3 vols.

Hodgett, Les J.L., *The Correspondents of John Nelson Darby 1800-1882 with a Geographical Index and a Chart of his Travels through his Life* (Ramsgate: L.J.L. Hodgett, 1995).

Hogg, C.F., and W.E. Vine, *Touching the Coming of the Lord* (London: Oliphants Ltd., 1919).

Holland, Margaret Jean (Viscountess Knutsford), *Life and Letters of Zachary Macaulay* (London: Edward Arnold, 1900).

Homes, Nathaniel, *The Resurrection Revealed: or The Dawning of the Day-Star, about to rise, and radiate a visible incomparable glory, far beyond any, since the Creation, upon the Universal Church on Earth, for a Thousand Years yet to come, before the ultimate Day, of the General Judgment: To the raising of the Jews, and the ruin of all Antichristian, and secular powers, that do not love the Members of Christ, submit to his Laws, and advance his interest in this Design* (London: 1654).

Hooper, John, *The Doctrine of the Second Advent, briefly stated in an address to the Members of the Church of England, in the Parish of Westbury, Wilts* (London: James Nisbet, 1829).

— 'The Church's Expectation', *The Morning Watch*, 4 (1832), 317-327.

— *The Translation: or, The Changing of the Living Saints, and their Deliverance from the Judgments which are coming on the earth* (London: William Edward Painter, 1846).

Hopkins, Hugh Evan, *Charles Simeon of Cambridge* (London: Hodder and Stoughton, 1977).

Horsley, Samuel, *Biblical Criticism on the first fourteen Historical Books of the Old Testament; also, on the first nine Prophetical Books, Vol. II*, 2nd edn (London: Longman, Brown, Green, & Longmans, 1844).

House, H. Wayne, (ed.), *Israel, the Land and the People: An Evangelical Affirmation of God's Promises* (Grand Rapids, MI: Kregel Publications, 1998).

House, H. Wayne, 'Apostasia in 2 Thessalonians 2:3: Apostasy or Rapture?', in Ice and Demy, *The Return*, pp. 147-182.

Howse, Ernest Marshall, *Saints in Politics: The 'Clapham Sect' and the Growth of Freedom* (London: George Allen & Unwin Ltd., 1976).

Hudson, John, *Cyrus and the Restoration of the Jews. A Poem which obtained the Seatonian Prize in the University of Cambridge for 1902* (Cambridge: Macmillan and Bowes, 1902).

Huebner, R.A., *The Truth of the Pre-Tribulation Rapture Recovered* (Millington, NJ: Present Truth Publishers, 1976).

— *Elements of Dispensational Truth*, 2nd edn (Morganville, NJ: Present Truth Publishers, 1998), 2 vols.

Hull, William L., *The Fall and Rise of Israel: The Story of the Jewish People during the time of their Dispersal and Regathering* (Grand Rapids, MI: Zondervan Publishing Company, 1959).

Hunt, Dave, *Global Peace and the Rise of Antichrist* (Eugene, OR: Harvest House Publishers, 1990).

— *A Woman Rides the Beast* (Eugene, OR: Harvest House Publishers, 1994).

— *A Cup of Trembling: Jerusalem and Bible Prophecy* (Eugene, OR: Harvest House Publishers, 1995).

— 'O Jerusalem, Jerusalem!', *The Berean Call*, September (2000), 1-2.

— *Judgment Day! Islam, Israel and the Nations*, 2nd edn (Bend, OR: The Berean Call, 2006).

Hunting, Joseph H., *The Set Time is Come* (Carnegie: The David Press, 1980).

Hutchings, Noah W., *25 Messianic Signs in Israel Today* (Oklahoma City, OK: Hearthstone Publishing, 1999).

Hutchinson, F.E., (ed.), *The Works of George Herbert* (Oxford: Clarendon Press, 1978).

Hyamson, Albert M., (ed.), *The British Consulate in Jerusalem in Relation to the Jews of Palestine 1838-1914, Part I: 1838-1861* (London: Edward Goldston Ltd., 1939).

Ice, Thomas D., 'Francisco Ribera', in Couch, *Dictionary of Premillennial Theology*, pp. 378-379.

— 'Hermeneutics and Bible Prophecy', in LaHaye and Ice, *The End Times Controversy*, pp. 67-81.

— 'The 70 Weeks of Daniel', in LaHaye and Ice, *The End Times Controversy*, pp. 307-353.

— 'Why Futurism?', in LaHaye and Ice, *The End Times Controversy*, pp. 399-418.

Ice, Thomas, and Randall Price, *Ready to Rebuild: The Imminent Plans to Rebuild the Last Days Temple* (Eugene, OR: Harvest House Publishers, 1992).

Ice, Thomas, and Timothy J. Demy, (eds.), *The Return: Understanding Christ's Second Coming and the End Times* (Grand Rapids, MI: Kregel Publications, 1999).

— *The Coming Cashless Society* (Eugene, OR: Harvest House Publishers, 1996).

ICEJ, *Declaration of the International Christian Zionist Leadership Congress* (1985).

— *Proclamation of the Second International Christian Zionist Congress* (1988).

— *Proclamation of the Third International Christian Zionist Congress* (1996).

Idel, Moshe, *Messianic Mystics* (New Haven, CT: Yale University Press, 1998).

Ingrams, Doreen, *Palestine Papers 1917-1922: Seeds of Conflict* (London: John Murray, 1972).

Ironside, H.A., *A Historical Sketch of the Brethren Movement* (Neptune, NJ: Loizeaux Brothers, 1985).

Irving, Edward, 'Preliminary Discourse', in Ben-Ezra, *The Coming of Messiah*, pp. iii-cxciv.

— *Babylon and Infidelity Foredoomed of God: A Discourse on the Prophecies of Daniel and the Apocalypse which relate to these latter times, and until the Second Advent*, 2nd edn (Glasgow: 1828).

— *The Last Days: A Discourse on the Evil Character of these our Times, Proving them to be the 'Perilous Times' of the 'Last Days'* (London: R.B. Seeley and W. Burnside, 1828).

— 'The Times and Seasons', *The Morning Watch*, 1 (1830), 36-44.

— 'Interpretation of all the Old-Testament Prophecies quoted in the New. Interpretation III.', *The Morning Watch*, 1 (1830), 315-350.

— 'Signs of the Times, and the Characteristics of the Church (Part I)', *The Morning Watch*, 1 (1830), 641-666.

— 'Interpretation of all the Old-Testament Prophecies quoted in the New. Interpretation VI-VII.II.', *The Morning Watch*, 2 (1831), 287-319, 529-563, 777-804.

— 'Signs of the Times, and the Characteristics of the Church (Part II)', *The Morning Watch*, 2 (1831), 141-162.

— 'What Caused Mr. Baxter's Fall?', *The Morning Watch*, 7 (1833), 129-140.

Isaac, Jad, Marla Schrader, and Suhail Khalilieh, 'The Colonisation of Palestine', in Ateek and Prior, *Holy Land Hollow Jubilee*, pp. 122-134.

Jerram, Charles, *An Essay Tending to Shew the Grounds Contained in Scripture for Expecting a Future Restoration of the Jews* (Cambridge: 1796).

Jerusalem Post, *Front Page Israel: Major Events 1932-1979 as Reflected in the Front Pages of The Jerusalem Post* (Jerusalem: The Palestine Post Ltd., 1978).

Jesse, Henry, *A Narrative of the Late Proceeds at Whitehall, concerning the Jews* (London: 1656).

Johnson, Paul, *A History of the Jews* (London: Phoenix, 1993).

Johnston, Philip, and Peter Walker, (eds.), *The Land of Promise: Biblical, Theological and Contemporary Perspectives* (Leicester: Apollos, 2000).

Jurieu, Pierre, *The Accomplishment of the Scripture Prophecies, or the Approaching Deliverance of the Church*, 2nd edn (London: 1687).

Katz, David S., *Philo-Semitism and the Readmission of the Jews to England 1603-1655* (Oxford: Clarendon Press, 1982).

— *The Jews in the History of England 1485-1850* (Oxford: Clarendon Press, 1994).

Keith, Alexander, *Evidence of the Truth of the Christian Religion derived from the Literal Fulfilment of Prophecy; Particularly as Illustrated by the History of the Jews, and by the Discoveries of Recent Travellers*, 37th edn (London: T. Nelson and Sons, 1859).

Kelly, William, *Lectures Introductory to the Study of the Minor Prophets* (London: W.H. Broom, 1871).

— *The Rapture of the Saints: Who Suggested it, or rather on what Scripture?* (London: T. Weston, 1903).

— *John Nelson Darby as I Knew Him* (Belfast: Words of Truth, 1986).

Kilde, Jeanne Halgren, 'How did Left Behind's Particular Vision of the End Times Develop? A Historical Look at Millenarian Thought', in Forbes and Kilde, *Rapture*, pp. 33-70.

King, Edward, *Remarks on the Signs of the Times* (London: 1798).

Kitson, Hugh, *Jerusalem, the Covenant City* (Steyning: Hatikvah Ltd., 2000).

Klausner, Joseph, *Menahem Ussishkin: His Life and Work* (London: The Joint Zionist Publication Committee, [1944]).

Kleinfeld, Daniel J., 'Staging a Nation: Mordecai Noah and the Early Republic', in Schuldiner and Kleinfeld, *The Selected Writings*, pp. 69-76.

Knox, Vicesimus, *Elegant Extracts: or, Useful and Entertaining Passages in Prose, Selected for the Improvement of Young Persons*, 8th edn (London: [1803]).

Kobler, Franz, *The Vision was There: A History of the British Movement for the Restoration of the Jews to Palestine* (London: Lincolns-Prayer Publishers Ltd., 1956).

— 'Sir Henry Finch (1558-1625) and the first English Advocates of the Restoration of the Jews to Palestine', in The Jewish Historical Society of England, *The Jewish Historical Society of England*, pp. 101-120.

— *Napoleon and the Jews* (Jerusalem: Massada Press Ltd., 1975).

Koenig, William R., *Eye to Eye: Facing the Consequences of Dividing Israel* (Alexandria, VA: About Him, 2004).

Kollek, Teddy, and Moshe Pearlman, *Jerusalem, Sacred City of Mankind: A History of Forty Centuries*, Revised edn (Jerusalem: Steimatzky's Agency Ltd., 1976).

Krapohl, Robert Henry, *A Search for Purity: The Controversial Life of John Nelson Darby* (PhD: Baylor University, Waco, 1988).

Kraus, C. Norman, *Dispensationalism in America* (Richmond, VA: John Knox Press, 1958).

Kromminga, Diedrich H., *The Millennium in the Church: Studies in the History of Christian Chiliasm* (Grand Rapids, MI: William B. Eerdmans Publishing Company, 1945).

Ladd, George Eldon, *Crucial Questions about the Kingdom of God* (Grand Rapids, MI: William B. Eerdmans Publishing Company, 1977).

— *The Blessed Hope* (Grand Rapids, MI: William B. Eerdmans Publishing Company, 1978).

LaHaye, Tim, *No Fear of the Storm: Why Christians will Escape all of the Tribulation* (Sisters, OR: Multnomah Press Books, 1992).

— *Rapture under Attack* (Sisters, OR: Multnomah Publishers, 1998).

— 'The Signs of the Times Imply His Coming', in Van Diest, *10 Reasons*, pp. 191-212.

— 'Twelve Reasons why this could be the Terminal Generation', in Ice and Demy, *The Return*, pp. 183-200.

LaHaye, Tim, and Jerry B. Jenkins, *Are We Living in the End Times?* (Wheaton, IL: Tyndale House Publishers, Inc., 1999).

LaHaye, Tim, and Thomas Ice, (eds.), *The End Times Controversy: The Second Coming Under Attack* (Eugene, OR: Harvest House Publishers, 2003).

— *Charting the End Times: A Visual Guide to Understanding Bible Prophecy* (Eugene, OR: Harvest House Publishers, 2001).

Lambert, Lance, *Till the Day Dawns* (Eastbourne: Kingsway Publications, 1982).

— *The Uniqueness of Israel* (Eastbourne: Kingsway Publications, 2002).

Lamont, William M., *Godly Rule: Politics and Religion, 1603-60* (London: Macmillan and Co. Ltd., 1969).

Langley, Michael, '"Back to the Land" in Palestine', *The Geographical Magazine*, July (1936), 185-206.

Laqueur, Walter, *A History of Zionism* (New York: Schocken Books, 2003).

Larkin, Clarence, *The Greatest Book on "Dispensational Truth" in the World: Dispensational Truth or God's Plan and Purpose in the Ages*, Revised edn (Glenside, PA: Rev. Clarence Larkin Est., 1920).

Larsen, Timothy, (ed.), *Biographical Dictionary of Evangelicals* (Leicester: Inter-Varsity Press, 2003).

Latourette, Kenneth Scott, *A History of Christianity* (London: Eyre and Spottiswoode Limited, 1954).

Lazarus, Emma, *The Poems of Emma Lazarus* (New York: Houghton Mifflin Company, 1888).

Learsi, Rufus, *Fulfilment: The Epic Story of Zionism* (New York: The World Publishing Company, 1951).

— *The Jews in America: A History* (New York: The World Publishing Company, 1954).

Lee, Sidney, (ed.), *Dictionary of National Biography* (London: Smith, Elder, & Co., 1891-1900), 37 vols.

Lerner, Robert E., *The Feast of Saint Abraham: Medieval Millenarians and the Jews* (Philadelphia, PA: University of Pennsylvania Press, 2001).

Lewis, Donald M., (ed.), *The Blackwell Dictionary of Evangelical Biography 1730-1860, Vol. I* (Oxford: Blackwell Publishers Ltd., 1995).

Liechty, Joseph, *Irish Evangelicalism, Trinity College Dublin, and the Mission of the Church of Ireland at the End of the Eighteenth Century* (PhD: St. Patrick's College, Maynooth, 1987).

Lindsay, Lord [Alexander William Crawford], *Letters on Egypt, Edom, and the Holy Land*, 4th edn (London: Henry Colburn, 1847).

Lindsey, Hal, *The Rapture: Truth or Consequences* (London: Bantam Books, 1985).

— *The Late Great Planet Earth* (Basingstoke: Marshall Pickering, 1988).

— *The Road to Holocaust* (New York: Bantam Books, 1989).

— *The Final Battle* (Palos Verdes, CA: Western Front, Ltd., 1995).

Lipman, Vivian D., 'America-Holy Land Material in British Archives, 1820-1930', in Davis and Meyer, *With Eyes Toward Zion*, pp. 25-71.

Littell, Franklin H., *The Crucifixion of the Jews: The Failure of Christians to Understand the Jewish Experience* (Macon, GA: Mercer University Press, 1986).

Lochery, Neill, *Why Blame Israel? The Facts behind the Headlines* (Cambridge: Icon Books Ltd., 2004).

Loizeaux, Marie Duvernoy, *A Century of Christian Publishing 1876-1976* (Neptune, NJ: Loizeaux Brothers, 1976).

'London Society for Promoting Christianity among the Jews', *Falmouth Packet and Cornish Herald*, 2 October (1830), 320a.

Lord, John, *Duty, Honour, Empire: The Life and Times of Colonel Richard Meinertzhagen* (London: Hutchinson & Co. Ltd., 1971).

Lowdermilk, Walter Clay, *Palestine: Land of Promise* (London: Victor Gollancz Ltd., 1944).

Lowrie, Donald, 'Chambon-sur-Lignon', in Glatstein, *Anthology of Holocaust Literature*, pp. 375-381.

LSPCJ, *The Eighth Report of the Committee of the London Society for Promoting Christianity amongst the Jews; read at the General Meeting, May 3rd, 1816. To which is prefixed, A Sermon, Preached before the Society, on the same day, at St. Anne's, Soho, by Rev. Daniel Wilson, Minister St. John's Chapel, Bedford Row* (London: 1816).

— *The Ninth Report of the Committee of the London Society for Promoting Christianity amongst the Jews; read at the General Meeting, May 9, 1817. To which is prefixed, A Sermon, Preached before the Society, on the same day, at Tavistock episcopal chapel, by Rev. Lewis Way* (London: 1817).

— *The First Report of the Committee of the London Society for Promoting Christianity amongst the Jews*, 2nd edn (London: 1819).

Lutz, Charles P., and Robert O. Smith, *Christians and a Land Called Holy: How We Can Foster Justice, Peace, and Hope* (Minneapolis, MN: Fortress Press, 2006).

Lutz, Charles P., 'What's So Special About This Space?', in Lutz and Smith, *Christians and a Land Called Holy*, pp. 7-34.

Macaulay, Thomas Babington, *The Miscellaneous Writings and Speeches of Lord Macaulay*, New edn (London: Longmans, Green, Reader, & Dyer, 1873).

Mackintosh, C.H., *Papers on the Lord's Coming* (Chicago, IL: The Moody Press, n.d.).

MacLeod, David J., 'Walter Scott, A Link in Dispensationalism between Darby and Scofield?', *Bibliotheca Sacra*, 153 (Apr-Jun, 1996), 156-179.

Macleod, John, *Scottish Theology in Relation to Church History since the Reformation*, 2nd edn (Edinburgh: The Banner of Truth Trust, 1946).

Macnaughtan, Keith A., *Israel and the Coming King* (Murrumbeena: The David Press, 1974).

MacPherson, Dave, *The Incredible Cover-Up: Exposing the Origins of Rapture Theories* (Medford, OR: Omega Publications, 2001).

MacRae, Allan A., 'Hath God Cast Away His People?', in Feinberg, *Prophetic Truth Unfolding Today*, p. 95.

Mahaffy, J.P., *An Epoch in Irish History: Trinity College, Dublin, Its Foundation and Early Fortunes 1591-1660*, 2nd edn (London: T. Fisher Unwin, 1906).

Maitland, Charles, *A Brief and Connected View of Prophecy: being An Exposition of the Second, Seventh, and Eighth Chapters of the Prophecy of Daniel; together with the Sixteenth Chapter of Revelation. To which are added Some Observations respecting the period and manner of the Restoration of the Jews* (London: 1814).

Maitland, Samuel, *An Enquiry into the Grounds on which the Prophetic Period of Daniel and St. John has been supposed to consist of 1260 Years* (London: Hatchard and Son, 1826).

Maltz, Steve, *The Land of Many Names: Towards a Christian Understanding of the Middle East Conflict* (Milton Keynes: Authentic Lifestyle, 2003).

— *The People of Many Names: Towards a Clearer Understanding of the Miracle of the Jewish People* (Milton Keynes: Authentic Media, 2005).

Mansfield, Stephen, *The Faith of George W. Bush* (New York: Jeremy P. Tarcher, 2003).

Maoz, Baruch, *Judaism is not Jewish: A Friendly Critique of the Messianic Movement* (Fearn: Christian Focus Publications Ltd., 2003).

Marcus, Jacob R., *The Colonial American Jew 1492-1776* (Detroit, MI: Wayne State University Press, 1970), 3 vols.

Marmur, Dow, 'The Future of the Jews', in Romain, *Renewing the Vision*, pp. 173-181.

Marsden, George M., *Fundamentalism and American Culture* (New York: Oxford University Press, 1980).

Marsh, William, *A Few Plain Thoughts on Prophecy* (Colchester: n.d.).

— *Israel's Sins, and Israel's Hopes. Being Lectures delivered during Lent, 1846, at St. George's, Bloomsbury. By twelve Clergymen of the Church of England. With a Preface by the Rev. William Marsh* (London: James Nisbet and Co., 1846).

Martin, L.C., (ed.), *The Works of Henry Vaughan*, 2nd edn (Oxford: The Clarendon Press, 1957).

Massil, Stephen W., (ed.), *The Jewish Year Book 2006* (London: Vallentine Mitchell, 2006).

Matar, Nabil I., 'George Herbert, Henry Vaughan, and the Conversion of the Jews', *Studies in English Literature 1500-1900*, 30.1 (Winter, 1990), 79-92.

Mather, Increase, *The Mystery of Israel's Salvation, Explained and Applied: or, A Discourse Concerning the General Conversion of the Israelitish Nation* (London: 1669).

Maton, Robert, *Israel's Redemption, or the Propheticall History of our Saviours Kingdome on Earth* (London: 1642).

— *Israel's Redemption Redeemed* (London: 1646).

McCall, Thomas S., and Zola Levitt, *Satan in the Sanctuary* (Chicago, IL: Moody Press, 1974).

McCaul, Alexander, *New Testament Evidence to Prove that the Jews are to be Restored to the Land of Israel*, 6th edn (London: London Society's House, 1878).

McDowell, R.B., and D.A. Webb, *Trinity College Dublin 1592-1952: An Academic History* (Cambridge: Cambridge University Press, 1982).

McGrath, Alister E., *Christian Theology: An Introduction* (Oxford: Blackwell Publishers, 1994).

McNeile, Hugh, *Popular Lectures on the Prophecies Relative to the Jewish Nation* (London: J. Hatchard and Son, 1830).

— *Lectures on the Prophecies relative to the Jewish Nation*, New edn (Liverpool: E. Howell, 1866).

McNeill, John T., (ed.), *Institutes of the Christian Religion, by Jean Calvin* (London: SCM Press, 1961), 2 vols.

Mede, Joseph, *A Paraphrase and Exposition of the Prophecie of Saint Peter, concerning the Day of Christ's Second Comming; described in the Third Chapter of his Second Epistle* (London: 1642).

— *Daniels Weekes: An Interpretation of Part of the Prophecy of Daniel* (London: 1643).

— *The Key of the Revelation*, trans. by Richard More (London: 1643).

Meinertzhagen, Richard, *Middle East Diary 1917-1956* (London: The Cresset Press, 1959).

Meir, Golda, *My Life* (London: Futura Publications Limited, 1978).

Melton, J. Gordon, *The Encyclopedia of American Religions, Vol. I* (Detroit, MI: Gale Research Company, 1978).

Merkley, Paul C., *The Politics of Christian Zionism 1891-1948* (London: Frank Cass, 1998).

— *Christian Attitudes towards the State of Israel* (London: McGill-Queen's University Press, 2001).

Metzger, Bruce M., and Michael D. Coogan, (eds.), *The Oxford Companion to the Bible* (Oxford: Oxford University Press, 1993).

Miller, Andrew, *The Brethren: A Brief Sketch of their Origin, Progress and Testimony* (London: G. Morrish, n.d.).

Miller, Edward, *The History and Doctrines of Irvingism, or of the So-called Catholic Apostolic Church* (London: C. Kegan Paul & Co., 1878), 2 vols.

Mitchell, Bob, *Rome, Babylon the Great and Europe* (Cambridge: St. Matthew Publishing Ltd., 2003).

Morrison, Walter, (ed.), *The Recovery of Jerusalem: A Narrative of Exploration and Discovery in the City and the Holy Land by Capt. Wilson, R.E., Capt. Warren, R.E., with an introduction by Arthur Penrhyn Stanley* (London: Richard Bentley, 1871), 2 vols.

Moscrop, John James, *Measuring Jerusalem: The Palestine Exploration Fund and British Interests in the Holy Land* (London: Leicester University Press, 2000).

Moule, H.C.G., *Charles Simeon* (London: Methuen & Co., 1892).

Murray, Iain H., *The Puritan Hope: A Study in Revival and the Interpretation of Prophecy* (London: The Banner of Truth Trust, 1971).

Myss, Lilli, *A Call to the Nations: Warning Signals for the Coming Russian Exodus* (Chichester: New Wine Press, 1999).

Napier, John, *A Plaine Discovery of the Whole Revelation of Saint John* (1593).

Neatby, William Blair, *A History of the Plymouth Brethren*, 2nd edn (London: Hodder and Stoughton, 1902).

Nebeker, Gary L., *The Hope of Heavenly Glory in John Nelson Darby (1800-1882)* (PhD: Dallas Theological Seminary, 1997).

— 'John Nelson Darby and Trinity College, Dublin: A Study in Eschatological Contrasts', *Fides et Historia*, 34.2 (2002), 87-108.

Nerel, Gershon, 'Spiritual *Intifada* of Palestinian Christians and Messianic Jews', in Wright, *Israel*, pp. 205-219.

Netanyahu, Benjamin, *A Place among the Nations: Israel and the World* (London: Bantam Press, 1993).

New General Index to the Writings of J.N. Darby (Oak Park, IL: Bible Truth Publishers, 1971).

Newman, Francis W., *Phases of Faith* (London: Trübner & Co., 1881).

Newport, Kenneth G.C., *Apocalypse and Millennium: Studies in Biblical Eisegesis* (Cambridge: Cambridge University Press, 2000).

Newton, Benjamin Wills, *The Second Advent of our Lord not Secret but in Manifested Glory* (London: Houlston and Wright, 1862).

— *Five Letters on Events Predicted in Scripture as Antecedent to the Coming of the Lord*, 3rd edn (London: Houlston and Sons, 1877).

— *Prophecies Respecting the Jews and Jerusalem Considered. In the Form of a Catechism*, 4th edn (London: Houlston and Sons, 1888).

— *Babylon, Its Future History and Doom: With Remarks on the Future of Egypt and other Eastern Countries*, 3rd edn (London: Houlston & Sons, 1890).

Newton, Thomas, *Dissertations on the Prophecies, which have remarkably been fulfilled, and at this time are fulfilling in the world* (London: 1754-1758), 3 vols.

— 'The Fulfilment of the Mosaical Prophecies concerning the Jews as Unanswerable Argument for the Truth of the Bible', in Knox, *Elegant Extracts*, pp. 230-236.

Nicholas, Edward, *An Apology for the Honourable Nation of the Jews, and all the Sons of Israel* (London: 1648).

Noah, Mordecai, 'Discourse on the Restoration of the Jews', in Schuldiner and Kleinfeld, *The Selected Writings*, pp. 125-147.

— 'The Ararat Proclamation and Speech', in Schuldiner and Kleinfeld, *The Selected Writings*, pp. 105-124.

Noakes, David, 'The Restoration of all Things', in Wright, *Israel*, pp. 271-283.

Noel, Napoleon, *The History of the Brethren 1826-1936* (Denver, CO: W.F. Knapp, 1936), 2 vols.

North, Gary, *Rapture Fever: Why Dispensationalism is Paralyzed* (Tyler, TX: Institute for Christian Economics, 1993).

Norton, Robert, *Memoirs of James & George MacDonald of Port-Glasgow* (London: John F. Shaw, 1840).

— *The Restoration of Apostles and Prophets in the Catholic Apostolic Church: A Letter to the Right Rev. the Lord Bishop of Ripon* (London: 1854).

Oddy, John Arthur, *Eschatological Prophecy in the English Theological Tradition c.1700 - c.1840* (PhD: University of London, 1982).

Oliphant, Margaret, *The Life of Edward Irving* (London: Hurst and Blackett, 1862), 2 vols.

Oliver, W.H., *Prophets and Millennialists: The Uses of Biblical Prophecy in England from the 1790s to the 1840s* (Auckland: Auckland University Press, 1978).

'On the Gradual Unfolding of Prophecy', *The Morning Watch*, 1 (1830), 525-542.

'On the Extraordinary Manifestations in Port-Glasgow', *The Morning Watch*, 2 (1831), 869-873.

O'Neill, Dan, and Don Wagner, *Peace or Armageddon? The Unfolding Drama of the Middle East Peace Accord* (London: Marshall Pickering, 1993).

Onne, Eyal, (ed.), *Photographic Heritage of the Holy Land 1839-1914* (Manchester: Institute of Advanced Studies, Manchester Polytechnic, 1980).

Oulton, John E.L., *The Study of Divinity in Trinity College Dublin since the Foundation* (Dublin: Hodges, Figgis, & Co., 1941).

Overton, John H., *The English Church in the Nineteenth Century (1800-1833)* (London: Longmans, Green, & Co. 1894).

Paldiel, Mordecai, *Sheltering the Jews: Stories of Holocaust Rescuers* (Minneapolis, MN: Fortress Press, 1996).

Palestine Exploration Fund, 'Brief Narrative of the Proceedings of the Palestine Exploration Fund', *Palestine Exploration Fund*, 1 (1870), 10-12.

'Palestine for the Jews: Copy of Memorial presented to President Harrison, March 5th, 1891', in *Christian Protagonists*, pp. 1-14.

Parkes, James, *Whose Land? A History of the Peoples of Palestine*, Revised edn (Harmondsworth: Penguin Books Ltd., 1970).

Patai, Raphael, (ed.), *The Complete Diaries of Theodor Herzl* (New York: Herzl Press, 1960).

— *Encyclopaedia of Zionism and Israel* (New York: Herzl Press, 1971).

Patterson, Mark Rayburn, *Designing the Last Days: Edward Irving, the Albury Circle, and the Theology of The Morning Watch* (PhD: University of London, 2001).

Pawson, David, *The Challenge of Islam to Christians* (London: Hodder & Stoughton, 2003).

Pearce, Tony, *The House Built on the Sand* (Chichester: New Wine Press, 2006).

Penstone, John Jewell, *A Caution to the Readers of 'A Caution Against the Darbyites' [by John Eliot Howard]. With a few words on 'The Close of Twenty-Eight Years' Association with J.N.D.'* (London: G. Morrish, 1867).

Pentecost, J. Dwight, *Things to Come: A Study in Biblical Eschatology* (Findlay, OH: Dunham Publishing Company, 1958).

Perry, Joseph, *The Glory of Christ's Visible Kingdom in this World, asserted, proved, and explained, in its two-fold branches; first spiritual, secondly personal* (Northampton: 1721).

Perry, Yaron, *British Mission to the Jews in Nineteenth-Century Palestine* (London: Frank Cass, 2003).

Peters, George N.H., *The Theocratic Kingdom of our Lord Jesus, the Christ, as Covenanted in the Old Testament and Presented in the New Testament* (Grand Rapids, MI: Kregel Publications, 1978), 3 vols.

Peters, Joan, *From Time Immemorial: The Origins of the Arab-Jewish Conflict over Palestine* (Chicago, IL: JKAP Publications, 2001).

Pickering, Henry, *Chief Men among the Brethren*, 2nd edn (London: Pickering & Inglis, 1961).

Poliakov, Léon, *The History of Anti-Semitism: Volume 3 - From Voltaire to Wagner* (London: Routledge & Kegan Paul, 1975).

Pollard, Arthur, and Michael Hennell, (eds.), *Charles Simeon (1759-1836): Essays written in Commemoration of his Bi-Centenary by Members of the Evangelical Fellowship for Theological Literature* (London: SPCK, 1959).

Pollard, Arthur, 'The Influence and Significance of Simeon's Work', in Pollard and Hennell, *Charles Simeon*, pp. 159-184.

Pollock, John, *Moody without Sankey* (London: Hodder and Stoughton, 1983).

Popkin, Richard H., ed., *Millenarianism and Messianism in English Literature and Thought 1650-1800* (Leiden: E.J. Brill, 1988).

Powell, Vavasor, *An Useful Concordance to the Holy Bible, with the various Acceptations contained in the Scriptures, and Marks to distinguish Commands, Promises, and Threatenings. Also a Curious Collection of Similies, Synonymous Phrases, and Prophecies, relating to the Call of the Jews, and the Glory that shall be in the Latter Days*, 2nd edn (London: n.d.).

Poythress, Vern S., *Understanding Dispensationalists*, 2nd edn (Phillipsburg, NJ: Presbyterian and Reformed Publishing Company, 1994).

Pragai, Michael J., *Faith and Fulfilment: Christians and the Return to the Promised Land* (London: Vallentine, Mitchell and Company Ltd., 1985).

Prager, Dennis, and Joseph Telushkin, *Why the Jews? The Reason for Antisemitism* (New York: Touchstone, 2003).

'Present State of Prophetic Knowledge, and Progress in the Interpretation of the Apocalypse', *The Morning Watch*, 5 (1832), 357-383.

Price, Randall, *Jerusalem in Prophecy: God's Stage for the Final Drama* (Eugene, OR: Harvest House Publishers, 1998).

— *Unholy War: America, Israel and Radical Islam* (Eugene, OR: Harvest House Publishers, 2001).

Price, Tim, 'The Restoration of Israel and the Kingdom of God', in Wright, *Israel*, pp. 15-37.

Prince, Derek, *The Last Word on the Middle East* (Eastbourne: Kingsway Publications, 1982).

— 'Epilogue: Drama in Three Acts', in Prince, *Appointment in Jerusalem*, pp. 176-189.

— 'A Letter from Derek Prince', *Israel & Christians Today*, Autumn (2003), 3.

— *Promised Land: The Future of Israel Revealed in Prophecy* (Grand Rapids, MI: Chosen Books, 2005).

Prince, Lydia, *Appointment in Jerusalem* (Eastbourne: Kingsway Publications, 1984).

Prior, Michael, (ed.), *They Came and They Saw: Western Christian Experiences of the Holy Land* (London: Melisende, 2000).

— (ed.), *Speaking the Truth: Zionism, Israel, and Occupation* (Northampton, MA: Olive Branch Press, 2005).

— 'A Perspective on Pilgrimage to the Holy Land', in Ateek, Duaybis, and Schrader, *Jerusalem*, pp. 114-131.

— *Zionism and the State of Israel: A Moral Inquiry* (London: Routledge, 1999).

— 'Zionism and the Bible', in Ateek and Prior, *Holy Land Hollow Jubilee*, pp. 69-88.

— 'Studying the Bible in the Holy Land', in Prior, *They Came and They Saw*, pp. 104-127.

— 'The Holy Land and the Scandalous Performance of the Churches', *Cornerstone*, 30 (Winter, 2003), 5-7.

— 'Zionism and the Challenge of Historical Truth and Morality', in Prior, *Speaking the Truth*, pp. 13-50.

Provan, Charles D., *The Church is Israel Now* (Vallecito, CA: Ross House Books, 1987).

Raheb, Mitri, *I am a Palestinian Christian* (Minneapolis, MN: Fortress Press, 1995).

— 'The Third Kingdom', in Ateek, Duaybis, and Tobin, *Challenging Christian Zionism*, pp. 263-270.

Railton, Nicholas M., '"The Dreamy Mazes of Millenarianism": William Graham and the Irish Presbyterian Mission to German Jews', in Gribben and Holmes, *Protestant Millennialism*, pp. 174-201.

Rantisi, Audeh G., and Ralph K. Beebe, *Blessed are the Peacemakers: The Story of a Palestinian Christian* (Guildford: Eagle, 1990).

Rausch, David A., *Zionism within early American Fundamentalism 1878-1918* (New York: The Edwin Mellen Press, 1979).

— *Arno C. Gaebelein 1861-1945 Irenic Fundamentalist and Scholar* (New York: Edwin Mellen Press, 1983).

Raviv, Moshe, *Israel at Fifty: Five Decades of Struggle for Peace* (London: Weidenfeld and Nicolson, 1998).

Reardon, Bernard M.G., *Religious Thought in the Nineteenth Century Illustrated from Writers of the Period* (Cambridge: Cambridge University Press, 1966).

Reese, Alexander, *The Approaching Advent of Christ: An Examination of the Teaching of J.N. Darby and his Followers* (London: Marshall, Morgan & Scott Ltd., n.d.).

Reeves, Marjorie, *Joachim of Fiore and the Prophetic Future* (London: SPCK, 1976).

Reid, John, *F.W. Grant: His Life, Ministry and Legacy* (Plainfield, NJ: John Reid Book Fund, 1995).

Reid, William, *Plymouth Brethrenism Unveiled and Refuted*, 2nd edn (Edinburgh: William Oliphant and Company, 1876).

Reif, Stefan C., 'Some Notions of Restoration in Early Rabbinic Prayer', in Scott, *Restoration*, pp. 281-304.

Reinharz, Jehuda, and Anita Shapira, (eds.), *Essential Papers on Zionism* (London: Cassell, 1996).

Rennie, Ian S., 'Nineteenth-Century Roots of Contemporary Prophetic Interpretation', in Armerding and Gasque, *A Guide to Biblical Prophecy*, pp. 41-59.

Rice, John R., *The Coming Kingdom of Christ* (Murfreesboro, TN: Sword of the Lord Publishers, 1979).

Richards, Rob, *Has God finished with Israel?* (St. Albans: Olive Press, 1994).

Richardson, Joel, *Antichrist: Islam's Awaited Messiah* (Enumclaw, WA: Pleasant Word, 2006).

Richardson, Peter, *Israel in the Apostolic Church* (Cambridge: Cambridge University Press, 1969).

Riggans, Walter, *Israel and Zionism* (Edinburgh: The Handsel Press, 1988).

Robinson, Edward, and Eli Smith, *Biblical Researches in Palestine, Mount Sinai and Arabia Petraea. A Journal of Travels in the Year 1838* (London: John Murray, 1841), 3 vols.

Rogers, P.G., *The Fifth Monarchy Men* (London: Oxford University Press, 1966).

Romain, Jonathan A., (ed.), *Renewing the Vision: Rabbis Speak Out on Modern Jewish Issues* (London: SCM Press Ltd., 1996).

Rose, Norman, (ed.), *From Palmerston to Balfour: Collected Essays of Mayir Vereté* (London: Frank Cass & Co. Ltd., 1992).

Rosenberg, Joel C., *Epicenter: Why the Current Rumblings in the Middle East will Change Your Future* (Carol Stream, IL: Tyndale House Publishers, Inc., 2006).

Rossing, Barbara R., *The Rapture Exposed: The Message of Hope in the Book of Revelation* (New York: Basic Books, 2004).

Roth, Cecil, ed., *Anglo-Jewish Letters (1158-1917)* (London: The Soncino Press, 1938).

— *Magna Bibliotheca Anglo-Judaica: A Bibliographical Guide to Anglo-Jewish History* (London: The Jewish Historical Society of England, 1937).

— *A History of the Jews in England*, 3rd edn (Oxford: Clarendon Press, 1964).

Rowdon, Harold H., *The Origins of the Brethren 1825-1850* (London: Pickering & Inglis, 1967).

Rowdon, Harold H., 'John Nelson Darby', in Ferguson and Wright, *New Dictionary of Theology*, pp. 186-187.

Rubinstein, William D., and Hilary L. Rubinstein, *Philosemitism: Admiration and Support in the English-Speaking World for Jews, 1840-1939* (Basingstoke: Macmillan Press, 1999).

Ruether, Rosemary Radford, 'Western Christianity and Zionism', in Ateek, Ellis, and Ruether, *Faith and the Intifada*, pp. 147-157.

Ruether, Rosemary Radford, and Herman J. Ruether, *The Wrath of Jonah: The Crisis of Religious Nationalism in the Israeli-Palestinian Conflict*, 2nd edn (Minneapolis, MN: Fortress Press, 2002).

Rydelnik, Michael, 'Israel: The Linchpin in God's Program for the Future', in Dyer, *Storm Clouds on the Horizon*, pp. 11-32.

Ryle, J.C., *Are You Ready for the End of Time?* (Fearn: Christian Focus Publications, 2001).

Ryrie, Charles C., *Dispensationalism Today* (Chicago, IL: Moody Press, 1965).

— *The Basis of the Premillennial Faith* (Neptune, NJ: Loizeaux Brothers, 1966).

— *The Living End* (Old Tappan, NJ: Fleming H. Revell, 1976).

Sabeel, 'Conference Statement [of the Third International Sabeel Conference]', in Ateek and Prior, *Holy Land Hollow Jubilee*, pp. 313-314.

— 'The Beginning of the Center', *Cornerstone*, 1 (Spring, 1994).

Sachar, Howard M., *A History of Israel from the Rise of Zionism to our Time*, 2nd edn (New York: Alfred A. Knopf, 1996).

Sale-Harrison, Leonard, *The Remarkable Jew*, 11th edn (London: Pickering and Inglis Ltd., 1939).

Sandeen, Ernest R., *The Roots of Fundamentalism: British and American Millenarianism 1800-1930* (Chicago, IL: University of Chicago Press, 1970).

Saphir, Adolph, *Christ and Israel: Lectures and Addresses on the Jews* (London: Morgan and Scott Ltd., 1911).

Sarna, Jonathan D., *Jacksonian Jew: The Two Worlds of Mordecai Noah* (New York: Holmes & Meier Publishers, 1981).

Sarna, Jonathan D., and David G. Dalin, *Religion and State in the American Jewish Experience* (Notre Dame, IN: The University of Notre Dame Press, 1997).

Sauer, Erich, *From Eternity to Eternity: An Outline of the Divine Purposes* (Carlisle: The Paternoster Press, 1994).

— *The Dawn of World Redemption: A Survey of the History of Salvation in the Old Testament* (Carlisle: The Paternoster Press, 1994).

— *The Triumph of the Crucified: A Survey of the History of Salvation in the New Testament* (Carlisle: The Paternoster Press, 1994).

Schlink, M. Basilea, *Israel My Chosen People: A German Confession before God and the Jews* (London: The Faith Press, 1963).

Scholem, Gershom, *Sabbatai Sevi: The Mystical Messiah 1626-1676*, trans. by R.J. Zwi Werblowsky (Princeton, NJ: Princeton University Press, 1973).

— *The Messianic Idea in Judaism* (New York: Schocken Books, 1974).

Schuldiner, Michael, and Daniel J. Kleinfeld, (eds.), *The Selected Writings of Mordecai Noah* (Westport, CT: Greenwood Press, 1999).

Schwarzfuchs, Simon, *Napoleon, the Jews and the Sanhedrin* (London: Routledge & Kegan Paul, 1979).

Schweid, Eliezer, 'The Rejection of the Diaspora in Zionist Thought: Two Approaches', in Reinharz and Shapira, *Essential Papers on Zionism*, pp. 133-160.

Scofield, C.I., *Prophecy made Plain: Addresses on Prophecy* (London: Pickering & Inglis, n.d.).

— *The Scofield Bible Correspondence School Course of Study, Vol. I: The Old Testament*, 7th edn (London: Morgan and Scott, n.d.).

— *The Scofield Bible Correspondence School Course of Study, Vol. II: The New Testament*, 9th edn (London: Morgan and Scott, n.d.).

— *The Scofield Bible Correspondence School Course of Study, Vol. III: Synthesis of Bible Truth*, 14th edn (Chicago, IL: Moody Bible Institute, n.d.).

— *Rightly Dividing the Word of Truth* (Neptune, NJ: Loizeaux Brothers, 1896).

— *The First Scofield Reference Bible* (Sunbury, PA: Believers Bookshelf Inc., 1986).

Scott, James M., (ed.), *Restoration: Old Testament, Jewish, and Christian Perspectives* (Leiden: Brill, 2001).

Scott, Walter, *John Nelson Darby* (Hamilton: n.d.).

Scott, William, (ed.), *The Works of the Most Reverend Father in God, William Laud, D.D., Vol. I: Sermons* (Oxford: John Henry Parker, 1847).

Scroggie, W. Graham, *The Unfolding Drama of Redemption: An Inductive Study of Salvation in the Old and New Testaments, Three Volumes in One* (Grand Rapids, MI: Kregel Publications, 1994).

Scult, Mel, *Millennial Expectations and Jewish Liberties: A Study of the Efforts to Convert the Jews in Britain, up to the Mid Nineteenth Century* (Leiden: E.J. Brill, 1978).

Seiss, Joseph A., *The Last Times and the Great Consummation: An Earnest Discussion of Momentous Themes*, Revised edn (Philadelphia, PA: Smith, English & Co., 1863).

Shaftesley, John M., (ed.), *Remember the Days: Essays on Anglo-Jewish History presented to Cecil Roth by Members of the Council of the Jewish Historical Society of England* (London: The Jewish Historical Society of England, 1966).

Shaftesley, John M., and Norman Bentwich, 'Forerunners of Zionism in the Victorian Era', in Shaftesley, *Remember the Days*, pp. 207-239.

Sharif, Regina S., *Non-Jewish Zionism* (London: Zed Press, 1983).

Shaw, P.E., *The Catholic Apostolic Church Sometimes Called Irvingite: A Historical Study* (New York: King's Crown Press, 1946).

Shema Yisrael: Testimonies of Devotion, Courage, and Self-Sacrifice 1939-1945, trans. from *The Shema Encyclopedia* by Yaakov Lavon (Southfield, MI: Targum Press, Inc., 2002).

Shepherd, Naomi, *The Zealous Intruders: The Western Rediscovery of Palestine* (London: Collins, 1987).

Sherman, A.J., *Mandate Days: British Lives in Palestine 1918-1948* (London: Thames and Hudson, 1997).

Shoebat, Walid, *Why I Left Jihad: The Root of Terrorism and the Return of Radical Islam* (USA: Top Executive Media, 2005).

Showers, Renald E., *There Really is a Difference! A Comparison of Covenant and Dispensational Theology* (Bellmawr, NJ: The Friends of Israel Gospel Ministry, Inc., 1990).

Sibthorpe, W.M., *A Defence of the Truth: Called for by Neatby's 'History of the Plymouth Brethren'*, 2nd edn (London: James Carter, 1903).

Sidebotham, Herbert, *Great Britain and Palestine* (London: MacMillan and Co. Limited, 1937).

Sief, Israel, *The Memoirs of Israel Sief* (London: Weidenfeld and Nicolson, 1970).

Silberman, Neil Asher, *Digging for God and Country: Exploration, Archaeology, and the Secret Struggle for the Holy Land 1799-1917* (New York: Alfred A. Knopf, 1982).

Simeon, Charles, *The Jews Provoked to Jealousy. A Sermon preached on Wednesday, June 5, 1811, at the Church of the United Parishes of St. Antholin and St. John Baptist, Watling Street* (London: 1811).

— *A Sermon, Preached before the Society on May 8, 1818, at the Parish Church of St. Paul, Covent Garden, prefixed to The Tenth Report of the London Society for Promoting Christianity amongst the Jews* (London: 1818).

— *The Conversion of the Jews; or, Our Duty and Encouragement to Promote it. Two Discourses, preached before the university of Cambridge, on February 18th and 25th, 1821* (London: 1821).

— *A Sermon, Preached in the Parish Church of St. George, Dublin, on Saturday, April 20, 1822, before the Irish Auxiliary Society, for Promoting Christianity amongst the Jews* (Dublin: 1822).

— *Sovereignty and Equity Combined: or The Dispensations of God towards Jews and Gentiles Illustrated. A Sermon preached before the University of Cambridge, May 5, 1822* (Cambridge: 1822).

Simon, Merrill, *Jerry Falwell and the Jews* (Middle Village, NY: Jonathan David Publishers, Inc., 1984).

Sinclair, James S., (ed.), *Rich Gleanings after the Vintage from 'Rabbi' Duncan* (Glasgow: Free Presbyterian Publications, 1984).

Sirr, Joseph D'Arcy, *A Memoir of the Honourable and Most Reverend Power Le Poer Trench, Last Archbishop of Tuam* (Dublin: William Curry Jr & Company, 1845).

Sitwell, Francis, *The Purpose of God in Creation and Redemption: and the Successive Steps for Manifesting the Same in and by the Church*, 3rd edn (London: Hamilton, Adams, & Co., 1868).

Sizer, Stephen R., 'Christian Zionism: A British Perspective', in Ateek and Prior, *Holy Land Hollow Jubilee*, pp. 189-198.

— 'Christian Zionism and its Impact on Justice', *Al-Aqsa Journal*, 3.1, October (2000), 9-15.

— 'Christian Zionism, True Friends of Israel?', *Evangelicals Now*, December (2000), 14.

— 'Dispensational Approaches to the Land', in Johnston and Walker, *The Land of Promise*, pp. 142-171.

— 'The Premised Land: Palestine and Israel', in Prior, *They Came and They Saw*, pp. 144-161.

— *The Promised Land: A Critical Investigation of Evangelical Christian Zionism in Britain and the United States of America since 1800* (PhD: Middlesex University, 2002).

— *Christian Zionism: Road-map to Armageddon?* (Leicester: Inter-Varsity Press, 2004).

— 'The International Christian Embassy, Jerusalem: A Case Study in Political Christian Zionism', in Prior, *Speaking the Truth*, pp. 104-125.

— 'The Historical Roots of Christian Zionism from Irving to Balfour: Christian Zionism in the United Kingdom (1820-1918)', in Ateek, Duaybis, and Tobin, *Challenging Christian Zionism*, pp. 20-31.

— 'The Theological Basis of Christian Zionism: On the Road to Armageddon', in Ateek, Duaybis, and Tobin, *Challenging Christian Zionism*, pp. 59-75.

Smith, Geoffrey, 'Christians, Israel and the Struggle for Peace', in Wright, *Israel*, pp. 122-141.

Smith, George Adam, *The Historical Geography of the Holy Land* (London: Collins, 1966).

Smith, Henry, *The Protestant Bishopric in Jerusalem: Its Origin and Progress from the Official Documents published by Command of His Majesty the King of Prussia and from other Authentic Sources* (London: B. Wertheim, Aldine Chambers, 1847).

Smith, Nigel, 'The Uses of Hebrew in the English Revolution', in *Language, Self and Society: A Social History of Language*, ed. by Peter Burke and Roy Porter (Cambridge: Polity Press, 1991), pp. 51-71.

Smith, Robert O., 'Politics, Faiths, and Fundamentalisms', in Lutz and Smith, *Christians and a Land Called Holy*, pp. 35-62.

Smith, Wilbur M., *Israeli-Arab Conflict and the Bible* (Glendale, CA: Regal Books, 1967).

Sokolow, Nahum, *History of Zionism 1600-1918* (London: Longmans, Green and Co., 1919), 2 vols.

Spurgeon, Charles Haddon, *The Restoration and Conversion of the Jews: A Sermon Preached on Thursday Evening, June 16th, 1864...at the Metropolitan Tabernacle, Newington, in Aid of the Funds of the British Society for the Propagation of the Gospel amongst the Jews* (Pasadena, TX: Pilgrim Publications, n.d.).

— *12 Sermons on the Second Coming of Christ* (Grand Rapids, MI: Baker Books, 1993).

Standring, G.L., *Albury and the Catholic Apostolic Church: A Guide to the Personalities, Beliefs and Practices of the Community of Christians commonly called the Catholic Apostolic Church* (Guildford: 1985).

Stanley, Arthur P., *Sinai and Palestine in Connection with their History* (London: John Murray, 1910).

Stanton, Gerald B., *Kept from the Hour: A Systematic Study of the Rapture in Bible Prophecy* (Grand Rapids, MI: Zondervan Publishing House, 1956).

Stein, Leonard, *Zionism* (London: Ernest Benn Ltd., 1925).

— *The Balfour Declaration* (London: Vallentine-Mitchell, 1961).

Stephen, Leslie, (ed.), *Dictionary of National Biography* (London: Smith, Elder, & Co., 1885-1890), 21 vols.

Stephen, Leslie, and Sidney Lee, (eds.), *Dictionary of National Biography* (London: Smith, Elder, & Co., 1890-1891), 5 vols.

Stewart, James Haldane, *Thoughts on the Importance of Special Prayer for the General Outpouring of the Holy Spirit* (London: 1821).

Stirling, A.M.W., *The Ways of Yesterday: Being the Chronicles of the Way Family from 1307 to 1885* (London: Thornton Butterworth, Limited, 1930).

St. John, Robert, *Tongue of the Prophets: The Life Story of Eliezer Ben Yehuda* (Gordon City, NY: Dolphin Books, 1952).

Stott, John, 'Foreword', in Johnston and Walker, *The Land of Promise*, pp. 10-11.

Strandberg, Todd, and Terry James, *Are You Rapture Ready? Signs, Prophecies, Warnings, Threats, and Suspicions that the Endtime is Now* (New York: Dutton, 2003).

Stunt, Timothy C.F., *From Awakening to Secession: Radical Evangelicals in Switzerland and Britain 1815-35* (Edinburgh: T.&T. Clark, 2000).

— 'Influences in the Early Development of J.N. Darby', in Gribben and Stunt, *Prisoners of Hope?*, pp. 44-68.

— 'John Nelson Darby: Contexts and Perceptions', in Gribben and Holmes, *Protestant Millennialism*, pp. 83-98.

Swindoll, Charles R., et al., *The Road to Armageddon* (Nashville, TN: Word Publishing, 1999).

Tal, Eliyahu, *You Don't Have to be Jewish to be a Zionist: A Review of 400 Years of Christian Zionism* (Jerusalem: International Forum for a United Jerusalem, 2000).

Talmon, J.L., *Political Messianism: The Romantic Phase* (London: Secker & Warburg, 1960).

Tarazi, Paul Nadim, 'Covenant, Land and City: Finding God's Will in Palestine', *The Reformed Journal*, 29 (1979), 10-16.

Tatford, Frederick A., *Five Minutes to Midnight* (London: Victory Press, 1970).

— *The Middle East Problem: Israel in History and Prophecy* (Scarborough, ON: Everyday Publications Inc., 1983).

— *It's Never Been So Late Before* (Belfast: Ambassador Productions Ltd., 1986).

Tayler, W.E., *Passages from the Diary and Letters of Henry Craik, of Bristol* (London: J.F. Shaw & Co., 1866).

Teichthal, Yissakhar Shlomo, *Em HaBanim Semeha: Restoration of Zion as a Response during the Holocaust*, ed. and trans'd by Pesach Schindler (Hoboken, NJ: KTAV Publishing House, Inc., 1999).

Telchin, Stan, *Abandoned: What is God's Will for the Jewish People and the Church?* (Grand Rapids, MI: Chosen Books, 2003).

Teplinsky, Sandra, *Why Care About Israel? How the Jewish Nation is Key to Unleashing God's Blessings in the 21st Century* (Grand Rapids, MI: Chosen Books, 2004).

Teulon, J.S., *The History and Teaching of the Plymouth Brethren* (London: SPCK, 1883).

'The Alphabet of Prophecy', *The Morning Watch*, 7 (1833), 140-160.

'The Ark of God in the Temple of Dagon', *The Morning Watch*, 5 (1832), 441-456.

The Christian Witness: Chiefly on Subjects Connected with the Present State of the Church, Vols. 1 and 2 (Plymouth: J.B. Rowe, 1834-1835).

The Christian Witness: Chiefly on Subjects Connected with the Present State of the Church, Vols. 3 and 4 (London: Simpkin, Marshall, and Co., 1836-1837).

The Christian Witness: Chiefly on Subjects Connected with the Present State of the Church, Vols. 5 and 6 (Plymouth: The Christian Witness and Tract Depot, 1838-1839).

The Christian Witness: Chiefly on Subjects Connected with the Present State of the Church, Vols. 7 and 8 (Plymouth: J. Clulow and H. Soltau, 1840-1841).

'The Hour of Christ's Appearance', *The Morning Watch*, 4 (1832), 251-254.

The Institute for Palestine Studies, (ed.), *Christians, Zionism and Palestine: A Selection of Articles and Statements on the Religious and Political Aspects of the Palestine Problem* (Beirut: The Institute for Palestine Studies, 1970).

The Jewish Historical Society of England: Transactions - Sessions 1945-1951: Vol. XVI (London: The Jewish Historical Society of England, 1952).

The Last Days of J.N.D. (John Nelson Darby) From March 3rd to April 29th, 1882, With Portrait, 2nd edn (Christchurch: N.C.M. Turner, 1925).

The Morning Watch; or, Quarterly Journal on Prophecy and Theological Review, Vols. 1-4 (London: James Nisbet, 1830-1832).

The Morning Watch; or, Quarterly Journal on Prophecy and Theological Review, Vols. 5-7 (London: James Fraser, 1832-1833).

'The Out-Pouring of the Holy Spirit', *The Morning Watch*, 2 (1831), 608-622.

Thomson, William McClure, *The Land and the Book; or, Biblical Illustrations drawn from the Manners and Customs, the Scenes and Scenery of the Holy Land* (London: T. Nelson and Sons, 1901).

Tibawi, A.L., *British Interests in Palestine 1800-1901: A Study of Religious and Educational Enterprise* (Oxford: Oxford University Press, 1961).

— *American Interests in Syria 1800-1901: A Study of Educational, Literary and Religious Work* (Oxford: Clarendon Press, 1966).

Toon, Peter, (ed.), *Puritans, The Millennium and the Future of Israel: Puritan Eschatology 1600-1660* (Cambridge: James Clarke & Co. Ltd., 1970).

— *Evangelical Theology 1833-1856: A Response to Tractarianism* (London: Marshall, Morgan & Scott, 1979).

Torrey, R.A., *The Lord's Return* (Belfast: Ambassador, 1997).

Toynbee, Arnold J., *A Study of History, Vol. XII: Reconsiderations* (London: Oxford University Press, 1961).

Tregelles, Samuel P., *Pastoral Relations* (London: Houlston & Sons, n.d.).

— *The Hope of Christ's Second Coming*, 7th edn (Chelmsford: Sovereign Grace Advent Testimony, n.d.).

— *Three Letters to the Author of 'A Retrospect of Events that have taken place amongst the Brethren'*, 2nd edn (London: Houlston & Sons, 1894).

Trotter, William, *Plain Papers on Prophetic and Other Subjects*, Revised edn (London: G. Morrish, n.d.).

Trumbull, Charles Gallaudet, *The Life Story of C.I. Scofield* (New York: Oxford University Press, 1920).

Tuchman, Barbara W., *Bible and Sword: How the British came to Palestine* (London: Papermac, 1982).

Tudor, John, 'The Study of Prophecy a Question of Degree', *The Morning Watch*, 1 (1830), 184-186.

— 'Prophetic Aspect of the Church; its Privileges and Powers', *The Morning Watch*, 3 (1831), 1-14.

— 'Conclusion of the Morning Watch', *The Morning Watch*, 7 (1833), 399-403.

Turner, W.G., *John Nelson Darby, A Biography* (London: C.A. Hammon, 1926).

Tutu, Desmond, 'Foreword', in Prior, *Speaking the Truth*, pp. 9-12.

Twain, Mark, *The Innocents Abroad* (London: Readers Library Publishing Co. Ltd., n.d.).

Twisse, William, 'A Preface written by Doctor Twisse, showing the Method and Excellency of Mr Mede's Interpretation of this Mysterious Book of the Revelation of Saint John', in Mede, *The Key of the Revelation*, pp. 1-10.

Tyso, Joseph, *An Inquiry after Prophetic Truth relative to the Restoration of the Jews and the Millennium* (London: Holdsworth and Ball, 1831).

— *The Year-Day System of Interpreting the Prophecies Examined* (Wallingford: 1845).

Urquhart, Carment, 'The World-wide Jewish Problem', in Urquhart, *Wonders of Prophecy*, pp. 187-195.

Urquhart, John, *Wonders of Prophecy: The Testimony of Fulfilled Prediction to the Inspiration of the Bible* (London: Pickering & Inglis Ltd., 1945).

Van der Hoeven, Jan Willem, *Babylon or Jerusalem?* (Shippensburg, PA: Destiny Image, 1993).

Van Diest, John, (ed.), *10 Reasons why Jesus is Coming Soon* (Sisters, OR: Multnomah Books, 1998).

Veitch, T.S., *The Story of the Brethren Movement* (London: Pickering and Inglis, n.d.).

Vital, David, *The Origins of Zionism* (Oxford: Oxford University Press, 1975).

Wachmann, Doreen, 'Anti-Israel Man Cut Down to Sizer', *Jewish Telegraph*, 7 July (Manchester, 2006), 29.

Wacker, Grant, 'Planning Ahead: The Enduring Appeal of Prophecy Belief', *The Christian Century*, 111 (January, 1994), 48-52.

Wagner, Jr, Clarence H., 'The Error of Replacement Theology', in Koenig, *Eye to Eye*, pp. 321-324.

Wagner, Donald, *Anxious for Armageddon* (Scottdale, PA: Herald Press, 1995).

— 'Marching to Zion: Western Evangelicals and Jerusalem approaching the Year 2000', in Ateek, Duaybis, and Schrader, *Jerusalem*, pp. 73-93.

— 'From Zion to Palestine: A Journey from Christian Zionism to Justice in the Holy Land', in Prior, *They Came and They Saw*, pp. 199-209.

Walker, Andrew, *Restoring the Kingdom: The Radical Christianity of the House Church Movement* (Guildford: Eagle, 1998).

Walker, Peter W.L., (ed.), *Jerusalem Past and Present in the Purposes of God*, 2nd edn (Carlisle: The Paternoster Press, 1994).

Wall, Moses, 'Considerations upon the Point of the Conversion of the Jews', in Menasseh ben Israel, *The Hope of Israel*, pp. 47-62.

Walmesley, Charles [Signor Pastorini], *The General History of the Christian Church, from her Birth to her Final Triumphant State in Heaven, chiefly Deduced from the Apocalypse of St. John the Apostle* (1771).

Walvoord, John F., *Israel in Prophecy* (Grand Rapids, MI: Zondervan Publishing House, 1962).

— *The Millennial Kingdom* (Grand Rapids, MI: Zondervan Publishing House, 1969).

— *Armageddon, Oil, and the Middle East Crisis* (Grand Rapids, MI: Zondervan Publishing House, 1975).

— *The Rapture Question*, 2nd edn (Grand Rapids, MI: Zondervan, 1979).

— *The Blessed Hope and the Tribulation: A Historical and Biblical Study of Posttribulationism* (Grand Rapids, MI: Zondervan Publishing House, 1977).

Walvoord, John F., and Mark Hitchcock, *Armageddon, Oil, and Terror: What the Bible says about the Future* (Carol Stream, IL: Tyndale House Publishers, 2007).

Wasserstein, Bernard, *Britain and the Jews of Europe 1939-1945* (London: Institute of Jewish Affairs, 1979).

Watson, Sydney, *In the Twinkling of an Eye* (London: W. Nicholson and Sons, n.d.).

— *Brighter Years: The Second Part of the Autobiography of Sydney Watson* (London: Hodder and Stoughton, 1898).

— *The New Europe: A Story of Today and Tomorrow* (London: William Nicholson & Sons Limited, 1915).

— *Plucked from the Burning, or the Bride of the False Church: The Snare of Ritualism* (London: William Nicholson & Sons Limited, [1915]).

— *The Mark of the Beast* (Edinburgh: B. McCall Barbour, 1977).

Way, Lewis, *Reviewers Reviewed; or, Observations on Article II of the British Critic for January 1819, New Series, entitled, 'On the London Society for Converting the Jews'*, 2nd edn (London: 1819).

— *The Latter Rain; with Observations on The Importance of General Prayer, for the Special Outpouring of the Holy Spirit*, 2nd edn (London: 1821).

— *Poems* (Stansted: 1822).

Webb, J.B., *Naomi; or The Last Days of Jerusalem* (Edinburgh: W.P. Nimmo, Hay, & Mitchell, 1887).

Weber, Timothy P., *Living in the Shadow of the Second Coming: American Premillennialism, 1875-1982* (Chicago, IL: The University of Chicago Press, 1987).

— *On the Road to Armageddon: How Evangelicals became Israel's Best Friend* (Grand Rapids, MI: Baker Academic, 2004).

Weizmann, Chaim, *Trial and Error: The Autobiography of Chaim Weizmann* (London: Hamish Hamilton, 1949).

Wenham, Gordon J., *Word Biblical Commentary, Genesis 16-50* (Dallas, TX: Word Books, 1994).

Weremchuk, Max S., *John Nelson Darby, A Biography* (Neptune, NJ: Loizeaux Brothers, 1992).

Wertheim, Charlotte, *War on God's People* (Chichester: New Wine Press, 2002).

Wesley, John, *A Collection of Hymns, For the Use of the People called Methodists* (London: Wesleyan Conference Office, n.d.).

West, Nathaniel, *The Thousand Year Reign of Christ* (Grand Rapids, MI: Kregel Publications, 1993).

Whalen, Robert K., '"Christians Love the Jews!" The Development of American Philo-Semitism, 1790-1860', *Religion and American Culture*, 6.2 (Summer, 1996), 225-259.

— 'Dispensationalism', in Brasher, *Encyclopedia of Fundamentalism*, pp. 134-139.

Wheatcroft, Geoffrey, *The Controversy of Zion* (London: Sinclair-Stevenson, 1996).

Whitaker, Edward W., *A Dissertation on the Prophecies relating to the Final Restoration of the Jews* (London: 1784).

Whitelam, Keith W., *The Invention of Ancient Israel: The Silencing of Palestinian History* (London: Routledge, 1996).

Wilkinson, John, *God's Plan for the Jew* (London: The Messianic Testimony, 1978).

Wilks, Michael, (ed.), *Prophecy and Eschatology* (Oxford: Blackwell Publishers, 1994).

Williams, Peter W., *America's Religions: From their Origins to the Twenty-First Century*, 2nd edn (Chicago, IL: University of Illinois Press, 2002).

Williams, Robert Folkestone, (ed.), *The Court and Times of James the First* (London: Henry Colburn, 1848).

Wilson, Daniel, 'Recollections of the Rev Charles Simeon (1837)', in Carus, *Memoirs*, pp. 833-848.

Wilson, Dwight, *Armageddon Now! The Premillenarian Response to Russia and Israel since 1917* (Tyler, TX: Institute for Christian Economics, 1991).

Wilson, John F., (ed.), *A History of the Work of Redemption* (New Haven, CT: Yale University Press, 1989).

Wilson, Marvin R., *Our Father Abraham: Jewish Roots of the Christian Faith* (Grand Rapids, MI: Centre for Judaic-Christian Studies, 1989).

Witherby, Thomas, *An Attempt to Remove Prejudices concerning the Jewish Nation by way of Dialogue* (London: 1804).

Witherby, William, *A Review of Scripture, in Testimony of the Truth of the Second Advent, the First Resurrection, and the Millennium: with an Appendix, containing extracts from Mr. Joseph Eyre's Observations on the Prophecies Relating to the Restoration of the Jews* (London: 1818).

Witherington III, Ben, *The Problem with Evangelical Theology: Testing the Exegetical Foundations of Calvinism, Dispensationalism and Wesleyanism* (Waco, TX: Baylor University Press, 2005).

Wolf, Lucien, (ed.), *Menasseh ben Israel's Mission to Oliver Cromwell. Being a reprint of the Pamphlets published by Menasseh ben Israel to promote the Re-admission of the Jews to England 1649-1656* (London: Macmillan & Co., Limited, 1901).

— *Notes on the diplomatic history of the Jewish question: with texts of protocols, treaty stipulations and other public acts and official documents* (London: 1919).

Wood, Arthur Skevington, *Prophecy in the Space Age: Studies in Prophetic Themes* (London: Marshall, Morgan & Scott, 1964).

Wouk, Herman, *This is My God: The Jewish Way of Life*, Revised edn (London: Collins, 1979).

Wrangham, Francis, *The Restoration of the Jews: A Poem* (Cambridge: 1795).

Wright, Fred, (ed.), *Israel: His People, His Land, His Story* (Eastbourne: Thankful Books, 2005).

Wright, N.T., *The Climax of the Covenant* (Edinburgh: T.&T. Clark, 1991).

— *The New Testament and the People of God* (London: SPCK, 1992).

— 'Jerusalem in the New Testament', in Walker, *Jerusalem*, pp. 53-77.

Wuest, Kenneth S., *Wuest's Word Studies from the Greek New Testament, Vol. III* (Grand Rapids, MI: Wm. B. Eerdmans Publishing Company, 1973).

— 'Great Truths to Live By', in Wuest, *Wuest's Word Studies*, pp. 138-142.

Younan, Munib, *Witnessing for Peace: In Jerusalem and the World* (Minneapolis, MN: Augsburg Fortress, 2003).

Young, G. Douglas, 'An Open Letter to Dr. A.C. Forrest, Editor of the United Church Observer', in Hanson, *A Gentile*, pp. 203-208.

Zagorin, Perez, (ed.), *Culture and Politics from Puritanism to the Enlightenment* (London: University of California Press, Ltd., 1980).

Zaru, Jean, 'Theologising, Truth and Peacemaking in the Palestinian Experience', in Prior, *Speaking the Truth*, pp. 165-189.

Zimpel, Charles F., *An Appeal to all Christians and the Jewish Nation to Liberate Jerusalem* (London: G.J. Stevenson, 1865).

— *Railway between the Mediterranean, the Dead Sea, and Damascus, by way of Jerusalem, with branches to Bethlehem, Hebron, Nablous, Nazareth, and Tiberias* (London: G.J. Stevenson, 1865).

Zoughbi, Zoughbi Elias, 'Faith, Non-violence, and the Palestinian Struggle', in Ateek, Ellis, and Ruether, *Faith and the Intifada*, pp. 101-107.

Zwicker, Stephen N., 'England, Israel, and the Triumph of Roman Virtue', in Popkin, *Millenarianism*, pp. 37-64.

Web-Sites

Ateek, Naim, 'Jerusalem Easter Message', 10 April 2001, <http://www.hcef.org/hcef/index.cfm/mod/news/ID/16/SubMod/NewsView/NewsID/220.cfm, 9 June 2006>.

Boyer, Paul S., 'John Darby meets Saddam Hussein: Foreign Policy and Bible Prophecy', *The Chronicle of Higher Education: The Chronicle Review*, 14 February (2003), <http://chronicle.com/weekly/v49/i23/23b01001.htm, 5 June 2006>.

Christ Church Virginia Water, 'Published Writings of Stephen Sizer: Commendations', <http://www.christchurch-virginiawater.co.uk/articles/ivp.html, 7 June 2006>.

Church and Society Council, 'Christian Zionism: Hope or Despair?', <http://www.churchofscotland.org.uk/generalassembly/downloads/gareports07churchsociety.txt, 24 July 2007>.

Currie, William E., 'God's Little Errand Boy', <http://www.amfi.org/errandboy.htm, 6 June 2005>.

Eisen, Paul, 'Jewish Power', *RighteousJews.org*, 19 August (2004), <http://www.righteousjews.org/article10.html, 8 June 2006>.

— 'The Holocaust Wars', *The Zundelsite*, 20 May (2005), <http://www.zundelsite.org/zundel_persecuted/may20-05_eisen.html, 8 June 2006>.

Episcopal Diocese of Jerusalem, 'The Jerusalem Declaration on Christian Zionism, 22 August 2006', <http://www.j-diocese.com/DiocesanNews/view.asp?selected=238, 2 September 2006>.

Flannery, Edward H., 'Christian Zionist Ethos should be Revived', *Providence Journal-Bulletin*, 26 April (1997), <http://pqasb.pqarchiver.com/projo/results.html?QryTxt=christian+zionist+ethos&submit=Go, 6 June 2006>.

Friends of Al-Aqsa, <http://www.aqsa.org.uk/page_detail.aspx?id=357, 8 May 2007>.

Goodenough, Stan, 'Christian Zionists are our Enemy: Hamas Authority has pro-Israel Christians in its Sights', *Jerusalem Newswire*, 9 May (2006), <http://www.jnewswire.com/article/896, 5 June 2006>.

Haaretz.com, 'Prime Minister Ehud Olmert's Address Before Congress (24 May 2006)', <http://www.haaretz.com/hasen/spages/719462.html, 31 May 2006>.

Huntington, Samuel P., 'The Clash of Civilisations?', *Foreign Affairs*, Summer (1993), <http://www.alamut.com/subj/economics/misc/clash.html, 17 August 2006>.

Knox Theological Seminary, 'An Open Letter to Evangelicals and Other Interested Parties: The People of God, the Land of Israel, and the Impartiality of the Gospel', <http://www.knoxseminary.org/Prospective/Faculty/WittenbergDoor/, 3 June 2006>.

Lind, Michael, 'George W. Bush's Holy War', *theGlobalist*, 23 March (2003), <http://www.theglobalist.com/DBWeb/StoryId.aspx?StoryId=3025, 23 May 2005>.

Lipset, Seymour Martin, 'The Socialism of Fools: The Left, the Jews and Israel', *Encounter*, (December, 1969), 24, <http://www.wzo.org.il/en/resources/view.asp?id=1823, 7 June 2006>.

Netanyahu, Benjamin, 'Christian Zionism and the Jewish Restoration, 1985', <http//:www.internationalwallofprayer.org/A-091-Christian-Zionism-and-the-Jewish-Restoration.html, 15 June 2006>.

Obenzinger, Hilton, 'In the Shadow of "God's Sun-dial": The Construction of American Christian Zionism and the Blackstone Memorial', *Stanford Electronic Humanities Review*, 5.1, <http://www.stanford.edu/group/SHR/5-1/text/obenzinger.html, 6 June 2006>.

Phillips, Melanie, 'Christians who hate the Jews', *The Spectator*, 16 February (2002), <http://www.melaniephillips.com/articles/archives/000765.html, 6 June 2006>.

Sabeel, 'Purpose Statement', <http://www.sabeel.org/etemplate.php?id=2, 9 June 2006>.

— 'The 5ᵗʰ International Sabeel Conference Statement: Challenging Christian Zionism', <http://www.sabeel.org/documents/5thConfStatementfinal.htm, 9 June 2006>.

— 'The Jerusalem Sabeel Document', <http://www.sabeel.org/documents/Jerusalem %20Sabeel%20Document.pdf, 9 June 2006>.

— 'A Call for Morally Responsible Investment', <http://www.sabeel.org/documents/ A%20nonviolence%20sabeel%20 second%20revision.pdf, 7 June 2006>.

Starr, Richard, 'The Big Jenin Lie', *The Daily Standard*, 8 May (2002), <http://www.weeklystandard.com/Content/Public/Articles/000/000/001/218vnicq .asp, 1 June 2006>.

The Temple Institute, <http://www.templeinstitute.org/main.htm, 1 August 2006>.

Wagner, Donald, 'Beyond Armageddon', *The Link*, 25.4 (Oct-Nov, 1992), 1-13, <http://www.ameu.org/uploads/vol25_issue4_1992.pdf, 7 June 2006>.

WZO, 'Theodor Herzl's Opening Address to the First Zionist Congress', <http://www. wzo.org.il/en/resources/view.asp?id=1367&subject=28, 1 May 2006>.

General Index

Studies in Evangelical History and Thought
(All titles uniform with this volume)
Dates in bold are of projected publication

Andrew Atherstone
Oxford's Protestant Spy
The Controversial Career of Charles Golightly
Charles Golightly (1807–85) was a notorious Protestant polemicist. His life was
dedicated to resisting the spread of ritualism and liberalism within the Church of
England and the University of Oxford. For half a century he led many
memorable campaigns, such as building a martyr's memorial and attempting to
close a theological college. John Henry Newman, Samuel Wilberforce and
Benjamin Jowett were among his adversaries. This is the first study of
Golightly's controversial career.
__2006__ / 1-84227-364-7 / approx. 324pp

Clyde Binfield
Victorian Nonconformity in Eastern England
Studies of Victorian religion and society often concentrate on cities, suburbs,
and industrialisation. This study provides a contrast. Victorian Eastern
England—Essex, Suffolk, Norfolk, Cambridgeshire, and Huntingdonshire—was
rural, traditional, relatively unchanging. That is nonetheless a caricature which
discounts the industry in Norwich and Ipswich (as well as in Haverhill,
Stowmarket and Leiston) and ignores the impact of London on Essex, of
railways throughout the region, and of an ancient but changing university
(Cambridge) on the county town which housed it. It also entirely ignores the
political implications of such changes in a region noted for the variety of its
religious Dissent since the seventeenth century. This book explores Victorian
Eastern England and its Nonconformity. It brings to a wider readership a
pioneering thesis which has made a major contribution to a fresh evolution of
English religion and society.
__2006__ / 1-84227-216-0 / approx. 274pp

John Brencher
Martyn Lloyd-Jones (1899–1981) and Twentieth-Century Evangelicalism
This study critically demonstrates the significance of the life and ministry of
Martyn Lloyd-Jones for post-war British evangelicalism and demonstrates that
his preaching was his greatest influence on twentieth-century Christianity. The
factors which shaped his view of the church are examined, as is the way his
reformed evangelicalism led to a separatist ecclesiology which divided
evangelicals.
__2002__ / 1-84227-051-6 / xvi + 268pp

Jonathan D. Burnham
A Story of Conflict
The Controversial Relationship between Benjamin Wills Newton and
John Nelson Darby
Burnham explores the controversial relationship between the two principal leaders of the early Brethren movement. In many ways Newton and Darby were products of their times, and this study of their relationship provides insight not only into the dynamics of early Brethrenism, but also into the progress of nineteenth-century English and Irish evangelicalism.
2004 / 1-84227-191-1 / xxiv + 268pp

Grayson Carter
Anglican Evangelicals
Protestant Secessions from the Via Media, c.1800–1850
This study examines, within a chronological framework, the major themes and personalities which influenced the outbreak of a number of Evangelical clerical and lay secessions from the Church of England and Ireland during the first half of the nineteenth century. Though the number of secessions was relatively small—between a hundred and two hundred of the 'Gospel' clergy abandoned the Church during this period—their influence was considerable, especially in highlighting in embarrassing fashion the tensions between the evangelical conversionist imperative and the principles of a national religious establishment. Moreover, through much of this period there remained, just beneath the surface, the potential threat of a large Evangelical disruption similar to that which occurred in Scotland in 1843. Consequently, these secessions provoked great consternation within the Church and within Evangelicalism itself, they contributed to the outbreak of millennial speculation following the 'constitutional revolution' of 1828–32, they led to the formation of several new denominations, and they sparked off a major Church–State crisis over the legal right of a clergyman to secede and begin a new ministry within Protestant Dissent.
2007 / 1-84227-401-5 / xvi + 470pp

J.N. Ian Dickson
Beyond Religious Discourse
*Sermons, Preaching and Evangelical Protestants in Nineteenth-Century
Irish Society*
Drawing extensively on primary sources, this pioneer work in modern religious
history explores the training of preachers, the construction of sermons and how
Irish evangelicalism and the wider movement in Great Britain and the United
States shaped the preaching event. Evangelical preaching and politics,
sectarianism, denominations, education, class, social reform, gender, and revival
are examined to advance the argument that evangelical sermons and preaching
went significantly beyond religious discourse. The result is a book for those with
interests in Irish history, culture and belief, popular religion and society,
evangelicalism, preaching and communication.
2005 / 1-84227-217-9 / approx. 324pp

Neil T.R. Dickson
Brethren in Scotland 1838–2000
A Social Study of an Evangelical Movement
The Brethren were remarkably pervasive throughout Scottish society. This study
of the Open Brethren in Scotland places them in their social context and
examines their growth, development and relationship to society.
2003 / 1-84227-113-X / xxviii + 510pp

Crawford Gribben and Timothy C.F. Stunt (eds)
Prisoners of Hope?
Aspects of Evangelical Millennialism in Britain and Ireland, 1800–1880
This volume of essays offers a comprehensive account of the impact of
evangelical millennialism in nineteenth-century Britain and Ireland.
2004 / 1-84227-224-1 / xiv + 208pp

Khim Harris
Evangelicals and Education
*Evangelical Anglicans and Middle-Class Education in
Nineteenth-Century England*
This ground breaking study investigates the history of English public schools
founded by nineteenth-century Evangelicals. It documents the rise of middle-
class education and Evangelical societies such as the influential Church
Association, and includes a useful biographical survey of prominent
Evangelicals of the period.
2004 / 1-84227-250-0 / xviii + 422pp

Mark Hopkins
Nonconformity's Romantic Generation
Evangelical and Liberal Theologies in Victorian England
A study of the theological development of key leaders of the Baptist and Congregational denominations at their period of greatest influence, including C.H. Spurgeon and R.W. Dale, and of the controversies in which those among them who embraced and rejected the liberal transformation of their evangelical heritage opposed each other.
2004 / 1-84227-150-4 / xvi + 284pp

Don Horrocks
Laws of the Spiritual Order
Innovation and Reconstruction in the Soteriology of Thomas Erskine of Linlathen
Don Horrocks argues that Thomas Erskine's unique historical and theological significance as a soteriological innovator has been neglected. This timely reassessment reveals Erskine as a creative, radical theologian of central and enduring importance in Scottish nineteenth-century theology, perhaps equivalent in significance to that of S.T. Coleridge in England.
2004 / 1-84227-192-X / xx + 362pp

Kenneth S. Jeffrey
When the Lord Walked the Land
The 1858–62 Revival in the North East of Scotland
Previous studies of revivals have tended to approach religious movements from either a broad, national or a strictly local level. This study of the multifaceted nature of the 1859 revival as it appeared in three distinct social contexts within a single region reveals the heterogeneous nature of simultaneous religious movements in the same vicinity.
2002 / 1-84227-057-5 / xxiv + 304pp

John Kenneth Lander
Itinerant Temples
Tent Methodism, 1814–1832
Tent preaching began in 1814 and the Tent Methodist sect resulted from disputes with Bristol Wesleyan Methodists in 1820. The movement spread to parts of Gloucestershire, Wiltshire, London and Liverpool, among other places. Its demise started in 1826 after which one leader returned to the Wesleyans and others became ministers in the Congregational and Baptist denominations.
2003 / 1-84227-151-2 / xx + 268pp

July 2005

Donald M. Lewis
Lighten Their Darkness
The Evangelical Mission to Working-Class London, 1828–1860
This is a comprehensive and compelling study of the Church and the
complexities of nineteenth-century London. Challenging our understanding of
the culture in working London at this time, Lewis presents a well-structured and
illustrated work that contributes substantially to the study of evangelicalism and
mission in nineteenth-century Britain.
2001 / 1-84227-074-5 / xviii + 372pp

Herbert McGonigle
'Sufficient Saving Grace'
John Wesley's Evangelical Arminianism
A thorough investigation of the theological roots of John Wesley's evangelical
Arminianism and how these convictions were hammered out in controversies on
predestination, limited atonement and the perseverance of the saints.
2001 / 1-84227-045-1 / xvi + 350pp

Lisa S. Nolland
A Victorian Feminist Christian
Josephine Butler, the Prostitutes and God
Josephine Butler was an unlikely candidate for taking up the cause of
prostitutes, as she did, with a fierce and self-disregarding passion. This book
explores the particular mix of perspectives and experiences that came together to
envision and empower her remarkable achievements. It highlights the vital role
of her spirituality and the tragic loss of her daughter.
2004 / 1-84227-225-X / xxiv + 328pp

Don J. Payne
The Theology of the Christian Life in J.I. Packer's Thought
*Theological Anthropology, Theological Method, and the Doctrine
of Sanctification*
J.I. Packer has wielded widespread influence on evangelicalism for more than
three decades. This study pursues a nuanced understanding of Packer's theology
of sanctification by tracing the development of his thought, showing how he
reflects a particular version of Reformed theology, and examining the unique
influence of theological anthropology and theological method on this area of his
theology.
2005 / 1-84227-397-3 / approx. 374pp

Ian M. Randall
Evangelical Experiences
A Study in the Spirituality of English Evangelicalism 1918–1939
This book makes a detailed historical examination of evangelical spirituality between the First and Second World Wars. It shows how patterns of devotion led to tensions and divisions. In a wide-ranging study, Anglican, Wesleyan, Reformed and Pentecostal-charismatic spiritualities are analysed.
1999 / 0-85364-919-7 / xii + 310pp

Ian M. Randall
Spirituality and Social Change
The Contribution of F.B. Meyer (1847–1929)
This is a fresh appraisal of F.B. Meyer (1847–1929), a leading Free Church minister. Having been deeply affected by holiness spirituality, Meyer became the Keswick Convention's foremost international speaker. He combined spirituality with effective evangelism and socio-political activity. This study shows Meyer's significant contribution to spiritual renewal and social change.
2003 / 1-84227-195-4 / xx + 184pp

James Robinson
Pentecostal Origins
Early Pentecostalism in Ireland in the Context of the British Isles
Harvey Cox describes Pentecostalism as 'the fascinating spiritual child of our time' that has the potential, at the global scale, to contribute to the 'reshaping of religion in the twenty-first century'. This study grounds such sentiments by examining at the local scale the origin, development and nature of Pentecostalism in Ireland in its first twenty years. Illustrative, in a paradigmatic way, of how Pentecostalism became established within one region of the British Isles, it sets the story within the wider context of formative influences emanating from America, Europe and, in particular, other parts of the British Isles. As a synoptic regional study in Pentecostal history it is the first survey of its kind.
2005 / 1-84227-329-1 / xxviii + 378pp

Geoffrey Robson
Dark Satanic Mills?
Religion and Irreligion in Birmingham and the Black Country
This book analyses and interprets the nature and extent of popular Christian belief and practice in Birmingham and the Black Country during the first half of the nineteenth century, with particular reference to the impact of cholera epidemics and evangelism on church extension programmes.
2002 / 1-84227-102-4 / xiv + 294pp

Roger Shuff
Searching for the True Church
Brethren and Evangelicals in Mid-Twentieth-Century England
Roger Shuff holds that the influence of the Brethren movement on wider evangelical life in England in the twentieth century is often underrated. This book records and accounts for the fact that Brethren reached the peak of their strength at the time when evangelicalism was at it lowest ebb, immediately before World War II. However, the movement then moved into persistent decline as evangelicalism regained ground in the post war period. Accompanying this downward trend has been a sharp accentuation of the contrast between Brethren congregations who engage constructively with the non-Brethren scene and, at the other end of the spectrum, the isolationist group commonly referred to as 'Exclusive Brethren'.
2005 / 1-84227-254-3 / xviii+ 296pp

James H.S. Steven
Worship in the Spirit
Charismatic Worship in the Church of England
This book explores the nature and function of worship in six Church of England churches influenced by the Charismatic Movement, focusing on congregational singing and public prayer ministry. The theological adequacy of such ritual is discussed in relation to pneumatological and christological understandings in Christian worship.
2002 / 1-84227-103-2 / xvi + 238pp

Peter K. Stevenson
God in Our Nature
The Incarnational Theology of John McLeod Campbell
This radical reassessment of Campbell's thought arises from a comprehensive study of his preaching and theology. Previous accounts have overlooked both his sermons and his Christology. This study examines the distinctive Christology evident in his sermons and shows that it sheds new light on Campbell's much debated views about atonement.
2004 / 1-84227-218-7 / xxiv + 458pp

Kenneth J. Stewart
Restoring the Reformation
British Evangelicalism and the Réveil at Geneva 1816–1849
Restoring the Reformation traces British missionary initiative in post-Revolutionary Francophone Europe from the genesis of the London Missionary Society, the visits of Robert Haldane and Henry Drummond, and the founding of the Continental Society. While British Evangelicals aimed at the reviving of a foreign Protestant cause of momentous legend, they received unforeseen reciprocating emphases from the Continent which forced self-reflection on Evangelicalism's own relationship to the Reformation.
2006 / 1-84227-392-2 / approx. 190pp

Martin Wellings
Evangelicals Embattled
Responses of Evangelicals in the Church of England to Ritualism, Darwinism and Theological Liberalism 1890–1930
In the closing years of the nineteenth century and the first decades of the twentieth century Anglican Evangelicals faced a series of challenges. In responding to Anglo-Catholicism, liberal theology, Darwinism and biblical criticism, the unity and identity of the Evangelical school were severely tested.
2003 / 1-84227-049-4 / xviii + 352pp

James Whisenant
A Fragile Unity
Anti-Ritualism and the Division of Anglican Evangelicalism in the Nineteenth Century
This book deals with the ritualist controversy (approximately 1850–1900) from the perspective of its evangelical participants and considers the divisive effects it had on the party.
2003 / 1-84227-105-9 / xvi + 530pp

Haddon Willmer
Evangelicalism 1785–1835: An Essay (1962) and Reflections (2004)
Awarded the Hulsean Prize in the University of Cambridge in 1962, this interpretation of a classic period of English Evangelicalism, by a young church historian, is now supplemented by reflections on Evangelicalism from the vantage point of a retired Professor of Theology.
2006 / 1-84227-219-5 / approx. 350pp

Linda Wilson
Constrained by Zeal
Female Spirituality amongst Nonconformists 1825–1875
Constrained by Zeal investigates the neglected area of Nonconformist female spirituality. Against the background of separate spheres, it analyses the experience of women from four denominations, and argues that the churches provided a 'third sphere' in which they could find opportunities for participation.

2000 / 0-85364-972-3 / xvi + 294pp

Paternoster
9 Holdom Avenue,
Bletchley,
Milton Keynes MK1 1QR,
United Kingdom
Web: www.authenticmedia.co.uk/paternoster

July 2005